EFFECTIVE MANAGEMENT and EVALUATION of INFORMATION TECHNOLOGY

Robert J. Thierauf

Q
QUORUM BOOKS
Westport, Connecticut • London

Library of Congress Cataloging-in-Publication Data

Thierauf, Robert J.
Effective management and evaluation of information technology / Robert J. Thierauf.
p. cm.
Includes index.
ISBN 0–89930–838–4 (alk. paper)
1. Industrial management—Data processing. 2. Management information systems. I. Title.
HD30.2.T48 1994
658.4'038'011—dc20 93–41816

British Library Cataloguing in Publication Data is available.

Library of Congress Catalog Card Number: 93–41816
ISBN: 0–89930–838–4

First published in 1994

Quorum Books, 88 Post Road West, Westport, CT 06881
An imprint of Greenwood Publishing Group, Inc.

Printed in the United States of America

The paper used in this book complies with the Permanent Paper Standard issued by the National Information Standards Organization (Z39.48–1984).

10 9 8 7 6 5 4 3 2 1

Effective Management and Evaluation of Information Technology

Copyright Acknowledgments

The author and publisher gratefully acknowledge permission to reprint material from the following copyrighted sources.

J. Daniel Couger and Robert A. Zawacki, *Motivating and Managing Computer Personnel*, New York: John Wiley & Sons, 1980. Copyright © 1980 by John Wiley & Sons. Reprinted by permission of John Wiley & Sons, Inc.

Russell Kay, "Business and Law Enforcement: Partners Against Computer Crime," *Infosecurity News*, November/December, 1992.

Russell Kay, "Calculating the Cost of Computer Crime," *Infosecurity News*, November/December, 1992.

James A. Champy, "Grand Designs," *CIO Magazine*, January, 1993. Reprinted through the courtesy of CIO. © 1993 CIO Publishing.

A Manager's Complete Guide to Effective Information Systems: A Questionnaire Approach by Robert J. Thierauf. Copyright © 1983 by The Free Press, a Division of Macmillan, Inc.

Statement on Auditing Standards (SAS) No. 3, The Effect of EDP on the Auditor's Study and Evaluation of Internal Controls, New York: AICPA, 1974.

David B. Mallinson, "The Humble Art of Estimating," *Journal of Systems Management*, December, 1987.

There is nothing more difficult to take in hand, more perilous to conduct, or more uncertain in its success, than to take the lead in the introduction of a new order of things.

Machiavelli

Contents

Figures

Preface

The skills required of effective management information system (MIS) managers in the near future and beyond 2000 center on competence in handling information technology (IT). Computers with far reaching data communications capabilities are reshaping competition. This information technology is an expensive resource with many hidden costs and now amounts to about half of most large firms' annual capital expenditures. This fact alone makes it part of the responsibility of top management who need to work with MIS managers. Electronic data interchange is the norm of everyday operations whereby companies are linked directly to major suppliers and customers in electronic partnerships. The electronic linkage found outside the typical company is complemented by image processing, where paper is replaced by an electronic image medium.

This new IT direction needs effective MIS managers to exploit it, that is, ones who are proactive and understand how to develop information technology to its maximum advantage. Too often in the past, companies have learned that it is not the information technology that creates a competitive edge, but top management working with MIS managers that exploit the technology. Basically, there are no instant solutions, only creative ones that involve organizational, technical, and market-related risks. Competitive advantage comes from doing something other organizations cannot match. If information technology were able to create competitive advantage, then there would be no competitive edge for any company.

This textbook for effective MIS managers takes into account the newer information technology as a means of leveraging it for the benefit of the total company. The starting point for pursuing competitive positioning through IT is for top management and MIS managers to understand where and how IT provides the capability to change the dynamics of competition; identify potential winners and avoid ideas that turn out to be unusable; understand what makes an IT-based competitive advantage sustainable; and determine the time to use IT as part of a major business initiative or to provide the technical infrastructure for later initiatives. In this textbook, the tie-in of top management with MIS managers is discussed where appropriate to leveraging information technology.

Throughout this textbook are references to past and current research I have undertaken on management information systems (MIS). This research is useful in developing new directions for MIS managers to employ so as to leverage information technology. For the most part, the important new directions center on the managerial functions (planning, organizing, directing: i.e., motivating and controlling) used by MIS managers. In the area of *planning,* the focus is on *problem finding,* which refers to bringing future problems back to the present time for solution as well as identifying future opportunities for implementation today. Equally important today is the implementation of a total quality management program for the MIS organization.

To help reduce the conflict between MIS personnel and end users, there is need for a new direction in *organizing* MIS. Essentially, this means bringing the MIS and end-user departments together by using *a functional end-user departmental approach.* By doing so, it is possible to undertake a new direction in *motivating* MIS personnel and end users. More specifically, the main thrust is on going beyond self-actualization of one's self and reaching out to others in terms of *mutual actualization* and, in certain cases, *self-donation.*

For *controlling,* the focus is on the utilization of *soft controls* to replace stringent controls that have had a tendency to restrict personal freedom on the job. All of the foregoing new directions plus others underlie effective guidelines that will be presented in this textbook for MIS managers. Overall, these major new directions are an integral part of this textbook. These directions indicate where MIS managers should be headed not only today, but also well into the twenty-first century.

From an MIS manager's perspective, a logical framework for successful management is contained in this textbook. More to the point, its structure is as follows:

PART I: INTRODUCTION TO EFFECTIVE MIS MANAGEMENT

Chapter 1 focuses on current and future information technology that can be leveraged to further organization objectives and goals. Because IT centers on gaining competitive advantage and improving organizational productivity, there is need for a new direction to assist MIS managers in these fast-changing times. Chapter 2 addresses past and current problems facing MIS managers that I have researched. In turn, these research results are useful in predicting future MIS problems that are to be faced by MIS managers. This background is helpful in developing the MIS guidelines that are found in the later chapters of this textbook.

PART II: EFFECTIVE STRATEGIC PLANNING AND TOTAL QUALITY MANAGEMENT

In Chapter 3, a new direction in MIS strategic planning is presented, namely, problem finding—the antithesis of problem solving. This is followed by a discussion of MIS objectives, goals, and strategies that are related to critical success factors and key performance indicators. Chapter 4 builds upon the preceding material of strategic planning by relating it to total quality management (TQM). The accent is on continuing quality improvements in the MIS organization. Also, performance standards are utilized to help facilitate a TQM program.

PART III: EFFECTIVE MIS ORGANIZATION STRUCTURES

As a starting point, Chapter 5 examines the current MIS organization structures and the difficulties with them; this discussion is followed by a new direction, that is, a functional end-user departmental approach. Staffing requirements necessary when using this new direction are also treated. In Chapter 6, informal relationships that tie in with the formal structures are discussed, along with the MIS organizationwide committee and project management.

PART IV: EFFECTIVE INFORMATION TECHNOLOGY

In order for MIS managers to put together an effective IT program, it is helpful to present the current state of the art in computer hardware and software, which is discussed in Chapter 7. In a similar manner, the latest database and data communications developments are found in Chapter 8. This exposition results in helpful guidelines for MIS managers to follow when leveraging information systems technology.

PART V: EFFECTIVE SYSTEMS DEVELOPMENT PROCESS AND END-USER COMPUTING

Since MIS managers are concerned with keeping the cost of the entire systems development process as low as possible, effective development procedures are found in Chapter 9. In turn, effective procedures that complement the development process are found in Chapter 10 for systems implementation and maintenance. Systems development procedures that are found in end-user computing are the subject matter of Chapter 11. These procedures are offered by the functional end-user information center as a way of providing an effective way for end users to leverage information technology to its fullest.

PART VI: EFFECTIVE DIRECTION OF MIS PERSONNEL AND END USERS

For new directions in MIS to be effective, new concepts and ideas that motivate MIS personnel and end users are needed. They are found in Chapter 12, where the accent is on satisfying an individual's higher-level needs. Similarly, the need for proper leadership and selection of MIS personnel is treated. In Chapter 13, training needs are addressed along with performance evaluation and career planning of MIS personnel.

PART VII: EFFECTIVE CONTROL OVER THE MIS ORGANIZATION

Control is an important aspect when implementing the new directions on planning, organizing, and directing MIS activities. Chapter 14 focuses on utilizing "soft controls" rather than "hard controls" to accomplish better results for control over organizationwide computing activities, especially in terms of end-user activities. Security concerns are addressed along with data integrity. Current audit practices for MIS managers to follow are addressed in Chapter 15 and a detailed two-part MIS questionnaire is presented. This questionnaire can be utilized to evaluate the degree of control over the entire MIS organization. In turn, this evaluation tool is useful in identifying MIS problems that need to be solved.

In a project of this magnitude, a number of individuals need to be acknowledged. First, I wish to thank Mr. Eric Valentine, publisher, for his helpful comments throughout the entire project. Second, I wish to thank the many MBA students at Xavier University for their help in the research reported in this textbook. Third, I am very thankful to all those who published materials that were helpful in developing the manuscript. Without their help, this publication would not have been possible.

Abbreviations

AA	Affirmative Action
AHS	American Hospital Supply
AI	artificial intelligence
AICPA	American Institute of Certified Public Accountants
AMP	access module processor
ANSI	American National Standards Institute
API	application program interface
APPI	Advanced Peer-to-Peer Internetworking
APPN	Advanced Peer-to-Peer Networking
ATM	asynchronous transfer mode
AT&T	American Telephone & Telegraph
BISDN	broadband integrated services digital network
BLOB	binary large object
CAD	computer-aided design
CASE	computer-aided software engineering
CCITT	Consultative Committee on International Telegraph and Telephone
CIO	chief information officer
CPA	certified public accountant
CRT	cathode ray terminal
CSF	critical success factor
DBA	database administrator
DBMS	database management system

D-DBMS	distributed-database management system
DDP	distributed data processing
DEC	Digital Equipment Corporation
DES	Data Encryption Standard
DP	data processing
DSS	decision support system
DSU	disk storage unit
EDI	electronic data interchange
EDP	electronic data processing
EEOC	Equal Employment Opportunity Commission
EIS	executive information system
E-mail	electronic mail
ENS	Enterprise Network Services
FDDI	Fiber Distributed Data Interface
4GLs	fourth-generation languages
GDSS	group decision support system
GUI	graphical user interface
IBM	International Business Machines
IC	information center
IMP	interface module processor
IPS	image processing system
IRM	information resource management
ISDN	integrated services digital network
ISO	International Standards Organization
IT	information technology
JAD	joint application development
JDS	Job Diagnostic Survey
JIT	just in time
K	thousand
KISS	Keep It Simple Stupid
KPI	key performance indicator
LAN	local area network
LCD	liquid crystal display
LCQM	life-cycle quality metrics
MAN	metropolitan area network
MBO	management by objectives
Mbps	megabits per second
MHS	Message Handling System

MIS	management information system
MIT	Massachusetts Institute of Technology
NDS	NetWare Directory Services
NN	Network Node
NNU	Neural Network Utility
OOAD	object-oriented analysis and design
OODBMS	object-oriented database management system
OOP	object-oriented programming
ONA	Open Network Architecture
OSHA	Occupational Safety and Health Act
OSI	Open Systems Interconnection
PC	personal computer
PERT	Performance Evaluation and Review Technique
QA	quality assurance
QI	quality improvement
RAD	rapid application development
RAM	random access memory
RDBMS	relational database management system
SAA	Systems Application Architecture
SEC	Securities and Exchange Commission
SLA	service-level agreement
SNA	Systems Network Architecture
SNMP	simple network management protocol
SPA	Software Publishers Association
SQL	Structured Query Language
TCP/IP	Transmission Control Protocol/Internet Protocol
3GLs	third-generation languages
TI	Texas Instruments
TQM	total quality management
UPS	United Parcel Service
WAN	wide area network

PART I

INTRODUCTION TO EFFECTIVE MIS MANAGEMENT

1

Effective MIS Management Leverages Information Technology

OUTLINE

INTRODUCTION TO EFFECTIVE MIS MANAGEMENT THAT LEVERAGES INFORMATION TECHNOLOGY

In today's world, the MIS organization which includes the MIS department and end users is continually undergoing changes in its information technology (IT). Structural changes in the world economy are elevating an organization's need for information technology to a new and higher level. MIS management is playing for higher stakes than ever before because the information asset they control is worth more. Robert B. Reich (Harvard University political economist), author of *The Work of Nations: Preparing Ourselves for 21st Century Capitalism,* contends that information technology professionals will play a leading role in corporate life. That is, the successful organization is organized around people and information technology in much the same way that a successful manufacturer was organized some fifty years ago around capital assets. The organization is defined by the quality of its people and its information technology infrastructure. This focus includes an orientation in which the latest insights and inventions around the world are continuously applied to finding and solving new problems of customers and organization personnel. It is from this perspective that effective MIS management is presented in this text.

In this opening chapter, the concept that information is a sixth resource of an organization is set forth. This is followed by a discussion on leveraging information technology along with real-world examples. Additionally, current and future directions of information technology are set forth. This background serves as a basis for presenting management information systems of all types that affect organizationwide computing activities under the jurisdiction of MIS management. The appropriate utilization of these current and future developments of management information systems should be of great assistance to management in gaining a competitive advantage and, at the same time, in improving the productivity of organization personnel. Last, there is a discussion on what makes for an effective MIS manager.

EFFECTIVE MIS MANAGEMENT RECOGNIZES THAT INFORMATION IS A CORPORATE ASSET

For successful organizationwide computing activities, MIS management must recognize that information is of vital importance to an organization's managers at all levels to achieve short- to long-range goals and objectives. There is now an awareness that accurate and timely information is a corporation's vital resource and that an effective management information system which is the center of organizationwide computing activities is a means of providing the needed information. Many senior corporate managers are finding that information is the source of competitive power; it gives them the ability to outmaneuver their rivals at critical times, especially when introducing new products and services. If the management information system does not produce the information necessary for management to handle its operations effectively, an "out-of-control" condition may result and the organization may never recover. An examination of companies that have experienced difficult times over the years will verify this point.

Information Can Be Viewed as a Sixth Organization Resource

Because of the importance of infor*m*ation in these fast-changing times, it can be looked upon as a sixth resource of a typical organization. It is not only useful for assisting the traditional 5Ms (*m*en or people, *m*achines, *m*oney, *m*aterials, and *m*anagement) in coordinating an organization's diverse activities, but it also supports them in planning and controlling activities from the highest management level to the lowest operational level.[1] It is the basic rationale for spending large sums of money on management information systems. Even though it is not as tangible as the 5Ms, nevertheless, it is a way of bringing together an organization's resources in an economical and efficient manner. The net result is *effectiveness* of the organization's operations. In light of these comments on information, it is the job of MIS management to make sure that functional managers at all levels have the appropriate information available at the right time and place for decision making. In order to carry out this awesome task, MIS management must move in newer directions as discussed in this chapter so that information is truly a sixth organization resource.

IRM CONCEPT TIED IN TO SIXTH ORGANIZATION RESOURCE

Information resource management (IRM) is a concept in which information is considered a sixth organization resource (as discussed previously). IRM focuses on users and their business needs and takes advantage of integrated technologies, ensuring that information and its management are considered vital resources in business planning and operations. In adopting the IRM concept, it is necessary to integrate previous separate, often competitive, departments and adjust their philosophies accordingly. The traditional MIS organization is often structured for the convenience of the systems and service providers rather than customers within and outside the organization. With IRM, all management information functions are under the direction of the MIS manager. To emphasize the authority of the chief information officer (CIO) or the top MIS manager, the position is typically placed at a level in the organization that allows information technology to play a vital role in strategic and operational business planning. Ideally, the CIO should report directly to the president or the chief executive officer (CEO).

Essential Elements of the IRM Concept

Essential elements of the information resource concept include (1) an appropriate business strategy for the times, (2) advanced development technologies, (3) the latest MIS methods, and (4) an organizational infrastructure. The successful integration of these elements enables organizations to build MIS applications that enhance their ability to differentiate themselves in national and international markets. Examples are the Chicago Board of Trade with a twenty-four-hour-a-day trading system, Federal Express with the introduction of a package management system, IBM with an on-line customer support system, and Phillips 66 with a worldwide management information system.

For the IRM concept to be effective within an organization, it must be related to a corporate business strategy that encompasses the entire organization. MIS management must understand fully the fundamental business activities performed within the organization. Otherwise, MIS management will have to guess at what the business needs to be successful. Only by understanding the needs of customers within and outside the organization and the strategy employed by senior corporate managers to meet these needs can MIS management supervise the building and implementing of the necessary applications architecture. This can only be done by instituting an effective systems development framework and an approach to utilizing advanced techniques and methodologies. An effective approach for adopting an effective strategy from an IRM perspective is found later in the text, namely, in Chapter 3.

Currently, advanced development technologies and newer MIS methodologies allow the MIS organization to respond quickly to changes in the business environment. Companies are adopting object-oriented and/or information engineering–based methodologies and combining them with advanced techniques such as joint application development (JAD) and rapid application development (RAD). The net result is that systems can be developed much faster because of the high degree of application modularity and system reusability that these methods provide. In addition, prototyping, computer-aided software engineering (CASE) tools, and fourth-generation languages (4GLs) are helpful to automating the project development life cycle. That is, systems analysis, systems design, development, and testing are supported by CASE and 4GL toolsets. But more importantly, these development tools provide the user with a central repository where previously defined data and process constructs (including databases and programs) can be stored and accessed for reuse—an important factor for boosting the productivity of systems developers. These important elements of IRM will be explored in more detail in later chapters. It should be noted that these toolsets are also available to end users for their development projects.

With the introduction of new tools and techniques comes the need for new organizational designs, a change in the MIS organizational infrastructure. The traditional overhead-rich MIS staffs that characterized the MIS organization in the past can be characterized by managers managing managers. Within an IRM operating mode, a leaner and more streamlined design is appropriate. MIS departments of tomorrow will be less like the job shops of today. Instead of using traditional development approaches, the MIS department will be more like an automated information technology factory where work is passed from station to station via a computerized conveyor belt using CASE technology that inspects for defects as the work is performed. This new structure will make it easier for the MIS department to employ total quality management (TQM). The new structure will focus more on integrating end users in the development process as well as allowing them to undertake their own systems projects. The net result is producing a quality system that works well the first time around. TQM throughout the development process will be covered in later chapters.

Supplementary and complementary to the IRM concept are open systems and client/server computing. Basically, *open systems* implement specifications for interfaces, services, and supporting formats which enable properly engineered application software to be ported across systems, interoperate with other applications, and interact with users in a consistent manner. In contrast, *client/server* offers a cost-effective alternative to traditional processing that allows users to develop flexible management information systems that span the organization such that large volumes of data can be converted into usable information. These two topics are covered in Chapter 7.

LEVERAGING INFORMATION TECHNOLOGY FOR A TYPICAL ORGANIZATION

For a typical organization to leverage information technology effectively under the guidance of MIS management, two important items must be considered. First, the organization must be responsive to rapidly changing competitive conditions and, at the same time, produce a positive return on its information technology. In this manner, new opportunities may be more quickly exploited and competitive vulnerabilities may be reduced. Second, the organization must enhance the efficiency and productivity of its personnel. This includes better coordination of the organizational functional components such as sales and marketing, manufacturing and production, distribution, support and service, finance and accounting, and administration. Related to both of these items is improving the creativity and effectiveness of individual decision makers as well as group decision makers in the organization. This centers on determining what accurate and timely information is needed; improving the analysis of the information and the quality of the decisions from it; and expediting, supporting, and monitoring the implementation of management actions and decisions. It is from this perspective that these important items are discussed.

Gaining Competitive Advantage

From past surveys of American competitiveness, the consensus is that U.S. competitiveness has deteriorated and that diminished competitiveness will hurt America's economic performance for the forseeable future. The net result is that the current situation represents a threat to the country's standard of living and economic power. In light of these comments, there is need for organizations to "shift gears" by employing an appropriate information technology to gain a competitive advantage. It is the job of MIS management to bring about the needed change in the *competitive landscape* by employing the proper approach to organizationwide computing activities. Formerly, the MIS manager's job was basically as a "storekeeper" of data and information. In today's world, the MIS manager has to facilitate change with information technology so that the organization remains competitive. The importance of information technology as a competitive weapon in furthering the organization's strategies, goals, and objectives is no less applicable for the small- to medium-size company than for the large-size company. Essentially, information technology offers a "window" on the competition and on changing market conditions.

For example, an office supply company with about $7 million in annual sales used communications technology to restructure its entire business, thereby changing from a retailer to a wholesale distributor. The company developed an efficient computer-based network to process orders from retail stores and deliver office furniture and supplies to them anywhere in the country the next day. This just-in-time (JIT) inventory approach, in effect, meant that an office supply dealer could work from a store front, with no inventory, and furnish customers anything from the wholesale supplier in one day. As a result, the wholesaler saw its sales multiply several times over in a relatively short period. In retrospect, the wholesaler applied a strategy of vendor lock-in. It created a relationship with its customers so attractive and so profitable that it became undesirable and costly for them to switch vendors. At the same time, the wholesaler's strategy changed distribution patterns and customer/supplier relationships up and down the supply chain. Overall, this illustration of changing customer/supplier relationships is a typical example of what can be done to gain competitive advantage through efficient and effective information technology. Needless to say, the MIS manager was an integral part of the entire transformation process.

Improving Productivity of Organization Personnel

Related to the MIS manager's job of assisting in gaining competitive advantage is the area of improving the productivity of organization personnel, in particular, those in management. For the most part, discussions of productivity to date have ignored the productivity of higher-level managers. Most attention has focused on robots on the assembly line or the implementation of the electronic "paperless" office, that is, on increasing the productivity of individual workers at the lower levels of the organization. However, when viewed from a strictly financial perspective, the productivity of labor and clerical workers is only one element in achieving organization productivity. The financial community measures productivity in terms of return on stockholders' equity, return on capital, and other financial tests. If the management of an organization decides to launch a new product that the customer will not buy, it is irrelevant whether the workers actually assembling the product are performing their jobs efficiently. Having the right product at the right time, however, has a much greater impact on the organizational productivity than gaining an incremental improvement in labor or clerical productivity.

From a forward-looking viewpoint, managers need to see important trends and relationships in widely disparate data in the form of computer graphics. For graphic representations to accomplish anything, they must communicate relationships—in contrasts, comparisons, and trends. These are the important elements from which decisions are formed. The right kind of graphics system overcomes the inability of tabular data to represent relationships. In another way, the output of computer graphics is quite helpful to managers and support personnel. Many times, managers must go before a high-level committee and present the analysis for the decision reached. Computer graphics allow them to present it in any number of ways: pie charts, bar charts, or three-dimensional images; on a black-and-white or color terminal; and on paper, overhead transparencies, or thirty-five-millimeter slides. Current interactive computer systems enable managers and support personnel to manipulate images on a cathode ray tube (CRT) screen until they are ready to be produced as hard-copy output. Future systems can be expected to be more helpful to management because of the increased capabilities of not only these systems themselves, but improved software. In summary, computer graphics are an important means to improve the managers' productivity and, at the same time, support their managerial decision making.

EXAMPLES OF ORGANIZATIONS LEVERAGING INFORMATION TECHNOLOGY

Today, there are a number of organizations that leverage information technology to gain competitive advantage and improve the productivity of organizational personnel. These organizations are changing the very nature of their industries by providing themselves with a strategic edge and increased productivity. Examples include (1) automating paper flow between the organization and its sales representatives, (2) giving customers terminals for direct-order entry to prevent costly and timely delays, (3) using information technology to place important information in the hands of marketing executives, (4) using information to target potential customers, (5) monopolizing the distribution channels by doing all of the customer's order-entry processing, (6) finding new electronic-processing mediums to promote potential as well as present customers, and (7) locking up a channel to customers by making it somewhat burdensome for a competitor to establish another channel. Generally, these methods along with those discussed later recognize that information technology will fundamentally change the way in which an organization does business. Thus, MIS management cannot afford to overlook this important fact.[2]

McKesson Corporation

The McKesson Corporation is an excellent example since this drug distributor helped to spearhead and continues to lead in distribution that has transformed retailing. It pioneered the electronic linkage of distributor and retailer in the midseventies to gain the advantages of just-in-time inventory. Today's druggist uses a laser scanner. With one swipe over the shelf label, bar-coded with the product's name and usual order quantity, the order is entered instantly. But that is only a refinement of the original system. Now McKesson has gone a step further. It has carried information technology into the warehouses. Although orders enter their depots electronically (with no order taker to introduce mistakes), errors can still creep in since the order filler can pick wrong items or wrong quantities. The solution is a twelve-ounce computer laser scanner with a two-way radio that is worn like a plaster cast on the hand and forearm.

Essentially, this device receives an order by radio from the warehouse's central computer and displays it on a three-square-inch screen strapped to the order filler's arm. It tells the person where the items are and plans the most efficient route through the 22,000-item warehouse to get them. As the employee chooses each item, the individual points a finger at the bar-coded shelf label beneath it, shooting a laser beam that scans the label and confirms that the person has picked the right product. When the order is complete, the arm-borne computer radios the warehouse's main computer, updating inventory numbers and the bill. The results are a substantial reduction in order errors and a rise in the productivity of order fillers.

Texas Instruments

Texas Instruments (TI) has long used its resources worldwide to design new products. In the past, days used to be lost when designers and engineers around the world worked together. Drawings they needed to see before they could talk might take two weeks to arrive. Faxing helped only a little since blurry faxes of blueprints cut into letter-size pieces and taped back together at the other end were often undecipherable. Now, with detailed designs sent instantly over the computer network so that TI employees anywhere can work on them simultaneously, development time has been reduced. The time needed to develop a calculator, for example, shrank by 20 percent as soon as TI began sending drawings electronically.

Today, far-flung units of Texas Instruments work simultaneously and speedily on separate parts of a project, keeping everything coordinated over the computer network. Time gets compressed in another way since departments scattered across the globe can work on a project twenty-four hours a day. When a U.S. financial exchange asked TI to come up with a quote to make a hand-held electronic bidding device for traders, the company's design department began working on the problem in Dallas, then at quitting time sent electronically what they had done to designers in Tokyo, who when their workday ended passed it on to designers in Nice, France. By the next day in Dallas, TI could also show the customer a computer-generated photograph of what the product would look like.

USAA

USAA, the San Antonio financial services company specializing in insurance for military officers and their families, decided early that information technology could be used to advantage (i.e., a strategic advantage). Management decided in the eighties that the capability to scan documents electronically and store them on optical disk would expedite daily operations. Because the technology was not available at that time, USAA joined with IBM in 1986 to develop it. Today, the system scans all incoming mail into USAA's computer network. When a customer buys insurance on jewelry, say, which takes effect twenty-four hours after the postmark on the appraisal mailed to USAA, the customer can telephone a service representative and get an instant answer to any question. A customer who needs to close quickly on a house but has not yet received the required confirmation of its insurability can learn whether the inspection report has reached USAA and whether the policy is being written. The net result is much better service to customers at much lower costs. At this point, no competitor is as advanced as USAA in its systems.

USAA has just installed a new system to process claims. When a customer calls to say he or she has had an accident, the system will digitize and store the phone call and scan the photos and the reports from doctors, lawyers, and appraisers that are sent in. Claim dossiers that fill a filing cabinet are recorded onto an optical disk or two. USAA currently is working with IBM to develop in the future a multimedia system that in a lawsuit, for example, will allow a USAA employee to hold a conference call with a lawyer in Miami and a doctor in Fort Lauderdale in which all participants can hear the recording of the original telephone accident report and review on their screen documents, X-rays of injuries, and color videos of damage to the car.

MANAGEMENT INFORMATION SYSTEMS THAT FOCUS ON EFFICIENCY OF OPERATIONS

The preceding discussion on information technology provides a background on current and most recent MIS developments that are under the control of MIS management. In the material to follow, those systems that help a typical organization leverage information technology will be stressed. However, in the past management information systems have not, for the most part, focused on leveraging information technology, but rather on improving the efficiency of everyday operations.

Integrated MIS

Generally, past management information systems have not provided managers with the potential to offer creative solutions to an organization's problems. That is, *integrated management information systems* provided selected decision-oriented information needed by management to plan, control, and evaluate the activities of the organization. They were designed within a framework that emphasized profit planning, performance planning, and control at all levels. Integrated MIS centered on the integration of required business information systems, both financial and nonfinancial, within the organization. In the past, the primary interest of information systems was in developing financial statements. When an integrated MIS was installed, its *primary purpose* was the production of reports to assist management. In contrast, its *secondary purpose* was the preparation of periodic financial reports representing a by-product of the information processed to assist in planning and controlling operations.

Although integrated management information systems rectified the problem posed by prior accounting-oriented systems by providing feedback in the form of reports through its various systems and subsystems, they were still deficient in one important respect. Data had to be accumulated for a period of time before processing was feasible. Whether sequential or random-access files were used, there was still the problem of time lag. For this reason, all prior systems, including integrated MIS, were called *backward-looking systems*. The methods, procedures, and equipment looked to past history before reports were produced for feedback. What was needed was *forward-looking systems*—ones that look to the present and the future. Such an approach is found in newer management information systems, in particular, real-time MIS and distributed MIS (discussed later). However, it should be noted that these systems do not stress leveraging information technology to gain competitive advantage or improve productivity of organization personnel for a typical organization.

Real-Time MIS

Although integrated MIS is operating in a few organizations of various sizes, it has been replaced by the implementation of *real-time management information systems,* sometimes referred to as *on-line real-time systems*. Like prior systems, they are essentially transactional processing systems that also provide essential information for management. Typical applications in such an environment include accounts receivable, airline reservation systems, bank deposit and withdrawal accounting, hotel accounting and reservations systems, law enforcement intelligence systems, patient hospital records, savings and loan deposit accounting, and stock market information.

Such systems focus on the on-line real-time concept. All data are *on-line:* that is, all data are sent directly to a computer system as soon as they come into being. The whole operation takes place in *real time,* which means that data are processed and fed back to the appropriate source in sufficient time to change or control the operating environment. Basically, then, any system that processes and stores data or reports them as they are happening is considered to be an on-line real-time system. Company personnel will receive a response from the system in time to satisfy their own real-time environmental requirements. The response time may range from a fraction of a second to minutes, hours, or days, depending on the attendant circumstances.

The integrated data accumulated from the many detailed on-line transactions are commonly referred to as the database elements or the organization's database. In addition to having all data collected in one place, the same inventory database, for example, may be used by a number of departments, such as manufacturing, production planning and control, inventory control, purchasing, and accounting. In another example, a database element is an employee skill number that can assist in preparing weekly payroll, referencing personnel records, filling new job openings, preparing contract negotiations, and the like. A database, then, contains elements or data bits in a common storage medium that form the foundation for operational information, although a database may be physically dispersed. Because designing a structured database for accommodating the various levels of management is a formidable task, real-time MIS satisfies the needs of lower and middle management for organizing, directing, and controlling activities around the established plans, in conformance with the organization's objectives. Although real-time MIS does respond to the managerial needs of the first two levels and does provide immediate feedback on present operations, it falls short of the information desired by top-level executives.[3] As will be seen shortly, this is not the case with decision support systems.

Distributed MIS

Distributed MIS, commonly referred to as *distributed data processing* (DDP), is one of the major thrusts in current management information systems. These systems represent a decentralized approach to placing low-cost computing power, starting at the various points of data entry, and linking these points, where deemed necessary, with a centralized computer via a distributed communications network. Like that of the previous systems, their essential focus is on transactional processing of business activities at the lower level of operations along with simultaneous supply of appropriate managerial information. In effect, distributed data processing is an approach to placing computing power where it is needed in an organization for efficient and economical data processing operations. Similarly, it is a feasible alternative to centralized data processing because of the declining costs of programmable terminals, microcomputers, minicomputers, and small business computers. Because the focus of current distributed data processing systems is placing power at the lower levels in an organization, their output generally centers on assisting lower and middle management.

An integral part of a distributed processing system is the use of data communications equipment from the remote processors to the central computer facility. The system allows a number of small computers to be combined to form an operational data center at more than one location. A network of these centers sharing computerized files provides powerful data processing capability at local and regional levels. The system provides on-line data entry to the local and regional databases for concurrent processing of multiple independent jobs. An operational data center performs the required MIS requirements of the remote site while it maintains concurrent high-speed communication with the central computer and other data centers in the network. It permits the development of network applications that can be solved by the existing MIS staff where the accent is on simplicity of operations. The system provides for generating reports within the network that give operational management control over their operations as well as for generating summary information for higher levels of management. Various network configurations can be developed by connecting network elements through communication lines. The attendant circumstances must be surveyed for the proper DDP network. In addition, to overcome objections to a large, centralized database, MIS strategists came up with the idea of *distributed databases* whereby the user's files are placed at or near the point where transactions occur. This way, the user's data are always available; concern about data communications failures is no longer necessary.[4]

MANAGEMENT INFORMATION SYSTEMS THAT LEVERAGE INFORMATION TECHNOLOGY

Management information systems, as noted in the previous discussion, center on producing periodic reports designed not only to recap past operations with an accent on exception items, but also to pinpoint possible control problems in current and upcoming operations for lower and middle management. Although these factors represent improvements over prior management information systems, they can be viewed from a ''two-dimensional'' framework: that is, the computer gives a periodic answer that is indicative of what should have been done or what should be done to control operations. However, there is a need to include a ''third-dimensional'' viewpoint, namely, that of the manager, who brings judgment, expertise, and the like, to bear on the problem. Whereas traditional MIS focuses on structured problem solving, decision support systems (DSSs) extend the range of problem structure to include semistructured and unstructured problems. DSS allows managers and their staffs to use the query capabilities of the computer to obtain requested information and be at the center of the decision-making process as changes occur. This is in contrast to relying on periodic control reports, as found in traditional MIS.

In the discussion to follow, the focus is initially on electronic data interchange (EDI) systems outside an organization with its trading partners and image processing systems (IPSs) within the organization. Next, decision support systems are viewed from both an individual and a group perspective. Additionally, executive information systems (EISs) are covered. Essentially, these management information systems are related to the utilization of computers to leverage information technology.

Electronic Data Interchange Systems

Electronic data interchange systems represent the exchange of documents and transactions by a computer in one company with the computer(s) of one or more companies in an open-system environment. Prior to EDI, the data flow focused on paper documents. The paper documents, for example, were mailed by the buyer to the seller, and the seller moved the documents to the proper departments for appropriate processing. In turn, the buyer undertook the necessary processing as well as the receipt of the goods. In contrast, the application of EDI involves the conversion of a written document into a machine readable form so that a computer in one company can communicate directly with the computer of the other company. Generally, the bulk of these documents relate to events that would generate input transactions for accounting systems to be processed into information.

EDI transmissions go from application to application between buyers and sellers without human intervention. An EDI system is involved in electronically exchanging purchase orders, invoices, payments, shipping notices, and similar transactions. In the process, staffing needs are cut by reducing paper handling, reducing errors by eliminating the need to rekey data, and improving transaction turnaround time. The net result of utilizing an EDI system is a computerized exchange of business documents in a specific format between companies. Fundamentally, an EDI system can be defined as a computer-to-computer exchange of routine paper documents, such as purchase orders, material releases, or receipt advices, by one company with other companies. This computerized information is transmitted in a standard format between a company and other companies. In an EDI system, electronically transmitted data replace paper documents throughout a company's transaction cycle.[5]

Image Processing Systems

From another perspective, electronic processing can be viewed only from within the organization—i.e. *image processing systems*—whereby electronic imaging is used to replace paper-intensive information systems. From an overall standpoint, there is an advantage to automating existing business processes with image processing systems. That is, the present method of paper processing is replaced by capturing all data initially in an electronic form. In turn, all subsequent processing refers to the same electronic images. Also, there is need to go a step further: to find applications for image processing that transform the business.

Organizations that have faced up to the issue of their survival can be very innovative in changing their business culture. As an example, the Xerox Corporation revolutionized its own methods of designing and manufacturing copiers when extreme competitive pressures came from Canon. Companywide integration and systems coordination is another key to improving customer service and guaranteeing success. Procter & Gamble pulled together under the umbrella of ''product delivery'' three separate functions that covered suppliers, manufacturers, and finished goods delivery. In effect, image processing systems can provide a competitive edge while also making employees more productive.[6]

Decision Support Systems

Essentially, an individually oriented *decision support system* is designed to satisfy the needs of a manager at any level in a distributed data processing environment. The system is designed to support the problem-finding (future problems related to the present) and problem-solving decisions of the manager. It incorporates features found in management information systems and in quantitative models of management science. Such a system emphasizes direct support for the manager in order to enhance the professional judgments required in making decisions, especially when the problem structures tend to be semistructured and unstructured. The use of interactive systems and CRT displays in a decision support system is an example of this point. Emphasis is placed on helping the manager to make decisions by being at the center of the decision-making process rather than on actually making decisions for the manager. This interplay results in a total effort that is greater than that of the manager or computer operating independently (as in traditional MIS), thereby providing *synergistic decision making*. Also, information is presented in a useful form rather than as a mass of all information that might be useful. From this perspective, an individually oriented decision support system builds on present management information systems as well as complements them.[7]

Since there is a move toward *group decision support systems* (GDSSs), there is need to define such an approach. Fundamentally, group decision support systems combine computers, data communications, and decision technologies to support problem finding and problem solving for managers and their staffs, which may also include operating personnel in the newer work environments. Technological advancements, such as electronic boardrooms, local area networks, teleconferencing, and decision support software, have spurred an interest in this area. In addition, fundamental changes in the external environment of organizations are encouraging organizations to head in this direction. Typically, organizations currently are experiencing the emergence of a postindustrial environment characterized by greater knowledge, complexity, and turbulence. One important effect of this trend is that decision-related meetings are becoming more frequent and more important. At the same time, the decisions confronting groups are becoming more complex and must be made more quickly and with greater participation than in the past. As part of the transition into this new environment, organizations are exploring advanced information technologies which might be employed in group meetings. Overall, group DSS has the capability to allow marketing executives, for example, to outmaneuver their competition and assist in resolving issues that center on making employees more productive.[8]

Executive Information Systems

To a degree, an extension of DSS is *executive information systems (EISs).* EISs are used mostly for highly structured reporting, sometimes referred to as status access. DSS has become almost synonymous with modeling and unstructured, ad hoc querying. Executive information systems are aimed at senior executives who currently have few, if any, computer-based systems to assist them in their day-to-day responsibilities. EIS brings together relevant data from various internal and external sources, delivering important information quickly and in a useful way. More important, it filters, compresses, and tracks critical data as determined by each executive end user. EIS performs the conceptually simple task of informing senior executives on matters relevant to their organizational responsibilities. Unlike traditional MIS functions that focus on the storage of large amounts of information, EIS focuses on the retrieval of specific information and on status access. The emphasis is on reducing the time and effort that the executive user must expend to obtain useful information for making the organization more competitive and its employees more productive.[9]

LATEST MANAGEMENT INFORMATION SYSTEMS THAT LEVERAGE INFORMATION TECHNOLOGY

The latest management information systems that can be related directly or indirectly to helping MIS managers leverage information technology are expert systems, neural networks, and multimedia systems. Additionally, idea processing systems that employ idea generators can be a rich source of developing new ways to utilize information technology effectively. The latest direction in information technology is virtual reality systems. These types of systems are discussed in the following sections.

Expert Systems

An *expert system* arrives at intelligent solutions to user queries by using the rules contained in the system's knowledge base. A *knowledge base* consists of IF-THEN rules, mathematical formulas, or some other knowledge representation structure to represent the knowledge of experts in a certain domain. The expert system scans through its knowledge base to find the appropriate rules, formulas, or some other knowledge structure to apply. Knowledge for such a system is extracted from human experts (i.e., domain experts) on the subject in which the expert system is expected to specialize. The knowledge in the form of rules is then stored in the expert system's knowledge base for use when needed.

Knowledge engineers who have been trained in the techniques of obtaining knowledge from domain experts procure the knowledge necessary to develop rules, formulas, or other knowledge structure for the problem under study. In effect, knowledge engineers develop the expert system that is designed to parallel decisions made by recognized experts in a field by acquiring knowledge about the particular problem and applying appropriate rules. Once the rules are captured and programmed, a panel of domain experts reviews the program's recommendations in a series of test cases to verify the newly designed expert system.

For typical business applications, most often the knowledge is stored in the form of "If . . . , then . . . " statements known as rules. This collection of rules is interpreted by an *inference engine*. Fundamentally, an inference engine navigates through the knowledge base much as a human would reason through a problem. Each rule can have one or more statements in its IF and THEN parts. If all the premises of the IF part hold *true,* the conclusions reached by the expert system in the THEN parts are also *true* and the rule is said to "fire." Furthermore, the conclusion of a certain rule may exist as a premise of another rule, that may itself "fire" and "ignite" other rules in succession, until a final conclusion is reached.

Basically, expert systems are designed to mimic the problem-solving abilities of experts in a particular domain. Because an expert system works roughly the way human experts do, it combines factual knowledge with rules that experience teaches (i.e., heuristics), and then makes inferences about the situation at hand, whether it be diagnosing the financial portfolio of a client or the cost of a new product. In light of these facts, an expert system can be defined as a computer program that embodies the expertise in a specific domain that would otherwise be available only from a human expert. It represents a codification of the knowledge and reasoning used by human experts. Once operational, it can be copied and distributed at little marginal cost to assist users whether they be experts or inexperienced personnel. From this perspective, experts systems can assist company employees in being more productive when assisting users inside or outside the organization.[10]

Neural Networks

Since an expert system contains expertise in the form of a knowledge base, the system goes through its knowledge base and picks out the most appropriate response. The real problem is that if a person queries the expert system about something outside its knowledge domain, it cannot respond. This is where *neural networks* come into play. The key distinction between expert systems and neural networks is that neural nets do not involve specific recordings or transcriptions of someone else's thinking. Neural networks can learn from experience.

Neural networks supposedly imitate the way actual neurons operate in a human's brain. The brain contains 100 billion or so neurons. Axons carry a signal away from the neuron, and dendrites carry the signal toward another neuron; synapses are where nervous impulses pass between neurons. Individual neurons thereby reach out to 10,000 or so other neurons. Related to the number of neurons is another item, that is, the connections per second that a neural net can make. Hardware vendors, such as Intel, are starting to show off specialized chips that increase the number of connections per second between these neurons. Intel, in fact, is claiming something like a billion-plus connections per second. Even with this increase in processing speed, neural nets still have a long way to go before they truly imitate the human brain. However, they can be useful in gaining a competitive advantage and in improving employee productivity.[11]

Multimedia Systems

Another current direction in leveraging information technology is *multimedia systems* that are networked. Making a video call from a personal computer (PC) is as easy as making a phone call. The purpose of meeting face to face on a video screen is to share work and information interactively. In this collaborative computing mode, there can be distributed meetings with coworkers and customers or vendors. Participants interact using the same documents while seeing each other on PCs. From another perspective, on-demand, stored video can be used in many different applications and environments. Video workstations located on the manufacturing floor can help workers get video reference information for complex operations. Multimedia information will help office workers receive "just-in-time" training at their desktops, that is, when it is most convenient and timely. Distributing training on the desktop will increase productivity by giving access to material without waiting for scheduled classes and will save travel costs. Organization communications can improve by distributing sales and business video information to employees at their desktops.

Other digital video applications promise to improve computer-based education and collaboration among medical workers. Advertising will take on a whole new look as advertisers will be able to tailor messages to specific people at the point of sale. Information video kiosks will be used in many different environments, from business to consumer applications. Travel agencies will use on-line video to show vacation spots or hotels. On-demand movies delivered to the home are possible with video-capable networks and end-user devices.

To be useful, video applications need to be networked. Only recently has networking video become practical. Networks are important because of the characteristics of multimedia data, especially the audio and video components. Multimedia has huge storage requirements relative to other kinds of data, a limiting factor for installation at every desktop. Most multimedia applications support work group or organizationwide activities, requiring access by many simultaneous users. In addition, future applications such as desktop videoconferencing will mandate networked solutions. Thus, networked multimedia may well prove to be an important means to leverage information technology for a company's customers, vendors, and employees.[12]

Idea Processing Systems

Generally, *idea processing systems* are considered to be related to decision support systems. Some in the field consider them a subset of group DSS. No matter how idea processing systems are looked upon, they are essentially systems designed to capture, evaluate, and synthesize individual ideas into a broad context that has real meaning for problem solving. From this perspective, idea generators are generally used to assist in the idea formulation stage. To understand this type of system better, it would be helpful initially to examine the meaning of ideas. An *idea* can be thought of as a formulated thought or opinion. Ideas spring from knowledge, which is essentially derived from observation of the environment in which one lives as well as from an awareness of one's internal emotions and feelings on these observations. Knowledge implies more than observations of past experience, but also includes some form of interpretation of past experience. Ideas can be thought of as the conscious expression of these interpretations. It should be noted that ideas are separate notions that a person is conscious of, but that may or may not be relevant to any specific purpose that has been predefined.

The basic stages of an idea processing system center on *inputs* in the form of problem statement and observation about the problem. In turn, *processing* involves idea generation and evaluation of ideas for solving the problem. The end result is *outputs,* that is, report preparation and dissemination of information about specific ideas to solve the problem. Regarding idea generation, the behavioral sciences have not been able to explain how a person's mental process operates nor how a person's knowledge is organized. However, there is ongoing research by behavioral psychologists as well as by computer scientists who are attempting to imitate such functions through a computer. Needless to say, idea processing systems are a natural for helping management and their staffs in gaining competitive advantage and improving employee productivity.[13]

Virtual Reality Systems

Another way of improving organization productivity is to employ *virtual reality systems.* In a virtual reality experience, sophisticated interactive computer programs, written in Forth, C, and Pascal, put a person inside a world of computer graphics. This allows the person to treat system-generated objects almost as if they were real things. The person interacts with the environment using special clothing and fiber-optic sensors that interpret body positions as computer commands. In theory, the person can create a world limited only by his or her imagination and programming capabilities.

Researchers are looking into ways to use what they call "augmented" or "see-through" reality. Workers would wear clear goggles with 3-D images reflected onto the lenses. The goggles would superimpose a virtual image of the desired result on a real object, so that workers would know what to do with the object without consulting manuals or blueprints. For example, an assembler inside a fuselage would see the real openings for hydraulic ducts or communications cables with a virtual image of the installed ducts or cables superimposed on them. The goggles could also reflect schematic and wiring diagrams, location of drill holes, and other information. The end result is better quality in less time. Some virtual reality experts predict that virtual reality will eventually have an impact as great as the invention of writing. If they are wrong, it will not be for any want of ambition or confidence among pioneers in the field. The major drawbacks are the ability to write complex software programs and the speed of light: that is, the limitations of the physical world.[14]

CHANGE UNDERLIES THE NEED FOR NEWER INFORMATION TECHNOLOGY

An underlying theme of the material in this chapter is *change*. In this fast-changing world of information technology, change is a simple fact of life. Yesterday's tools and techniques will not solve tomorrow's problems. A typical remark from a MIS manager is "I know information technology is going to change the industry and the whole business in which my company operates. Although my MIS department may do a very good job as a support function, it is now a new game. What I need is some kind of new focus for changing times. In other words, how do I organize the entire MIS function that includes end users to get there? Where do I go from here?"

Although some MIS managers may not welcome the fact or admit that a major transition is occurring, the consequences of failure are much higher than they were in the past. Hence, MIS managers would do well to reexamine their focus and direction by developing policies and procedures that recognize change as an inevitable part of doing business. In turn, the reality of future changes is incorporated into new directions that they must understand and make an integral part of the MIS strategic planning process for successful organizationwide computing activities in the future.

Even though most organizations have already recognized information as a competitive weapon to some extent and a way to improve management productivity in some way, a wide gap still exists between current organizationwide computing activities and future activities. Closing the gap will become an economic imperative as new and improved information technology becomes a key determinant of competitiveness and productivity in the years ahead. The gap exists because information technology is still viewed by MIS management within a relatively narrow technical or organizational framework. Small-, medium-, and large-size organizations need to go beyond the purely operational uses of information technology and apply it strategically in order to further the objectives and goals of the organization and break new ground.

In the next chapter, problems associated with current computing activities are presented. As a way of overcoming or, at least, reducing them, new directions for MIS management to follow are in order. They are related to what an MIS manager does, that is, planning, organizing, directing, and controlling information technology. In effect, current problems are used as a means to develop new directions that MIS management should follow in the future to leverage information technology successfully. Under the leadership of MIS management, these new directions are helpful in making organizations lithe and flexible. MIS managers are able to restructure quickly in order to keep pace with a changing world. The challenge is to maintain that resilience through years of steady growth. New and improved information technology under the leadership of MIS management, then, assumes a special role for the typical organization to help it remain supple and responsive to change.

WHAT MAKES FOR AN EFFECTIVE MIS MANAGER

The myriad advances in information technology, including integrated distributed computers, data communications and networking, and imaging systems, have risen in strategic importance to the level of human and financial assets. Effective leveraging of the information asset is rapidly defining a new breed of corporate leaders. Technology advances have driven forward-thinking organizations to reorganize in support of the information technology asset. The MIS manager must help position his or her organization for the future. Improvements in productivity and leveraging IT as a competitive weapon are chief components of the MIS manager's job description. In a similar manner, senior corporate management must be made aware of how advancing information technologies are changing the very nature of how business is done. Gone are the days when the computer simply displaced groups of clerical workers. Tomorrow's organizations will use the technology investment to streamline corporate hierarchies, enhance individual job performance, and reach out and touch customers down the street and around the globe. Essentially, the prior material in this chapter has focused on information technology, particularly, newer management information systems that exemplify this technology. It is MIS management's job to provide the necessary leadership to see that their organizations reap the rewards of this rapidly expanding information technology. It is from this viewpoint that the essentials of what constitutes an effective MIS manager are developed.

Is a Manager First and a Technician Second to Leverage Information Technology

An important starting point for effective MIS managers is that they must be managers first and technicians second to leverage information technology successfully. The wall between the technical back shop and the corporate business office must come down. MIS managers must learn to communicate more effectively with the front office. To do this, they need to shed their technical cloaks; they must learn the business and effectively integrate corporate and MIS strategic planning. Conversely, they must get senior corporate management and functional end-user management more involved in the business of leveraging information technology and in understanding the impact of today's technical trends on the organization. Closing the communications gap between MIS managers and senior corporate managers will be critical to success in the years to come. Failure to do so will likely result in an acceleration of the already growing trend to put nontechnical managers from the functional business units of the organization in charge of the MIS function. End-user literacy is improving, computers are much lower in cost and friendlier, and more and more people will want to "do their own thing." Let there be no mistake about the new directions in organizationwide computing.

MIS management in this new information technology world will be quite different from the monolithic MIS management of the past. Smart MIS managers will lead and not fight this movement so that their organizations will be assured of compatibility, consistency, efficiency, and effectiveness from its distributed resources. No one else in the organization has the corporate view and skill to do this job. *Proactive* MIS managers who provide the leadership and learn to adapt to distributed processing resources will lead their organizations into controlled and sensible computer-aided business management. Those who adopt a siege mentality in relation to end users in this distributed processing environment will ultimately lose when trying to leverage information technology.

Is Concerned That Information Technology Pays for Itself

Most effective MIS managers are concerned with employing information technology that pays for itself. Despite all the money their organizations have spent on information technology, typically they struggle to explain the benefits of an IT investment in hard dollars. They are more likely to justify IT expenditures by citing nonfinancial measures, such as improvements in productivity and response time as well as reduction in customer complaints and error rates, than by measuring the return on investment in information technology. Although nonfinancial measures are useful and valid, they are generally not considered sufficient by senior corporate management. These ultimate arbiters frequently insist on proof that money spent on information technology results in earnings and savings that surpass the investment. MIS managers often feel caught between an irresistible force and an immovable object as they are compelled to provide financial justification for an investment that resists such hard measurements.

To resolve this senior corporate management issue, there is a need to view cost justification from a different perspective. More specifically, the initial focus of MIS managers is on customer-oriented effectiveness issues. Efficiency gains that can be measured in dollars are usually the next consideration. The well-known customer order-entry system of American Hospital Supply (AHS) was initiated by marketing personnel who were trying to solve a customer service problem. Only later did MIS management realize the cost-justifiable efficiency gains that emerged as a by-product: gains achieved by eliminating AHS's order-entry clerical function and allowing customers the convenience of placing their orders directly.

On the other hand, if the initial focus is on cost-cutting efficiency issues, then customer service and effectiveness are usually compromised and the idea has less appeal. For example, it is much more interesting to talk about a system such as National Car Rental's, in which customers can go directly to the lot, select cars, and leave, only having to use their Emerald Cards at the checkout gate, than it is to talk about reducing the clerical staff by, say, 20 percent. The net result is that most of the breakthrough ideas in competitive and productivity applications do not get sold by hard-numbered cost justification but rather because they are winners and easily recognized as such.

Utilizes a Total Quality Management (TQM) Approach

To leverage information technology successfully, the MIS manager needs to implement a total quality management (TQM) program that is an integral part of an organizationwide quality program. Such a program is usually implemented through quality teams set up in functional business units. Typical tasks include identifying customer needs, defining problems, analyzing business processes, measuring critical factors that affect quality, and implementing corrective action. The tasks involved in running an organizationwide quality improvement program point to a starring role for the MIS organization. Typically, MIS measures critical factors such as the number of customer service calls or the flow of material to a just-in-time manufacturing operation. A tenet of TQM is "You only improve what you measure." But aggregate numbers planned and measured high in the organization have little relevance to the work of most people in that organization. Hence, total quality management requires all to be working on measurable improvement meaningful in their own jobs.

Within the MIS organization itself, the MIS managers must insist that quality cannot be added to software as a final or remedial step. Instead, it must be an important consideration at every stage of the MIS project life cycle. This means it has to be incorporated into the organization's culture. In staffing, managing, designing, testing, and deployment, total quality must be a dominant consideration. This is opposed to the present approach where schedule pressures drive almost all MIS project considerations in a programming department. This department often views quality as a luxury that can be indulged in if time permits. As soon as it becomes clear to programmers that MIS management does not insist on quality, a downward spiral starts; it stops only when minimum functionality is reached. The devaluation of quality inevitably damages the morale of the programming staff, and this, in turn, further damages quality. Needless to say, a TQM takes time to overcome this problem. Because of the importance of TQM, it is discussed at length in Chapter 4, where consideration is given to understanding the customer first. The discussion also focuses on the concept of continuous improvement, the empowerment of employees, and the basic tenets of TQM.

NOTES

1. Robert J. Thierauf, *New Directions in MIS Management: A Guide for the 1990s,* New York: Quorum Books, 1988, p. 5.
2. Myron Magnet, ''Who's Winning the Information Revolution,'' *Fortune,* November 30, 1992, pp. 110–117.
3. Robert J. Thierauf, *Systems Analysis and Design of Real-Time Management Information Systems,* Englewood Cliffs, N.J.: Prentice-Hall, 1975.
4. Robert J. Thierauf, *Distributed Processing Systems,* Englewood Cliffs, N.J.: Prentice-Hall, 1978.
5. Robert J. Thierauf, *Electronic Data Interchange in Finance and Accounting,* New York: Quorum Books, 1990.
6. Robert J. Thierauf, *Image Processing Systems for Business: A Guide for MIS Professionals and End Users,* New York: Quorum Books, 1992.
7. Robert J. Thierauf, *Decision Support Systems for Effective Planning and Control, A Case Study Approach,* Englewood Cliffs, N.J.: Prentice-Hall, 1982; and *User-Oriented Decision Support Systems, Accent on Problem Finding,* Englewood Cliffs, N.J.: Prentice-Hall, 1988.
8. Robert J. Thierauf, *Group Decision Support Systems for Effective Decision Making, A Guide for MIS Professionals and End Users,* New York: Quorum Books, 1989.
9. Robert J. Thierauf, *Executive Information Systems, A Guide for Senior Management and MIS Professionals,* New York: Quorum Books, 1991.
10. Robert J. Thierauf, *Expert Systems in Finance and Accounting,* New York: Quorum Books, 1990.
11. Franco Vitaliano, ''Expert Systems and Neural Networks,'' *Digital Review,* June 10, 1991, p. 15.
12. Jim Long and Barbara M. Baker, ''Distributed Computing,'' *Network Computing,* November 1, 1992, pp. 22–26.
13. Robert J. Thierauf, *Creative Computer Software for Strategic Thinking and Decision Making: A Guide for Senior Management and MIS Professionals,* New York: Quorum Books, 1993.
14. Gene Bylinsky, ''The Marvels of 'Virtual Reality','' *Fortune,* June 3, 1991, pp. 138–139.

2

Problems Facing MIS Management

OUTLINE

INTRODUCTION TO PROBLEMS FACED BY MIS MANAGEMENT

In order to assist MIS management (i.e., the MIS manager and his or her supervisors) in the future, it is helpful to look at past and present problems and what has happened and what is happening in management information systems. A measuring device is necessary to evaluate the performance of MIS management and their operations. This chapter centers on such a device in terms of research results using a two-part management information systems questionnaire that can be used by external or internal auditors/consultants to determine how effective MIS management is in the discharge of their duties and responsibilities over the entire management information system. Because this comprehensive MIS questionnaire centers on evaluating *general* and *application* controls over management information systems, it is also useful to MIS managers and their supervisors as a means to determine what areas need to be improved for daily operations. Thus, the MIS questionnaire can be used by parties external to the MIS department or by the MIS department itself as a means for self-evaluation. However, our main concerns are the actual research results from using this questionnaire as well as their relevance to the development of future guidelines to assist MIS management.

To be considered truly effective today as well as in the future, MIS management must stand back and assess their proper place in the overall organization and prepare it for changing times. They must be willing to manage MIS personnel and end users (where necessary) and provide incentives for those who have the desire and potential to bring business and information processing together. In other words, MIS management must make the transition from being hardware/software specialists to being generalists for the MIS organization plus assisting end users in the functional areas of a typical organization.

Additionally, MIS management must exert effective leadership over the MIS organization. An effective starting point is the establishment of MIS *plans,* from the *broad* to the *specific.* This, in turn, is followed by the development of an MIS *organization structure* to accomplish these plans. In addition, there is need for effective *information systems technology* and *systems development,* which includes *end-user computing* that complements the MIS plans and organization structure. In the process, MIS personnel and end users need to be *directed,* that is, motivated and led by MIS management. Finally, there is need for effective *control* over the MIS organization, a control that goes from the overall MIS plans to the detailed aspects of these plans, the day-to-day MIS operations, and the inclusion of end-user computing. Thus, MIS management must integrate the plans of the MIS organization, including end users, with appropriate controls over daily MIS activities and, at the same time, provide the appropriate structure and direction for MIS personnel and end users using the latest information systems technology and development tools.

MANAGEMENT INFORMATION SYSTEMS QUESTIONNAIRE TO PINPOINT MIS PROBLEMS

A two-part MIS questionnaire is used to determine how effective an MIS manager and his or her supervisors are in discharging their managerial functions (planning, organizing, directing, and controlling). This questionnaire follows the guidelines of the American Institute of Certified Public Accountants (AICPA) *Statement on Auditing Standards*. In addition, it follows the *Foreign Corrupt Practices Act,* which makes bribes to foreign officials by U.S. companies a criminal offense and establishes Internal Accounting Control Standards. Although this questionnaire is not presented in this chapter, it is sufficient to say that it is comprehensive enough to evaluate a typical MIS department. For the complete two-part MIS questionnaire, reference can be made to Robert J. Thierauf, *A Manager's Complete Guide to Effective Information Systems.*[1] However, a revised and up-to-date two-part questionnaire that is comprehensive enough to include the major parts of this text is found in Chapter 15. Like the previous questionnaire, it can be used by external or internal auditors/consultants for an objective evaluation as well as by the MIS organization for self-evaluation.

CLASSIFICATION OF TWO-PART MIS QUESTIONNAIRE

Controls developed by the AICPA are segregated into two major categories. Those controls that relate to all MIS activities are termed *general controls* and form the basis for Questionnaire 1. Those controls that relate to specific MIS tasks are called *application controls* and provide the basis for Questionnaire 2. MIS Questionnaire 1 and 2 do not give answers but simply ask questions. If the questions are all answered "yes," the function or area under investigation is operating as desired. On the other hand, if there are some "no" answers, it is experiencing difficulty, and the negative answers must be expanded upon in writing. If the question does not apply, the "N.A." (not applicable) is checked. As will be seen, the two-part MIS questionnaire serves as a tool to analyze current MIS management and operations under their control. But more importantly, it allows the external or internal auditors/consultants to synthesize those elements causing difficulties and deficiencies. The capability to assess all negative answers helps separate problems from symptoms.

General Controls—Questionnaire 1

According to the AICPA's *Statement on Auditing Standards No. 3, general controls* comprise a five-part breakdown which can be segregated as follows[2]:

1. MIS department controls
2. System and program procedures controls
3. Built-in hardware and software controls
4. Computer center controls
5. Security controls

This segregation will be the focus of discussion for the research results in this chapter.

Application Controls—Questionnaire 2

Referring again to the AICPA's *Statement on Auditing Standards No. 3, applications controls* which relate to the specific tasks performed by the MIS department can be segregated as a five-part breakdown for Questionnaire[23]:

1. Input controls
2. Processing controls
3. Output controls
4. Database controls
5. Data communication controls

Like the previous breakdown, this segregation will be the focus of discussion for research results in this chapter.

RESEARCH RESULTS USING THE TWO-PART MIS QUESTIONNAIRE

Research results over management information systems are related to both large corporations and small companies. Results for Questionnaires 1 and 2 are compiled to show where MIS organizations are having difficulties, which turn up as "no" answers on the questionnaires. An evaluation of the questions receiving negative answers then provides a basis for determining important problem areas. When problem areas have been located through the questions most frequently checked "no," these areas are then identified for improvement. Discussion will be centered on past research (early and middle 1980s) and current research (early 1990s) on problem areas as a way to determine future potential problems.

Current Research Versus Past Research

The author was assisted by a number of MIS professionals in determining important problems for improvement. *Past* research using Questionnaires 1 and 2 was conducted in 1982 while similar research was conducted approximately five years later, that is, in 1986 and 1987. The results of past research were published in 1983[4] and in 1988[5], respectively. *Current* research results are set forth in this chapter for combined 1991–1992. In this manner, research results are brought together as a way of comparing the past with the present. It should be noted that most of the organizations are located in the Midwest. Essentially, they represent a cross section of industries. The questionnaires' results represent a broad spectrum of computerized management information systems; hence, they allow general conclusions to be drawn about problem areas that would be found in a typical management information system.

Large Corporations Versus Small Companies

For past research conducted in 1982, nine large corporations and nine small companies were used in the evaluation of Questionnaire 1. Also, eleven large corporations and eleven small companies were utilized in past research in 1986–1987. In contrast, twelve large corporations and six small companies were used in the evaluation of Questionnaire 1 for current research in 1991–1992. In terms of Questionnaire 2 for past research in 1982, three large corporations and three small companies were evaluated, while the comparable number for 1986–1987 is four large corporations and four small companies. In contrast, there were eight large corporations and five small companies in 1991–1992 for current research in terms of Questionnaire 2. The totals of organizations for past and current research were fifty-four and thirty-one, respectively.[6] Not only do these organizations represent a large number of industries, but they can also be considered representative of other firms in the same or similar types of industries.

From an overall MIS standpoint, the past and current research results indicate that large corporations typically have fewer problems than small companies. However, some small companies are better managed than large ones.

MAJOR PROBLEMS UNCOVERED FOR GENERAL CONTROLS—QUESTIONNAIRE 1

The starting point for determining problem areas for general controls is the five-part breakdown of Questionnaire 1, which consists of (1) MIS department controls, (2) system and program procedures controls, (3) built-in hardware and software controls, (4) computer center controls, and (5) security controls. As indicated previously, an important requirement in using this Questionnaire 1 as an evaluation tool is that all of the "no" questions be so marked.

Past and Current Problems Facing MIS Management

A way of identifying major problems for general controls using Questionnaire 1 is to look at the number of "no" answers. The percentages based on the number of no's for fifty-eight business organizations (thirty-two large corporations and twenty-six small companies) in 1982, 1986–1987, and 1991–1992 have been calculated as follows:[7,8]

	1982	*1986–1987*	*1991–1992*
MIS department controls	24.6%	21.6%	22.6%
Security controls	21.6%	20.5%	13.7%
System and program procedures controls	19.5%	13.8%	21.3%
Computer center controls	13.3%	17.2%	12.3%
Built-in hardware and software controls	5.8%	4.4%	6.4%

The order of the five parts is the same in large corporations and small companies for both past and current research results. The largest decrease is found in security controls. The principal reason is that the current focus on improving computer security is found not only within the MIS department, but within the functional end-user units of a typical organization. Additionally, there is a greater concern for security issues when interfacing with an organization's customers, vendors, and other outside concerns than in the past.

From an overall standpoint, the average percentages of "no" answers to the total questions is *18.8 percent for all organizations:* 13.5 percent for large corporations and 24.0 percent for small companies in *1982*. In a similar manner for *1986–1987,* the average percentage of "no" answers to the total questions is *16.1 percent for all organizations:* 14.1 percent for large corporations and 18.1 percent for small companies. Also, the percentages for *1991–1992* of "no" answers to total questions is *17.7 percent for all organizations:* 13.7 percent for large corporations and 25.8 percent for small companies.

The major problem areas (using Questionnaire 1 from past research) are shown in Figure 2.1. In terms of 1982, the *first* problem of general controls is the lack of proper documentation over standards and procedures. Typically, this problem has been "the scourge of the data processing [DP] industry" from its beginnings. The *second* problem is the lack of security protection measures over the management information system. MIS managers often fail to plan for security protection measures over their computer systems; many times, only after a really bad problem concerning security protection has arisen do they undertake the planning necessary to prevent an unfortunate condition in the near future. They react to a bad present situation rather than apply a preventive approach to the future.

In a somewhat similar manner, regarding the *third* problem, MIS management fail to develop appropriate short- to long-range plans for their management information systems. This means that many MIS managers are "flying by the seats of their pants"; hence, they are not truly in charge of their MIS organi-

Figure 2.1
Past and Current Research Results of The Ten Major General Controls Problems (from the Highest to the Lowest) Using Questionnaire 1

1982		1986–1987		1991–1992		
Ranking	*Number*	*Ranking*	*Number*	*Ranking*	*Number*	*Problem*
1	13	4	13	1	15	Lack of proper documentation over standards and procedures
2	10	1	17	2	11	Lack of security protection measures over the management information system
3	10	3	14	3	10	Lack of short- to long-range plans for management information systems
4	8	2	17	4	10	Lack of an independent third party to review MIS operations
5	7	6	7	5	6	Lack of a contingency recovery program
6	5	8	4	6	6	Lack of career pathing
7	5	-	-	-	-	Lack of control over new or about-to-be-discharged MIS personnel
8	4	5	10	7	6	Lack of training programs for new and experienced MIS personnel
9	4	9	4	8	5	Lack of control over computer center operations
10	4	-	-	-	-	Lack of control over methods and procedures in MIS operations
-	-	7	6	9	5	Lack of performance standards to evaluate MIS personnel
-	-	10	4	10	5	Lack of an adequate performance appraisal program

Source: 1982 — Robert J. Thierauf, *A Manager's Complete Guide to Effective Information Systems: A Questionnaire Approach* (New York: Free Press, 1983), pp. 96-97; 1986–1987 — Robert J. Thierauf, *New Directions in MIS Management: A Guide for the 1990s* (New York: Quorum Books, 1988), p. 34: 1991–1992 — Research performed by part-time M.B.A. graduate students in the graduate-level course Managerial Aspects of Management Information Systems, conducted by Robert J. Thierauf at Xavier University (Cincinnati, Ohio). The students are full-time professionals, systems analysts, or analysts/programmers who have been on the job for several years.

zations. They tend to practice "management by exception," reacting to bad MIS conditions, rather than "management by perception," perceiving future trends in MIS and their impact on their operations before they happen. They are *reactive* and not *proactive*. In terms of the *fourth* problem, there is lack of an independent third party to review MIS operations. The independent third party can be an internal auditor or auditors schooled in computers or an outside auditing/consulting firm hired to perform a review of the MIS organization. The *fifth* problem is the lack of a contingency recovery program. This means that in case of fire, flood, disaster, or the like, the recovery program is inadequate to handle these extreme conditions. Only temporary power outages, dropped disks, and so on, are provided for in the contingency recovery program.

The *sixth* problem is the lack of career pathing. Many times, because MIS personnel see no discernible career paths in their organizations, they tend to switch to organizations that have clearly defined opportunities for personal growth and development. The high turnover rate in the past can be attributed, in part, to the lack of definite career paths. The lack of control over new or about-to-be-discharged MIS personnel has been identified as the *seventh* problem. New and inexperienced personnel see a lack of direction and control as well as a lack of guidance as an indication that an organization will be deficient in concern for them in the future. The individual feels like a forgotten person who is clearly expendable as the situation dictates. There is also a need to prevent experienced personnel who are about to be discharged from taking opportunities for "getting even" or "settling old scores." The *eighth* problem is the lack of training programs for new and experienced MIS personnel. Too often, MIS personnel feel that they are stagnating and not growing in their field; the result is a high level of anxiety and frustration. This can be sufficient reason for leaving an organization.

Lack of control over the computer center operations, the *ninth* problem, can take the form of ease of entry into the computer room, lack of computer run books, an improperly maintained equipment log, and similar items. The practice of allowing the computer room to operate "as loose as a goose" can cause numerous problems in terms of not meeting computer production schedules, not to mention the possibility of collusion or fraud in manipulating data files, issuing unauthorized checks, and so forth. Finally, the *tenth* problem is the lack of control over standards and procedures in MIS operations, which complements the prior problem. Adequate control over standards and procedures in systems analysis and design as well as in programming is a must for effective MIS operations.

Past research results for 1986–1987 are also shown in Figure 2.1. The same categories prevail as in 1982, except for two changes: lack of control over new or about-to-be-discharged MIS personnel and lack of control over standards and procedures in MIS operations. These two are missing from the top ten problem areas. The new problem areas are shown as the seventh and tenth items, namely, the lack of performance standards to evaluate MIS personnel and the lack of an adequate performance appraisal program. Because of the high growth needs of MIS personnel, typically there is a need to review their performance at least twice a year, especially for new MIS personnel. In this manner, the MIS person can be counseled as to his or her good and bad characteristics as well as what must be done to overcome barriers to meeting career goals.

An examination of the current research results for 1991–1992 in Figure 2.1 versus past research results indicates that no new categories have been added. The current ordering of the ten major problems is more in line with 1982 than 1986–1987. The change from the number 4 position in 1986–1987 to the number 1 position in 1991–1992 for documentation can be explained by the fact that MIS managers believe that the rapid rise of end-user computing is going through the same problems experienced by the MIS department many years ago. That is, documentation was always a problem since systems analysts and programmers tended not to use the appropriate documentation procedures in order to make themselves somewhat indispensable. However, with improved design and programming software, documentation has become almost second nature to systems analysts and programmers, along with the urging of MIS managers. In contrast, since end users have not been taught proper documenting procedures, this problem is again surfacing in the 1990s. Similar analyses can be made among the other items in Figure 2.1. Overall, current research results are in line with past research results.

MAJOR PROBLEMS UNCOVERED FOR APPLICATION CONTROLS—QUESTIONNAIRE 2

A beginning point for specifying problem areas using Questionnaire 2 comprises five parts: (1) input controls, (2) processing controls, (3) output controls, (4) database controls, and (5) data communications controls. As in Questionnaire 1, an important part of completing the questionnaire is to answer all of the "no" questions. The negative answers to questions are helpful to identify specific application control problems. Thus, there is a logical sequence to interpreting the research results with a view to offering recommendations to improve MIS operations.

Past and Current Problems Facing MIS Management

To understand the basis for the major problems of application controls, there is need to look at the "no" answers of Questionnaire 2. Using these answers for twenty-seven business organizations (fifteen large corporations and twelve small companies) in 1982, 1986–1987, and 1991–1992, the percentages (from the highest to the lowest) have been calculated as follows[9,10]:

	1982	*1986–1987*	*1991–1992*
Input controls	21.8%	14.6%	15.0%
Output controls	19.0%	19.0%	15.9%
Processing controls	15.2%	14.2%	17.7%
Database controls	13.7%	11.8%	14.7%
Data communications controls	10.5%	12.2%	17.8%

For both past research results, this ordering of the five parts is not the same for both large corporations and small companies although for the most part they approximate the ranking. For 1991–1992, the order of these five categories is not identical for large corporations and small companies. Essentially, the current percentages are not out of line with those set forth previously, except that data communications controls scored much higher. The rationale is that the trend today and tomorrow is in the direction of not only local area networks, but also metropolitan area networks and wide area networks, including global communications in multinational corporations. Hence, data communications can be expected to have a large number of problems today and into the future.

The average percentage of "no" answers for the total questions is *15.9 percent for all organizations* in *1992*. When viewing the percentages for large corporations versus small companies, a different picture emerges. The percentage for the former is 12.6 percent and for the latter is 19.3 percent. Similarly, for *1986–1987*, the average percentage of "no" answers to the total questions is *14.2 percent for all organizations:* 11.9 percent for large corporations and 16.4 percent for small companies. Also, the percentage of "no" answers to total questions is *16.7 percent for all organizations* in *1991–1992:* 12.6 percent for large corporations and 23.2 percent for small companies.

Using Questionnaire 2, the major problems in terms of past research for 1982 are shown in Figure 2.2. Half of these problems were noted in Figure 2.1 and discussed in a previous section, namely, lack of third-party auditing, training, documentation, security, and contingency recovery program. The other five problems are explored in the following sections.

In terms of 1982, the *second* problem of Figure 2.2 refers to the lack of control over input and/or output data. In some cases, input and output errors were found to be chronic, a problem that can be corrected by additional data-entry operator training. Another circumstance is poor control over input and output from the functional areas of the organization. In yet another situation, there was a lack of proper editing of input and/or output data. Generally, the end result is that the output is unacceptable because of errors in input data.

In light of the increased use of on-line databases, the *fourth* problem is lack of or poor database administration. The problem was absent from large corporations and very pronounced in small companies, which tend to lack a database administrator (DBA). The introduction of numerous interactive programs has given rise to the need for a DBA to control the contents of the database. Other-

Figure 2.2
Past and Current Research Results of The Ten Major Application Controls Problems (from the Highest to the Lowest) Using Questionnaire 2

1982		1986–1987		1991–1992		
Ranking	*Number*	*Ranking*	*Number*	*Ranking*	*Number*	*Problem*
1	5	1	8	1	11	Lack of an independent third party to review MIS operations
2	4	2	5	4	6	Lack of control over input and/or output data*
3	3	5	2	6	4	Lack of training programs for new and experienced MIS personnel
4	3	6	2	2	8	Lack of or poor database administration
5	3	7	2	7	4	Lack of proper documentation over standards and procedures
6	2	3	5	3	7	Lack of security protection measures over the management information system
7	2	4	3	8	3	Lack of communication in the MIS area*
8	1	8	2	-	-	Lack of a contingency recovery program
9	1	-	-	-	-	Lack of encryptian devices in data communications*
10	1	-	-	-	-	Lack of obsolescence dates on labels of data files*
-	-	9	2	10	2	Lack of control over information centers*
-	-	10	2	-	-	Lack of MIS flexibility and adaptability
-	-	-	-	5	5	Lack of adherence to established methods and procedures
-	-	-	-	9	3	Lack of strategy and methods for network communications management*

* Not found in Figure 2.1 using Questionnaire 1.

Source: 1982 — Robert J. Thierauf, *A Manager's Complete Guide to Effective Information Systems: A Questionnaire Approach* (New York: Free Press, 1983), p. 135; 1986–1987 — Robert J. Thierauf, *New Directions in MIS Management: A Guide for the 1990s* (New York: Quorum Books, 1988), p. 37: 1991–1992 — Research performed by part-time M.B.A. graduate students in the graduate-level course Managerial Aspects of Management Information Systems, conducted by Robert J. Thierauf at Xavier University (Cincinnati, Ohio). The students are full-time professionals, systems analysts, or analysts/programmers who have been on the job for several years.

wise, the same information may be stored on the database for different users and in different formats, yet be capable of serving several needs at one time.

The lack of communication in the MIS area is the *seventh* problem. In one case, little information was exchanged by systems developers and users. In the other case, there was a lack of communication to the users of periodic changes to the system. In either case, the principles of effective communication have been violated. In the area of data communications, the *ninth* problem is the lack of encryption devices. The utilization of data encryption devices reduces the possibility that someone on the outside will steal valuable company information. A desirable approach to overcome theft of data is the use of encryption devices at the sending and receiving ends of data transmission. The *tenth* problem is the lack of obsolescence dates on labels of data files. As a result, computer operators mount the incorrect tapes when processing data. The end result is that many processing runs must be rerun.

Past research results for 1986–1987 using Questionnaire 2 are also shown in Figure 2.2. The first eight categories from 1982 are still on the list: lack of third party auditing, control over input and/or output data, training, documentation, database administration, security, communication, and contingency recovery program. However, two new problems have appeared as the last two items, namely, the lack of control over information centers and the lack of MIS flexibility and adaptability. The *ninth* problem refers to the emergence of information centers to assist end users not only in procuring appropriate micro software and hardware, but also in training them in their use. The *tenth* problem relates to the inability of the management information system to be flexible and adaptable to meet end-user needs. Basically, the ninth problem centers on poor external help to end users, while the tenth problem focuses on the lack of interest in helping them.

An analysis of the current research results for 1991–1992 in Figure 2.2 versus the past research results indicates that the ordering is somewhat different from past research, in particular 1986–1987. That is, the lack of or poor database administration has risen to the number two position while the other categories are somewhat alike. The rise in the importance of the database administrator has resulted from the need for integrated databases so that data can be shared across the whole organization versus separate functional units as in the past. Additionally, two new categories have been appended, namely, the lack of adherence to established methods and procedures and the lack of strategy and methods for network communications management and control. The *fifth* problem can be related to end users who do not follow through with the proper methods and procedures practiced by the MIS organization. This problem was alluded to earlier in relation to current research using Questionnaire 1 where lack of proper documentation of standards and procedures is the number one problem, caused principally by the rapid growth of end-user computing. In reference to the *ninth* problem for current research, it relates to the comments about data communication controls. The proliferation of local area networks (LANs), metropolitan area networks, and wide area networks, including global communications, will probably cause this problem to go even higher in the future. This is particularly true since LANs are replacing computer mainframes of all sizes at a rapid rate.

COMBINED MAJOR PROBLEMS FOR GENERAL AND APPLICATION CONTROLS—QUESTIONNAIRES 1 AND 2

In order to obtain an overview of the preceding materials, this section of the chapter brings together past and current research. More specifically, *past* problems for 1982 and 1986–1987 using Questionnaires 1 and 2 are combined, followed by the same approach for *current* problems for 1991–1992. Next, past and current research results are compared in order to determine whether a major problem is increasing or decreasing in importance. This presentation alerts MIS management to the more important critical problems that need to be addressed today. Additionally, this material provides the background for the next section, which develops the future problems that need to be addressed by MIS management currently in order to practice "management by perception." That is, future problems should be solved today so that their impact on the MIS organization will be minimal tomorrow.

Past Problems Facing MIS Management

On the basis of past research results for 1982 and 1986–1987, the most significant problems when Questionnaires 1 and 2 are combined are illustrated in Figure 2.3. These results are taken from the combination of Figures 2.1 and 2.2. In Figure 2.1, the total number of organizations is forty (twenty large corporations and twenty small companies), while the number in Figure 2.2 is fourteen (seven large corporations and seven small companies). Thus, the total number of participating organizations in Figure 2.3 is fifty-four (twenty-seven large corporations and twenty-seven small companies). As shown, the top six most significant past problems relate to (1) third-party auditing, (2) security, (3) documentation, (4) short- to long-range plans, (5) training, and (6) contingency recovery program. All of these top past problems are compared to current ones to determine whether their significance has increased or decreased. However, before doing so, it is necessary to bring together current research results.

Current Problems Facing MIS Management

The previous approach is used again to bring together current problems facing MIS management for 1991–1992. The combined results from Questionnaires 1 and 2 are found in Figure 2.4. These results are from Figures 2.1 and 2.2. In Figure 2.1, the total number of problems for eighteen organizations (twelve large corporations and six small companies) was set forth. In a similar manner, the

Figure 2.3
Combined Past Research Results (1982 and 1986–1987) of Fifteen Major General and Application Controls Problems (from the Highest to the Lowest) Using Questionnaire 1 (Twenty Large Corporations and Twenty Small Companies) and Questionnaire 2 (Seven Large Corporations and Seven Small Companies) — Based on Data in Figures 2.1 and 2.2

Ranking	1982	1986–1987	Combined	Problem
1	13	25	38	Lack of an independent third party to review MIS operations
2	12	22	34	Lack of security protection measures over the management information system
3	16	15	31	Lack of proper documentation over standards and procedures
4	10	14	24	Lackof short- to long-range plans for management information systems
5	7	12	19	Lack of training programs for new and experienced MIS personnel
6	8	9	17	Lack of contingency recovery program
7	5	4	9	Lack of career pathing
8	4	5	9	Lack of control over input and/or output data
9	4	4	8	Lack of control over computer center operations
10	-	6	6	Lack of performance standards to evaluate MIS personnel
11	5	-	5	Lack of control over new or about-to-be-discharged MIS personnel
12	3	2	5	Lack of or poor database administration
13	2	3	5	Lack of communication in the MIS area
14	4	-	4	Lack of control over standards and procedures in MIS operations
15	4	-	4	Lack of an adequate performance appraisal program

number of problems for thirteen organizations (eight large corporations and five small companies) was illustrated in Figure 2.2. For these thirty-one organizations, the top six problems in order of importance are related to a lack of (1) third-party auditing, (2) documentation, (3) security, (4) short- to long-range plans, (5) training, and (6) database administration. In the next section, these current top six will be compared to the past top ones.

Going beyond the problems set forth in Figure 2.4, several new problems are

Figure 2.4
Combined Current Research Results (1991–1992) of Fifteen Major General and Application Controls Problems (from the Highest to the Lowest) Using Questionnaire 1 (Twelve Large Corporations and Six Small Companies) and Questionnaire 2 (Eight Large Corporations and Five Small Companies) — Based on Data in Figures 2.1 and 2.2

	1991–1992			
Ranking	*20 Large Corporations*	*11 Small Companies*	*Combined*	*Problem*
1	11	10	21	Lack of an independent third party to review MIS operations
2	11	8	19	Lack of proper documentation over standards and procedures
3	11	7	18	Lack of security protection measures over the management information system
4	6	4	10	Lack of short- to long-range plans for management information systems
5	6	4	10	Lack of training programs for new and experienced MIS personnel
6	4	4	8	Lack of or poor database administration
7	3	3	6	Lack of a contingency recovery program
8	2	4	6	Lack of control over input and/or output data
9	4	2	6	Lack of career pathing
10	3	2	5	Lack of performance standards to evaluate MIS personnel
11	3	2	5	Lack of control over computer center operations
12	5	-	5	Lack of an adequate performance appraisal program
13	2	3	5	Lack of adherence to established methods and procedures
14	2	1	3	Lack of a strategy and methods for network communications management
15	1	1	2	Lack of control over information centers

emerging that were not previously reported. Among those mentioned are the proliferation of end-user computing and the lack of MIS management guidance and control along with the ensuing conflict between the two, the inflexibility of the MIS department in meeting end-user needs, the lack of control and inefficient use of microcomputers (i.e., personal computers), and the lack of compatibility between micros and mainframes. In addition, problems were reported concerning the lack of end-user involvement in the systems review and design process; lack of concern for user ergonomics, that is, users' new working environmental factors; as well as a general need for an improved communicating process between the MIS department and end users. Essentially, these problems have arisen as a result of the vast inroads of microcomputers throughout the typical business organization. The micro proliferation problem will continue to make the MIS manager's job more difficult. Typical ones include those related to security, training, and documentation. In fact, the top six problems reported in Figure 2.4 within the MIS department are resurfacing outside the department.

Even within the MIS department, problems were reported in terms of a need for new systems methodology, too much time spent on program and system maintenance, a need for a report on the progress of the MIS projects, lack of quality assurance for MIS programs and operations, and a better match between MIS project needs and manpower planning. All in all, several new problems are emerging and replacing those that have been with the MIS department for some time. These problems and others will be explored further in the next section.

COMPARISON OF PAST AND CURRENT PROBLEMS FACING MIS MANAGEMENT

In order to compare the *past* research results (Figure 2.3) to results of *current* research (Figure 2.4), it is necessary to determine the relative increase or decrease of importance of each item. As a result of the number of problems, comparison will be limited to the top six, namely, (1) third-party auditing, (2) security, (3) documentation, (4) short- to long-range plans, (5) training, and (6) contingency recovery program. Figure 2.5 compares the relative significance of the top six major problems for past and current research.

The *lack of an independent third party to review MIS operations* is the past and current *topmost* problem facing MIS management. Actually, its significance has gone down, from .703 to .677. MIS practitioners involved in the past and current research felt that the amount of review is much too narrow and short for assuring MIS management of adequate performance of MIS department activities. Even the periodic review by external auditors/consultants was a cause for concern. In essence, too little time and effort is spent on assuring that the entire MIS organization is functioning as desired.

The *number two* problem, namely, the *lack of security protection measures over the management information system,* has decreased in importance in relation to past research: that is, it is currently number three. Additionally, its significance

Figure 2.5
Comparison of the Relative Significance of Past Research (Figure 2.3) to Current Research (Figure 2.4) for the Top Six Problems Facing MIS Management

Rankings			Past Research 54 Organizations		Current Research 31 Organizations		
Past Research	*Current Research*	*Problem*	*Number*	*Percentage*	*Number*	*Percentage*	
1	1	Lack of an independent third party to review MIS operations	38	.703	21	.677	Dec.
2	3	Lack of security protection measures over the management information system	34	.630	18	.580	Dec.
3	2	Lack of proper documentation over standards and procedures	31	.574	19	.613	Inc.
4	4	Lack of short- to long-range plans for management information systems	24	.444	10	.323	Dec.
5	5	Lack of training programs for new and experienced MIS personnel	19	.352	10	.323	Dec.
6	7	Lack of contingency recovery program	17	.315	6	.193	Dec.

has decreased from .630 to .580. This should come as a surprise since the number of users has increased steadily over the years. However, more recently, MIS management has focused on security and will continue to do so with the continual usage of microcomputers throughout a typical organization. Not only is the MIS department subject to internal security problems, but the threat to security is also coming from outside the company, such as from *hackers,* as well as from the fact that many MIS activities are being operated in a distributed data processing mode. It is conceivable that this problem may well be number one in the future.

The *third* top problem in terms of past research not only has increased in importance to number two; in addition, the number of times it was mentioned has increased from .574 to .613 (Figure 2.5). One reason for this change is that although newer-generation languages are easier to use and to implement since they resemble or are the English language for MIS practitioners, this may not always be true for end users. Hence, the *lack of proper documentation over standards and procedures* is still an important concern for MIS management. The proliferation of microcomputers is causing a change in the significance of documentation.

The *lack of short- to long-range plans for management information systems* of the entire organization has been ranked the number *four* problem currently as it has been in the past. Its importance has gone from .444 to .323. This has been caused, in part, by a more effective usage of microcomputers. So the question can be asked; "Is the typical organization getting expected results from its microcomputers?" This question can be answered by stating that if well-laid plans have been made, the organization probably is. If adequate MIS plans have not included these micros, the organization is generally not getting its money's worth.

The number *five* problem, the *lack of training programs for new and experienced MIS personnel,* has gone from .352 to .323. The reason that this problem is in the top six is that the MIS department must staff information centers which did not exist a few years ago. Hence, their resources have been spread too thin, making fewer personnel available to give the training for new and experienced MIS personnel. Also, the backlog of MIS projects puts a strain on training; that is, there is the eternal rush to meet deadlines of new systems. As a result, training to cover all situations for efficient operations is seldom or never undertaken.

An integral part of the security problem is the *lack of a contingency recovery program.* This problem has slipped in importance, from .315 to .193. However, it is ranked *sixth* of the problems facing MIS management. After reading many scare stories in the MIS literature, some organizations have taken appropriate action to anticipate the unforeseen. However, with the rise of violence and terrorism around the world, this problem may increase in importance in the future.

FUTURE PROBLEMS FACING MIS MANAGEMENT

In order to obtain an understanding of future problems facing MIS management, it is helpful to look at what the computing environment might be. Several leading computer authorities predict that 80 percent of all computing will be done by end users by the year 2000. From this perspective, end users will be relying very heavily on information centers that may or may not be a part of their functional departments. Similarly, they will look to these centers for training to realize the full potential of their microcomputers, that will probably be linked to local, metropolitan, or wide area networks or some type of computer mainframe. The increasing involvement of end users in future computing, then, brings to the forefront new problems and extensions of present problems.

As a way of "getting a handle" on these future problems, reference can be made to the six most important current problems. The top three problems—third-party auditing, documentation, and security—will be even more evident in the future. To overcome these problems, MIS management must take a new direction to provide user incentives for adhering to MIS standards and guidelines. Support of "user freedom" can yield subtle but valuable rewards. By replacing "the MIS department versus end users" mentality that rigid controls generate with an attitude that encourages users to experiment with applications, the organization can experience important breakthroughs. For example, typical end users, left to develop their own applications, tend to drift toward *prototyping*. Despite its approximations of reality, the system often produces useful results quickly. In turn, it provides a basis that end users can develop more completely or turn over to the MIS department for development and implementation. By being involved in the development of systems, end users will begin to recognize the need for documentation and security over the system as well as the need for a periodic review of the system. Thus, the message should be clear—get end users involved from a positive viewpoint and not from a negative one so that these top three current problems can be minimized in the future.

Future problems are likewise expected for the next three most current problems—short- to long-range plans, training, and a contingency recovery program. In terms of planning and its detailed parts, MIS management must have a definitive hardware and software policy. This means limiting the PC selection to compatible machines. The same must be done for operating systems. Generally, it is best to support one PC operating system and one or two integrated spreadsheet packages and/or a fourth-generation language as opposed to a multitude of them. This is particularly true of spreadsheet packages and fourth-generation languages since the output from one user serves as input for another user. Hence, the *need for compatibility is paramount.*

Typically, many MIS problems with end users can be overcome or reduced by providing effective training. While such training will not transform first-time developers into effective systems analysts, it can teach them shortcuts and easy ways to perform system functions. In the training process, the end users should be instructed in how to develop a contingency recovery program in case of unforeseen circumstances. This problem of today, like tomorrow, can be minimized by having the end users sufficiently trained to meet their computing needs. Overall, the need for planning, training, and development of a contingency recovery program that represents the next three top problems can be minimized by effective MIS management in the future.

Although the foregoing presentation has centered on end-user problems of tomorrow, problems within the MIS department are expected to occur along the continuum of problems presented in Figure 2.4. That is, more of the same is expected with a much greater accent on interface problems between MIS personnel and end users. As noted previously, the best approach is for MIS management to be prepared by taking a *proactive* approach rather than a *reactive* one. Essentially, this means not only having well-managed information centers in the functional units of the organization or stand-alone information centers, but also providing hardware and software capabilities with more user-friendly access in an integrated manner. MIS management needs to improve their departments and information centers so that functional-level management can easily accomplish computational and data retrieval functions through easy-to-use English commands.

PROBLEMS SERVE AS A BASIS FOR DEVELOPMENT OF NEW DIRECTIONS TO LEVERAGE INFORMATION TECHNOLOGY

Although these future observations can be garnered from the current problems, there is need to go beyond these generalized conclusions and develop specific new directions for MIS management. More specifically, the accent is on new directions in the following areas: MIS strategic planning and total quality management (TQM); MIS organization structures; hardware, software, database, and data communications; systems development, implementation, and maintenance; end-user computing; direction of MIS personnel and end users; and control over MIS organizationwide computing activities. Although each of these areas is briefly noted later, this introduction serves as a basis for developing the remaining chapters of this text along with appropriate principles and guidelines for MIS management to follow.

New Directions in MIS Strategic Planning and Total Quality Management (Part II)

As discussed in the current research on management information systems, there is one overriding problem that is related directly to MIS planning, that is, the lack of short- to long-range plans for MIS and other problems related indirectly to this area. Although taking a proactive approach is recommended for these planning problems and others facing MIS management, this generalized approach needs to be refined further so that a proactive approach is implemented effectively. Essentially, this refinement takes the form of a *problem-finding approach:* that is, the focus of problem finding is on bringing future MIS problems back to the present time for solution as well as identifying future MIS opportunities for implementation today.

In Chapter 3 on strategic planning, the main thrust is on ways of assisting MIS management in developing short- to long-range plans, starting with the problem-finding approach. A new management principle underlies this approach, namely, ''management by perception''—perceiving the future in a way that will be beneficial to the organization. Not only are the essentials of developing one-year and longer-term MIS plans discussed; in addition, the need for creativity in the development of such plans is presented. Overall, this early chapter sets the stage for looking at important strategic planning issues that should be at the forefront of the typical MIS manager's thinking about the direction that his or her MIS organization should be taking today as well as tomorrow.

Related to strategic planning is the employment of a total quality management (TQM) approach which is tied in with performance standards in Chapter 4. Because MIS management needs to develop a corporationwide information policy, it is helpful to utilize TQM as a meaningful way of setting forth a comprehensive framework for what the MIS manager does. In this manner, the end product of providing a computing service to customers (i.e., users), whether within or outside the MIS department, is paramount in this pervasive MIS policy.

New Directions in MIS Organization Structures (Part III)

Closely related to MIS strategic planning is the area of MIS organization structures. If short- to long-range plans do not include changing the MIS structure in relation to the times, there can be significant problems facing the typical MIS manager. For example, the establishment of information centers as an integral part of functional departments or as stand-alone units should be prevalent today to meet end-user needs. Those organizations that do not have such centers in some shape or form are probably experiencing a certain level of conflict between the MIS department and the functional departments, not to mention out-of-control conditions over the widely scattered microcomputers. In addition to the organization problems related to MIS planning, current research indicates that there is a lack of training programs for new and experienced MIS personnel. The same can be said if information centers are lacking in the organization. End users are not being properly trained to utilize the micros in a productive manner.

In light of the foregoing problems, there is need for the MIS department to take a new direction. This means bringing the MIS and end-user departments together by using a combined functional and computing department approach. In essence, an information center is located in each major functional area of an organization so that MIS personnel serve the specific needs of that operational functional unit while its information manager reports to the MIS department. Such an approach is discussed in Chapter 5 and refined further in Chapter 6 in terms of specific formal roles that MIS personnel can assume in this MIS and end-user relationship.

New Directions in Information Technology (Part IV)

As suggested in the preceding discussion, future problems may revolve around the proper acquisition of computer hardware and software by end users. These problems can be related directly or indirectly to control over information centers set up in functional end-user departments or stand-alone units operated by the MIS department and independent of the functional end-user departments. In Chapter 7, appropriate procedures to assist all organization personnel in acquiring computer hardware and software will be delineated. Similarly, in Chapter 8, database systems and data communications will be examined from the standpoint of utilizing newer information technology to assist the total organization in getting a better understanding of its operations and possibly gaining a competitive advantage. Also, they will be related to current problems found in Figure 2.4, namely, the lack of or poor database administration and the lack of a strategy and methods for network communications management and control. Overall, both chapters will focus on ways of leveraging information technology to serve the total organization better.

New Directions in the Systems Development Process and End-User Computing (Part V)

In Chapter 9, the main thrust is on current approaches to systems development. Not only the MIS department is included in this discussion; the functional end-user units are also discussed since the bulk of systems development by the year 2000 is expected to be undertaken by end users. Examination of Figure 2.4 discloses a number of problems that are related to systems development, such as lack of proper documentation over standards and procedures, lack of security over the management information system, and lack of a contingency recovery program. In addition, there is need for training programs for new and experienced MIS personnel so that the newer and more productive design approaches are taught and used to speed up the implementation of MIS projects. For example, a fourth-generation language can be a productive substitute for a third-generation language when information processing tasks are straightforward and when processing time requirements are not critical.

Appropriate systems development methodologies are extended to Chapter 10 to include systems implementation and maintenance. From this view, MIS management needs to adhere to established methods and procedures—a current problem found in Figure 2.4. Needless to say, the problems of end-user activities which encompass systems development, implementation, and maintenance may be magnified outside the MIS department. In Chapter 11, end-user system activities are examined and appropriate guidelines are set forth to assist MIS management of daily operations in the functional end-user units. Thus, all systems development activities within and outside the MIS department must be managed so that the organization reaps the rewards of this time-consuming and costly effort.

New Directions in Directing MIS Personnel and End Users (Part VI)

Although current research results (refer to Figure 2.4) do not highlight a motivation problem per se facing MIS management, nevertheless, motivation problems typically underlie many MIS problems. For example, lack of proper planning and organization over widespread microcomputers usually causes many end users to be insufficiently motivated to utilize their micros productively. Another example relates to MIS personnel who identify more with their profession than with the organization for which they work. Inasmuch as the MIS and functional end-user departments are brought together, it is possible to undertake a new direction in motivating them. More to the point, this means going beyond self-actualization by centering on *mutual actualization* and, in certain cases, *self-*

donation. This area is covered in Chapter 12 and tied in with leadership by MIS management.

Additionally in Chapter 13, a number of problems identified through current research (Figure 2.4) are discussed. Proper approaches to training new and experienced MIS personnel, career pathing, and an adequate performance appraisal program are set forth. In this manner, MIS management can turn "human liabilities" into "human assets" by making MIS employees more productive as well as improving the productivity of end users.

New Directions in Control over the MIS Organization (Part VII)

Current research results (Figure 2.4) that relate to major control problems facing MIS management center on the following: There is a lack of an independent third party to review MIS operations, and there is a lack of proper documentation over standards and procedures along with a lack of control over computer center operations and a lack of performance standards to evaluate MIS personnel. Also, there is a lack of control over information centers and over input and/or output data. The planning problems are, in turn, related to controls directly: that is, the lack of security protection measures over MIS and the lack of a contingency recovery program. An evaluation of these problems indicates that the typical MIS manager has a wide range of control problems.

In keeping with the preceding new directions, it is appropriate that one be included for MIS control. More specifically, there is need for *soft controls* to replace stringent controls that have a tendency to restrict personal freedom on the job. In Chapter 14, the use of soft controls is discussed along with the need for data security and data integrity. The end result should be an improvement of MIS control over organizationwide computing activities. A complementary discussion to this area is found in Chapter 15, where the focus is on computer crime and auditing.

As a way of integrating control over the MIS organization, a revised two-part MIS questionnaire is presented in Chapter 15. The original two-part questionnaire was the instrument used for the research data in this text. However, the revised questionnaire is useful for evaluating the MIS department and end users in the functional units.

PRINCIPLES AND GUIDELINES TO ASSIST MIS MANAGEMENT IN OVERSEEING ORGANIZATIONWIDE COMPUTING ACTIVITIES

Throughout the remainder of the text, appropriate principles underlying the subject matter are stated at the beginning of each chapter. These principles provide a logical framework to assist in the development of topics that need to be overseen by MIS management. In turn, a rich discussion of a specific area of MIS management concern provides the basis to synthesize appropriate guidelines for the typical MIS manager to follow—found at the end of each chapter. Basically, the underlying structure for these guidelines is provided by the new directions set forth in each chapter. In effect, these management guidelines for the 1990s and beyond are helpful to the typical MIS manager on a day-to-day basis.

NOTES

1. Robert J. Thierauf, *A Manager's Complete Guide to Effective Information Systems: A Questionnaire Approach,* New York: Free Press, 1983, Questionnaire 1, pp. 38–49, and Questionnaire 2, pp. 61–68.

2. *Statement on Auditing Standards (SAS) No. 3: The Effect of EDP on the Auditor's Study and Evaluation of Internal Controls,* New York: AICPA, 1974, p. 3, paragraph 7.

3. Ibid., pp. 3–4, paragraph 8.

4. Robert J. Thierauf, *A Manager's Complete Guide to Effective Information Systems: A Questionnaire Approach,* New York: Free Press, 1983, pp. 89–108 and pp. 129–143.

5. Robert J. Thierauf, *New Directions in MIS Management: A Guide for the 1990s,* New York: Quorum Books, 1988, pp. 29–43.

6. Part-time graduate students in the graduate-level course Managerial Aspects of Management Information Systems were to complete one of the questionnaires (Questionnaire 1 or 2) as a requirement for completing the course. They are full-time systems professionals, systems analysts, or analysts/programmers who have been on the job for several years.

7. Robert J. Thierauf, *A Manager's Complete Guide to Effective Information Systems: A Questionnaire Approach,* New York: Free Press, 1983, p. 76.

8. Robert J. Thierauf, *New Directions in MIS Management: A Guide for the 1990s,* New York: Quorum Books, 1988, p. 33.

9. Robert J. Thierauf, *A Manager's Complete Guide to Effective Information Systems: A Questionnaire Approach,* New York: Free Press, 1983, p. 121.

10. Robert J. Thierauf, *New Directions in MIS Management: A Guide for the 1990s,* New York: Quorum Books, 1988, p. 36.

PART II

EFFECTIVE STRATEGIC PLANNING AND TOTAL QUALITY MANAGEMENT

3

Strategic Planning of the MIS Organization

OUTLINE

Guidelines to Assist MIS Management in Strategic Planning
Notes

INTRODUCTION TO STRATEGIC PLANNING OF THE MIS ORGANIZATION

After the human element, MIS strategic planning is the MIS manager's most important resource. This important fact means that MIS strategic planning should be approached from a new and different perspective. This involves future information in the form of problems and related opportunities that should be evaluated and resolved currently because they will impact the MIS organization tomorrow. This way of thinking, defined as *problem finding,* underlies the approach taken here. To set the stage for effective MIS strategic planning, the underlying principle of problem finding, ''management by perception,'' is highlighted and related to the problem-finding process. In contrast, the management-by-exception principle underlies the current approaches to *problem solving* in resolving MIS strategic planning problems.

In addition, the chapter looks at those factors that provide a starting point for effective MIS strategic planning. Similarly, the need for creative thinking by MIS management; the need for clearly defined MIS objectives, goals, and strategies; and their linkage to a company's critical success factors and key performance indicators are discussed. Next, the development of short- to long-range strategic plans is treated. Overall, the chapter looks at those important factors that focus on the planning aspects of a typical MIS manager's job.

STRATEGIC PLANNING VERSUS TACTICAL PLANNING AND OPERATIONAL PLANNING

From an overview, *strategic planning* requires a clear and complete understanding of the organization, its mission, its business, its customers, and its competitors. If MIS management can exploit information technology to its fullest to impact these important factors and people, they, in turn, can make a major impact on the total organization. Similarly, if MIS management can identify uses of information in the pursuit of organization objectives, goals, strategies, and critical success factors at the highest level, they can help their organizations use the latest information technology to further the organization's mission. From this perspective, productive MIS strategic planning can evolve.

Basically, there are two key elements underlying effective strategic planning. The first is a strategic vision which serves as a cornerstone for everyone in the organization for daily decision making. The second key element is a complete understanding of the business environment and its current and future movement, that is, customer needs and their perceptions of new products and services, competitor effectiveness in satisfying those needs and perceptions, and opportunities and threats derived from social, political, and economic changes. An integral part of this second element is understanding the evolving business environment whereby the environment is monitored regularly for changes that may signal the beginning of a trend. Many business failures can be attributed to the lack of detailed or current understanding of the business environment.

In contrast, *tactical planning* is concerned with developing action plans for the acquisition and deployment of organization resources to carry out the strategies identified in strategic planning. Budgets, plans for specific projects, and master manufacturing plans are examples of tactical plans. Information resource plans often are more tactical in approach than strategic plans despite their longer time frames. Generally, they are carried out by middle management as opposed to senior corporate management or top management. From a very short-term viewpoint, *operational planning* deals with day-to-day operations that are necessary for accomplishing the action plans. Shop-floor scheduling in manufacturing and production scheduling by an MIS department are examples. At this level, there is need for detailed practices and procedures, desk or workstation instructions, and other detailed plans that ensure the execution of operational plans. Operational planning is under the control of lower management.

Need of Creative Thinking for Effective Strategic Planning

The main thrust of creative thinking for effective strategic planning of the MIS organization is on new and untried approaches. The unusual approach and the exploration of generally nonstandard approaches and methods can often bring MIS management in the planning process—from the short range to the long range—to the point where new alternatives can be devised for a problem under study. The period of *incubation* where new decision alternatives are fermenting finally results in the *illumination* state. Too often, time for creative thinking is unduly restricted because there is the pressing demand for immediate results.

Creativity requires a good logical mind that can reduce a complex situation to its essential elements. Effective MIS managers must think analytically and be highly imaginative in their approaches to decision making. Not only must they be able to visualize the possibilities of alternatives; they also must be capable of communicating their ideas in an understandable manner. They must take the initiative when required and answer valid objections to their work. In essence, they must operate effectively in two worlds—the *conceptual* one of creative problem finding and the *real* one of effective decisions.

During decision making, MIS managers who possess these attributes should work with managers from the functional end-user departments, who can then act as a sounding board for new ideas and alternatives. Departmental managers who have the answers to the proverbial questions of who, what, where, when, how, and why should be imaginative enough to recommend improvements to the new ideas. Likewise, they should be objective in their thinking and should accept worthwhile changes. Facts that may be needed subsequently can be gathered under their direction. MIS planners and departmental managers can complement one another. Their teamwork can produce better decisions than if MIS management works alone on short- to long-range MIS strategic plans.

PRINCIPLES OF EFFECTIVE MIS STRATEGIC PLANNING

A newer principle (as noted) that has not been widely promulgated in the MIS literature or elsewhere is the principle of management by perception. As will be seen in a later section of this chapter, it is a means by which MIS management can perceive future problems and bring them back to the present time for solution. In addition, this principle includes identifying future problems that can be turned into opportunities. Specific steps will be set forth so that the MIS manager can become familiar with this important management process. Hence, the first principle can be stated as the *Principle of Future-Based Management of the MIS Organization.*

Once the future of the MIS organization has been explored in terms of problems and related opportunities, the MIS manager needs to apply the *Principle of Developing Appropriate MIS Objectives and Goals.* Specific objectives and goals need to be developed that not only reflect the organization's mission, but also take into account adjustments that may be necessary to reflect changing times. Additionally, if an organization changes its mission, there is need for the MIS manager to adjust the MIS organization's objectives and goals.

Closely tied in with the prior principle is one relating to MIS in terms of its critical success factors, that is, the *Principle of Focusing on MIS Critical Success Factors.* Because these factors are critical to the success of the MIS organization, they must be first identified. In turn, appropriate measurement of these factors by the MIS manager is necessary. Generally, key performance indicators are used in the measurement. Because of the importance of critical success factors and key performance indicators, they are treated later in the chapter.

The essential part of the strategic planning process by MIS management centers on a very important principle, namely, the *Principle of Developing Short- to Long-Range MIS Strategic Plans.* Typically, MIS critical success factors are integrated with the development of short- to long-range MIS strategic plans. In this way, appropriate MIS strategic plans can be developed over a time frame that allows those factors that are really necessary for success to be even more successful. In other words, successful MIS does not just happen: It must be planned; otherwise, chaos might be the order of the day. In essence, the MIS manager might be proactive or forward looking as opposed to being reactive or backward looking.

In the development of short- to long-range MIS strategic plans, it may become necessary to adjust these plans because of changes in the economy as well as unforeseen circumstances, such as mergers and acquisitions. Also, the organization may be experiencing financial difficulties that need to be addressed. Hence, the MIS manager must be aware of the need for the *Principle of Flexibility in*

Strategic MIS Plans. What may be appropriate today may be inappropriate tomorrow.

Last, but not least, the MIS manager must include provision for end-user involvement in the MIS strategic planning effort. Hence, there is need for the *Principle of End-User Involvement in MIS Strategic Plans.* The rationale is that end-user computing expenditures for stand-alone microcomputers, local area networks, and data communications networks plus all types of software have exceeded and will continue to exceed those spent by the MIS department directly. There is need for the entire company to march to the same step in terms of hardware and software acquired. Not only can training problems be reduced, but maintenance problems of computer hardware and software can be minimized. Overall, it is recommended that end users be included in the MIS organization-wide committee to help plan current and future hardware/software acquisitions and their implementation.

RELATIONSHIP OF CURRENT RESEARCH TO MIS STRATEGIC PLANNING

Current research results in Chapter 2 on management information systems (Figure 2.4) indicate the following *planning* problems:

- Lack of security protection measures over the management information system (rated no. 3)
- Lack of adequate short- to long-range plans for management information systems (rated no. 4)
- Lack of a contingency recovery program (rated no. 7)

An examination of these current problems indicates that the utilization of problem finding would be of great assistance to the MIS manager when engaging in MIS strategic planning. To visualize this important point, each problem area is related directly or indirectly to problem finding later.

The *lack of security protection measures over the management information system* can relate to problem finding in the following manner. Because security is an organizationwide problem caused by the proliferation of microcomputers, MIS management needs to interact with the managers of functional end-user departments not only to solve current security problems, but also to engage in problem finding in order to determine the organization's potential exposure to fraud, theft, and the like. MIS management must determine the organization's potential for loss that would prevent it from realizing its objectives today and tomorrow. A critical review of security using problem finding will undoubtedly uncover some unfavorable security scenarios that must be dealt with today by MIS and functional departmental management.

In relation to the *lack of adequate short- to long-range plans for management information systems,* problem finding is a natural. Information to assist MIS management will be given in this chapter. Additionally, there is a need for integrating MIS objectives, goals, and strategies with the organization's critical success factors for effective problem finding. Discussion of their importance to MIS management for successful MIS strategic planning will be addressed in this chapter.

Another problem that can be related to problem finding is the *lack of a contingency recovery program.* More specifically, problem finding can assist MIS management in determining what type of contingency recovery program is needed. This may center on restructuring the organization's one or more centralized and decentralized databases or may involve methods and procedures to get started again after the organization's computer mainframes have been down for several hours or possibly days. No matter the type of recovery program, problem finding can be helpful in assessing the program needed today that can be expanded or contracted as the situation demands over time. Setting up a contingency recovery program without giving consideration to changing times can be wasteful. A problem-finding approach, as opposed to a problem-solving approach, helps MIS management to place current and future events into their proper perspective.

EFFECTIVE MIS STRATEGIC PLANNING FOCUSES ON PROBLEM FINDING

For a broad-based and objective viewpoint of MIS strategic planning, two approaches to the problem-finding process are presented, namely, the problem-centered approach and the opportunity-centered approach. Underlying the problem-finding process is the management by perception principle mentioned previously. This principle refers to the ability of management to perceive future external and internal trends before they occur and to determine their impact on new products and/or services so as to improve overall organizational performance.[1] On the other hand, management by exception focuses on comparison after the fact. However, both have their place in a typical organization for making appropriate MIS strategic planning decisions.

To elaborate further on management by perception, management must be able to perceive developing computer, economic, and social trends that have relevance to the organization, including a tie-in with organizationwide computing activities. By perceiving these trends before they occur, MIS management can adjust its strategic (long-range) MIS plans and, in turn, its tactical (medium-range) and operational (short-range) plans for the coming external and internal environmental changes. In this manner, MIS managers can improve overall MIS performance today to meet the demands placed on the MIS organization in the future.

Problem-Centered Approach

For the *problem-centered* approach, there is need to examine the environment with the idea of looking out into the future and exploring those problems that will have impact on the organization now and at some time in the future. Because the process is one of going out into the future and determining important problems (i.e., problem finding), these problems are brought back to the present time to examine their cause-and-effect relationship. The problem-centered approach includes dividing problems into their component parts, employing operational decision rules when deemed necessary, utilizing the language of numbers to quantify the parameters surrounding the problem, and searching for convergence, that is, for an answer. All in all, the main thrust is on logical-analytical thinking that will identify future problems having a great impact on the organization not only today, but also in the future. Of equal importance is the fact that these future problems are related directly to organizationwide computing activities. MIS managers can get a handle on what must be done to improve the organization's computing capabilities.

The six steps of the problem-centered approach to problem finding consist of (1) generation, (2) evaluation, (3) validation, (4) establishment of boundaries, (5) solution, and (6) implementation. The first four steps are the actual search for and identification of future problems, while the remaining two steps represent the actual solution to one or more problems and the implementation of the solution. These steps are as follows:

Step 1. *Generation* is the probe for potential problems that might exist in the future that will have impact on the organization. A popular technique is to utilize the well-known *brainstorming* approach. The analysis is initially forward looking; it later becomes backward looking.

Step 2. *Evaluation* reviews problems uncovered and determines whether they merit managerial concern. In most situations, there is need to utilize a *cost/benefit analysis* to determine what impact the problem has on the organization.

Step 3. *Validation* is an extension of problem evaluation in that one or more actual problems are validated for managerial concern. The validation is generally backed up by a cost/benefit analysis. If such an analysis is not available, alternative means are needed to substantiate this selection of problem(s).

Step 4. *Establishment of boundaries* defines each potential problem within its boundaries so as to uncover the whole area that the problem encompasses. There may be need for "fine tuning" so that the appropriate boundaries are established.

Step 5. *Solution* uses an appropriate method that is dictated by the type of future problem(s) being solved.

Step 6. *Implementation* focuses on utilizing the proper implementation procedures and establishing control over the solution to the problem(s).

The preceding steps are generally conducted in the order presented. However, there may be circumstances that warrant changing the sequence. In addition, there is need of *feedback,* the means to start anew if necessary.

Opportunity-Centered Approach

Within the *opportunity-centered approach,* the perspective is somewhat different from that of the problem-centered approach. The main focus is on identifying opportunities for the organization to pursue that generally arise from the problems uncovered. In effect, there is need to change an organizational liability into an asset, that is, identify problems that can result in important opportunities for the organization. From this enlightened view, the opportunity-centered approach identifies important opportunities that are often overlooked when the problem-solving process has been employed in the past. Logical-analytical thinking allows the individual to look inside the problem and examine it thoroughly in order to identify opportunities that are typically overlooked by the traditional approach to problem solving. Additionally, the opportunity-centered approach need not always be related to future problems. Rather, it can center on opportunities that have been identified currently. From this perspective, specific opportunities can be addressed directly by MIS management to allow their organizations to meet and, many times, to beat competition by having advanced computing capabilities.

The five steps of the opportunity-centered approach to problem finding are as follows: (1) exploration, (2) selection, (3) examination of boundaries, (4) solution, and (5) implementation. The first three steps are the actual search for and identification of present and future opportunities, while the remaining two steps reflect the actual solution to one or more opportunities and the implementation of the solution. These steps are as follows:

Step 1. *Exploration* examines the environment for opportunities that arise from problems uncovered. Generally, a *brainstorming* approach is used by top management and the corporate planning staff.

Step 2. *Selection* determines that one or more opportunities should be explored by top management and corporate planners. The selection process should focus on those opportunities that relate to an organization's *critical success factors.*

Step 3. *Examination of boundaries* surveys the environment for each opportunity and determines the proper boundaries. Because of the nature of some opportunities, the boundaries may be quite wide.

Step 4. *Solution* uses an appropriate method that is dictated by the type of opportunity(ies).

Step 5. *Implementation* focuses on implementing the opportunity(s) and on establishing control over the solution to the opportunity(s).

The preceding steps are generally conducted in the order presented although there may be conditions that warrant changing this order. As before, *feedback* is necessary, to provide a means for recognizing new opportunities.

For the most part, problem-centered and opportunity-centered approaches are oriented toward semistructured and unstructured problems for the following time periods—some short-range and most medium- to long-range periods. Also, the problems found in problem finding require a thorough search, which is typically not the case with problem solving. For more information on the problem-finding process, reference can be made to another publication by the author.[2]

ASSESSING AN MIS MANAGER'S CAPABILITY TO ENGAGE IN PROBLEM FINDING

Building upon the foregoing discussion, the question can be asked, "How effective is the MIS manager when engaging in MIS strategic planning?" An effective MIS manager is not born, but is made by going beyond problem solving and being alert to acquiring problem-finding skills, namely, knowledge about problem-finding techniques and the problem-finding process. These skills, in turn, are internalized by the MIS manager over time, becoming an integral part of his or her personality in everyday dealings with organizational personnel whether senior corporate managers, end users, or MIS personnel.

As with any new management approach, it is necessary for the MIS manager "to crawl before he or she walks." That is, the individual should recognize that his or her first encounters with problem finding may not be as rewarding as the individual would like. However, encountering common difficulties that are a part of problem finding and overcoming them one by one as more experience is gained results in an improved problem-finding approach to MIS strategic planning. The essential message, then, is that "practice makes perfect." To try to make the first tries at problem finding "remarkable successes" is unrealistic and does not speak well of the MIS manager. The very nature of problem finding does not lend itself to the "perfect practice" of MIS strategic planning. The MIS manager must recognize the multitude of difficulties related to poorly structured problems and opportunities that have a long-range time frame.

To determine whether you are an effective MIS manager in the area of problem finding, the questions in Figure 3.1 are offered as a means of assessing your qualifications. If you answer many of these questions negatively, the subject matter of this text should be of great interest for improving your problem-finding skills. Even if you score very well, there will be many helpful hints given throughout this text to sharpen your skills.

STARTING POINT FOR EFFECTIVE STRATEGIC PLANNING OF THE MIS ORGANIZATION

MIS management can significantly influence the effectiveness and success of the organizations they support by building a solid working relationship with their colleagues in senior management. Traditional long-range MIS plans continue to ensure the "bread-and-butter role" of the information resource. They also provide the foundation on which a new planning approach must be built. This new approach focuses on MIS strategic planning considerations—the nature of the organization and the business environment in which it operates. This new ap-

Figure 3.1
Questions to Assess the MIS Manager's Capability to Engage in Problem Finding

- Do you recognize the need for exploring potential MIS problems now and in the future?
- Are you alert to signs pointing to the need to explore potential MIS problems?
- Do you recognize the need for exploring profitable opportunities now and in the future that are related to MIS?
- Are you alert to signs pointing to the need to explore profitable opportunities that are related to MIS?
- Do you take time for sorting things out from the short run to the long run?
- Do you face difficult MIS problems head on?
- Do you act rather than drift and "let things happen"?
- Do you keep an open mind to new MIS opportunities and ideas?
- Do you keep up with small MIS problems to prevent being overwhelmed by them?
- Do you set priorities in the MIS planning process?
- Do you review long-standing problems and opportunities to see whether they are still valid?
- Do you do your own thinking or are you a chronic advice seeker?
- Do you try to have an MIS backup plan on difficult problems?
- Do you take the time for careful consideration when needed?
- Can you sense when to make a quick decision?
- Do you face the fact that "the buck stops here"?
- Do you see a possible opportunity in every crisis?
- Do you recognize the need for new approaches to MIS strategic planning?
- Do you employ newer planning techniques to improve MIS strategic plans?
- Do you integrate MIS strategic plans with corporate objectives, goals, strategies, and critical success factors?

proach produces business plans that include strategic uses of the information technology in conjunction with the other organization resources to take advantage of business opportunities and achieve business objectives. This section of the chapter suggests appropriate means for strengthening information technology components of a corporatewide planning effort.

Establishment of an MIS Organizationwide Committee

A starting point for an effective corporatewide planning effort is to get the involvement of functional end-user departments with the MIS department such that the total MIS organization is marching to the same drummer. Essentially, this means the establishment of an *MIS organizationwide committee* that gives overall direction to exploiting information technology for the total organization. This MIS committee is charged with the development of appropriate organizationwide information technology policies. Such a formal planning process forces an organization's management to articulate their policies, priorities, and action plans. The advantages of a formal, documented information resource plan that emanates from an organizationwide committee include the following:

- Easier cost justification for information technology projects, helping to ensure that resources will be available when needed
- Better use of the money spent on information technology
- Improved information that is in accessible and usable form
- Smoother running of all components in a complex information technology environment
- Reduction of costly maintenance and corrective work
- Identification of cost-saving and cost-sharing opportunities in a distributed environment
- More effective responses to changes in the business environment, thereby avoiding crisis management

Among the many duties of the MIS organizationwide committee is the development of short- to long-range MIS plans, that is, the preparation of one- to five-year projections of MIS needs. Other duties include establishing new and challenging MIS standards of performance for organizationwide computing activities, analyzing current and future MIS operations with the purpose of improving them, coordinating and monitoring the preparation of a comprehensive MIS plan for longer than five years, and finding future MIS problems as a means to recommending MIS opportunities for growth.

After MIS management has reviewed the work of this committee, evaluated the one- to five-year forecasts, and become convinced that the financial figures are reasonable and feasible, the composite documents thus gathered constitute the organizationwide computing plan for the years ahead. Typically, these "working papers" are regarded as the future MIS plans. In turn, their significant elements are brought together to ensure compatibility with organizationwide objectives, goals, and strategies as well as critical success factors and key performance indicators.

Development of Appropriate Organizationwide Information Technology Policies

The most important work of MIS management, assisted by the MIS organizationwide committee, centers not only on developing and executing MIS plans, but also on setting information technology policies. An MIS organization without guiding policies typically wanders in search of its objectives and goals. Policies are the means by which senior corporate management sets guidelines for consistent decision making by its subordinates. As such, MIS policies represent the formal vehicle for delegating *authority* and *responsibility* to lower levels in the MIS organization. In turn, they become the means for holding subordinates *accountable for results*. Essentially, MIS policies provide the means by which the rest of the MIS organization sets its course. Although most organizations today rely heavily on management information systems for their well-being, their corporate policies often do not reflect this dependence. Organizationwide information policies that tie in with information technology policies are imperative.

Information technology policies that specify authority, responsibility, and accountability over specific MIS operations must take into account two separate but overlapping areas. First, policies covering MIS operations must be developed on an organizationwide basis. Second, policies that govern the use and distribution of MIS information must be developed. Thus, MIS management must develop and distribute a list of appropriate IT policy issues to senior corporate management for discussion. In turn, the group's conclusions and suggestions provide the framework for developing organizationwide information technology policies. For the most part, MIS policies that affect the MIS department and end users are set forth in an MIS Policies and Procedures Manual. Essentially, this manual details the internal policies and procedures that apply to all MIS personnel and end users in the organization. As usual, there is need for periodic updating of this manual. This is the job of the MIS manager's staff.

EFFECTIVE STRATEGIC PLANNING OF THE MIS ORGANIZATION

For the MIS department and end users to make optimum use of information technology and to support the organization aggressively as a whole, MIS management must have effective strategic plans to guide them through the short to the long term. This section of the chapter discusses the need to establish clearly defined MIS objectives, goals, and strategies that are based on the organization's mission. In turn, there is linkage of these items for the total organization to the MIS organization to clearly stated critical success factors (CSFs) and their measurement using key performance indicators (KPIs).

Need for Clearly Defined MIS Objectives, Goals, and Strategies Based on the Organization's Mission

As a starting point, MIS management must have a clear vision of where the MIS organization is headed tomorrow, which might be different from today. For example, MIS management might be considering outsourcing, which is quite a different direction than the MIS organization is taking currently. Needless to say, this vision must be tied in with the organization's mission, which is found in its mission statement. A company's *mission* statement generally states its intent of servicing a certain market segment such that customers and employees are better served by the organization than if it did not exist. Related directly to realizing an organization's mission are its objectives, goals, and strategies. In the material to follow, the focus is from the MIS organization's viewpoint.

Basically, an *objective* is a statement of intent—what there is to accomplish. It is a statement of what will be accomplished when it has been achieved successfully. Every objective means an *action* toward a predetermined end. In establishing an objective, both the action to be used (how) and the *object* or end (what) to which action is applied must be described. Thus, an objective has two parts—an action and the object of the action. As an example, the objective of being the lowest-cost MIS organization in a certain industry contains the action to be undertaken (lowest-cost MIS organization) and the end (in a certain industry).

A statement of an objective must indicate measurable characteristics. Otherwise, it is impossible to determine whether the objective has been achieved. From this perspective, there is a need to set forth *measurable goals* in terms of a time frame. When clearly defined goals are lacking, it is impossible to evaluate the plan of action, and there is no sound basis for selecting appropriate people, equipment, or methods. As an example that relates to the previous objective of being the lowest-cost MIS organization in a certain industry, goals could include reducing total MIS automation efforts by 12 percent next year and achieving a 20 percent return on investment. In essence, MIS planners will function "in a fog" until they know just what is to be achieved. In addition, an important reason for stating clearly measurable goals is that MIS planners provide a means for evaluating their progress at any time and are able to organize their efforts into appropriate activities. Extrapolating from these factors concerning objectives and goals, MIS objectives are essentially those things the organization will achieve today and in the future for its organizationwide computing activities that are clearly measurable in terms of specific MIS goals.

Related to MIS objectives and goals are appropriate MIS strategies. Basically, a *strategy* centers on the acquisition, use, and disposition of resources required to meet an established objective. As an example that is tied in with the previous MIS objective (being the lowest-cost MIS organization in a certain industry), a strategy could include reviewing and upgrading all performance standards as well as negotiating lower information processing costs by outside service vendors. Hence, MIS strategies relate to the acquisition, use, and disposition of MIS resources required to meet stated MIS objectives in terms of organizationwide computing activities as well as specific MIS goals.

Need for Clearly Stated MIS Critical Success Factors (CSFs)

For any business, *critical success factors* (CSFs) are the limited number of areas in which results, if they are satisfactory, will ensure successful competitive performance for an organization. They were developed by John F. Rockart at MIT. They are the few important areas where things must go right if the organization is to flourish. If results are not adequate in these areas, the organi-

Figure 3.2
The Relationship of Organization Goals to Critical Success Factors and Key Performance Indicators

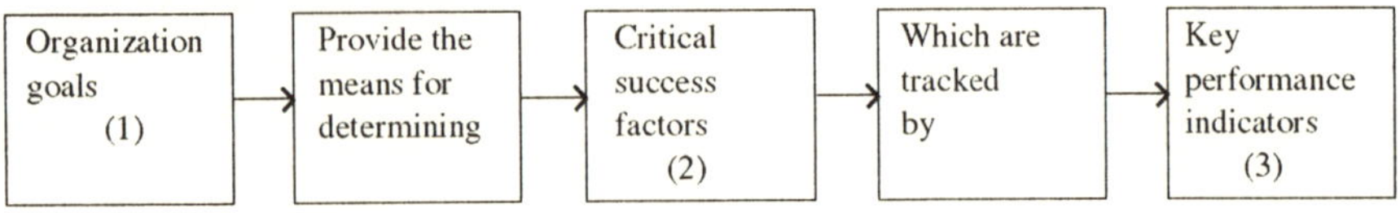

zation's efforts for the period will be less than desired. As a result, the CSFs are the areas of activity that should receive constant and careful attention from lower to top management. The current status of performance in each area should be made available to higher levels of management.[3] The process of identifying CSFs can be extended to the MIS organization. More specifically, knowing what the CSFs are and determining how they are measured enable MIS management to identify the appropriate system needed to monitor the CSFs.

Critical success factors that are essential to an MIS organization need to be defined quite clearly and discussed by the MIS organizationwide committee. These factors are related to the major problems found in the prior chapter (refer to Figure 2.5). By way of review, they include need for more thorough independent third-party auditing, more security protection measures, improved documentation over standards and procedures, better short- to long-range MIS plans, improved training programs of MIS personnel, and an adequate contingency recovery program. Although these factors have been critical to the MIS organization in the past, the same may not be true in the future, particularly if the MIS organization is engaged in a fair amount of outsourcing. Thus, the MIS organizationwide committee needs to state CSFs that are critical to the success of the MIS organization as it changes over time. For example, the greater tie-in with an organization's trading partners using EDI may signal the need for new CSFs that focus on reliable electronic exchange of information among the partners.

Measurement of CSFs Using Key Performance Indicators (KPIs)

The concept of key performance indicators (KPIs), developed at MIT's Sloan School of Management, is a way of formalizing and describing John Rockart's critical success factors. Fundamentally, the CSF system has three basic components, as shown in Figure 3.2. Essentially, overall organization goals are broken down into appropriate goals for divisions and business units. In turn, each business unit identifies a number of critical activities that must be performed well to achieve its goals. These activities are then assigned to the people responsible for their completion and are tracked by key performance indicators.

From an MIS perspective, typical overall key performance indicators that are linked to CSFs would include the following: productivity of the organization's data centers, the level of security that minimizes an organization's exposure to large financial losses, and financial analysis for assessing MIS projects. In a specialized area such as data communications and networking, key performance indicators include network downtime in hours per month, user response times on a daily basis, and network help-desk calls by the hour of the day. Similarly, in the area of database administration, KPIs center on the number of incorrect records processed on a daily basis, the number of breaches of data security daily, and the number of incorrect records stored on-line on a daily basis. Hence, a number of KPIs can be determined for each major functional area of a typical MIS organization.

LINKAGE OF MIS OBJECTIVES, GOALS, AND STRATEGIES WITH CSFs AND KPIs

To synthesize the preceding materials, the following example will be helpful. The RT Manufacturing Company is a textile firm with annual sales of about $300 million; it manufactures towels, bath mats, drapes, and tablecloths, and it sells cloth at intermediate stages in the production process. Production is handled at a number of plants; there are three cloth mills, a yarn mill, a dye house, and a finishing plant. The company's management reviewed its corporate strategic plans. To prevent competition from foreign imports, the company chose to focus on being the low-cost producer in the market niches selected. Because the company values employee satisfaction as much as profitability, the company's mission is twofold: first, to be the dominant supplier of textile products for the most profitable segments of the domestic textile market, and second, to provide a high-quality work life for its employees. Senior corporate management has determined its corporate objectives to be (1) to compete in profitable markets, (2) to operate as a low-cost producer, and (3) to offer high-quality products. In Figure 3.3, the first of these three objectives is broken down into the goals and strategies needed to accomplish these corporate objectives. It should be noted that the company's goals are very specific and target dates are identified and, in turn, related to specific corporate strategies.

Next, the critical success factors were selected. CSFs important to the company for achieving the first objective included effective market intelligence, new product development, and dominance in chosen market segments. For the second corporate objective set forth previously (operate as a low-cost producer), the critical success factors are high labor productivity and low material cost. Similarly, the CSFs related to the third corporate objective (offer high-quality products) center on updating the production process with new methods so as to improve or at least maintain product quality and installing new equipment that can improve final product quality. Finally, it was necessary to determine and

Figure 3.3
Relationship of Corporate Objectives, Goals, and Strategies with Critical Success Factors and Key Performance Indicators for the First Objective of the RT Manufacturing Company (Compete in Profitable Market Segments)

Corporate Objective	Corporate Goals	Corporate Strategies	Critical Success Factors	Key Performance Indicators
Compete in profitable market segments	Identify and enter five new market segments with high-profit potential next year	Upgrade market research to identify high-profit potential market segments	Effective market intelligence	Market research data
	Increase market share 15 percent in high-profit market segments in which the company is the dominant supplier within two years	Develop a product line that fits the requirements and needs of the high-potential market segments	New product development	Evaluation of new products and market share

communicate the key performance indicators to appropriate company personnel. Key performance indicators related to CSFs are shown in Figure 3.3.

The corporate objectives, goals, and strategies plus CSFs and KPIs are extended to MIS management. When they are known, it is incumbent upon MIS management through its organizationwide computing activities to measure these items, that is, CSFs via KPIs, so that the right information is available to ensure that the company is moving in the right direction. It makes no sense for the company to develop elaborate management information systems that measure factors that are not critical to its operations. Similarly, it makes no sense to spend considerable amounts of money to develop such systems that are not helpful to all managers.

As a starting point, the first MIS objective, from among a number of possible ones, is oriented toward effective organizationwide computing activities that assist functional end-user managers and their operating personnel to meet their organizational financial objectives (refer to Figure 3.4). Essentially, this objective is then related to the goal of providing a certain level of computing for the entire company that costs 5 percent of sales. As shown in Figure 3.4, this goal plus two others—increase end-user productivity by 5 percent each year and provide end users with accurate and timely information—are complemented by appropriate MIS strategies which are defined to meet these measurable MIS goals. These strategies focus on upgrading organizationwide computing activities so that end users are utilizing state-of-the-art hardware and software, utilizing pro-

Figure 3.4
Relationship of MIS Objectives, Goals, and Strategies with Critical Success Factors and Key Performance Indicators for the First MIS Objective of the RT Manufacturing Company. It Centers on Effective Organizationwide Computing Activities that Assist Functional End-User Managers and Their Operating Personnel in Meeting Their Financial Objectives

MIS Objective	MIS Goals	MIS Strategies	Critical Success Factors	Key Performance Indicators
Centers on effective organization-wide computing activities that assist functional end-user managers and their operating personnel in meeting their organizational financial objectives	Provide a certain level of computing for the entire company that costs 5 percent of sales	Utilize state-of-the-art hardware and software in assisting end-users to meet their computing needs	Effective functional end-user departmental computing	Measurement of the number of new systems implemented
	Increase end-user productivity by 5 percent each year	Utilize prototyping to get systems up and running fast	Quality systems development	Measurement of quality of the new systems
	Provide end-users with accurate and timely information	Develop appropriate systems which include MIS controls	Effective data security and integrity	Measurement of level of internal control in the new systems

totyping to get systems up and running fast, and developing appropriate systems that include MIS controls. In turn, these MIS strategies are related to operational critical success factors that are germane to MIS activities. Typical CSFs for the RT Manufacturing Company include an effective functional end-user departmental computing approach, quality systems improvement, and effective data security and integrity. In turn, appropriate KPIs include measurement of the number of new systems implemented, the quality of new systems, and the level of internal control in the new systems.

Tie-In with Problem Finding

Once the MIS objectives, goals, strategies, CSFs, and KPIs have been clearly defined and integrated, they provide the stepping-stones for MIS management to undertake *problem finding* for organizationwide computing activities. For the RT Manufacturing Company, this centers on finding the important computing problems that will impact the organization in the future which should be considered today. Such problems relate to the company's information needs of tomorrow, the utilization of electronic systems in the various functional departments of the company in the near future, and the relevance of the newer languages to systems and development. A thorough evaluation of these typical problems using the problem-centered approach, then, can be extremely beneficial to MIS management over time.

A SCENARIO APPROACH TO MIS STRATEGIC PLANS

An approach widely used by senior corporate management as well as MIS management centers on using different scenarios of the future. This approach is generally supported by group decision support systems and driven by the key words "what if." In MIS planning, the scenario approach provides an orderly method for managing the assumptions required for strategic planning by creating scenarios that combine trends, events, environmental factors, and the relationships among them. Essentially, this approach presents a picture of how strategies for introducing new information technology might be developed under good, average, and bad scenarios over the next five years.

The scenarios help identify important problem areas that could arise if some factors changed. Once these scenarios have been generated, managers choose those that could happen. Then one *most likely scenario* is selected as the basis for long-range strategic plans. In the MIS area, scenarios for good, average, and bad economic conditions can also be helpful to determine the most likely scenario for the MIS organization. As such, this most likely scenario can help MIS management in deciding whether outsourcing, downsizing, or maintaining the status quo is appropriate.

In addition, scenarios provide flexibility in the strategic plans and a means of escape should it be necessary. This is the role of the other scenarios that are less likely but still feasible. They identify the causes of changes that management should monitor. In these fast changing times, about the only thing certain is that some of the views of the future will prove to be somewhat wrong. The selected scenario of the future is used to develop long-range on down to short-range strategic plans for achieving desired results. Another role that scenario creation can play is to protect against errors of judgment by management, by flushing out basic assumptions that are no longer relevant. In this period of major changes, many old assumptions based on things that happened commonly in the past may no longer apply.

It should be noted that the scenario approach presented here expects things to change; hence, midcourse corrections are part of the whole scenario process. As scenarios of the future are regenerated at later points in time, they will certainly show new directions of the future. That is the time for senior corporate management as well as MIS management to assess the changes to determine whether plans must be modified, and decide whether a new approach should be implemented.

Current Issues That Impact a Scenario Approach

Currently, a number of issues affect scenarios in the future. Typical ones that most MIS organizations face are as follows. *First,* there may be need to downsize or upsize the MIS organization so that it is compatible with the total organization. In these fast changing times, downsizing has become a way of life for many organizations. *Second,* the amount of integration of the MIS organization with its trading partners using electronic processing is an important factor that establishes new relationships not found in the past. Electronic data interchange outside the organization and image processing within the organization essentially eliminate the mounds of paper used in past management information systems. *Third,* reengineering is a very important factor in the development of long-term MIS strategic plans. Currently, there is need to reengineer inefficient, long-standing business processes so that orders get filled faster and more accurately, new products hit the market faster, customers are served better, and goods and services are produced efficiently and with high quality. *Fourth,* improving the software development quality is necessary not only for the MIS department, but also for end users. This is an important factor that impacts the organization's customers whether they be outside or inside the organization. *Fifth,* there is a significant movement of information technology (i.e., information processing, database, and application development) to distributed organizational (departmental) levels. Basically, this movement will provide the necessary integration across the organization's business functions. *Sixth,* the rapid increase in computers devoted to end-user computing will cause MIS management to develop new policies and control mechanisms for managing end-user computing. These policies will differ from the traditional ones concerned with managing the supply of computing services. *Seventh,* the combination of office/end-user systems will substantially increase information technology spending as a percentage of total sales revenue. The growth will be almost impossible to contain because of the economics of the new information technology. *Eighth,* the primary value of a centralized MIS utility will be in providing interconnectability to the organization. This will be reflected in the change of emphasis by information processing from managing computer local operations to managing all types of networks. *Ninth* and last, the increasing productivity of application development by systems analysts/programmers and end users due to better CASE development tools and programming languages will affect the organization's ability to move in step with the times.

To get a good idea of what important issues are facing MIS management more recently, reference can be made to the Sixth Annual CSC/Index survey of senior MIS executives. They are (1) reengineering business practices, (2) aligning MIS and corporate goals, (3) improving systems development, (4) instituting cross-functional information systems, (5) organizing/utilizing data, (6) cutting MIS costs, (7) creating an information architecture, (8) updating obsolete systems, (9) developing an MIS strategic plan, and (10) changing technology platforms. Reengineering was called "most important" more frequently than any other management issue by the 224 U.S. and Canadian respondents polled.[4] Typically, many applications supporting reengineered processes will end up not on the computer mainframe, but on much smaller platforms.

DEVELOPMENT OF LONG-RANGE MIS STRATEGIC PLANS

The development of long-range MIS strategic plans must be linked initially to the organization's strategic vision of itself over the next five years. In some cases, the time frame can be a longer time basis. To generate an organization's strategic vision, senior corporate management must understand a highly complex set of interacting factors, including the industry's history and structure, the organization's and its competition's core capabilities, and the various strategic segments in which the organization competes. Senior corporate management must also take into account the unpredictable future, such as "What if there is a technological breakthrough?" and "What if new markets open up?" Once these areas have been discussed and analyzed fully, senior corporate management then articulates a strategic vision for the entire organization to follow. In turn, this vision can be utilized by MIS management to determine what long-range to short-range plans should be developed. In the process of this development, the problem-solving process along with the problem-finding process can be utilized where appropriate for resolving difficult problems and exploring forthcoming opportunities.

Today, a long-term view of the MIS organization by its management and the MIS organizationwide committee centers on incorporating the major issues set forth. A typical vision of the MIS organization is one that takes into account as many of these issues that apply as possible. For example, the MIS organization's strategic vision of the future is to employ appropriate information technology such that the organization's customers whether external or internal experience improved services, thereby making their operations easier.

The determination of which of these issues is to be the central focus of long-range MIS strategic plans is a difficult undertaking for MIS management and its MIS organizationwide committee. A recommended approach is to place each of the issues into the general framework of a cost/benefit analysis: that is, those issues that add value to the total organization should be implemented. For example, if an electronic data interchange mode with trading partners eliminates friction between the organization and its customers as well as reduces total processing costs, then a cost/benefit analysis will disclose a very positive return on investment. In a similar manner, if image processing within the organization eliminates the friction between departments and reduces total processing costs, then a cost/benefit analysis will disclose a very satisfactory return on investment. However, in other cases, cost justification might be difficult for newer types of systems that offer only marginal returns to users. It might be possible if competition has these types of systems. Thus, MIS projects which resolve important issues that are a major part of long-range MIS strategic plans and, in turn, are integrated into short-range MIS strategic plans are undertaken.

By using return on investment, that is, a quantitative measure, MIS management and the MIS organizationwide committee can ensure that MIS development resources are assigned with the greatest benefit to the organization. Although financial benefits of some MIS strategic projects are impossible to quantify or users will inflate the estimated benefits to ensure that their project receives a high priority, these arguments also apply to the capital allocation process, an activity in which most senior corporate managers have learned to screen out the fluff and make effective decisions despite ambiguous data.

Ranking projects by return on investment has several important payoffs. It encourages MIS management to use a disciplined estimating and project-control process to prevent project overruns. It establishes competitive parity between the MIS group and consulting firms, who most often bid a fixed price. It also gives senior corporate management greater control. If the quoted cost exceeds the business value of the project, the user can cancel the project request or reduce its complexity. Once the project is approved, the fixed price gives MIS management a quantitative measure for evaluating performance.

A sample cost/benefit analysis for an MIS project is found in Figure 3.5 for the ABC Company. As shown, estimated savings (i.e., benefits) are subtracted from estimated one-time costs and estimated operating costs over the five-year period. Since projected savings and costs are in the future, the difference between the two sums after federal income taxes should be discounted back to the present time to account for the time value of money. This also provides a sound economic comparative analysis of MIS projects. Such an analysis is found in Figure 3.6. It should be noted that the net savings—after federal income taxes—of $196,158 over the five-year period (anticipated life of the system), when discounted at 20 percent (a common cutoff for return on investment), shows a negative amount of $56,367 for this project. That is, the return is less than 20 percent. There will be a need to consider other factors, both tangible and intangible, that affect this project to determine the feasibility or infeasibility of undertaking this MIS project. It well may be that the project will be rejected.

Details of Long-Range MIS Strategic Plans

Once important MIS strategic projects have been determined over the next several years, MIS management can begin to determine the specific details of its long-range MIS strategic plans. The projected amounts for long-term projects provide the starting point for a three- to five-year budget plan. Next, MIS needs to determine which new information technology (i.e., new hardware and software) on the market today will serve as the foundation for the organization's changing information infrastructure. It is necessary that MIS management start with a three-year acquisition and upgrade cycle and build upon these IT assumptions for up to five years. Forward-looking products that are available now and can

Figure 3.5
A Sample Cost/Benefit Analysis of an MIS Project

The ABC Company: MIS Project No. 30

Estimated Net Savings on a Rental Basis over Five Years

	Years from Start of Systems Implementation					
	1	2	3	4	5	Five-Year Total
Estimated savings						
Reduction in personnel	$120,200	$400,500	$440,300	$490,500	$540,500	$1,992,000
Sale of equipment	150,000					150,000
Rental (space) savings	25,000	51,000	54,500	58,000	61,800	250,300
Elimination of rental equipment	2,050	4,380	4,690	5,000	5,300	21,420
Other savings	3,000	3,060	3,210	3,370	3,540	16,180
Total	$300,250	$458,940	$502,700	$556,870	$611,140	$2,429,900
Estimated one-time costs						
Feasability study	$75,000					$75,000
Training	50,000					50,000
Systems and programming	355,500					355,500
Master file conversion	262,500					262,500
Other conversion costs	95,500					95,500
Site preparation	55,400					55,400
Other one-time costs	2,300					2,300
Total	$896,200					$896,200
Estimated operating costs						
Equipment rental	$110,000	$120,800	$127,400	$134,100	$141,000	$633,300
Additional personnel	34,000	60,700	62,300	63,400	64,600	285,000
Program maintenance	20,000	30,700	32,200	33,800	36,000	152,700

Figure 3.5 (Continued)

Forms and supplies	10,000	21,500	23,000	24,500	26,00	105,000
Other operating costs	4,400	12,400	12,800	13,290	17,600	60,490
Total	$178,400	$246,100	$257,700	$269,090	$285,200	$1,236,490
Net savings (losses) before fed. inc. tax	($774,350)	$212,840	$245,000	$287,780	$325,940	$297,210

Figure 3.6
A Sample Analysis Considering the Time Value of Money for an MIS Project

The ABC Company: MIS Project No. 30

Discounted Cash Flow —20 Percent Return After Federal Income Taxes on a Rental Basis over Five Years

Year	Net savings (losses) before federal income taxes (Figure 3.5)	Federal income tax at 34 percent rate	Net savings (losses) after federal income taxes	At 20 percent Present value of $1,000	Present value of net savings (losses)
1	($774,350)	($263.279)	($511,071)	.833	($425,722)
2	212,840	72,366	140.474	.694	97,489
3	245,000	83,300	161,700	.579	93,624
4	287,780	97,845	189,935	.482	91,549
5	325,940	110,820	215,120	.402	86,693
Total	$297,210	$101,052	$196,158		($56,367)

serve as the foundation for the organization's evolving architecture include client/server, object-orientation, and wireless computing products. Going beyond proposed MIS projects and the acquisition of future hardware and software, MIS management must also include the projected expenses of operating an MIS department: systems development, systems operations, data centers, data communications and networking, database administration, and information centers.

In the development of three- to five-year MIS strategic financial plans, similar future expenditures must also be developed for end users. In this manner, the total projected long-range (three- to five-year) MIS strategic financial plans can be tabulated. In addition, separate financial plans must be tabulated for scenarios under good, average, and poor economic conditions. The initial totals will be much too high. Fine tuning for the three scenarios by MIS management working in conjunction with the MIS organizationwide committee will be necessary. It well may be that the next three- to five-year plans for the least desirable scenario require a substantial increase in IT outlays, thereby requiring the approval of the board of directors. To obtain their approval, the board of directors want assurance that the new information technology will help give the organization a competitive advantage or, at least, meet competition and improve productivity.

Overall, MIS management must take the steps necessary to ensure that long-range MIS strategic formal plans present MIS departments' and end users' needs appropriately and that they can be expected to meet their future needs regardless of the fortunes the organization may encounter. Success in meeting organizational and MIS objectives and goals may create a most difficult situation for MIS management. The long-range MIS strategic plans should provide for all contingencies, including success.

DEVELOPMENT OF SHORT-RANGE MIS STRATEGIC PLANS

Development of short-range MIS strategic plans for the coming year and the following year are an outgrowth of long-range plans discussed previously. Essentially, the MIS planning process is a hierarchy of short- to long-range documented plans. Since the long-range MIS strategic plans serve as a road map for implementing the strategies and achieving the objectives through the effective deployment of resources, they also provide a means for developing more detailed MIS budgets for the short term. *MIS budgets* are detailed statements of actions, including the use of resources, for accomplishing the tasks scheduled for the coming year and the following year. The *action plans* include management plans for each project, functional area, and organizational unit which are the actual plans through which work is accomplished. Overall, this hierarchy of MIS strategic plans provides snapshot views of the integrated planning process as well as documentation. Perhaps the principal value of these documented MIS plans is their use in the redeployment of resources in response to changing times.

When working with senior corporate management in the development of short-range MIS strategic plans, MIS management should keep an open mind, not only in regard to those factors that are critical to the entire organization, but to those that are essential to the MIS organization. For example, one of the critical success factors of the United Parcel Service (UPS) is reducing minutes off delivery times. Years ago, UPS had no local area networks (LANs), but one MIS manager saw that a LAN could process documents faster. In turn, that would allow UPS drivers to deliver packages faster. Several years later, UPS has more than 500 LANs and a benchmark for establishing a LAN's value.

Additionally, in the development of short-range MIS strategic plans (whether they revolve around CSFs or not), MIS management must convey to senior corporate management that when making infrastructure investments in information technology, an organization gets what it pays for since not all the costs and benefits are obvious during the initial analysis. MIS management should never put senior corporate managers in the position of making technology-based decisions they are ill-prepared to make. Needless to say, the consequences can be detrimental and sometimes disastrous to the organization.

An effective way to influence future decisions on corporate strategic plans is to have MIS management write annual as well as quarterly reports for its organization. Senior corporate managers respond to issues they can discuss in dollar terms. And writing a report that puts the financial picture on paper is a great way to get across the message that the MIS department is a profit center. In essence, MIS management can establish the strategic importance of the MIS organization for getting approval in implementing information technology on a more current basis.

Details of Short-Range MIS Strategic Plans

Building upon the long-range MIS strategic plans noted in the previous section, MIS management must develop more detailed short-range plans that include the major capital projects and anticipated changes for this coming year and the following year: that is, use a two-year basis. For the most part, these short-range plans should be stated in financial terms so that the MIS organization can be integrated into an organization's total budget plan. Although the second year can be stated financially in more general categories, the coming year must be developed with specific financial figures. More to the point, there is need to develop specific budgeted amounts for the centralized MIS department, systems development department, decentralized data center operations, database administration, centralized information centers, data communications, and networking operations, along with all costs to be incurred by functional end-user departments for information processing operations.

Costs for the total MIS organization include a number of specific categories that must be budgeted. Typically, MIS costs are the following:

- Salaries and wages
- Outside services
- Travel
- Purchased hardware
- Maintenance
- Supplies
- Information centers
- Miscellaneous
- Fringe benefits

- Education
- Rental/lease
- Purchased software
- Depreciation
- Telephone and communications
- Overhead

Since they must be budgeted for the coming year by departmental areas, there is need to have input from the MIS and end-user functional departments in the preparation of the final figures. Working in conjunction with these departments, MIS management prepares the final figures. Needless to say, there is a final review with the various departments to assure that both know what is expected for the forthcoming year. In turn, these budgets are reviewed by the MIS organizationwide committee for approval. If there is a problem with one or more items in the MIS budget, it needs to be resolved. In total, these short-range plans represent what is expected of MIS management in terms of financial performance for the coming year.

If there are unexpected changes to these plans caused by any number of factors, they should be resolved as soon as possible. In this manner, the final figures for the coming year are always current and reflect the real situation. It is recommended that the current year's budget be updated month-by-month throughout the year so there is a twelve-month standing plan. This is where the second-year budgeted figures come into play. In conjunction with these plans is the measurement of appropriate key performance indicators for the CSFs of the MIS organization. No matter the focus of CSFs, the accomplishment of them by KPIs can indicate whether or not MIS management is performing its duties.

DISASTER RECOVERY PLANNING

An integral part of an MIS organization's strategic plans is a disaster recovery plan. Such a plan should be in place at all times in case of earthquakes, fires, floods, riots, and even pestilences and plagues. A most important consideration is not whether something might happen or even what sort of event; what is important is to have a standing plan for what to do when any disruptive or disabling event occurs that shuts down all or part of the MIS organization. An important concept here is *maximum time to belly-up,* a term used by security expert Donn B. Parker of SRI International (refer to his 1976 book, *Crime by Computer*). This term carries with it the question, ''How long could your organization stay in business without this vital resource?'' Some organizations could go two or more weeks before being seriously inconvenienced. However, for airline reservation systems or brokerage firms that process thousands or millions of transactions a day, every minute of unavailability costs money, representing lost business and lost income that cannot be recaptured. Most businesses will fall in between and begin to feel the pinch within a few days. In addition to such considerations of business survival, some organizations, such as hospitals and banks, are required by law to have emergency plans in place.

In the past, a typical disaster recovery plan has focused mainly on one or more data centers of an organization where commercial hot sites, cooperative agreements, second-bank data centers, commercial cold sites, and service bureaus have been the mainstay of the recovery. However, today there is a pressing need for recovery planning for local, metropolitan, and wide-area networks. Generally, neither MIS organizations nor disaster recovery vendors are adequately prepared to recover these networks. The rationale is that the sheer variety of platforms, network operating systems, and other technologies makes it nearly impossible to cover every possible contingency or configuration. When dealing with computer mainframes only in data centers, there were a lot of shops in the customer community that had similar configurations.

One solution for MIS management to follow is to warehouse components that can be used to replicate the LANs in event of a disaster. That is, it is necessary to bring LANs back up in 24 to 48 hours. Another solution is to have disaster recovery vendors provide the LAN support that is required today. The moment that a customer deems it critical in a disaster recovery application, the vendor should be able to provide it. Actually, disaster recovery vendors have had local-area backup products for a couple of years now.

Steps in a Disaster Recovery Plan

To assist MIS management in the development of a disaster recovery plan, the following steps are recommended for a comprehensive approach. *First,* as in most areas of MIS operations that have great impact on the organization, it is important to make senior corporate management aware of the need and get their commitment to the standby disaster recovery plan. *Second,* MIS management must choose the team that will prepare the plan as well as identify who is in charge and clarify reporting relationships. *Third,* this team will determine what facilities and operations are at risk and identify potential threats and areas of vulnerability. This includes identifying critical and essential information systems and applications. *Fourth,* the team needs to make sure that data are backed up regularly and that the backups are stored off-site. Consideration should be given to using electronic vaulting services for backing up data. An alternative processing site should be selected where the organization can go to recover operations or make other arrangements for replacement equipment and needed space. Telecommunications needs are to be included in the plan, plus the hardware, software, communications, and physical facilities needed to restore operations. Many times, the organization can work with disaster recovery vendors to meet their disaster recovery plan needs. *Fifth,* the team needs to develop a set of written procedures to follow in the event of a disaster as well as determine who will make the decision to declare a disaster and initiate recovery operations. Once the individuals who will be needed to implement a recovery operation are assembled, they need to be trained so that they can carry out their jobs. *Sixth,* the plan needs to be tested to ensure that it works. Any needed modifications in light of test results should be made. The *seventh* and last step is to update the disaster recovery plan to reflect personnel transfers and moves, changes in computer equipment and applications, and changes in business operations or strategic objectives and goals. In brief, the plan is a set of procedures to follow in the event of a disaster. In such an event, many important decisions have to be made quickly and without being able to get individual, real-time approvals.

GUIDELINES TO ASSIST MIS MANAGEMENT IN STRATEGIC PLANNING

Guidelines that are tied in with the topics of this chapter stress a macro or overview perspective when MIS management engages in short- to long-range strategic planning. *First* and foremost is the guideline that a problem-finding approach centers on MIS management's taking a very broad view of future problems. The same can be said about exploring future opportunities. The importance of this perspective is that all important facets of the problems or opportunities will be uncovered. In turn, the proper approach can be applied to the problem's solution. If a problem is viewed too narrowly, a problem-solving approach may be used when, in fact, a problem-finding approach is more appropriate. For this desired benefit, MIS management needs to take a broad-based view so that the problem is defined within its proper framework. As a result, the problem is developed so that a problem-centered approach can be employed. In a similar manner, if the accent is on identifying future opportunities, the opportunity-centered approach can be used.

For MIS management to be truly effective in taking a broad-based view, a *second* guideline is that they must think strategically, that is, integrate the important MIS factors that have strategic impact on the organization in the short to long run. This centers on relating corporate objectives, goals, and strategies to critical success factors and key performance indicators that have impact on the MIS organization. In essence, there is need for a logical flow from corporate objectives that tie in with MIS objectives, that, in turn, are related to MIS goals and strategies. Then, there is linkage to critical success factors, and then measurement for the entire organization as well as the MIS organization. Within this relationship, the MIS manager must think strategically about the importance of critical information to the entire organization. The net result is that critical information provides a balance among these integrated factors (i.e., objectives, goals, strategies, critical success factors, and key performance indicators from the short run to the long run).

A *third* guideline for effective MIS management when engaging in MIS strategic planning is an openness to growth through a willingness to try new approaches. For example, a rightsizing decision is the point at which the MIS manager faces the challenge of how his or her IT resources will be utilized. Although this potential is attainable within a problem-solving approach, it is even more so within a problem-finding approach. Thus, an MIS manager must be open to growing on the job by employing new approaches to MIS.

A recommended *fourth* guideline is that MIS management use imagination when engaging in strategic planning of the MIS organization. From an MIS planning perspective, how "original" is the individual's thinking? How often is it "borrowed"? Is the individual too settled in comfortable mental habits? Does the MIS manager let the thoughts flow freely? Hence, imagination can often be an important part of effective problem finding. In some cases, however, imagination may well be the focal point of problem finding where strategic planning problems are extremely poorly structured or where problems have long time frames.

In order to reap the important benefits of strategic planning, there is need for a *fifth* guideline relating to flexibility. Many times, it is necessary to change tactics. When an impasse is reached, the following questions can be asked: Is there any other way to express the strategic planning problem? What random ideas come to mind when I relax and think about it? Can I turn the problem upside down? Can I shift the emphasis from one part to another? The main point is that rigid thinking in MIS strategic planning must be replaced by flexible thinking.

Underlying these guidelines for successful MIS management is a *sixth* guideline that stresses a proactive approach rather than a reactive one. Such an approach centers on identifying potential problems and opportunities via the strategic planning process before they occur. The accent is on solving them by using the management-by-perception principle. Fundamentally, problems and opportunities facing MIS management are better addressed today versus sometime in the future. A forward-looking approach that is proactive needs to replace one focusing on a backward-looking or reactive approach.

NOTES

1. Robert J. Thierauf, Robert C. Klekamp, and Daniel W. Geeding, *Management Principles and Practices: A Contingency and Questionnaire Approach,* Santa Barbara, California: Wiley/Hamilton, 1977, p. 773.

2. Robert J. Thierauf, *A Problem-Finding Approach to Effective Corporate Planning,* New York: Quorum Books, 1987.

3. John F. Rockart, "Chief Executives Define Their Own Data Needs," *Harvard Business Review,* March–April 1979, pp. 81–93.

4. James A. Champy, "Grand Designs," *CIO,* January, 1993, p. 26.

4

Total Quality Management and Performance Standards

OUTLINE

Introduction to Total Quality Management (TQM) and Performance Standards
Principles of Effective TQM and Performance Standards
Relationship of Current Research to TQM and Performance Standards
Effective MIS Management of a TQM Program
Getting a TQM Program Started
1. Develop a Consensus TQM Mission Statement
2. Plan for Quality Improvement
3. Focus on Constantly Improving Service
4. Team up with Vendors for Improvement

Organization for a TQM Program
- QI Teams
- Accent on Zero-Defects Software

TQM Program for Software Improvement
Linkage of TQM to Benchmarking
Linkage of TQM to Performance Standards and Performance Appraisal
Difficulty of Setting MIS Performance Standards for Personnel and Equipment
An Effective Approach to the Development of MIS Performance Standards
1. Get Broad Participation in the Development of MIS Performance Standards
2. Review the MIS Performance Standards Prior to Finalization
3. Ensure That MIS Performance Standards Are Widely Disseminated and Fully Understood
4. Monitor to Make Sure That MIS Performance Standards Remain Current

Performance Standards for MIS Personnel
- Traditional Approach to Setting Performance Standards
- Newer Function Point Analysis to Determine Total Project Time
- Development Activities by Systems Analysts
- Development Activities by Programmers

INTRODUCTION TO TOTAL QUALITY MANAGEMENT (TQM) AND PERFORMANCE STANDARDS

Although not discussed in the prior chapter, an integral part of the strategic planning process is the inclusion of total quality management (TQM). As will be seen in this chapter, TQM is not just for manufacturing firms. It is true that the concepts originated by such quality gurus as Dr. W. Edwards Deming and Dr. Joseph M. Juran focused on statistical process control (SPC) techniques for manufacturing companies. Since that time, a number of service organizations, including MIS organizations, have adopted various forms of SPC and other quality improvement techniques. In fact, the Japanese have embraced the work of Deming and Juran in the software development market and are on their way to becoming key players in the U.S. market. Thus, it can be said that TQM is a growing, worldwide movement within both the manufacturing and service sectors that is backed by senior corporate management.

The focus of TQM is on consistently meeting the customers' expectations. MIS managers deal most often with internal customers. However, when the emphasis is only on internal customers, the organization can lose sight of external customers. MIS managers should focus primarily on the needs of the internal customers as a means to achieve the ultimate needs of external customers. This perspective of customers (internal and external) will be very useful throughout the systems development process, particularly in the requirements analysis and design stages. MIS managers must make sure that requirements and design specifications reflect the ultimate customers' perception of quality, rather than solely the organization's internal perspective. This important subject area is covered in the first part of the chapter.

In order for total quality management to be successful, it should be related to MIS performance standards for personnel and equipment. That is, TQM requires that MIS management provide a means for measuring what is required of its personnel and equipment in terms of day-to-day operations. Effective MIS management of performance standards requires ongoing effort because of the changes in the organization's needs and the introduction of new information technology. Successful MIS management depends on the availability of appropriate performance standards as a most effective tool to meet its goals and objectives. Furthermore, measurement of the impact of MIS performance standards is necessary to determine whether or not they are fair and accurate. Within this framework, MIS performance standards are discussed in the second half of thc chapter.

PRINCIPLES OF EFFECTIVE TQM AND PERFORMANCE STANDARDS

The *Principle of Consistently Meeting Customers' Expectations* relates to the initial focus of a total quality management program. As noted in the opening part of this chapter, the customers or users of the MIS department's services can be those within or outside the organization. No matter where customers are located, the thrust of MIS services to them is meeting their current needs and, ideally, their future needs. Closely tied in with this principle is another one, namely, the *Principle of Planning for a TQM Program.* The MIS manager must set up a TQM group in the MIS department to meet customer expectations. Short- to long-range plans must be put in place and reviewed periodically for meeting or not meeting predetermined plans. A feedback mechanism should be set in place to alert the MIS manager to the shortcomings or failings of the current TQM program.

The *Principle of Continuous Quality Improvement* underlies a total quality management program. MIS managers and their personnel should strive for continuous improvements. These improvements should be a true motivator for all personnel in the MIS organization since they provide a means of lowering the cost of information services to users over time. Failure to subscribe to continuous quality improvement will cause the MIS organization to fall behind in information technology and be unable to supply the newer information services provided by its competition.

Underlying the total quality management concept from the standpoint of MIS personnel is the *Principle of MIS Personnel Taking Pride in Their Work.* The MIS manager has the capability to provide an environment in which employees can be proud of their work. In addition, MIS employees should look upon their jobs as an opportunity for advancement as opposed to a means to pay their bills.

In the setting of effective performance standards, MIS management must follow the *Principle of Setting High-Performance Standards.* MIS managers must demand a high level of performance from their employees as well as themselves in order to be successful. Mediocrity should never be acceptable, and standards should challenge people to operate at close to their best abilities. In other words, MIS personnel should be encouraged at all times to stretch their capabilities to meet challenging tasks. This approach relies to a large degree on applying creativity to the MIS tasks at hand. (The utilization of creativity is discussed in Chapter 9.)

The *Principle of Involving MIS Personnel in Setting Performance Standards* is also important. It is imperative that the performance standards be accepted as meaningful, useful, and fair by those who are expected to meet them. An effective way to gain this acceptance is for management to state clearly the reasons for the development of a set of standards and to define how the standards are to be used. They can then delegate to MIS personnel the responsibility of defining the specific details of the standards. This approach ensures broad participation and greatly increases acceptance.

A most important principle that MIS management should follow is the *Principle of Being Effective and Then Efficient.* MIS management must remember that *what* they do is much more important than *how* it is done. Too often, MIS standards focus too narrowly on "the right way" to do systems-related work. MIS performance standards should be broad enough to provide useful guidelines for determining project or activity priorities. In this way, standards can raise the level of effectiveness and the efficiency of the MIS organization.

MIS managers should review all performance standards to make sure that they conform to the *Principle of Appropriate Degree of Flexibility.* Every effort requires a balance between cost and quality, and standards provide a flexible frame of reference for this judgment. They should not be defined or interpreted so narrowly that they hamstring the managers and become a substitute for a careful and deliberate consideration of a specific situation.

The *Principle of Clear Definition of Responsibility and Accountability* ensures that performance standards will be met. An individual must be held responsible for conformance to a set of clearly identified performance standards. This person must also understand what expectations his or her manager has regarding compliance: that is, the individual will be held accountable for results. The standards must be documented in such a way that they are clearly defined, kept up to date, and are convenient to use.

RELATIONSHIP OF CURRENT RESEARCH TO TQM AND PERFORMANCE STANDARDS

A review of the current problems set forth in Figure 2.4 indicates that a large number of them can be related to a lack of a total quality management program and the lack of setting appropriate performance standards for MIS personnel and equipment. However, four are particularly important in terms of the chapter's subject matter:

- Lack of proper documentation over standards and procedures (rated no. 2)
- Lack of short- to long-range plans for management information systems (rated no. 4)
- Lack of performance standards to evaluate MIS personnel (rated no. 10)
- Lack of adherence to established methods and procedures (rated no. 13)

The first two problems can be related directly to total quality management. As will be stressed, TQM is a *continuous process* that requires a long-term commitment by the entire organization. Those organizations that have received a prestigious quality award, such as the Deming Prize or the Malcolm Baldrige National Quality Award, have worked at continuous quality improvement for years and are still working at it. Too often, MIS managers develop quality assurance programs with a short-term view. In fact, in many MIS organizations, the quality assurance (QA) function operates as an after-the-fact monitoring unit to ensure conformance with established standards and procedures. The focus of these efforts is on the review of software engineering end-products rather than on the total software engineering process. Thus, the result of the *lack of short- to long-range plans for management information systems* is a tacked-on QA function after the fact, that is, a reactive approach. Similarly, the incorrect approach to TQM is in line with the *lack of proper documentation over standards and procedures*. On the other hand, continuous quality improvement means that there is proper documentation so that where improvements are to be made, systems analysts and programmers know where they are currently to improve operational systems and programs.

In terms of the last two problems, they are linked directly with performance standards. The *lack of performance standards to evaluate MIS personnel* is ever present for systems analysts and programmers. As will be discussed, functional point analysis is useful in determining accurate time performance standards. *Lack of adherence to established methods and procedures* is caused in part by the lack of direction by MIS managers and supervisors under them as well as by the lack of newer design methodologies and programming languages. The focus is away from those approaches that have not served the MIS organization very well in the past. Overall, the development of newer approaches to performance standards will be helpful in overcoming these two problems.

EFFECTIVE MIS MANAGEMENT OF A TQM PROGRAM

Related to the prior chapter, that is, strategic planning of the MIS organization, is the whole subject of quality. As indicated in the opening part of this chapter, W. Edwards Deming's approach, or total quality management, is currently being implemented by many MIS organizations. There is little disagreement about its philosophy or its benefits. Total quality management focuses on customer satisfaction and continuous quality improvement as well as encourages teamwork and trust within the organization. Basically, it is an approach which states that the quality of products and services is number one and should be an integral and working part of the entire organization. The workplace should be set up on this basis and the organization should practice TQM on a day-to-day basis. Typically, this means a shifting of gears by employees throughout the organization. In terms of the MIS managers, this means that a total quality management program needs to be put in place. Such a program shows up on the company's bottom line, in user satisfaction and, ultimately, in advancement of their careers.

Overall, the focus of TQM is more on people and processes than on technology. TQM is about teamwork and trust whereby employees are empowered to make decisions about their work and to improve continuously the processes that affect the quality of the product or service delivered to the ultimate customer. The search for the best CASE tools is not the answer, although they do yield significant productivity gains. The key success factor is developing an effective TQM approach that enables MIS personnel to use CASE tools productively. Similarly, the search is not always for the best programming languages, but rather for an effective TQM approach that enables the languages being used to produce the systems that users want whether inside or outside the organization.

GETTING A TQM PROGRAM STARTED

Getting started on a TQM program means that MIS management needs to get the backing of senior corporate management. Typically, as suggested in the opening part of this chapter, a total quality management program is inaugurated for the whole organization by the president and CEO of an organization. Hence, MIS management needs to develop a TQM program for the MIS organization that has the backing of senior corporate management. Such an approach is found in the following steps:

1. Develop a consensus TQM mission statement
2. Plan for quality improvement
3. Focus on constantly improving service
4. Team up with vendors for improvement

Each of these steps is discussed in later sections.

1. Develop a Consensus TQM Mission Statement

Initially, it is necessary that the MIS manager determine what his or her management team is trying to accomplish. That is, who are the key internal and external customers? What is most important to their success? The MIS manager can then develop a consensus TQM mission statement for the MIS organization. Without it, supervisors under the MIS manager will be pulling in different directions, and the MIS support staff will lack job clarity. Having a clear mission and sticking to it confer what Deming calls "constancy of purpose," which provides guiding principles against which decisions can be made.

2. Plan for Quality Improvement

The MIS manager needs to plan for quality improvement. Quality does not just happen. An MIS organization's annual strategic plans are not complete unless they detail what will be done during the year to effect better quality, and who will do it. As with any other part of MIS's strategic plans, the quality effort will require that the MIS manager designate time and resources. The MIS manager should not take on more than he or she can handle. Proclaiming with much fanfare a new dawn of quality, putting up big "*Q*'s," and using quality buzzwords will get the MIS manager nowhere. If there are quality problems now, the cynicism of customers will only deepen. It is better to adopt a new way of life slowly, starting with development of a mission statement and then working on no more than one or two important problems.

Initially, the MIS manager can get started with the help of staff members. At a meeting, key project team members make a list of the problems they consider most pressing. Then, going around the room one at a time, each person reads a problem off the list and writes the problem on a flip-chart or whiteboard. Once all the problems are listed, they are consolidated so that the composite list eliminates all redundancies. Chances are very good that one, two, or three problems will stand out. In effect, they provide a good starting point for the first quality projects. If the problems chosen are too big or too vague for guidance, for example, knowing customers' real needs or staff communications problems, the same process can be used to break the problem into subproblems, which constitute manageable projects.

3. Focus on Constantly Improving Service

There is need to adopt an attitude that a TQM program will constantly improve service to internal and external customers. The MIS manager must state that he or she will be dissatisfied with any key work processes that yield less than excellent results. This dissatisfaction does not mean that the MIS manager will be tougher on employees; it is just the opposite. It means understanding that the bulk of the errors and problems happen not because of idiosyncratic foibles of MIS personnel, but because of the defects in the information systems by which work gets done. Seeking constant improvement of these systems is part of the MIS manager's job, one requiring cooperation among the MIS manager, MIS personnel, and end users.

4. Team up with Vendors for Improvement

Last, the MIS manager needs to team up with vendors for constant improvement by ending adversarial relationships of the past. Most equipment and service vendors want to do a good job and will work with the MIS manager if needs are made clear and concerns are documented with supporting data. It is recommended that the vendors be required to show statistical proof of their quality and be willing to provide quality guarantees to benchmark their own improvement efforts.

ORGANIZATION FOR A TQM PROGRAM

The organization structure for a companywide TQM process is essentially the same structure used to promote MIS quality improvements. This structure is based on quality improvement (QI) teams, who operate in parallel with the organization's existing structure. For the most part, each MIS employee is part of a QI team. When the TQM process is in full swing, an organization can have hundreds of QI teams working on the most critical problems affecting internal and external customers.

QI Teams

Using past experience as a guide, team size is typically limited to no more than seven members. One member serves as the team's facilitator. This person must not only be an effective listener and communicator, but also possess effective leadership skills and be proficient in problem solving and problem finding. QI teams typically meet for one or two hours per week. MIS managers select team members to work on implementing solutions to specific QI projects that relate to the needs of the ultimate customer. Once QI projects have been identified, the MIS managers can assemble the teams with members who are closest to the issues at hand. QI projects will include several projects that require participation by MIS staff. In fact, most of the projects will involve mission-critical information systems that affect the ultimate customer. The team members for such projects come from both the MIS and the end-user community. These joint-participation projects are great for improving processes within the organization, such as the order-entry process, the billing process, and the payment process. Equally important are projects that center on improving the software engineering process to achieve zero-defects software, which is discussed next.

Accent on Zero-Defects Software

Zero defects is the final goal that underlies continuous quality improvement. Without a goal of zero defects, the organization has no incentive to stretch its maximum capabilities. Within the MIS software development process, the focus is on the prevention and detection of software defects, which are broadly defined as flaws in the requirement specification, design, development, testing, or documentation. They include logical inconsistency, ambiguity in the software requirements, functional and design errors, inadequate testing, incorrect looping, improper branching, fixes that have introduced new defects, missing information, and incorrect or incomplete documentation. According to experts, software contains, on average, ten to fifty defects for every 1,000 lines of programming code. Also, they state that the most common type of defect is a program fragment that does the wrong thing: that is, incorrect logic. The next most common defect is failure to cope; that is, a program that was not written to handle a particular situation does something unexpected without warning when that situation arises.[1]

In the past, the optimum number of defects, that is, the point at which the cost per defect is minimized, is the point at which the cost of prevention equals the cost of failure. This argument assumes that the cost of prevention is inversely related to the number of defects. However, this is generally not the case; in fact, the cost of prevention in cost per defect is constant. In other words, the MIS organization makes a fixed investment in preventing defects, regardless of how many defects actually occur. Hence, the cost per defect is minimized at the point of zero defects. To achieve zero-defects software, there is need for a TQM program for software improvement.

TQM PROGRAM FOR SOFTWARE IMPROVEMENT

An important part of the overall TQM program for the MIS organization is the employment of software quality improvement teams under the direction of the MIS manager. Essentially, software QI teams follow these steps:

1. Establish and revise the software quality improvement plan
2. Define and adjust software metrics and implement procedures
3. Monitor quality indicators and check with customers
4. Improve the software engineering process

This software quality improvement process model is basically the Deming Wheel (Plan, Do, Check, Act) applied to the software engineering process. For more details, reference can be made to an article by Mary A. Zadrozny and Robert E. Tumanic.[2]

For an effective software quality improvement process, the quality assurance (QA) function within the MIS organization must take on a new direction. Traditionally, the MIS organization has the idea that quality is the responsibility of the QA function, which acts as an oversight group to ensure that standards and procedures are being followed. For continuous quality improvement, the traditional QA model is not effective since the role of the quality assurance function must go beyond "inspecting quality in" to the end product. Hence, quality assurance must be an active part of the software development process to facilitate process improvements with the QI teams. A separate quality assurance function is no longer necessary because all MIS personnel are responsible for quality.

LINKAGE OF TQM TO BENCHMARKING

Related to total quality management is the area of benchmarking. Implementation of a benchmarking program helps assure the MIS department that most effective procedures or practices are in place. The idea behind benchmarking is to research and find practices or performances which have proved to be the most successful and which can lead to improvements for the MIS department. Those who participate in benchmarking find out whether they are using the best practices or whether those of another MIS department would work more effectively. The information gathered is an invaluable tool in assessing quality of the MIS department on a day-to-day basis.

Initially, benchmarking meant taking a long, hard look at how the competition produced a better product and then having the courage to make changes in or at least match, if not surpass, that performance to create a new best for others to emulate. By the 1990s, the concept of benchmarking had expanded to include all of an organization's functional areas, including MIS. No longer limited to competitors within an industry, benchmarking now searches for the best wherever it may be found whether it be internally or externally, such as a superior accounting function found outside the organization that can be adapted to the MIS department. Individuals even "benchmark" themselves to see how they match up against other top performers, such as in the programming department.

For example, American Express goes to General Electric to pick up information on self-directed teams and to Motorola for ideas on training. As another example, GTE goes to American Express for guidance on billing. In a similar manner, L. L. Bean goes to 3M, IBM, and Disney to learn about human and management development, while Xerox and just about everybody else go to L. L. Bean to study how one of the best in the business handles warehousing and mail-order distribution.

Now, in the 1990s, benchmarking traverses the globe. Rather than looking for just the best in a given business, benchmarking companies are searching for the best in the world. For example, GTE Corporation modeled its billing system on that of worldwide American Express and set a new standard within its own industry. Motorola studied the First National Bank of Chicago's efficient electronic-data-transfer techniques for use in worldwide operations. By adopting their methods, Motorola spent considerably less time auditing its financial records.

Currently, benchmarking is so widely accepted that administrators of the Malcolm Baldrige National Quality Award view it as a vital element of a quality-management program. According to the National Institute of Standards and Technology, which bestows the Quality Award, benchmarks serve a useful purpose in stimulating breakthrough thinking since they offer the opportunity to achieve significant improvement based on adoption or adaptation of the current best practice. Also, benchmarks help encourage creativity through exposure to alternative approaches and results. In essence, benchmarks represent an important challenge to best the best, thereby encouraging major improvements as opposed to incremental refinements to existing approaches.

LINKAGE OF TQM TO PERFORMANCE STANDARDS AND PERFORMANCE APPRAISAL

Also related to total quality management is the area of performance standards, which is an integral part of performance appraisal (covered in Chapter 13). In reference to performance appraisals, Deming cites them for poor quality. He identifies many problems associated with them: they nourish short-term performance and annihilate long-term planning; they are destructive to the individual being reviewed; they are detrimental to teamwork because they foster rivalry, politics, and fear; they focus on the end product, not leadership to help people; they do not reward attempts to improve the system or take a risk; the measures used to evaluate performance are not meaningful because supervisors and subordinates are pressured to use numbers and count something; the measures discourage quality; and despite apparent variation in performance, factors outside an employee's control account for the differences in performance.[3]

Despite Deming's criticisms of performance appraisals, they do perform a number of valuable services when implemented properly. There should be little doubt that the goal-setting process is powerful. Research during the last thirty years has repeatedly shown that goal setting enhances performance. Although these findings have been confirmed by experience in thousands of organizations, it has also been shown that setting the wrong goals can lead to undesirable results. Regardless of whether an organization conducts formal performance appraisals, research has not discovered one organization that did not give promotions.[4] Promoting one individual over another is, like it or not, an evaluation. It is far better to have formal criteria for promotion than an informal, subjective system. In essence, employees want to know how they are doing. Annual performance appraisals may cause consternation once or twice a year, but a lack of clear goals causes confusion and aimlessness every day. Moreover, performance appraisals are the basis for legal defensibility for any personnel action taken, from promotion to termination.

DIFFICULTY OF SETTING MIS PERFORMANCE STANDARDS FOR PERSONNEL AND EQUIPMENT

In light of the previous discussion, there is need for MIS management to set appropriate performance standards for MIS personnel. Similarly, MIS management must do the same for equipment. The fundamental purpose of setting performance standards for MIS personnel and equipment is to determine whether or not they are accomplishing their tasks effectively. Although computers and related peripheral equipment can be routinely scheduled for a desired level of productivity, the same cannot be said for MIS personnel. A most pervasive problem confronting the MIS manager is that of managing the personnel resource, particularly systems analysts and computer programmers. It is usually not very difficult to manage the operations portion of the problem because in comparison to the areas of systems, design, and programming, operations is a much more structured world of essentially repetitive tasks. But managing the analysis and computer specialist functions can be frustrating, especially when trying to increase productivity while maintaining quality.

Because systems analysis, design, and programming are subjective areas involving thought processes, they are difficult to quantify in terms of a standard. Fundamentally, the MIS manager is faced with managing an abstract function for which there are not valid work measurement criteria. Typically, there are many difficulties involved and the process relies on subjective judgment. One computer program is not like another, and it would be difficult to find two programmers who are precisely equal in ability and competence. In a system of programs, modules, or segments, it becomes extremely difficult to manage this resource effectively in attempting to get a job done by a specific date.

Although the foregoing present difficulties for MIS management, there are ways to assess productivity of systems analysts and programmers realistically. Past experience and historical statistics help and, in some cases, are the principal means of estimating productivity. History can also help dictate what an individual's or unit's workload should be. The MIS manager must consider individual proficiency and the specifics of an assignment to determine how profitably the individual is being employed. While experience and history considered in combination are not a panacea, they do offer some hope in what might otherwise be considered a hopeless task. Current performance standards for MIS personnel and equipment are covered later, along with a function point analysis approach.

AN EFFECTIVE APPROACH TO THE DEVELOPMENT OF MIS PERFORMANCE STANDARDS

Effective management of MIS performance standards for personnel and equipment requires continuous effort necessitated by changes in the organization's needs and the introduction of new information technology. Successful MIS management depends on setting appropriate standards as an effective way to meet stated MIS objectives and goals. Furthermore, measurement of the impact of performance standards is necessary to determine whether or not they remain effective. Within this framework, effective MIS performance standards of personnel and equipment are discussed later.

As is the case with most complex tasks, there are many ways in which a useful set of MIS performance standards can be developed. One approach which has proved effective involves the following steps:

1. Get broad participation in the development of MIS performance standards
2. Review the MIS performance standards prior to finalization
3. Ensure that MIS performance standards are widely disseminated and fully understood
4. Monitor to make sure that MIS performance standards remain current

Each of these steps is explored next.

1. Get Broad Participation in the Development of MIS Performance Standards

MIS management must specifically identify those areas in which MIS performance standards must be set. During the initial development, management should focus on key areas and not attempt to tackle all areas at once. For example, within the general area of the systems development process, MIS management may decide to concentrate on the specific areas of prioritization of MIS projects, documentation necessary for systems support and maintenance, and tasks to be completed during each phase of the system development life cycle.

It is essential that the MIS standards have the blessing of senior corporate management and support at all levels of the MIS organization. MIS management may occasionally need concurrence on proposed performance standards from high levels of management to ensure consistency with key corporate policies and legal requirements. Management cannot expect acceptance of performance standards unless those standards are viewed as meaningful, useful, and fair. Industry and other MIS organizations can be consulted as part of the performance standards definition effort.

2. Review the MIS Performance Standards Prior to Finalization

MIS management must review the progress of the standards development effort to ensure that standards will indeed support the objectives of the MIS organization. The internal audit group should check standards' compliance with corporate policy and legal regulations, such as the Foreign Corrupt Policy Act. But more importantly, this intensive review should allow key MIS personnel to pass judgment on the performance standards; if they do not like the way they were set, then there is need for both MIS management and key MIS personnel to pursue an approach that will be acceptable to both. As will be noted later in the chapter, many times the use of function point analysis can serve as an acceptable basis for both parties.

3. Ensure That MIS Performance Standards Are Widely Disseminated and Fully Understood

Once performance standards are defined and agreed upon, they must be communicated clearly to each person affected by them. In many MIS organizations, this takes place in the form of a performance standards manual. The manual must be written in a manner that makes it easy to use and should distinguish between requirements and recommended practices. An effective performance standards manual will also coordinate and cross-reference related materials, such as guides, manuals, and internal documents.

The performance standards effort is doomed to failure if the only form of communication is the manual. The teaching of performance standards needs to be integrated into the training program at every level: newly hired MIS employees, technical MIS managers, systems analysts, systems operators, programmers, and end users. It is imperative that MIS personnel as well as other appropriate organization employees understand the rationale behind the performance standards and know who is responsible for ensuring compliance.

4. Monitor to Make Sure That MIS Performance Standards Remain Current

The costs associated with the performance standards program must be reviewed to ensure that more than offsetting cost reductions or benefits are realized by following the standards. Elimination or modification of performance standards which do not lead to cost reductions or other benefits should be strongly considered.

The development of performance standards is an evolutionary process. As new equipment, programming languages, and design methodologies are introduced, the MIS organization must develop standards for their use. An integral part of developing performance standards is documentation. Complete and timely documentation is necessary to protect the company's computerized assets, prevent disruption of orderly operations when the unexpected occurs, and satisfy the ever-increasing demands of auditors. Hence, lack of performance standards, like lack of program documentation, can lead to numerous problems at a later date.

PERFORMANCE STANDARDS FOR MIS PERSONNEL

Performance standards are a means by which the MIS manager can determine whether or not people and equipment are operating according to established levels of performance. They are needed in the areas of systems development by systems analysts, program development by programmers, and processing activities by the operations group. In this section, a basis for determining performance standards of MIS projects is set forth. In the next section, performance standards for equipment are given.

Traditional Approach to Setting Performance Standards

The traditional approach to developing performance standards for MIS projects was somewhat straightforward: that is, past projects were reviewed in terms of what constituted these projects and the time to complete them. The complexity of the project, its processing mode (batch processing or interactive processing), and the software employed to complete the project were taken into account. Generally, the familiarity of MIS personnel with the computer technology was also considered. On the basis of an analysis of these type projects, the MIS manager constructed a list of projects, from the very simple to the very complex, that gave total past times. In turn, the MIS manager used this listing of MIS projects to estimate the time requirement for a comparable project. Although this approach worked reasonably well for straightforward projects, the same cannot be said for newer projects that are complex, such as the introduction of an image processing system or an EDI system. Typically, the MIS organization has no past experience it can draw upon, nor does it have the expertise, many times, to start such a project. Hence, the MIS manager needs to take a newer perspective, namely, the utilization of a function point analysis.

Newer Function Point Analysis to Determine Total Project Time

A newer and a more scientific approach to estimating the time of MIS projects is to utilize *function point analysis*, also referred to as *function points*. In this approach, four basic stages of estimating are required of the MIS manager[5]:

1. Identify the basic elements of which a proposed management information system is composed
2. Calculate the basic effort required
3. Apply factors to adjust the basic estimate for complexity of the proposed management information system and the environment
4. Apply factors to adjust for familiarity of the MIS staff with the methods, tools, and technology involved

In the *first* stage, the MIS encompasses major functions that process transactions and produce outputs. The means by which this is accomplished will depend upon the sophistication of the environment. However, three types of elements can be identified: inputs, major processes, and outputs. An input, such as a customer order or an expense voucher, is a transaction or other grouping of data that has meaning in the business world. A major process, such as updating customer records or calculating pay deductions, is one a proposed MIS will do again and again. Outputs are those products of an MIS that have relevance in the business world, such as invoices, checks, or even customer inquiry responses. When identifying the inputs, major processes, and outputs of a proposed MIS, it is helpful to document them for future reference.

In the *second* stage, values which represent the number of man-months needed to analyze, specify, develop, prototype, test, and implement that part of the MIS which deals with the type of element in question can be applied. Elements can vary in complexity, and this should be taken into account. By allowing these levels of complexity, the ratings would have these meanings: (0) not applicable, (1) very simple, (2) relatively simple, (3) relatively complex, (4) complex, and (5) very complex. A timetable in months based on this complexity rating is shown in Figure 4.1. For example, if inputs are relatively complex, the number of inputs needs to be multiplied by 0.50 man-month. Similarly, the complexity of the major processes and outputs needs to be rated in order to determine the

Figure 4.1
The Effort Required in Man-Months for the Basic Elements of a System

	Complexity Rating				
Man-Months per Element	**1**	**2**	**3**	**4**	**5**
Inputs	0.25	0.30	0.50	0.75	1.00
Major processes	0.50	0.75	1.00	1.50	2.00
Outputs	0.25	0.30	0.50	0.75	1.00

Source: David B. Mallinson, "The Humble Art of Estimating," *Journal of Systems Management*, December, 1987, p. 23.

appropriate man-months for them. Also, the three results are added together to obtain the total basic man-months.

The *third* stage centers on applying complexity factors of the proposed MIS. There may be a number of different aspects of the MIS that will contribute to the complexity of the project, such as a policy to build interactive systems, the use of data communications, a need to access corporate databases, and the use of a specific programming language. Once again, there is need for a table, such as that found in Figure 4.2, to accommodate the complexity of the MIS and the environment. To rate the complexity on a scale of one to five, the following are used: (0) not applicable, (1) application generator (generates actual code or pseudocode), (2) fourth-generation—advanced, (3) fourth-generation—basic, (4) third-generation (COBOL, etc.), and (5) assembler/machine language. Because a proposed MIS developed for use on a personal computer is likely to be developed faster than on a computer mainframe, this factor is reflected in this table. Essentially, each complexity factor represents an adjustment to the basic man-months calculated in Figure 4.1. For example, a factor of 1.20 for an interactive operation indicates that the environmental aspect for which one is trying to compensate will increase the development time for the proposed MIS by 20 percent. By multiplying all the factors together, an overall complexity factor is obtained. In turn, the basic man-months are multiplied by this factor to derive the *adjusted* man-months.

It should be noted that there may be other aspects of the MIS environment that the MIS manager wants to take into account. For example, if purchased system packages are to be installed to satisfy end-user needs, another set of factors can be added to the table (Figure 4.2) to adjust the development effort on the basis of how well a package fits the requirements. The better the fit, the fewer changes that the MIS manager will have to make.

The *fourth* stage in estimating is to make adjustments for the MIS staff's level of expertise or knowledge. The first projects to be tackled within a new information technology environment, for example, will inevitably take longer to

Figure 4.2
The Complexity of the System and Its Environment (Stated on a Man-Months Basis)

Complexity Factors (Adjustments)	Rating 1	2	3	4	5
Interactive operation	1.15	1.20	1.25	1.35	1.50
Data communications	1.05	1.10	1.15	1.20	1.25
Corp. database access	1.10	1.12	1.15	1.10	1.25
Language	0.50	0.60	0.75	1.00	1.35
PC system	0.55	0.60	0.65	0.70	0.75

Source: David B. Mallinson, "The Humble Art of Estimating," *Journal of Systems Management,* December, 1987, p. 23.

Figure 4.3
The Familiarity of the MIS Staff with Methods, Tools, and Technology (Stated on a Man-Months Basis)

Familiarity Factors	Rating 1	2	3	4	5
Technology	1.00	1.05	1.15	1.30	1.50
Methodologies	1.00	1.02	1.05	1.07	1.12
Analysis & design tools	1.00	1.02	1.05	1.07	1.12
Database	1.00	1.03	1.12	1.25	1.40
Language	1.00	1.07	1.12	1.25	1.40

Source: David B. Mallinson, "The Humble Art of Estimating," *Journal of Systems Management,* December, 1987, p. 24.

complete than those undertaken later. If the MIS manager makes the assumption that a particular MIS project will be first on the list, the individual can then apply factors that reflect the lack of his or her staff's familiarity with that environment to the estimates for that MIS project. The familiarity ratings found in Figure 4.3 have these meanings: (0) not applicable, (1) very familiar, (2) mostly familiar, (3) somewhat familiar, (4) somewhat unfamiliar, and (5) totally unfamiliar. The overall familiarity factor is derived by multiplying together all of the factors that the MIS manager has selected out of the table. The final adjusted man-months total is obtained by multiplying the man-months adjusted for complexity by the overall familiarity factor.

To place the foregoing into perspective, consider an MIS project whose basic elements for inputs, major processes, and outputs total 8.5 man-months by using Figure 4.1. Using the combined complexity factor which is calculated to be 1.20 from Figure 4.2, results in 10.2 man-months (adjusted for complexity). In addition, the total familiarity factor, derived from Figure 4.3, turns out to be 1.35. This value times 10.2 man-months results in 13.8 man-months (adjusted for familiarity).

The mathematics involved in this approach may appear to be tedious at first sight. However, the MIS manager can use a personal computer with a spreadsheet package such that the estimates can be calculated automatically. The actual values used in Figure 4.1 can initially be set by examining past MIS projects and determining what length of time is needed to develop each type of element. It is important that these values be reviewed periodically using reported results from MIS projects to ensure that they reflect the actual experience. The factors in Figures 4.2 and 4.3 can be set through discussion with MIS project leaders who have had experience in leading MIS projects in which project complexity has varied. For all values, *feedback* derived from experience is necessary to prevent them from becoming obsolete over time.

Development Activities by Systems Analysts

In order to assist the MIS manager in getting a handle on the current development activities of systems analysts, there is need for them to fill out a weekly systems analyst activity form, such as that found in Figure 4.4. The postings of their time to specific MIS projects provide the basis for updating the projects as well as for updating the approach to function point analysis periodically (reference can be made to Figures 4.1, 4.2, and 4.3).

As shown in this weekly systems analyst activity report, there is need for the systems analyst to record the activity code, project number, and project name along with total regular and overtime hours worked. Also, time estimates are needed before the week begins for such activities as interviews with managerial and operational personnel from end-user departments; observations of end users; preparation of system flowcharts and data flow diagrams; and definitions of input, major processes, outputs, and file specifications. In a similar manner, a detailed checklist can be developed for systems design activities like flowcharting proposed MIS alternatives; developing data flow diagrams; employing the modular design approach for a new system; designing new inputs, processes, outputs, and file specifications along with the appropriate forms; and preparing documentation. The implementation phase which begins with preparatory work includes such activities as developing system flowcharts, preparing logic descriptions, coordinating programming and testing activities, developing training materials for end users, and preparing end-user instructions. Operation of the new MIS includes all those activities necessary for a smooth transition from

Figure 4.4
A Typical Weekly Systems Analyst Activity Report Form

Weekly Systems Analyst Activity Report	Name:
	Week Ending:

5 Defining system specifications	45 Forms design	85 System maintenance
10 Interviewing	50 Program review	90 Documentation
15 Survey operations	55 Program test	95 Instruction
20 System flowcharting	60 System test	96 Training
25 Prepare data flow diagrams	65 Parallel test	97 Meetings
30 Program flowcharting	70 Vendor specification	99 Other (explain in writing)
35 Systems analysis	75 Vendor proposals	
40 Systems design	80 Follow-up on vendors	

Activity Code	Project Number	Project Name	Estimated Hours	Total Actual Hours	Hours Regular	Hours Overtime	Variance

the present system to the new MIS. It is recommended that the MIS manager add 10 to 15 percent to time estimates for normal delays.

Once the time estimates have been prepared and times have been accumulated weekly, a comparison can be made between the estimated times (based on function point analysis) and the actual times. It is recommended that an on-line interactive approach be utilized to give each systems analyst his or her weekly estimated times and to allow each analyst to report actual times on various MIS projects. When the systems analyst has completed entering his or her times, there should be instant feedback concerning the times reported: that is, over or under the estimates. When the systems analyst is running over actual times either periodically or continuously, the MIS manager should talk to the individual about the cause. Needless to say, there can be a wide range of reasons that times are too high. It may well be that time estimates used in certain MIS projects have been underestimated. Hence, one or more values in function point analysis tables (as in Figures 4.1, 4.2, and 4.3) may need modification.

Figure 4.5
A Typical Weekly Programming Activity Report Form

Weekly Programmer Activity Report	Name:
	Week Ending:

5 Define system specifications	55 Program test	90 Documentation
25 Prepare data flow diagrams	58 System data preparation	95 Instruction
30 Program flowcharting	60 System test	96 Training
33 Coding	63 Evaluate trial results	97 Meetings
50 Program review	65 Parallel test	99 Other (explain in writing)
53 Test data preparation	88 Program maintenance	

Activity Code	Project Number	Project Name	Estimated Hours	Total Actual Hours	Hours Regular	Hours Overtime	Variance

Development Activities by Programmers

Computer programmers are responsible for not only preparing program flowcharts of new computer programs, but also writing modular, utility, and conversion programs; maintaining existing computer programs; and interacting with database management about data required. In addition, they desk-check the coding and logic of other programmers, devise test data, compile or assemble computer source programs, test and debug programs, and prepare adequate documentation. In view of these activities, programmers need to prepare a weekly programming activity report that lists all of the individual's possible activities, such as that found in Figure 4.5.

In the development of time estimates, the MIS manager should consider the normal delays in programming projects by adding 10 to 15 percent to time estimates. As with the prior weekly report form, actual hours are recorded and compared weekly for variances. As before, if the programmer is periodically or continually over the time estimates, the MIS manager needs to determine the causes and rectify the problem(s).

From the information provided by the weekly programming activity reports, the MIS manager can update MIS programming projects to show the present status of all programming projects. Because activity codes are assigned the same number here as in the systems analyst activity report, there is a common means for reporting time spent on the various MIS projects. As before, feedback from this reporting process may mean that the values in the function point analysis tables (like those in Figures 4.1, 4.2, and 4.3) may have to be modified.

In most MIS programming departments, assignments are made on the basis of experience: a senior programmer would be given more complex tasks than a junior programmer. However, the newer CASE tools and programming languages can generally enhance productivity of senior and junior programmers. The MIS manager should take into account increased productivity from his or her programming staff. Hence, the most efficient programming methods should be employed. The end results of improved programming activity show up on the weekly programming activity reports in terms of reduced time taken to do the same work as in the past.

PERFORMANCE STANDARDS FOR CONTROL OF MIS OPERATIONS

The operations department of an MIS organization resembles a custom job shop production plant. The "customers" are the system users, and the "customer orders" are the sets of data or service requests they submit. The operations department "fills the customer orders" by providing the information processing service requested. If MIS management accepts this TQM approach to its operations, then they must be very sensitive to the two key considerations of every service organization: First, what are the demands of the system user, both now and in the future? Second, how can these demands be met in the most cost-effective way? Overall, MIS operations will set many standards to ensure that the proper emphasis is given to finding the answer to both these questions and, once the answers are known, to make sure that the solution is implemented. Although there are many areas in which performance standards may be set, this section will concentrate on just two MIS operations, MIS operations service levels and data and systems security. In Chapters 14 and 15, these areas plus others will be set forth for a comprehensive approach to evaluate the performance of the total MIS organization.

MIS Operations Service Levels

If the MIS operations department views itself as a true service organization, it should have a continual performance review process to ensure that it is meeting current and future service needs cost-effectively. The performance review process should (1) evaluate how effectively and efficiently current service needs are being met, (2) measure current resource usage and determine the current excess capacity, and (3) determine future service needs and performance resource planning to meet these needs.

First, the services provided by the MIS operations department should be reviewed to identify current problems. This review should reach into all aspects of operations: input processing and procedures, staging of jobs, distribution of output, and relationship with end users. End users of the services, MIS management, and other MIS personnel should be solicited for their ideas of problem areas and opportunities for improvement. A special effort should be made to identify specific service needs that are not being met. A review of this type for the typical MIS operations department will yield at least a dozen or more opportunities for improvement, many of which will be fairly easy and will yield immediate benefits. Also, performance standard service goals for key services should be set and performance against these standards tracked. The following typical service goals: 90 percent of all interactive system responses within five seconds, system unavailable no more than one hour per month, and 95 percent of all batch job outputs available to end users within six hours after job submission.

Second, it is necessary to maintain fairly accurate measurements of all major resource usage in the MIS operations department. The number of operation shifts, hours per shift, and people per shift should be determined. On what activities do these people spend their time? In terms of equipment, there are many hardware and software monitoring devices to measure the use of the CPU, main memory, printers, disk drives, channels, and the like. Many MIS operations departments have a performance review group that uses such monitors to help get the best performance from current equipment and recommend hardware and software upgrades.

Third, the long lead times associated with obtaining equipment, rapid business growth that creates heavier than anticipated work loads on all areas of the organization, and the difficulty of obtaining funds at a reasonable interest rate all are reasons why successful resource planning necessitates thinking ahead three to five years. This requires excellent communication with MIS personnel and end users to be aware of what applications are likely to come on line within the planning horizon. It also requires keeping abreast of new information technology as it is being developed. Having completed the previous two activities in this section, the MIS operations department has a clear picture of where things stand today; this activity will provide them with a picture (albeit somewhat fuzzy) of what the future holds. MIS management then takes a proactive approach to move from where the MIS operations department is today to where it should be three to five years hence.

Data and Systems Security

There is a widely recognized need for a comprehensive approach to protect and secure management information systems and their data. Data and systems security relates to ensuring that data and systems are not being compromised and that appropriate controls have been put in place to assure safe and secure information processing. Computer-related "white collar" crimes involving the manipulation of data and systems security have received much publicity. Destruction or theft of stored data in a retaliatory gesture by disgruntled employees is not uncommon. Public and private pressure for assurance of the privacy of computerized information has grown over time.

Essentially, there is a great need to set performance standards to ensure data and systems security in every functional area that generates, processes, or uses data. This is a particularly challenging task in light of today's sophisticated information technology employing distributed data processing, electronic data interchange among trading partners, and global data communications. MIS management along with internal and external auditors/consultants need to perform the following activities: (1) evaluate the adequacy of the present security of data and systems; (2) document current data and systems risks and exposures; (3) develop a list of prioritized recommendations to begin improving data and systems security; (4) establish a means for performing long-range strategic planning to develop and maintain an appropriate security program; and (5) define a set of performance standards for data and systems security to ensure that, over time, the long-range strategic plan will be implemented. Typically, a comprehensive approach to data and systems security should cover personnel, physical security, software protection, data protection, backup provision, insurance, and the like.

GUIDELINES TO ASSIST MIS MANAGEMENT IN TQM AND PERFORMANCE STANDARDS

A *first* and important guideline to assist MIS management in a successful total quality management program is to tie in with corporate strategic planning (refer to Chapter 3). More specifically, corporate long-term objectives can be integrated with continuous improvement in the quality of goods and services, responsiveness and flexibility of working with internal and external processes, and cost and waste elimination, all important elements of a TQM program. In turn, these objectives can become part of the MIS organization. MIS objectives provide a basis for specific programs for quality improvement. Such a TQM program for software development is given in Chapter 3.

A *second* guideline to assist MIS management in taking the route to a total quality management program is initially to get the MIS organization in order from a quality standpoint. The MIS organization needs to undertake TQM-type activities, such as surveying customer satisfaction, using performance metrics, and linking goals and objectives. It can also train its personnel in the fundamentals of TQM to determine what makes sense, that is, what methodology and tool set should be used. Hence, there is need for MIS management to exert leadership initially so that the MIS organization is known as a quality support function and a tool provider to extend quality throughout the organization. For example, the MIS department can supply E-mail and statistical packages that will assist the total organization in its TQM pursuits. The critical issue is not one of tools but involvement of the MIS organization in promoting the quality efforts of the functional end-user business units.

A *third* guideline is the recognition that total quality management starts at the systems specification stage in the MIS organization. Studies have shown that about 60 percent of the errors reported during system testing and production can be traced to the analysis stage of development. The most common causes of these errors are specifications that are missing, erroneous, ambiguous, or conflicting. Only a small percentage of errors have to do with code that does not meet specifications. To help identify and correct analysis stage specifications, system developers should apply TQM properly. That is, they should understand and document the detailed work steps required to produce analysis stage specifications; document criteria to judge the quality of the work steps through life-cycle quality metrics (LCQM); train employees to perform these detailed work steps and recognize defects in the work steps; and add more sophisticated LCQM as analysts become proficient in recognizing defects in specifications.

The LCQMs documented for the various tasks and subtasks necessary to produce data and process models for a system enable developers to recognize most cases of business rules that are incomplete. The most critical aspect of any quality improvement program for MIS development, then, is the ability to recognize a defect. LCQMs applied in the system specifications analysis stage can identify defects that would otherwise be propagated throughout the development and production life cycle. The net result is that correcting these defects results in a higher-quality analysis specification—a prerequisite to high-quality management information systems.

A *fourth* guideline for TQM relates to empowering employees in the organization as well as in the MIS area. Basically, this means giving them all the responsibility and authority as well as the information to back up the responsibility and the authority. In turn, organization personnel can be held accountable. Because this information needs to be accessible, a client/server architecture that is based on open systems has a higher probability of making information more accessible to people in the organization. If the MIS organization can get information at a place where people can look at it, and if they have the right cognitive skills and capabilities and tools, then they can come up with some very innovative and creative ways of running a business better. This represents a high level of empowerment. It is up to the MIS organization to create the ways that organization personnel can get information that they can use when they need it.

This guideline also can include the empowerment of employees through networking. The underlying thrust is that since knowledge is power, then the diffusion of knowledge through information networks empowers those on the network. The net result of such empowerment may be flatter organizational structures in which all employees act as team members. Thus, a total quality management program throughout an organization may require the help and guidance of the MIS organization for successful results.

A *fifth* guideline that underlies TQM is the concept of continuous improvement.

Although this item was included under principles in the first part of the chapter, it is also applicable here. Essentially, total quality management in MIS or elsewhere requires everyone to be working on measurable improvement meaningful to his or her own job. The process of progressive improvement should be a true motivator for everyone. In turn, the cost of producing a product or service will decline over time. A basic tenet of TQM is "You only improve what you measure." In the process, there is improvement from the standpoint of the customer. Hence, a win-win situation is the order of the day for the organization and the customer.

In the area of performance standards, there is a *sixth* guideline for MIS management to follow in regard to MIS personnel and end users. Namely, there is need for MIS management to make an ongoing effort to change performance standards in light of rapid changes in information technology. More to the point, as newer analysis and design methodologies, such as object-oriented and CASE technologies, are brought into the workplace, they reduce the time to analyze, design, and implement new management information systems and their maintenance. Hence, performance standards need to be maintained over time.

In a similar manner, a *seventh* guideline relates to developing and maintaining performance standards for MIS equipment throughout the organization. Not only must MIS managers and functional end-user managers develop appropriate equipment performance standards, but also they must be prepared periodically to review performance standards. Inappropriate performance standards must be identified and changed or discarded.

NOTES

1. Peter Coffee, "Sloppy Work Is Cheap, but Quality Is Cheaper," *PC Week,* April 5, 1993, p. 44.

2. Mary A. Zadrozny and Robert E. Tumanic, "Zero-Defects' Software: The Total Quality Management Approach to Software Engineering," *Chief Information Officer Journal,* Spring 1992, p. 14.

3. W. Edwards Deming, *Out of the Crisis,* Cambridge, Mass.: Massachusetts Institute of Technology, Center for Advanced Engineering Study, 1982, pp. 101–120.

4. Jim M. Graber, Roger E. Breisch, and Walter E. Breisch, "Performance Appraisals and Deming: A Misunderstanding?" *Quality Progress,* June 1992, p. 59.

5. David B. Mallinson, "The Humble Art of Estimating," *Journal of Systems Management,* December 1987, pp. 22–25.

PART III

EFFECTIVE MIS ORGANIZATION STRUCTURES

5

Formal Organization of MIS Personnel

OUTLINE

INTRODUCTION TO AN EFFECTIVE FORMAL ORGANIZATION OF MIS PERSONNEL

The MIS structures that have been developed in the past are being assaulted from so many directions that they need to be reevaluated for replacement. Typically, organizational restructuring, information technology integration, electronic processing, and growing end-user sophistication are acting as catalysts forcing the restructuring. The centralized MIS organization has seen its heyday as the only computer resource. End users throughout organizations believe they are getting better at doing things for themselves. As a result, many of the MIS departments with large mainframe platforms are being regarded as computer utilities whose services are being used only as needed. This is forcing a rethinking of the MIS role. Overall, the burgeoning PC or micro population using LAN technology is forcing MIS to change to an integrated end-user/MIS approach. With every local area network and departmental computer installed, there is a pool of information out of MIS direct span of control. In addition, these pools are still expanding currently at an increasing rate.

In light of these comments, this chapter will focus on the organizing function, that is, determining a new direction for MIS management to follow in structuring its organization. As organizations grow in size, business diversity, and organizational complexity, new demands will require a change in concepts underlying MIS structures. Initially, the chapter's focus is on where organizations are currently in terms of centralization and decentralization; this is followed by a discussion of current structures for the MIS department and end users. The difficulties with the current MIS organization structures are also discussed. This exposition provides the background for developing a functional end-user departmental approach. Occupational groupings of present MIS personnel are set forth, as are newer roles in MIS staffing and future roles that MIS personnel will tend to assume over time when using a functional end-user approach.

PRINCIPLES OF AN EFFECTIVE FORMAL MIS ORGANIZATION

The *Principle of Facilitating MIS Objectives* is a starting point for developing an organization structure to support the MIS organization which includes the MIS department and end users. The primary purpose of the structure is to facilitate the accomplishment of predetermined MIS objectives and goals. If the structure fails in this regard, the MIS organization is ineffective. In the final analysis, the organization's activities must be measured against the criterion of effectiveness in meeting established MIS objectives and goals.

The MIS organizational structure should also take into account the *Principle of Efficient Operations* to minimize costs. The MIS structure should not waste valuable resources, such as people and equipment. It should provide a means for personal development and a method for using computer equipment efficiently.

Another important principle is the *Principle of Making MIS an Integral Part of End-User Computing*. Too often in the past, end users have not been integrated into the MIS organization in terms of the formal MIS structure. Their only contact was with the centralized information centers. However, the newer direction in MIS organization structures makes them an integral part of the MIS organization, as will be demonstrated later in the chapter.

The MIS manager should consider very carefully the *Principle of the Span of Control*—the number of employees reporting to a single manager. In the data center operations area, where the work tends to be simple and straightforward, the number of subordinates reporting to an MIS superior can be large, perhaps ten to thirty. In contrast, in the systems area, where the work tends to be complex, more management personnel are needed. The span of control, then, is determined by the complexity of the job, the type of personnel, and similar factors.

The last principle, the *Principle of MIS Organizational Flexibility and Stability,* recognizes that external and internal environmental changes occur and must be incorporated into the MIS organization structure. The structure must be able to accommodate these changes, and this may necessitate redesign. The structure must be stable as well as flexible. Stability refers to the structure's ability to accommodate changes while continuing to meet stated objectives efficiently and economically. An important element of this principle is *rightsizing* the MIS organization structures to reflect changing times.

RELATIONSHIP OF CURRENT RESEARCH TO THE FORMAL MIS ORGANIZATION

An examination of the results of current research on the major problems confronting the MIS formal organization indicates that there is only one problem related directly to the MIS organization structure (see Figure 2.4). That problem, rated number five, centers on the *lack of training programs for new and experienced MIS personnel.* This problem takes the form of making MIS personnel focus their efforts on getting their current projects completed as quickly as possible. This is caused by the shortage of qualified MIS personnel in the typical organization. Hence, there is little time to train MIS personnel since the emphasis is on getting the job done. In the long run, this approach is counterproductive: that is, many MIS personnel experience "job burnout." There should be time for MIS personnel to rejuvenate themselves through appropriate training on current topics. This, in turn, will improve their productivity and performance on the job.

In addition, many of the other problems indicated by current research results are related directly or indirectly to the formal MIS structure. For example, the *lack of control over input and/or output data* is caused to a degree by the fact that the MIS department is isolated from end users who are involved in data entry on a daily basis. Improper control over input can go on for years if the MIS department is not interfacing periodically with those functional end-user departments responsible for entering data into the management information system. In a similar manner, the *lack of security protection measures over the management information system* is caused partly by the isolation of the MIS department from functional end-user departments. Overall, the tendency of the MIS department and end users "to march to a different step" underlies many of the problems uncovered by past and current research.

NEWER DIRECTIONS AFFECTING THE MIS ORGANIZATION STRUCTURES

Currently, there are a number of newer directions affecting the MIS organization structures whether they are centralized or decentralized. They are (1) downsizing, (2) upsizing, (3) netsizing, and (4) rightsizing. First, *downsizing* refers to a change from managed hosts, that is, computer mainframes and minicomputers, to microcomputer platforms in order to capture the benefits of plummeting price/performance ratios. Organizations are gradually turning their hosts into servers. They are reaching down to take control of desktop computers. Second, *upsizing* is just the reverse: that is, microcomputers and workstations are scaling up from stand-alone applications. They are adding concurrency control, security, and fault tolerance to their servers. They are taking microcomputers beyond their use as personal productivity tools and finding ways to associate them with corporate information. Third, *netsizing* refers to changing their local area networks. More specifically, more microcomputers and servers are being added. Organizations are growing their LANs with repeaters and hubs, interconnecting them with bridges and routers, and turning them around to talk back to their hosts through gateways. Although downsizing, upsizing, and netsizing represent three different directions in enterprise computing, there is a fourth direction, *rightsizing,* which is discussed next.

Rightsizing—Making Downsizing Appropriate

If downsizing is about the migration of applications from computer mainframes to smaller platforms, then rightsizing is concerned with the migration of those applications to the systems most suitable to an organization's needs. Rightsizing is made possible by the freedom that open systems, which are nonproprietary and standards-based, grant to choose among many products and vendors for the most appropriate implementation. Open systems protect an organization's investment in current installations because open technologies can be integrated with existing systems. Also, the ease with which open technologies can be incorporated into both present and future systems permits MIS managers to plan information technology growth more effectively.

Rightsizing is a first step toward combining the best of the computer mainframe with the best of the desktop computer without interfering with applications or end users. MIS managers want to continue to benefit from the large and diverse family of computer mainframe applications even as they profit from the price/performance improvements offered by open systems. The value added by rightsizing (focusing on a good fit between an application and the system on which it is implemented) is pivotal since not all applications should be offloaded from the computer mainframe. Some tasks, such as the processing of large volumes of transactions from thousands of concurrent users across hundreds of interdependent application platforms, are best left on the computer mainframe. Other tasks, however, like those that can capitalize on point-and-click interfaces to hike end-user productivity, are ideally implemented in an open, desktop systems environment. Obviously, any rightsizing decision involves a judgment call. It requires that MIS managers understand not only the inner workings of an application, but also the end-user environment that the application serves.

Rightsizing Must Be Properly Managed

The most challenging aspect of rightsizing facing MIS management is not implementing information technology but managing change and its impact on MIS personnel. Most organizations that rightsize from computer mainframes to local area networks or distributed processors lose between 15 percent and 30 percent of their programming staffs, depending on the speed at which the migration is carried out and the complexity of the new development environment. Needless to say, rightsizing is difficult on MIS personnel emotionally and in terms of their skills. People who have invested their whole careers developing a certain skill set all of a sudden are faced with the prospect of having to start over again.

MIS Management Must Help Staff Adjust to Change

To minimize attrition, MIS management must provide substantial training to ease their staff's transition to the new development environment. Also, it is necessary to communicate to MIS personnel the direction in which the organization is headed, the goals of the MIS department, and the skills and attitude that will be required to succeed in the long term. Although people dislike change because of its very nature, it has become a way of life in the MIS field. MIS management should try to convince their people that true job security comes from being able to adapt rapidly to new information technologies.

Whatever their long-term systems direction, MIS managers need to provide substantial training to their staff if they are going to acquire the necessary technical skills and help the organization migrate to a newer computing environment that has been downsized. For example, a company can provide its programmers with ten days of training a year using a mix of in-house and external training programs. In contrast, a company can rely exclusively on informal training conducted by peers who have gained skills either before joining the company or through previous projects. Junior and senior programmers can be paired so that they review each other's code. This pairing serves two purposes: it helps catch code errors and enables programmers to learn new techniques and skills from each other.

Although programmers can learn new technologies and development skills, it is generally more difficult for them to overcome fears about the future when their organization migrates to, say, client/server computing. Employees wonder whether there will be a place for them in the redesigned organization and whether they will retain their status and responsibility level. In order to deal with the staff's real or imagined fears, MIS managers need to communicate openly and honestly everything about the migration that is likely to affect these people's professional and personal lives. One approach for MIS managers to follow is to take their staff off-site to discuss potential obstacles to the organization's downsizing project and possible solutions. During the discussions, the fears that many MIS personnel had about the downsizing project surfaced and were addressed.

From another perspective, MIS managers can modify their compensation programs in order to reinforce work habits and techniques that further the migration effort. For example, a compensation program that pays programmers for the amount of code they reuse instead of the amount they write can be examined for implementation. Compensation helps MIS personnel hurdle one of the toughest aspects of downsizing: that is, they look and think about systems in a new way. Thus, there is need for MIS managers to think and innovate: in effect, to be more like system managers. System personnel succeed in their jobs by following specific rules and guidelines while systems managers work independently and resolve problems using whatever technique or tool is necessary.

EFFECTIVE MIS MANAGEMENT OF CURRENT ORGANIZATION STRUCTURES

Currently, the type of business will determine what information is important, whether it be marketing, manufacturing, or engineering. Related to these information requirements is the management information system that is needed to supply the required information at the right time and place—from top to lower management as well as for operating personnel. From this view, an MIS organization structure must be capable of accommodating changing conditions, whether externally or internally initiated.

Centralization versus Decentralization

Before discussing the pros and cons of centralization versus decentralization within an MIS environment, it would be helpful to define each. *Centralization* of processing creates a single functional unit with responsibility for providing information processing services to all functional operating units in the organization. In contrast, *decentralization* of processing creates a data center within each functional operating unit with responsibility for servicing the information processing needs of that functional operating unit. The basic difference, then, is the degree to which information-processing decision making, authority, and responsibility are disseminated throughout the organization.

In the past, organizations centralized their computer operations for the purpose of reducing MIS costs. Reduced costs result from several factors: decentralized small computers may have unused capacity; individual small computers may be overloaded, generating pressure for upgrading equipment or purchasing service bureau time; the costs of floor space, electricity, air-conditioning, and other facilities are lower in a single large installation than in multiple smaller ones; and one large installation needs fewer support personnel than several small installations. Likewise, large computer mainframes allow certain applications that are not feasible on smaller equipment. Another reason for centralization is improved efficiency in systems development and programming. Centralization permits the design and use of common databases as well as common standards for data entry and input validation. It can also facilitate the use of development and project techniques to produce specific benefits for the organization. Large installations are able to attract and retain highly qualified technical people who can provide management with a wide range of alternatives to reduce the cost of development, operation, and future maintenance.

The reasons advanced for *centralization* are generally based on *efficiency;* the arguments for *decentralization* deal with *effectiveness*. Although no one could argue that decentralization offered anything but added cost, microcomputers and minicomputers have demonstrated savings. A microcomputer programmed for a specific MIS application is relatively inexpensive. If it is an office machine, it may not require a trained operator or the programming and technical support of a general-purpose computer. More recently, local area networking of PCs provides extensive on-line inquiry, thereby reducing the cost of end-user computing substantially. The high cost of communications, the overhead associated with computer mainframes and minicomputers, and the possibility that an installation's capacity will not be fully utilized combine to weaken the case against decentralization.

Advocates of decentralization state that local systems analysts are more attuned to local needs and have a deeper understanding of local operations, managerial preferences, and organization structures. This enables them to establish requirement specifications and to design systems that are best suited for the local end users. The local systems analysts can respond more quickly to emergencies and priority changes. In addition, the close association between the systems analysts and end users means that end users will be better informed about the benefits and limitations of the management information system. End users can work better with MIS personnel and improve the quality of their systems. In contrast, a functional unit manager at the local level in a centralized environment has to battle with other end users for the central system's development resources.

Even though most centralized installations allocate their costs to end users according to the resources used, the local functional unit manager has little responsibility for total MIS costs. Salaries paid to central MIS personnel, overhead rates, choice of equipment, time spent on MIS projects, and share of resources used all seem to be beyond the manager's control at the local level. As a consequence, the allocations are viewed as arbitrary. The local functional unit manager's only objective is to obtain as much service as possible from the central installation. In the long run, this drives up costs. However, if the information processing resource is local, its manager has direct knowledge of all the elements of cost and an incentive to control them. Thus, local functional unit managers know that they have better control over operations in a decentralized environment.

Need to Study Both for Appropriate MIS Organization Structure

Now that some of the important reasons for both centralization and decentralization have been stated, which is the better approach? Currently, as well as in the future, most business organizations undertake or will continue to undertake a thorough study to determine which elements of both are best suited for them. If the organization's MIS problems are in the area of service, cost, or effectiveness, it will be necessary to balance the requirements of the decentralized units against those of the organization as a whole. The MIS manager should pay close attention to developing alternate organizational designs and comparative costs. In some cases, *cost* information may be all that MIS management needs to resolve the problem. However, if management is primarily concerned with *service* rather than cost, a different approach may be necessary. Thus, the study's objectives will determine what elements of centralization and decentralization are needed for the MIS organization today as well as in the future.

CURRENT CENTRALIZED STRUCTURES FOR EFFECTIVE MIS OPERATIONS

The degree of centralization or decentralization is one factor that determines the type of the MIS organization structure. However, for a small organization, centralization is the initial way to go because of the size of the operation. As the organization grows, the MIS organization structure may change. The structure that was loosely knit in the past becomes more formal, reflecting the larger number of people to be supervised. More formal lines of communication must be employed to accomplish the many tasks.

The organization structure necessary to accommodate an MIS also varies with the size of the organization and the complexity of the system. A system for a small company (say, sales of $20 million) will be different from that for a medium-size one (say, sales of $100 million) or a large one (say, sales of $1 billion). The degree of hardware and software sophistication in an organization should best serve its needs at the appropriate cost.

Small- to Medium-Size Company

It is impossible to design an MIS organization chart that fits all companies and their respective needs. Nevertheless, it is worthwhile to discuss the MIS organizational chart for typical companies of varying sizes. An MIS organization chart for a small- to medium-size company is depicted in Figure 5.1. Here, six supervisors report to the management information systems manager, who has an assistant. Two supervisors, for systems development and computer programming, direct the systems and programming effort. Two other supervisors, for data-entry and peripheral equipment and computer operations, control daily operational activities. There are also a supervisor over the information center(s) and a supervisor over data communications. As shown in the diagram, all supervisors are assisted by other personnel. Management levels are kept to a minimum.

Medium- to Large-Size Company

For a medium- to large-size company, the MIS organization chart (Figure 5.2) becomes larger and jobs become more specialized. The number of management levels also increases, as do equipment costs. Figure 5.2 shows that the organization is divided into four functions, (1) developmental, (2) operational, (3) information center, and (4) data communications, which are all under the direction of the MIS vice president. These areas are controlled by the systems and programming director, the data center director, the information center director, and the data communications director, respectively. The *first* function, developmental activities, includes:

- Feasibility studies of new computer systems
- Systems analysis and design of new computer systems
- Programming and testing of new computer systems
- Program maintenance
- Database administration
- Management science programs

Figure 5.1
Organization Chart of a Typical Centralized MIS Department in a Small- to Medium-Size Company

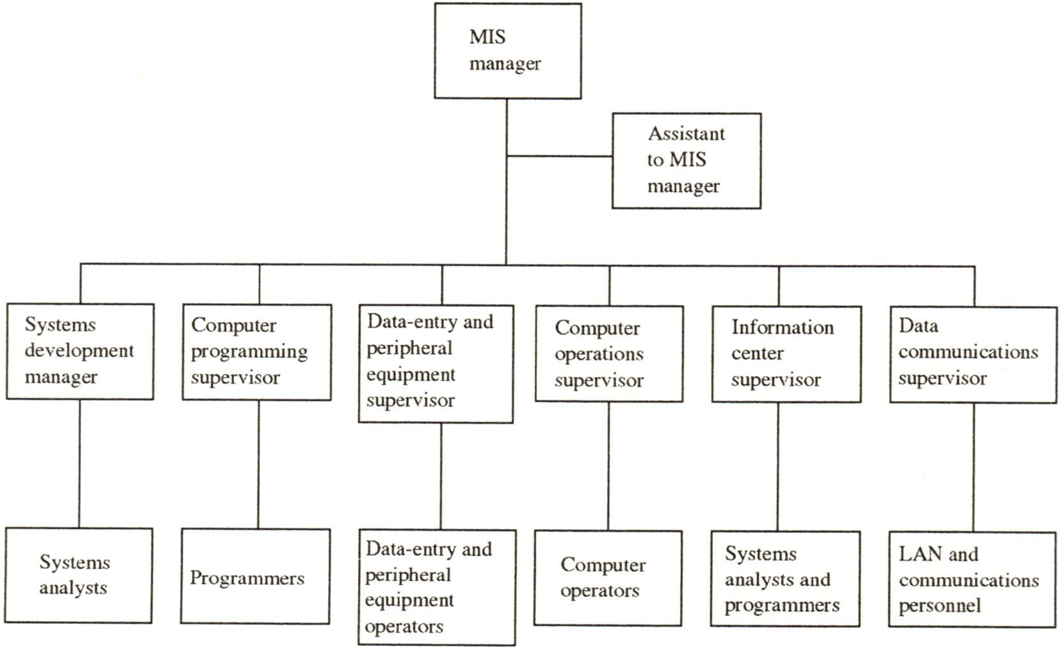

Figure 5.2
Organization Chart of a Typical Centralized MIS Department in a Medium- to Large-Size Company

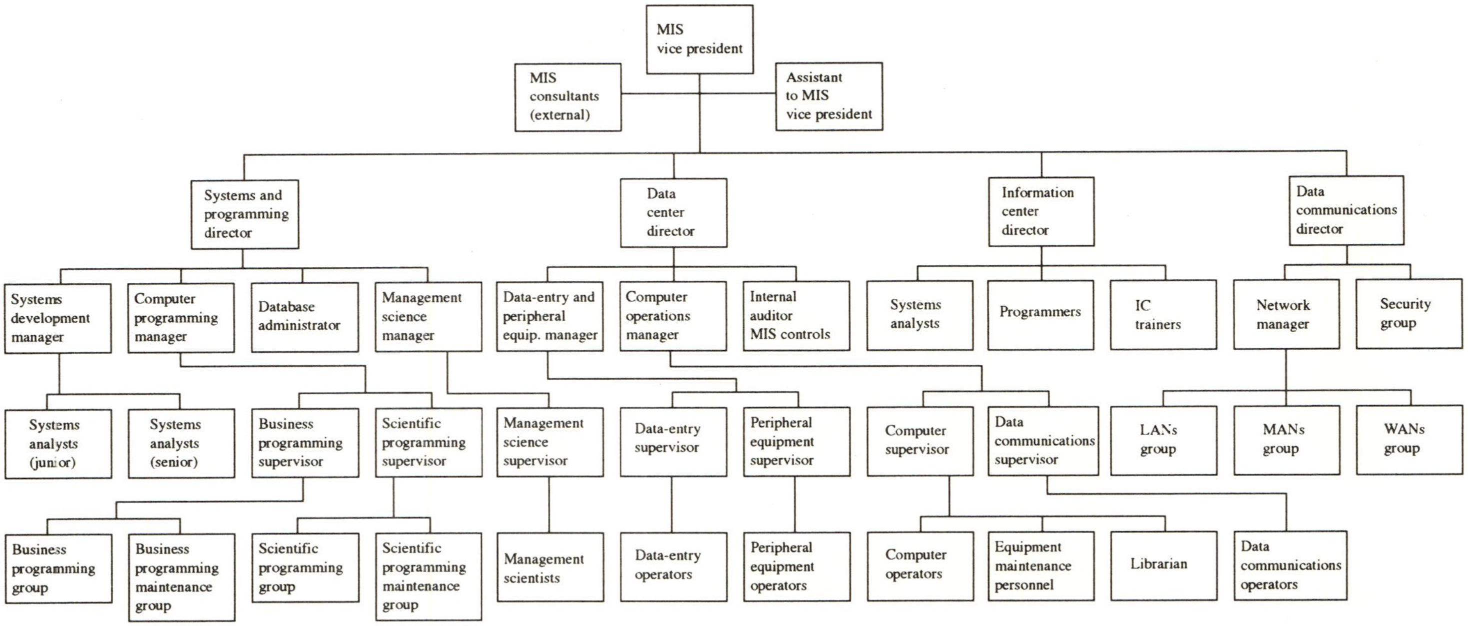

The *second* function, operational or day-to-day activities of the data center, encompasses:

- Data-entry and peripheral equipment operations
- Computer mainframe operations
- Internal control

The *third* function under the direction of the MIS vice president is the information center. Its activities center on the following:

- Systems analysis and design assistance for end users
- Programming assistance for end users
- Training of end users

All of these activities are directed primarily toward end users, unlike the first two functions discussed.

A *fourth* function under the control of the MIS vice president is data communications (and networking) direction. Basically, its daily activities focus on four areas:

- Local area networks
- Metropolitan area networks
- Wide area networks, including accent on global networks
- Security over all networks

Needless to say, there is a tie-in with the other three areas, in particular, systems and programming. With the increasing use of global networks, its importance in the MIS organization is increasing considerably.

CURRENT DECENTRALIZED STRUCTURES FOR EFFECTIVE MIS OPERATIONS

The preceding discussion of centralized structures centered on the familiar pyramidal MIS organization chart where authority and responsibility flow through a chain of command starting with the top MIS manager. This structure is currently undergoing changes, which will be evident later in the chapter. As a result of the great inroads of distributed processing over the years, decentralization has produced a set of division or operating MIS pyramids. The home office structure is smaller than it was under a wholly centralized approach. The local and/or regional levels have their own structures. Thus, a decentralized structure within a distributed operating mode is quite different from the traditional centralized approach. It makes great use of MIS consultants, some of whom may be from outside the organization and some from the organization itself. Their main focus is to try to maximize the usefulness of the system to meet as many local end-user needs as possible and, at the same time, provide information needed by the home office.

Small- to Medium-Size Company

An example of an MIS organization chart for a small- to medium-size company within a distributed operating mode is shown in Figure 5.3. Although this illustration is similar to Figure 5.1, the MIS structure at the lower level is represented by a systems and programming manager, a data center manager, an information center manager, and the appropriate LAN personnel. Generally, local area networks are handled by the local office. The assumption is that each local office has a LAN or a computer platform to process data and produce the operational and managerial reports desired at that level.

An important aspect of this structure is the role of MIS consultants from the centralized portion of the MIS organization at the home office. They assure that the work of the local office conforms with established guidelines and quality standards of effective use of equipment and personnel resources. In this manner, systems can be tailored to accommodate local processing needs and still meet overall corporate requirements. Finally, when comparing Figures 5.1 and 5.3, the number of employees has been reduced at the home office while a comparable number has been added at the local level. The total number of personnel has remained about the same between the two structures. The essential difference is that the MIS organization in a distributed operating mode allows more flexibility to accommodate the specific needs of local end users as long as they conform with stated MIS objectives and goals.

Medium- to Large-Size Company

A typical organization chart for a medium- to large-size company in a distributed environment is illustrated in Figure 5.4. The positions at the home office remain the same as in Figure 5.3; however, positions have been added for the local and/or regional levels. The total number of positions has not increased, but they have been distributed throughout the organization. Systems and programming personnel can tailor systems to meet local and/or regional needs and, at the same time, assure that they conform with home office mandates.

Because of the size of the MIS structure, consultants are extremely helpful in achieving MIS objectives. At the very top of Figure 5.4, external consultants assist the upper echelons of management with such areas as new information technology and rightsizing. In contrast, the internal MIS consultants are heavily involved with the home office as well as the local and regional personnel in such areas as LANs and MANs. In this manner, the expertise of MIS personnel can be applied in a consistent and effective manner throughout the organization.

Figure 5.3
A Typical MIS Organization Chart of a Small- to Medium-Size Company in a Distributed Environment

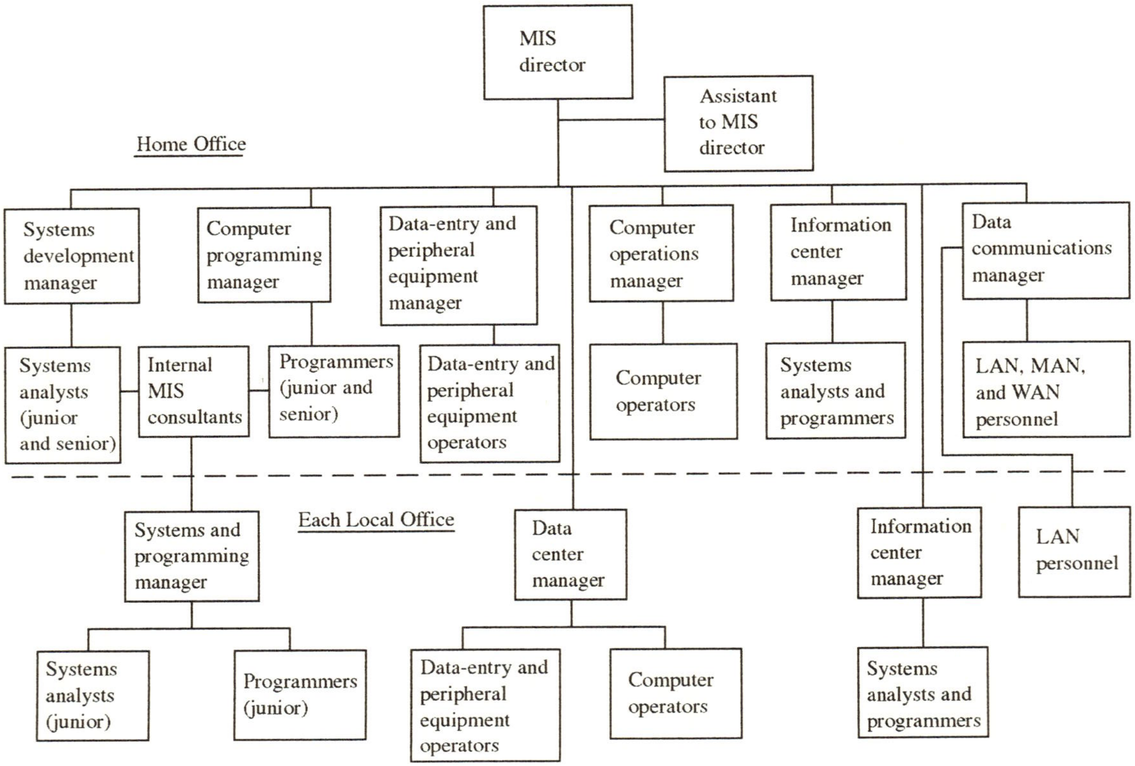

A Typical MIS Organization Chart of a Medium- to Large-Size Company in a Distributed Environment

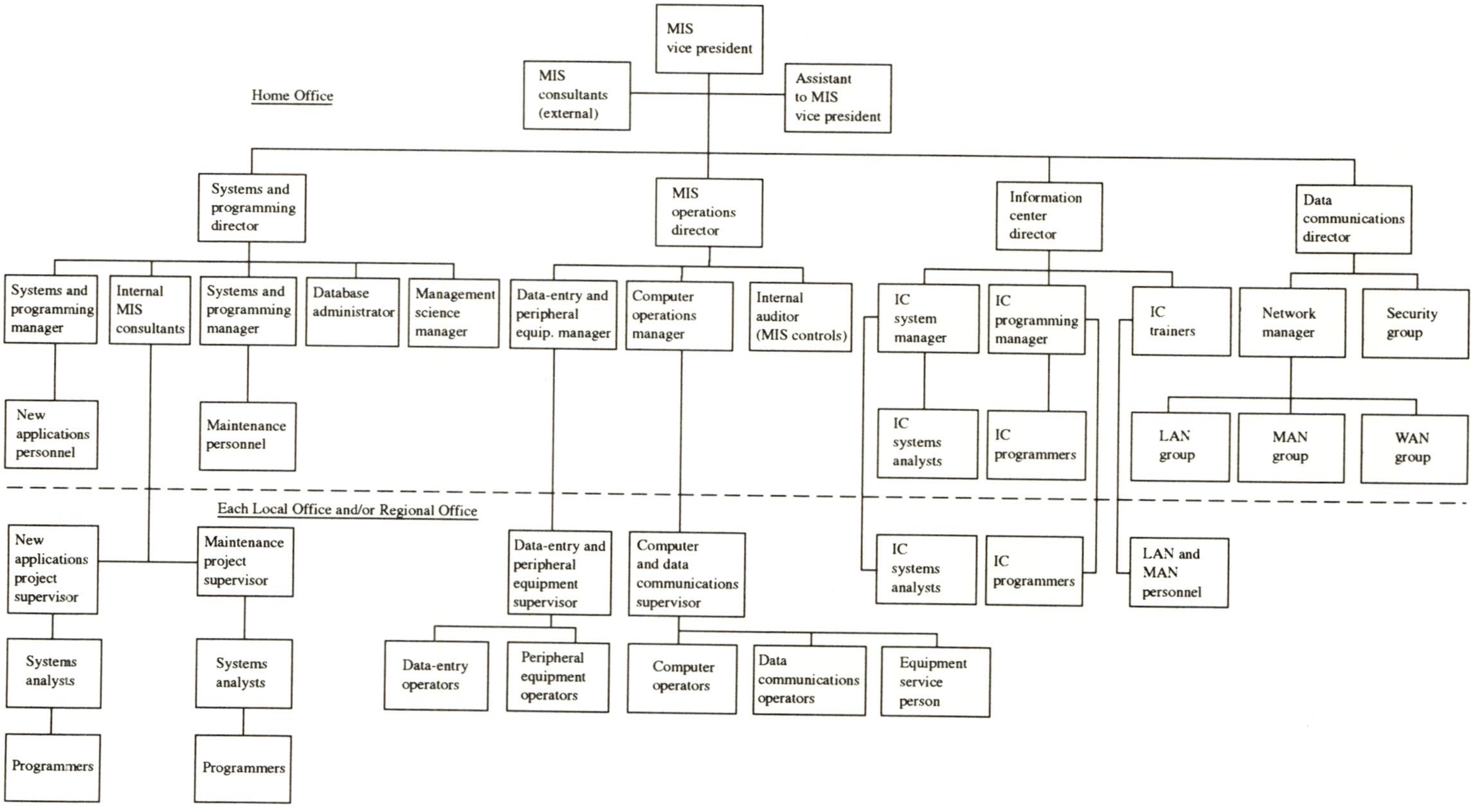

DIFFICULTIES WITH CURRENT MIS ORGANIZATION STRUCTURES

A thorough examination of the MIS organization structures indicates that they are centered around MIS personnel with little consideration for end users. This, in itself, is not bad. However, end users perceive this arrangement as "us" versus "them." Hence, a major difficulty with the present approach is that the functional end-user departments and the MIS department are considered separate entities so that "never the twain shall meet." This is particularly noticeable during breaks and lunchtime when MIS personnel congregate together and tend to isolate themselves from end users. Overall, this isolation from one another tends to be an underlying cause of conflict between the two groups.

Isolation is not only prevalent in the MIS department, but also is discovered by end users when interfacing with the organization's information centers. For example, end users perceive a somewhat hostile attitude when they are involved in the acquisition of microcomputer hardware and software since the information center staff utilizes a reactive approach to meet their needs. Under the *reactive* approach, those responsible for the information center plan its services around identifiable end-user demands. If end users begin requisitioning IBM personal computers in large numbers, for example, then training and assistance for this product are available in the information center. If the engineering department has a strong interest in graphics or the accounting department has made a commitment to acquire a certain spreadsheet package, these preferences provide leads to what the information center should emphasize.

NEW DIRECTION PLACES MAJOR MIS FUNCTIONS WITHIN END-USER DEPARTMENTS

In light of the previous comments, a new direction in MIS organization structures is needed. More specifically, it centers on the absorption of the major MIS functions within the functional end-user departments of the typical organization. Hence, MIS resources are made an integral part of the functional end-user units in terms of day-to-day operations. The underlying philosophy of MIS management behind this big move is that the MIS department, including its information centers, is not an entity isolated from the functional end-user departments; all are necessary to the well-being of the organization. As such, both MIS operations and end-user departments by functional areas should work together to meet stated corporate objectives and goals. They are linked with corporate strategic plans plus critical success factors and key performance indicators. Rather than isolate the MIS department with its information centers from the end-user departments, they should be merged together so that there is *synergism* between the two. This means that by working together, they are able to achieve stated corporate objectives as opposed to each working alone. Hence, "two plus two equals five" from a synergistic viewpoint as opposed to the traditional "two plus two equals four."

A new functional end-user departmental organization structure for a typical company is found in Figure 5.5. Essentially, three major functional areas are under the direction of the highest-level end-user departmental manager. These functional areas—line, staff, and MIS—are represented by functional line managers over day-to-day operations, functional staff members to plan and control departmental activities, and an MIS development and data center manager, respectively. Although not shown in Figure 5.5, there is linkage of each functional MIS operating unit with the MIS management of the centralized computing function that has control over organizationwide computing activities.

As shown in Figure 5.5, the MIS development and data center manager is assisted by the systems and programming supervisor. In turn, this supervisor is assisted by application (new and maintenance) personnel—systems analysts and programmers. Also, this individual has MIS consultants to assist departmental end users under his or her direction. The second supervisor, the functional data center supervisor, is assisted by data-entry operators, computer and peripheral equipment personnel, and local area network personnel. Not shown is the very active interface among line, staff, and MIS personnel so that the three groups form a synergistic approach to developing and employing information to assist the entire functional department. As such, the three groups are better able to fulfill information needs of the department as opposed to working alone.

Benefits of an End-User/MIS Departmental Approach

There are several benefits of an end-user/MIS departmental approach in the functional units for the average organization. An obvious advantage to this new direction in MIS organization structures is that decisions about management information systems are closely tied to competitive realities. Each functional end-user manager must now treat his or her applications backlog as another business issue, setting priorities that will increase profits. If a business plan or product dependent on a computer program fails, the blame falls on the functional end-user departmental manager. Because technical staffers work in narrow technical capacities, they must work closely with functional line managers and other end users in designing applications that support specific products or services.

Another benefit of an end-user/MIS departmental approach is that managers at all levels in a specific functional unit are given access to needed information about their operations. Because MIS personnel are located physically in the functional department and work full-time on the problems about which they are knowledgeable, managers and operating personnel get the systems they want. This enables end users to get their hands on information that is germane to their operations. This benefit is generally not found in the traditional approach to MIS organization structures.

This new organization structure provides for a wide range of new MIS roles.

Figure 5.5
A Typical Functional End-User Departmental Organization Structure That Includes the Functions Currently Performed by the MIS Department and the Information Centers

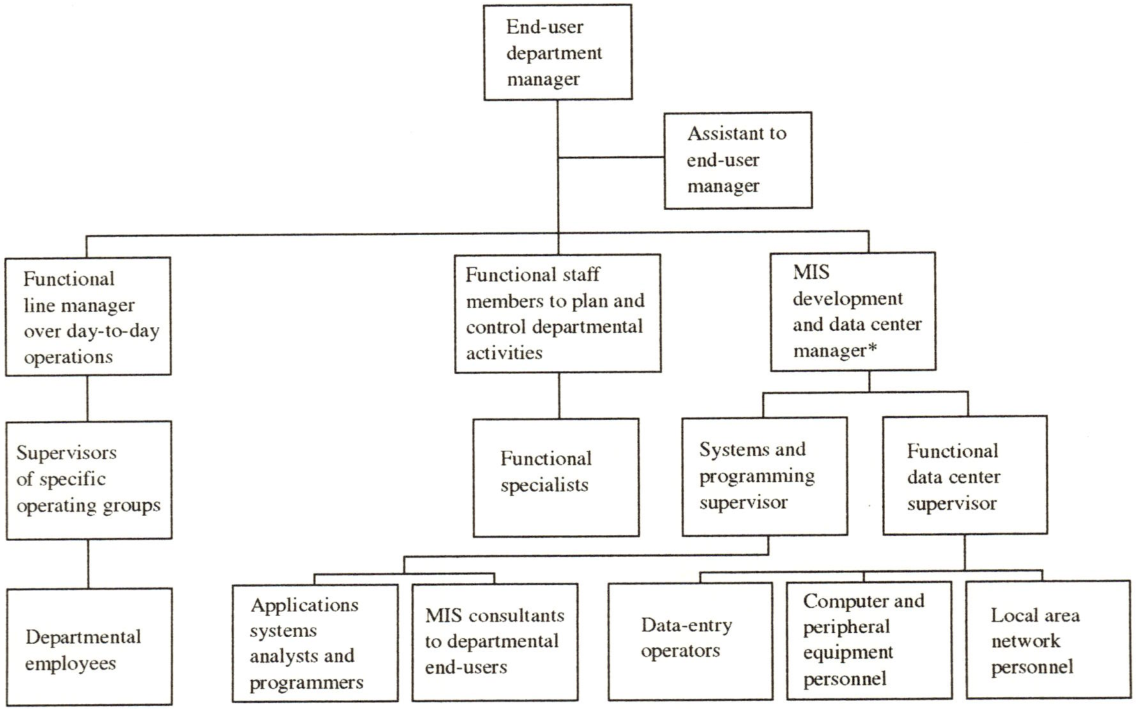

*Although not shown, MIS development and operations groups are linked with the centralized MIS function.

MIS roles, such as facilitators, advisers, consultants, and educators, can be developed, depending on the computing needs of the organization. Because these new roles are more attuned to realizing more of the higher-level needs of MIS personnel, they have the capacity to allow both MIS personnel and end users to benefit from their mutual "enriching" experiences. Underlying these benefits of an end-user/MIS departmental approach is the utilization of a *proactive approach:* that is, functional MIS personnel are better able to anticipate end-user needs before the fact rather than after the fact. They must aggressively seek to introduce new technology that offers the potential for increased productivity and enhanced end-user performance.

Overall, this new direction combines the computing power of microcomputers, minicomputers, and computer mainframe platforms found in the MIS data centers with the advice currently given by the organization's information centers. However, there is a big difference in that the energies of MIS personnel are directed toward one functional area rather than a wide range of functional areas. MIS personnel can utilize specialized software approaches that are not ordinarily applied when dealing with a multitude of functional areas. Thus, this end-user/MIS departmental approach plays an important role in producing newer information that would not have been available using the traditional MIS organization structure. In addition, because MIS personnel are better able to relate to the functional unit, there is a better match of departmental objectives and goals with overall corporate objectives and goals. The net result is that "the right hand knows what the left hand is doing."

EFFECTIVE MIS MANAGEMENT OF STAFFING END-USER/MIS DEPARTMENTS

Once there has been a move to an end-user/MIS departmental approach, it is necessary to change end-user/MIS staffing. The rationale for staffing changes focuses on the fact that end users possess more corporate power than MIS because they are, in essence, the organization. Microcomputers and local area networks are here to stay, and the number of end users who are proficient in the use of the machines increases daily. Departmental computing is putting more power into the hands of end users. The lines between MIS personnel and end users are becoming more blurred as end users become proficient. Hence, there is a need for a new direction in staffing that is related to the end-user/MIS departmental approach set forth here. However, first, the current approach to staffing the MIS department and the current organization roles of MIS personnel to assist end users are set forth.

CURRENT APPROACH TO STAFFING THE MIS DEPARTMENT

The current approach to staffing the MIS department essentially centers on five distinct types of personnel: (1) MIS management, (2) MIS application development and software support personnel, (3) data center personnel, (4) information center personnel, and (5) data communications personnel. Within these five categories, job titles and responsibilities vary greatly from one organization to another. Because of the importance of these categories, they are discussed individually. Basically, they serve as a starting point for newer organizational roles of MIS personnel to assist current end users.

MIS Management

No matter the size of the organization, MIS managers are responsible for planning, organizing, directing, and controlling MIS activities. For a large organization, they include the MIS vice president or chief information officer (CIO), MIS systems and programming director, data center director, information center director, data communications director, and the managers below them, who, in turn, are assisted by a wide range of supervisors. The assistant to the MIS vice president and outside MIS consultants provide additional support to MIS management and their staff as needed. A list of typical managerial positions for MIS is found in Figure 5.6(a).

MIS Application Development and Software Support Personnel

Just as there are a series of management positions in the MIS organization structure, so too there are a number of staff personnel to assist MIS management. These people are responsible for the analysis, design, implementation, and maintenance of management information systems. Within this occupational grouping, there are junior- and senior-level positions differentiated by experience and competence. A typical listing of positions is found in Figure 5.6(b).

Data Center Personnel

MIS data center personnel have the detailed tasks of daily operations. Their repetitive tasks form the basis for processing the necessary data for desired output and managerial reports. Failure to fill these positions with the required skills can cause considerable problems for MIS management. Typical positions for this third area are found in Figure 5.6(c).

Information Center Personnel

In addition to personnel within the MIS department currently, there are a number of information center (IC) personnel who work outside the department to assist end users in meeting their computing needs. Typically, they include most of the functions delineated previously, that is, systems analysts, programmers, and IC trainers. In addition, information center personnel can include hardware and

Figure 5.6
Occupational Groups of MIS Personnel

(a) *MIS Management*

MIS vice president or *CIO* (first level): provides overall direction to systems, programming, daily operations, and information center efforts.

MIS systems and programming director (second level): provides leadership and directs the efforts of several MIS systems and programming managers.

Data center director (second level): is responsible for data entry, data output, control, scheduling, quality control of information services, and efficient use of the equipment.

Information center director (second level): is responsible for the daily operations of the organization's information centers and thereby has control over MIS personnel who assist end users.

Data communications director (second level): is responsible for the entire data communications network, ranging from local area networks to global networks and thereby has control over data communications and security personnel.

Systems and programming manager (third level): gives direction to project supervisors (managers) who are in charge of new applications and maintenance of existing programs.

Database administrator (third level): has control over how data are arranged on the organization's database.

Management science (operations research) manager (third level): has the responsibility of directing management science (operations research) personnel who apply standard or custom-made mathematical models to computer projects.

Data-entry and peripheral equipment manager (third level): has control over data-entry and peripheral equipment in an organization. This individual is assisted by a number of supervisors.

Computer operations manager (third level): has the responsibility for controlling computer equipment for all areas of an organization. In turn, this individual is assisted by a number of supervisors.

Internal auditor (third level): is responsible for establishing controls before and after the data are processed by the computer system.

Network manager (third level): has control over daily operations of a company's data communications and networks as well as its security. This individual is assisted by a number of supervisors over local area networks, metropolitan area networks and wide area networks.

MIS project supervisor (manager) (fourth level): has administrative responsibilities for several systems analysts, programmer/analysts, programmers, and management scientists (operations researchers) in the areas of new applications and maintenance of existing systems and programs.

Supervisors of MIS operations (fourth level): include those in charge of data-entry, peripheral, computer, and data communications.

MIS consultants (external or internal): are the key link in the development of new ideas for the MIS organization and perform a review function of the entire MIS organization.

Figure 5.6 continued

(b) *MIS Application Development and Software Support Personnel*

Systems analyst: works closely with end users to define opportunities for system applications and/or works on system problems. The main focus is the development of new system applications for implementation.

Programmer and programmer/analyst: develops detailed computer program specifications based on more general guidelines provided by systems analysts.

Systems (software) programmer: is responsible for generating and maintaining the computer operating system and other generalized software systems.

Management science (operations research) analyst: assists systems analysts and programmers in implementing standard and custom-made mathematical models as an integral part of management information systems.

(c) *Data Center Personnel*

Data-entry operators: are responsible for operating data-entry devices that produce the basic MIS output.

Peripheral equipment operators: are in charge of operating all types of off-line peripheral equipment that assists in facilitating data processing operations.

Computer operators: maintain the operations of the computer, monitor systems performance, ensure that input data are entered as required, respond to messages from the computer system, and initialize the appropriate configuration of the operating system.

Data communication operators: monitor the equipment used to send and receive information from remote points and help rectify problems of data communications equipment

(d) *Information Center Personnel*

Systems analyst: works closely with end users to assist them in developing their own applications to meet their computing needs.

Programmer: assists end users in getting started on programming their own applications, with emphasis on newer-generation programming languages.

Hardware specialist: assists end users in determining what computer hardware is appropriate for solving the current computer applications.

Software specialist: works closely with end users on deciding what software packages to use for their own computing needs.

IC trainer: dispenses the appropriate training to meet end-user needs when interacting with micro or mainframe platforms and software packages.

(e) *Data Communications Personnel*

Data communications analyst: works with systems analysts to define opportunities for internal or external data communications and networking applications for the company as well as work on related problems.

Local area network specialist: works closely with specific groups of company personnel in functional units to develop and maintain local area networks.

Metropolitan and wide area network specialist: works with personnel throughout the organization to develop networks that extend beyond LANs, in particular, MANs and WANs.

software specialists. The information center positions are set forth in Figure 5.6(d).

Data Communications Personnel

Essentially, data communications personnel are responsible for developing data communications networks along with security over these networks. They include network managers, specialists in local area networks and metropolitan area networks as well as wide area networks, who can focus on global networking. Additionally, there is need for security specialists and, if necessary, internal auditors to ensure that security over the company's data communications network is not violated. Typical data communications positions are set forth in Figure 5.6(e).

CURRENT ORGANIZATIONAL ROLES OF MIS PERSONNEL TO ASSIST END USERS

On the basis of the current formal organization structures for staffing MIS departments, MIS personnel can assume a number of organization roles in order to assist end users. More specifically, they center on MIS consultants within a distributed environment, systems analysts as change agents in a decision support system environment, DSS coordinators to assist end users at the home office and remote locations, and information center staff members to assist end users. Each of these current organizational roles is discussed later.

MIS Consultants

Because MIS management at the central site must be involved in the development of end-user applications at every site, this involvement requires that senior systems analysts assume new duties as MIS consultants. Sometimes they are called internal consultants. Duties of MIS consultants include the following: (1) functional consulting, for example, planning order processing and physical distribution and helping end users to identify and design new areas of MIS applications; (2) technical consulting, for example, designing interactive system capabilities and database management systems, helping end users to evaluate, design, and implement new MIS applications; (3) establishing and demonstrating sound techniques, including project cost estimation, benefits analysis, and feasibility, to identify and assess potential MIS applications; (4) providing assistance in and tools for project planning and control; and (5) organizing and participating in task forces that evaluate, design, and develop MIS systems with multiuser applications (i.e., common MIS systems).

As can be seen from the duties described, the role of senior systems analysts changes from one of *doing* to one of *advising*. As MIS consultants, they plan operations throughout the organization and recommend appropriate controls over

MIS systems. The use of these consultants ensures that what is planned will be controlled from a broad viewpoint.

Systems Analysts Act as Change Agents

In a decision support system project, the systems analysts must go beyond the traditional involvement in an MIS project. They must assume the role of change agents by planning and gaining acceptance for changes in the way computers are used. However, a word of caution is necessary. A certain amount of change can cause a certain level of anxiety in the end user. In fact, too much change can cause people to become negative toward the changes. Thomas H. Holmes, a psychiatrist at the University of Washington, has quantified personal change, ranking a list of commonly stressful events that may lead to illness. Almost 20 percent of these events are work-related. Sample events (and point scores assigned them) are the following: fired at work (47 points), retirement (45), business readjustment (39), change to different line of work (36), change in responsibilities at work (29), trouble with the boss (23), and change in working hours or conditions (20).[1] According to Holmes, if a person's total points during a year approach 200, he or she may become ill. The successful change agent knows that people find change difficult, accept it to varying degrees, and can become ill and ineffective as a result of too much change.

Because systems analysts most often bring about a certain amount of change during a DSS project, how should they act when they want to change people in an organization? By being sensitive to the organizational setting, the systems analysts will have a better idea of the extent and force of change that will be acceptable and will accomplish the DSS project goals. In addition, the systems analysts have a variety of change-agent roles from which to select. Specifically, they may assume the role of persuader, catalyst, confronter, or imposer. The specific situation will determine which role is best.

DSS Coordinators

There is need for DSS coordinators who are basically liaison computer professionals with end users. There should be at least one coordinator specializing in each of the organization's functional areas. Ideally, the individual should have an acquaintance with the organization based on some actual line experience as well as confidence in the users. Also, the DSS coordinator should have training and knowledge of relevant disciplines, including computer technology; economics of computers and information; organizational, managerial, and decision-making theory; mathematical and statistical models; and behavioral sciences. With this background, the DSS coordinator should assist not only systems analysts in work redesign efforts, but also the end users in reaping the full benefits of decision support systems. Because decision support systems are generally never finalized and evolve over time in response to changing conditions, there is a need for this person to coordinate changes that are taking place. In effect, the DSS coordinator acts as a "continuous change agent" by alerting the users to newer and better ways to support decision making. Depending on the functions performed by the DSS coordinator and the structure of the organization, it is quite possible that an information center staff member can act as such.

Information Center Staff Members

Just as systems analysts within a DSS operating mode can act as change agents, information centers can also act as change agents. More to the point, information center staff members need to have a "teaching attitude": that is, they must study the various roles that they can assume as information center professionals and effectively use all of their interpersonal skills, such as listening, empathizing, and asking effective questions. They should have an affinity for technology without making the technology an end in itself. While one of their major jobs seems to be constant reading and updating of information and resources on the latest technological advances, their real aim is to help people make use of what is currently available in the information centers. At times, this requires using one or more roles of change agents.

NEW ORGANIZATION ROLES OF MIS PERSONNEL AND END USERS

Because the current organization roles governing the staffing of MIS departments are giving way to new roles planned to assist end users, these changes are oriented toward bringing MIS personnel and end users closer together. They represent the current state of the art in MIS personnel/end-user interaction. They also represent an attempt by MIS management to get their subordinates more fully involved in their jobs on a day-to-day basis. Hence, these newer organizational roles are designed to get away from the stereotyped roles typically found in an MIS department, including information centers. By utilizing the new end-user/MIS departmental approach, MIS management is trying to get its personnel more aligned with the total organization versus the MIS profession so that they are more motivated and loyal to the organization, thereby reducing MIS personnel turnover. In the placement of MIS personnel in functional end-user departments, MIS personnel take on new roles, including those of end-user coordinators and information knowledge analysts.

In terms of *end-user coordinators,* the change agent role of systems analysts evolves into one of facilitator of information about computer hardware and software desired by end users with emphasis on PC information technology. From this perspective, end users who wish to operate on their own for the most part can get brief periods of help from end-user coordinators. In addition, end-user coordinators can anticipate likely user demands in the future. They act, then, as continuous end-user facilitators by alerting end users to newer directions for making their jobs easier as well as improving their decision-making capability. In a somewhat similar manner, systems analysts will take on the role of *information knowledge analysts:* that is, they will assist end users in developing appropriate systems that will allow them to get new insights into as well as improving their decisions. Information knowledge analysts will go beyond helping individual decision makers by tying in their functional activities with others for a more coordinated approach to organizational effectiveness. Needless to say, this new direction represents a real challenge for MIS personnel.

Just as MIS personnel will take on new roles, so will end users. End users will be undertaking some of the straightforward tasks of MIS personnel by engaging in systems analysis and design as well as programming computer applications. In the systems area, end users will be reviewing present systems that run essentially on microcomputers under their jurisdiction with the view to designing better ones. In this role, they will be acting as *end-user systems analysts.* Likewise, in the programming area, end users will be programming with newer user-oriented programming languages to implement their own designed micro applications. As such, end users will be acting as *end-user programmers.*

GUIDELINES TO ASSIST MIS MANAGEMENT IN STRUCTURING AND STAFFING THE MIS ORGANIZATION

A *first* guideline for organizing MIS, that is, structuring and staffing the MIS organization, effectively ties in with predetermined MIS objectives, goals, and plans. Otherwise, as the organization grows, the MIS structure will not respond to the demands placed on it in an efficient and effective manner. For example, there will be missed report deadlines, long customer service times for order processing, and the like. Thus, MIS management needs to review the advantages and disadvantages of both centralization and decentralization or a combination to determine the best MIS organization structure for itself and end users. Within an appropriate organizational framework, there are a variety of information systems positions that need to be staffed. They are described in the chapter.

A *second* guideline centers on MIS management's taking a broad-based view of its organization that encompasses day-to-day operations. As indicated previously, there is no one best organization structure for all situations. Nevertheless, MIS management needs to operate at a level where they have a broad view; otherwise, they will cater to a narrow constituency and, in the process, neglect important areas. While the debate over the advisability of having MIS participate at the top (even though research studies indicate this is the direction to take) continues, there is a growing consensus that management information systems can no longer be relegated to the bottom. The value of information to the organization is simply too great.

As a result of the current trend of downsizing, a *third* guideline relates to MIS management's being in full control when this situation occurs. More specifically, organizational downsizing creates personnel-related stress problems. The mere rumor of layoffs will have a negative impact. Even normally reliable MIS employees may attempt to gain "their pound of flesh" from the organization which they perceive has sold them out. One way of reducing the trauma is to provide such services as outplacement counseling and assistance in writing resumes, refining interview skills, and developing contacts. Offering to assist MIS employees during this period of transition will help employees not to dwell on the negative aspects and perceived injustices. Giving MIS employees a helping hand makes it less likely they will want to get even with the company.

Related to the prior guideline is a *fourth* one that MIS management should follow. Call it downsizing or rightsizing, work force reduction creates a host of new security problems and intensifies virtually all the old ones. The information security and audit staff must be aware of what is going on, and they must have the full blessing of MIS management to react quickly to the changing situation. It is vital that organizations develop, in advance, contingency plans for such a period and then focus on making security controls a part of everyday work.

A *fifth* guideline that relates to all organization structures is accountability. That is, once a person is given authority and responsibility over one area, he or she is accountable for final results. Hence, accountability can be explained in terms of the need to know. Employees are given access only to the specific data they need to do their jobs. This minimizes the number of employees with access to critical systems and confidential information. Accountability is enhanced when information owners must review access lists regularly and purge employees who no longer require access. MIS and end-user functional managers must notify the information security officer when access needs change or are no longer required.

A *sixth* guideline for MIS management relates to the organization of MIS and end users. As discussed in the chapter, this entails a broad-based approach that integrates MIS personnel with functional end-user departments. The net result is an approach that allows end users to access data that will enable them to make more effective decisions. From this perspective, there is need for appropriate MIS organization structures that include an end-user/MIS department approach.

NOTE

1. James Connolly, "Survey Asks: What Makes a Good DPer?," *Computerworld*, January 23, 1984, p. 15.

6

Informal Organization of MIS Personnel

OUTLINE

INTRODUCTION TO AN EFFECTIVE INFORMAL ORGANIZATION OF MIS PERSONNEL

In the preceding chapter, *formal* relationships specified by the MIS organization structure were examined. Part of this structured environment is created by social interactions which are largely an outgrowth of the specific task and the authority relationships prescribed by the formal MIS organization. There are also many unofficial relationships that support the formal organization, which is usually structured along the lines of office or plant layout, machine processes, job specifications, physical proximity of workers to each other, and operating policies and procedures. The *informal* organization helps to fulfill workers' needs for companionship, affection, reputation, prestige, respect, and status.

For the most part, the basic purpose of this chapter is to examine the nature of the informal MIS organization from an MIS management viewpoint. Principles for effective use of the informal organization are discussed, and the basic reasons for its existence are identified. Popular types of informal organization structures are examined, along with the values and losses accruing from the informal organization. Finally, the MIS committee and the project management structures are discussed along with their advantages and disadvantages.

PRINCIPLES OF AN EFFECTIVE INFORMAL MIS ORGANIZATION

Failure to develop and use an effective informal MIS organization can severely limit the effectiveness of an MIS manager. The first of these principles is the *Principle of Supporting MIS Objectives.* If the informal MIS structure is compatible with and supportive of the MIS formal structure, MIS objectives are more easily realizable. Without the appropriate use of status, power, and politics, operations would be generally slow and inefficient. Overall, the informal MIS structure can be a vital force in supporting and carrying out desired MIS objectives.

A most important principle for assisting MIS management at various levels is the *Principle of Lengthening the Span of Control.* As the informal MIS structure interacts with the formal MIS structure, methods and procedures are developed informally by employees on the job. Because employees need not be told what to do at what time and place throughout the working day, the MIS manager is freed from specifying numerous detailed instructions. Such an environment allows the MIS manager to supervise more employees, thereby lengthening the span of control. Also, this individual can spend more time on the formal aspects of his or her job, such as planning future operations more thoroughly and motivating personnel.

The *Principle of Effective Usage of Informal Leaders* refers to finding out who are the leaders within the informal MIS organization or groups. Inasmuch as these people influence behavioral work patterns, it is wise to work with and through them to further organizational objectives.

The *Principle of Helping to Resolve Conflict* is important within the MIS organization. Too often, an attempt to resolve conflict must be undertaken by MIS management. A faster and more effective way is to let the informal structure take over and let the informal group resolve the conflict. In this manner, conflict which can be impeding system development or everyday MIS operations can be resolved in a timely manner versus letting it smolder over a period of time and getting MIS management involved.

Finally, the *Principle of Effective Usage of the Informal Channel of Communication* refers to the "grapevine." MIS management can use this as an additional channel of communication. Because the grapevine has a tendency to distort facts and form its own opinions (normally contrary to organization plans and objectives), it is wise for MIS management to feed accurate and useful information to this important channel.

RELATIONSHIP OF CURRENT RESEARCH TO THE INFORMAL MIS ORGANIZATION

Current research results (refer to Figure 2.4) indicate that there is no major problem area for the informal MIS organization. However, many current problems, as in the past, are related indirectly to the informal organization. For example, the lack of training programs for new and experienced MIS personnel (rated number 5) would indicate that the informal structure would be useful to disseminate information to MIS management about the need for specialized training. In effect, the informal structure is a way of informing MIS management where and when deemed necessary. In a similar manner, the lack of career pathing (rated number 9) would indicate that the informal structure would be able to disseminate valuable information to MIS personnel about their future. There are additional implications for other MIS problem areas, as set forth in Chapter 2. The other side of the formal organization structure is that it provides a way of helping MIS personnel to deal with anxiety and frustration on the job. Thus, the informal MIS organization goes beyond satisfying an individual's social needs by allowing a flow of information that may be necessary for MIS personnel to survive on the job.

EFFECTIVE MIS MANAGEMENT OF THE INFORMAL ORGANIZATION

Fundamentally, organization behavior, whether it occurs in formal or informal organization structures, has three basic elements: activities, interactions, and sentiments. Through the formal organization, managers generally specify what *activities* their subordinates will perform and what *interactions* with other workers will arise directly from these activities. Managers need to be aware of the *sentiments* or attitudes of workers insofar as willingness to perform the work is concerned. When doing so within the formal structure, managers assume *responsibility,* which is the obligation they have to perform assigned duties. A derivative of responsibility is the *authority* (the power to order or command) the managers have to perform assigned tasks. In turn, a derivative of authority is making managers answerable for final results. The name for this is *accountability.* These basic relationships within the formal structure are illustrated in Figure 6.1. However, while performing their tasks, employees develop activities, interactions, and sentiments other than those found in the formal organization structure.

Because of these relationships, the organization structure has another important dimension, commonly called the *informal organization.* Although informal relationships are highly varied in nature and virtually unlimited in scope, their principal relationships are status, power, and politics, which are affected by activities, interactions, and sentiments. Basically, *status* is defined as one's social rank or position in a group, and *power* is the ability to influence or exert force over group members against their will. As power moves into action, the result is *politics.* The degree of "politicking" is limited not only by the formal organization structure, but by an individual's personal ethics as well. Although status, power, and politics provide the underlying structure for the informal organization, they are not the exact counterparts for responsibility, authority, and accountability within the formal structure. Nevertheless, the manager should be aware of these important factors that influence not only his or her own personnel, but also all other organization personnel.

Importance of the Informal Organization to the MIS Manager

The MIS formal and informal structures are integrally related and combine to create the total organizational design. The major inputs shown in Figure 6.1 affect this total design. External factors, such as economic and social conditions, and internal factors, especially assumptions concerning human nature, determine what the final organization will be. In a similar manner, the structure of new formal relationships causes the development of new patterns of informal relationships. These relationships, as indicated in the illustration, can move toward expected results, such as high profitability and productivity for the organization, and satisfaction of personnel needs and opportunity for advancement for organization personnel or toward unexpected results. If both the formal and informal organization structures can be aligned with intended system outputs, the organization will benefit. An understanding of these structures by MIS management goes a long way toward resolving problems throughout the life cycle of a typical MIS project, particularly during the implementation phase.

Although many behavioral scientists have assumed that the informal organi-

Figure 6.1
Relationship of Inputs and Outputs to the Formal and Informal Structures Inside (and Outside) the MIS Organization

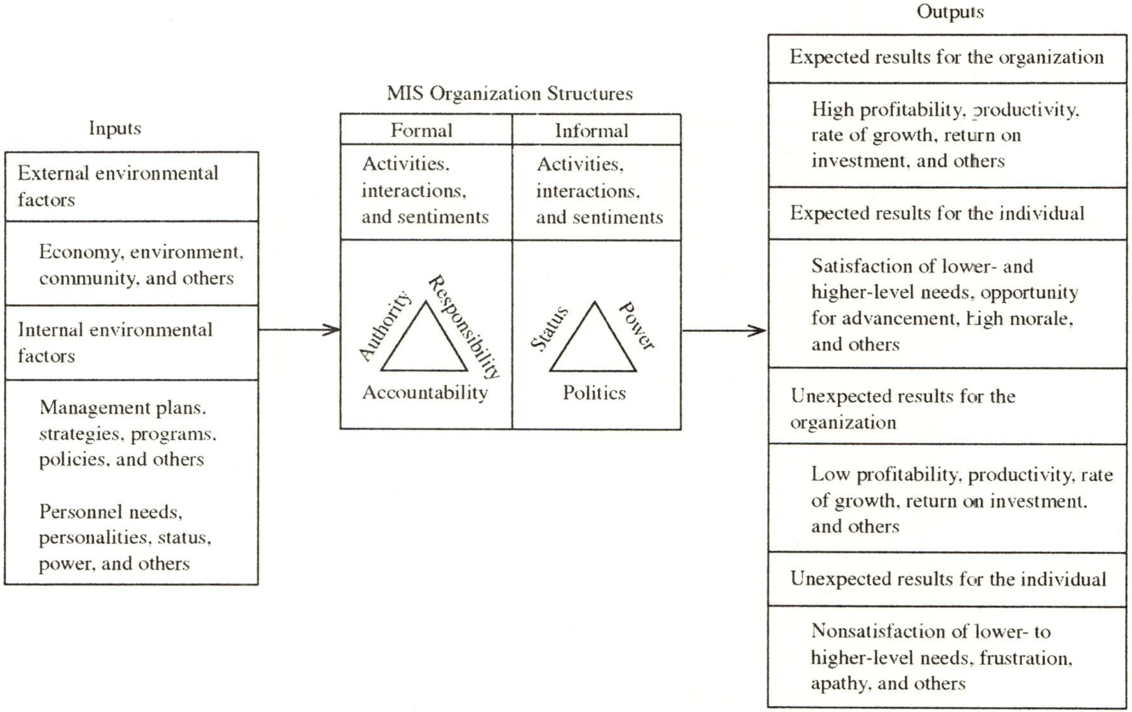

zation has a greater impact on organization effectiveness than the formal organization, past research surveying 341 managers and white-collar employees from 164 organizations indicated otherwise.[1] This research demonstrated that employees perceived the formal organization to be more valuable in satisfying individual needs and more influential in affecting behavior than the informal organization. However, if blue-collar and office workers in these same organizations had been surveyed, the results might have been significantly different. For this reason, the formal and informal structures may be viewed as two sides of the same coin. When they work together, the organization benefits.

THE INFORMAL MIS ORGANIZATION

There are several basic causes of the informal organization no matter where it is found in a typical organization: job specialization, psychological fatigue of routine tasks, and desire to escape from the work environment. But more importantly, organization personnel would still form informal groups because there is a need to socialize in order to satisfy their social and ego needs on the job. *Social* needs include physical contact and association and acceptance within the informal group; there must be a certain amount of respect, affection, and loyalty among members of the group. In contrast to social needs, *ego* needs focus on satisfying one's self in a certain manner. Some members need to be recognized as informal leaders; others need to display their expertise on a certain subject or hobby.

The degree of socializing within the informal group is dependent to a large extent upon the conditions of the work environment. If the organization structure is traditionally oriented and very formal, there will be a tendency to keep informal relationships to a minimum. On the other hand, if the formal structure has been designed quite loosely in the interest of encouraging individual initiative and self-regulation, there will tend to be more informal groups operating in an open atmosphere. In any case, social groups will arise and MIS management should use this phenomenon to facilitate the accomplishment of its objectives.

Groups Within the Informal Organization

In general, people form informal groups based on their contacts and common interests. The informal group develops a structure and life-style that are separate from, but overlapping, the prescribed work-centered relationships of the group members. Given a range of possible people, an individual tends to choose one similar to him or her. Unless an employee is completely isolated from fellow workers, he or she will normally belong to one or more informal groups.

Although groups are formed spontaneously and naturally, many times they are influenced by the formal structure. Workers may try to improve their chances of advancement within the formal structure by joining selected informal groups. Members within the group tend to be homogeneous when the social distances between members are not great. Within the groups, an informal leader will emerge after a period of time. Generally, leadership is accepted by the group members on the basis of expertise, respect, or some other criterion.

Informal groups not only are a means for employees to satisfy their needs on the job, but also effect changes in organizational activities within the formal structure. Several characteristics of informal groups should be clearly understood by MIS management for successful MIS projects. They are as follows:

- Goals—performing task and group maintenance
- Structure—tends to be highly complex
- Leadership—based on expertise, experience, knowledge, and so on
- Behavioral norms—each group has its own rules
- Cohesiveness—degree of attraction among its members
- Small membership—tendency to remain small, ideally five to seven members
- Stability—tendency to resist changes
- Internal and external boundaries—perceptual set that defines the group and environmental considerations

Generally, it is rather difficult for MIS managers to separate the formal groups from the informal ones inasmuch as the jobs and their locations have important bearings on the formation and continuance of informal groups. MIS managers must accept these groups as an essential and integral part of the total organization.

Values Accruing from the Informal Organization

As indicated previously (Figure 6.1), formal relationships by themselves will not accomplish all organizational tasks. In fact, MIS management is fully aware of the inner workings of its structure; it realizes that much of the work performed by its employees is done informally. Thus, an effective MIS manager will not depend solely upon the authority of his or her position, but rather understand the informal organization and use it to get desired results.

The values of the MIS informal organization which can make a great contribution to organization effectiveness are as follows:

- Aids in accomplishing MIS and organization objectives if the informal structure is compatible with and supportive of the formal structure.
- Allows for more creativity of the individual on the job since personnel are not constrained by the rigidity of the formal structure.
- Improves employee morale since employees feel that they are truly a part of the organization because of the positive interaction of employees within their informal group.
- Helps formal managers determine who are the leaders of tomorrow by assessing their performance within the informal group.
- Facilitates faster accomplishment of tasks within the work environment. If employees

followed standard orders from their superiors and contacted only those within the formal organization structure, operations would be slow and generally inefficient.

- Compensates for the formality of the organization structure. The formal structure deals with organization behavior as it *should* occur; the informal structure deals with behavior as it *actually* occurs.
- Allows a longer span of control. As the informal structure is permitted to interact with the formal one, management is able to devote less time to coordinating and controlling activities.
- Provides an additional channel of communication (i.e., the grapevine) to disseminate accurate and useful information quickly.
- Provides a means for satisfying employees' social needs. The informal structure counteracts the cold and impersonal qualities of the formal structure by providing a means for establishing friendships and being accepted by fellow workers.
- Assists in applying formal organization principles. Informal relationships often increase the effectiveness of traditional principles of formal organizations.
- Stimulates more effective management. If the organization's work is performed informally to a great degree, management will improve its understanding of the nature of group performance and individual interactions within a group.

Knowledge of these values will enable MIS managers to predict group behavior and reactions to their orders more accurately, thereby increasing their managerial effectiveness.

Losses Accruing from the Informal Organization

Just as there are values to be obtained from the informal structure, the reverse is also true: that is, losses can accrue from the informal organization:

- Works counter to organization objectives. Although the informal structure can be aligned with the formal structure to accomplish organizational objectives, informal relationships can be used to pressure other workers to restrict their output, exhibit indifference to company policies and procedures, cause insubordination, and, in general, promote unauthorized actions that work counter to the organization.
- Makes the organization somewhat inflexible. If informal groups that have evolved naturally over time are broken up by moving individual members in and out of them, the degree of cooperation with the formal structure can be greatly reduced.
- Reduces the degree of predictability and control. Since the human element is an integral part of the informal structure, it adds a degree of uncertainty to the effectiveness of the formal structure.
- Increases the cost of running the organization. Allowing informal groups to engage in talking, telling jokes, and general horseplay that meet some of the employees' social needs results in higher operating costs.

Even though these losses will tax the patience of MIS management, they must be tolerated. Informal groups should be allowed the time and opportunity to maintain themselves in good working order. For the most part, an individual will generally contribute more to the organization in an open, informal atmosphere than in a highly rigid, controlled environment.

INFORMAL MIS ORGANIZATION STRUCTURES

The number of relationships within the informal organization is almost unlimited because people are complex and dynamic. Although the MIS manager may not be able to identify all the informal groups and their corresponding structures, he or she will want to study the more common ones so that the informal structure can be employed to complement the formal structure in furthering MIS objectives.

Various types of informal organization charts have been developed to fit specific informal relationships. Several of these charting techniques will be explored: the contact chart, the sociogram, and the power or influence chart.

Contact Chart

The actual contacts among a group of MIS personnel are illustrated in Figure 6.2. Those contacts indicated by dotted lines do not go through the formal structure, but are an essential part of the informal structure. In some cases, levels of MIS management are completely bypassed, while others show cross-contact on the same level. As the illustration shows, employee 13 appears to be the most popular because the greatest number of people seek to contact him or her. Unfortunately, the contact chart does not show the reason for these contacts, which can range from having a certain MIS expertise within the work environment to being in charge of the football pool. The chart also does not show which informal relationships are facilitating work and which are countering it. Overall, the contact chart does show one or more MIS personnel who have some reason to be sought out. It may well be that such persons are viable candidates for higher-level positions of authority and responsibility in the MIS organization.

Sociogram

The sociogram depicted in Figure 6.3 goes a step further than the contact chart by showing the feelings of people toward each other. MIS department members in the illustration were asked to indicate with whom they prefer to work, with whom they do not like to work, and to whom they are indifferent. By analyzing workers' feelings toward one another, the MIS manager can identify informal leaders in order to form formal work tasks. In this manner, the formal and informal structures can be better aligned to accomplish specific organization goals. Additionally, MIS department members will be better motivated since they have an opportunity to work with those with whom they feel most comfortable.

Figure 6.2
A Contact Chart Showing Employee 13 to Be the Most Popular or Most Necessary — a Primary Source of MIS Expertise or Information

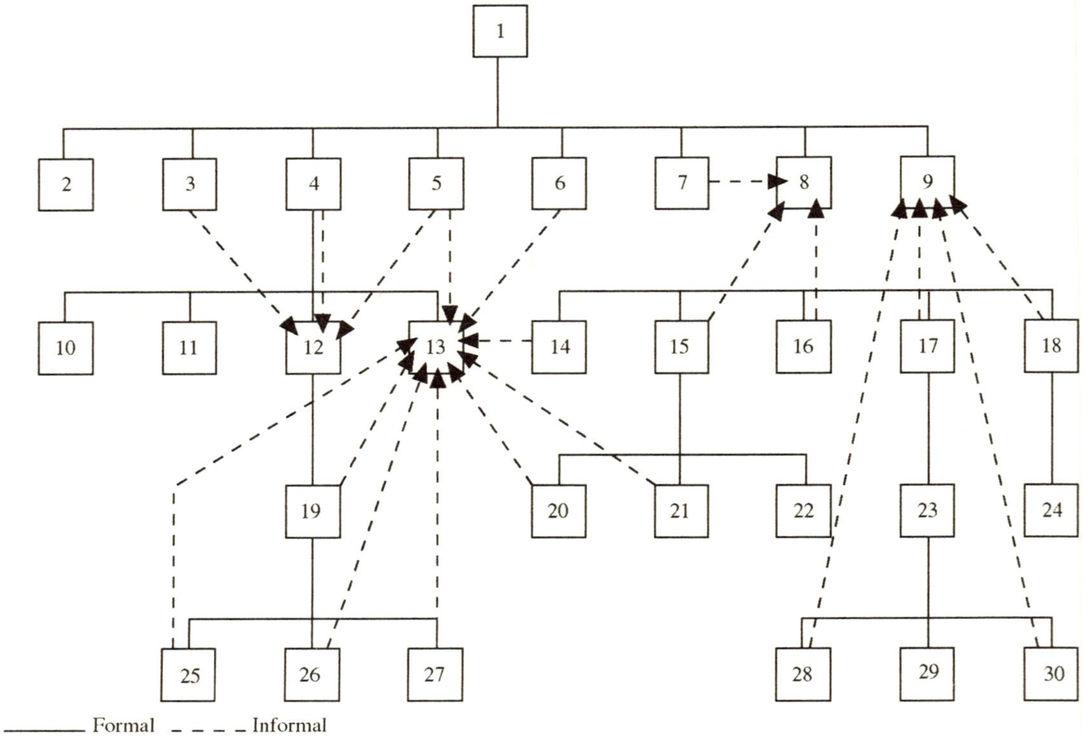

Figure 6.3
Sociogram Imposed on MIS Department Members

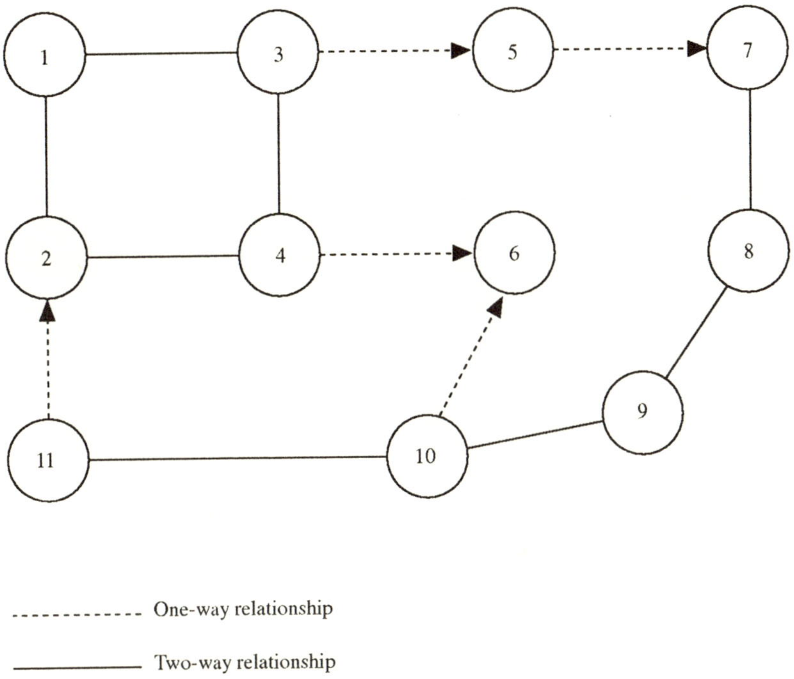

Power or Influence Chart

A further refinement of informal structures can be illustrated by showing the levels of power or influence within an MIS organization. Figure 6.4 depicts a simplified formal MIS structure for a small company, and Figure 6.5 indicates the influence or power level of its personnel. Within the formal structure, Cosgrove, Jansen, Faeth, and Overwein are on the same organization level. However, within the informal structure, Faeth has the greatest influence, followed by Cosgrove and Overwein. It is interesting to note that Thompson, the assistant to the MIS director, has equal influence with Gordon, the MIS director. Also, Brand, one of the programmer/analysts, is right below the MIS director and the assistant to the MIS director.

These charting techniques can shed some light on the underlying structure of the informal organization. As depicted in Figure 6.1, this structure is composed of the elements of status, power, and politics. The last chart discussed is basically a power chart, but it also gives some insight into status relationships, as do the

Figure 6.4
Simplified Formal MIS Organization Chart

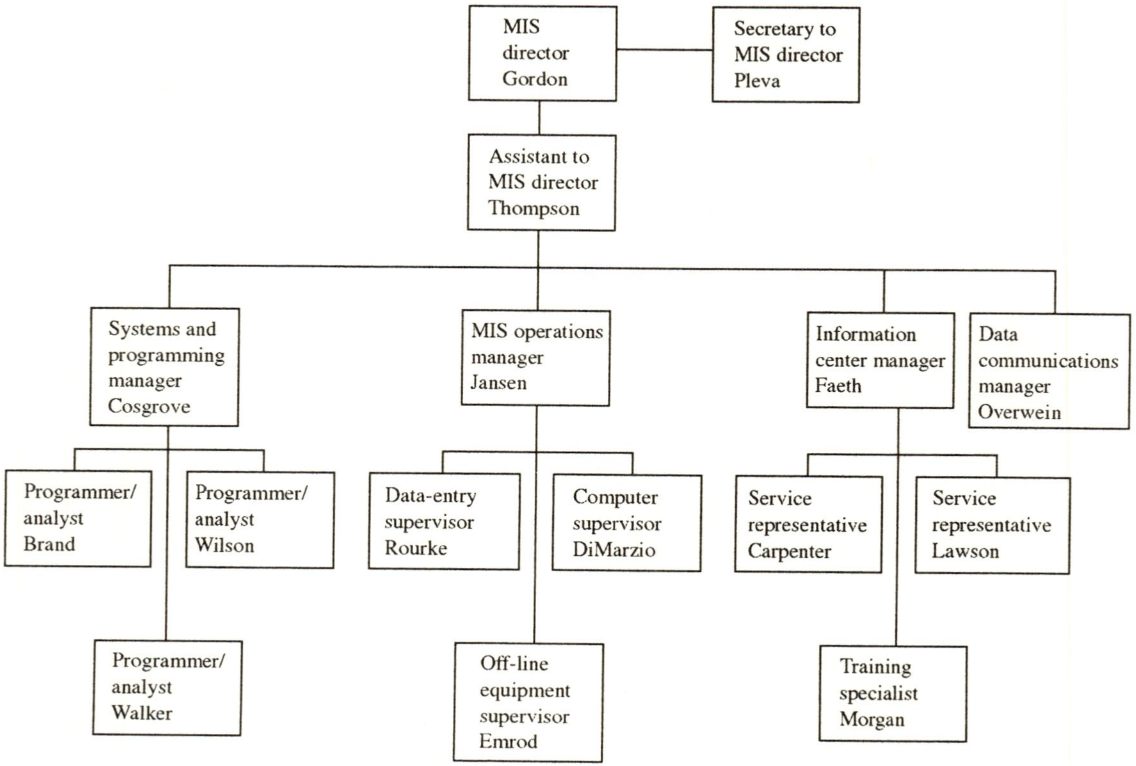

Figure 6.5
Organization Chart of Unofficial Power or Influence

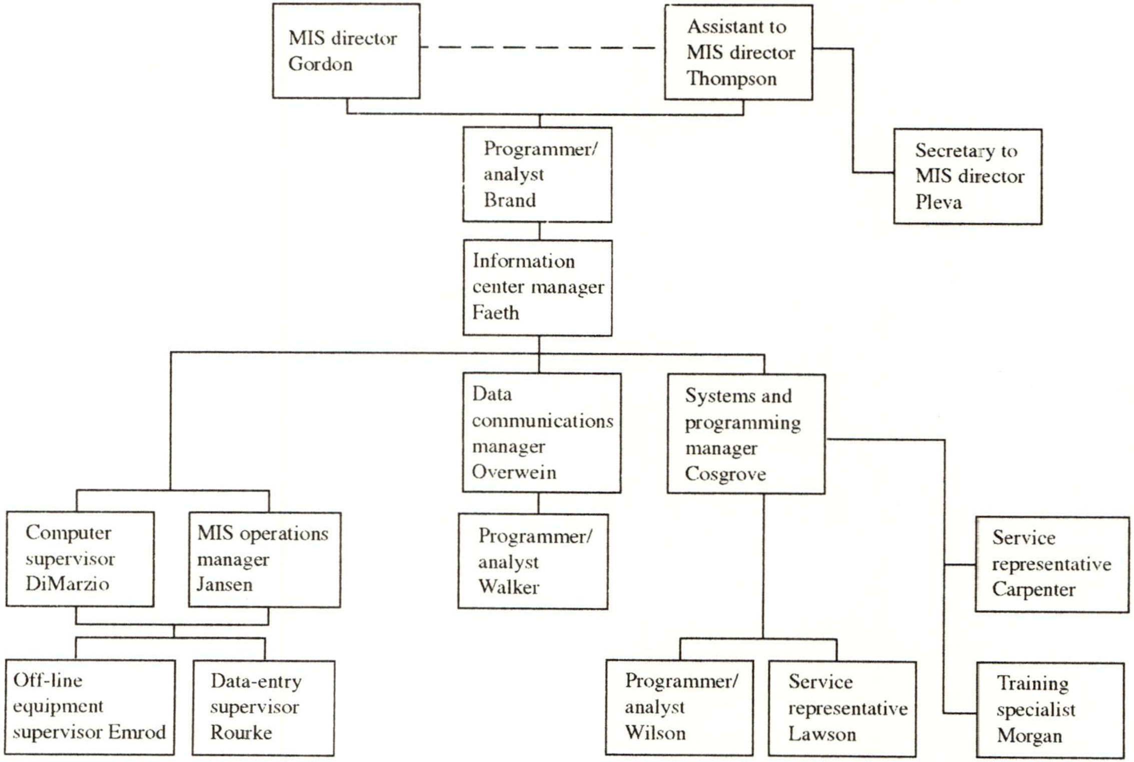

contact chart and the sociogram. It should be noted that all three techniques hint at the politics of the informal organization.

EFFECTIVE MIS ORGANIZATIONWIDE COMMITTEE AND PROJECT MANAGEMENT STRUCTURES

In addition to MIS formal and informal organizational structures, there are other common structures useful to an MIS organization. The MIS organizationwide committee and the project management structure complement and supplement more traditional structures. Note that both contain elements of both formal and informal relationships. Each of these structures is discussed.

MIS ORGANIZATIONWIDE COMMITTEE

As the accumulation and specialization of MIS increase, creative solutions to complex problems will increasingly involve group processes. This fact largely explains the establishment of an MIS organizationwide committee. A committee can be defined as a group of people who discuss and develop solutions to problems. It can be either line or staff and either *standing* or *ad hoc*. A committee may be granted authority to make or recommend decisions, or it may serve in an advisory capacity. Generally, large organizations tend to use committees more than small organizations. This is typically true of an MIS organizationwide committee.

The typical business committee is relatively small. Of the 1,658 committees recorded in a *Harvard Business Review* survey, the average membership was 8.[2] When asked for their preference, the 79 percent who answered suggested an ideal committee size that averaged 4.6 members. Similarly, Kriesberg reported that, for the 75 administrative conferences analyzed, there were typically 5 or 6 conferees at the meetings studied.[3] Overall, research findings indicate that the ideal committee is 5 when the 5 members possess the necessary skills to solve the problems facing the committee.[4] Viewed from the standpoint of the MIS committee members' ability to attend to both the group and its members, or from the standpoint of balanced interpersonal needs, it seems safe to suggest that this number is representative for an MIS organizationwide committee. For technical reasons, however, additional members may be added to ensure the inclusion of necessary skills.

Inclusion of PC and LAN Managers as Well as End Users

The establishment of an MIS organizationwide committee should include PC and LAN managers who have authority over and responsibility for a large segment of an organization or the entire organization. Typically, PC and LAN managers have responsibility for evaluating PC hardware and software, for supporting PC users, and for maintaining the network. Also, they have a key role in making sure the PCs connect, not only with each other, but also with the multitude of other management information systems. This involves much more interaction with MIS and end users than in the past.

Composition of the MIS organizationwide committee extends beyond computer professionals. The inclusion of PC and LAN managers with centralized MIS management means that the actual power of organizationwide computing is being shared with others. What it means, more often than not, is that considerable power rests in the hands of end users, with the PC, LAN, and MIS department managers acting more as consultants. Because microcomputers are an essential part of any organization's corporatewide policy, senior corporate management is paying more attention to what PC products are bought, and where they are installed. Thus, many PC, LAN, and MIS managers find themselves serving on the MIS organizationwide committee that includes business managers of functional units and representatives of the end-user community. It should be noted that the way that organizationwide computing policies are formulated can vary greatly from company to company. The organization's overall philosophy will have a great deal to do with how the company organizes its MIS organizationwide committee.

Advantages and Disadvantages

Perhaps the most important advantage of the MIS organizationwide committee is group deliberation and judgment: that is, "Two heads are better than one." An organizationwide group of imaginative people offer a wider range of experience, a more thorough probing of facts, and a more diverse and specialized background than any single person can possibly bring to a problem. The stimulation resulting from oral interchange can clarify problems and help develop new ideas and solutions. When problems are so diverse and complex that no one person can possibly have a balanced perspective, the results obtained by group judgment are generally superior to those obtained by individual judgment. In essence, the *error correcting properties* of a group process come into play and can help resolve difficult problems, such as alternative systems designs for an organization.

An MIS organizationwide committee is extremely useful in coordinating and executing MIS plans. Such a committee can give its members an overall picture of plans and their place in the plans and allow its members to contribute valuable suggestions on the spot for improving the plans. Of course, such a committee is not restricted to planning; it can be very effective in organizing, directing, and controlling all types of MIS activities. Also, since participation in decision making is required, personnel who take part may feel more enthusiastic in accepting and executing the final decision.

Though MIS organizationwide committees abound, they possess a number of disadvantages. When committee members are required to reach some decision or conclusion, there is always a chance that their recommendation will be watered down, and in some cases, meaningless. The point at which all or a majority of the committee members can agree will tend to be at the least common denominator. The best answer may not always be the most popular. On the other hand, there can be a tendency toward *group think:* the group thinks in terms of what the group leader wants rather than what is best for the situation being studied.

Indecision may also lead to a breakdown of group action. The difficulty in reaching agreement often results in adjournment without action. Indecisiveness gives the chairperson an opportunity to force the committee into action. Indecision also gives one or more members the opportunity to dominate the committee. Whoever is allowed to become dominant changes the essential nature of the committee: that is, a decision-making group of equals changes to that of a leader(s) and followers. Generally, an MIS committee that no longer operates as a group of equals makes weaker decisions than one based on the least common denominator of agreement. Another disadvantage is the difficulty of holding members accountable for the actions of the group. A group process tends to be slow and, therefore, an expensive way of reaching a decision. A typical executive, for example, can reach a decision in a fraction of the time. Despite the limitations of MIS organizationwide committees, they are highly recommended since their advantages outweigh their disadvantages.

PROJECT MANAGEMENT

MIS managers can point to a number of projects that have failed to meet schedules or overrun budgets or whose end results have not met user expectations. Some probably used elaborate techniques for cost and schedule control, while others have probably been run "by the seat of the pants." On the surface, it is often difficult to tell why one project turns out successfully while another fails. Looking at the experience with most MIS projects, the cause of success or failure is not readily apparent. MIS managers must learn how to evaluate the available alternatives to determine the best management approach for their projects. Identifying the alternatives is not a problem; the real questions are, What will work in this particular organization? Will the investment pay for itself?

Project management typically involves the organization and performance of an integrated effort leading toward a specific objective, such as the development of a management information system. The immediate project organization is usually established to meet that specific objective and to dissolve after it has been accomplished. However, the project supervisor of new applications and maintenance projects moves onto a new project. The type of project will determine whether it is a one-time or an ongoing operation.

Typically, the use of a project management methodology by MIS project leaders requires time and effort. However, this usually results in faster completion of projects and, more importantly, a higher-quality product. This can be accomplished by establishing an environment in which (1) general and specific goals are identified, (2) authority and responsibility are assigned, (3) communications at all levels are open and timely, (4) resources are available when needed, (5) change is manageable, (6) end users are involved on a continual basis, (7) progress can be accurately measured, and (8) problem areas can be quickly identified and addressed. With this environment in place, the project can be achieved only through clearly defined steps. A project management methodology provides the project leader with the means to accomplish project goals. With a means of measuring and monitoring the effort, the leader can control the project by ensuring that the proper resources are applied and by making adjustments when necessary.

Basically, project management methodology involves defining the tasks to be done and establishing their interdependencies, scheduling and assigning the tasks, and maintaining a status reporting system which permits management to track progress and initiate any necessary control actions. Although project management sometimes is not extended to costs, it normally should include budgeting, establishing cost targets, allocating human and other resources, and related reporting and controlling. MIS project managers typically use such tools as work breakdown structures, Gantt charts, PERT networks, resource allocation algorithms, and exception reports. Gantt charts and PERT charts are discussed separately.

Areas of Concern for Project Management

Areas where the success of an MIS project is determined are organization compatibility, collaborative environment, and technical adequacy. *Organization compatibility* relates to the management attitude, the expectations of the MIS systems and programming groups, and the real interests of managers and personnel when faced with the need for planning and controlling their work. The difference between situations is illustrated by the fact that management techniques successful in one situation often fail in another, less because of weaknesses in the systems than of incompatibility with the organization.

One of the principal and more difficult tasks is establishing a *collaborative environment*. MIS personnel must be able to work with end users and MIS groups must be able to work with other organization groups. The life and the performance of the MIS project team are influenced by such factors as (1) the leadership structure imposed on the project, (2) the technical competence of the team leader, (3) individual strengths and weaknesses, (4) the manner of setting goals, (5) the structure of the programs being produced, and (6) communication between the team and its environment. MIS managers of systems projects seldom have the training in human relations required to recognize these factors and the leadership qualities necessary to deal with them. Recognizing this, MIS project managers may be assisted by a counselor who is skilled in human relations.

In terms of *technical adequacy*, MIS projects usually require computer software to keep track of schedules, costs, and personnel assignments. Depending on the application, this can be a simple Gantt chart or a complex PERT software program to handle all aspects of a project's organization.

Advantages and Disadvantages

As expected, project management has a number of advantages and disadvantages. A most important advantage of project management is that it is an effective way of managing an MIS project. MIS project managers are chosen for their specific capabilities in terms of the goal to be accomplished. When the MIS project has been completed, the task force can be dissolved and personnel returned to their regular tasks or a new MIS project can be undertaken. Additionally, effective project management can help control the following problem areas: lack of project definition, inaccurate time and cost estimates, inability to accommodate changes, inadequate user support, and improper communication among MIS project members and end users.

On the other hand, a most pronounced disadvantage of project management is that MIS personnel, although qualified to undertake the designated tasks, may not like the other personnel assigned to the project, thereby creating numerous personnel problems. The high turnover of MIS personnel can also take a heavy toll on the members of the project. Continual motivation of members may be necessary to bring the project to a successful conclusion.

GANTT CHARTS

The Gantt chart was first formulated by Henry L. Gantt in 1917 as a means of controlling the production of war materials. Currently, it is used in the scheduling of MIS projects, starting from the first major phase to the last one. It can also be used for the various phases of an MIS study—systems analysis, systems design, equipment, and/or systems implementation. The complexity of the MIS project determines which phase(s) should be charted.

Within a Gantt bar chart, the horizontal axis depicts time; activities are listed vertically in the left-hand column. Ordinarily, the chart is used to compare planned performance against actual performance to indicate whether the MIS project is ahead of, behind, or on schedule. The solid line is the scheduled event, and the dotted line is the completed event. Different events can be depicted by differently colored bars. The scheduled events may appear in one color, and the actual times achieved may be filled in with another color. In this manner, a quick glance at the chart reveals the current status of the project.

Gantt Software Packages

Currently, several software packages create Gantt charts quickly. One such package is MacSchedule, which allows the user to create and manage a project calendar automatically. Schedules can be on a quarterly, monthly, half-monthly, weekly, daily, hourly, quarter-hourly, or custom basis. Schedules that take hours to draw manually can be drawn in a matter of minutes.

An important advantage of the bar chart over other time-charting techniques is simplicity. Managers are accustomed to working with charts; in relatively simple MIS projects, they can comprehend a schedule and its status easily from a Gantt chart. However, the Gantt chart fails to show relationships between events; this shortcoming is not found in PERT charts.

PERT CHARTS

PERT, an acronym for Performance Evaluation and Review Technique, builds upon the material discussed under project management. In a typical PERT network, the circled numbers are *events* which represent the completion of *activities*. An event does not consume time, but activities, depicted as arrows, do. All events are numbered from the lowest (beginning) to the highest (end). The expected time (t_e) is calculated as follows:

$$t_e = \frac{a + 4m + b}{6}$$

A equals the most optimistic time, *m* equals the most likely time, and *b* equals the most pessimistic time. Although space does not permit a complex study of the statistics to develop and prove the formula, it should be somewhat obvious that the most likely time should be weighted more heavily than the most optimistic or pessimistic time. The expected times are used in determining other times, such as earliest expected times and latest allowable times. Essentially, the difference between these two times represents the slack (extra) time available for each activity within the project. In those cases where the earliest expected and latest allowable times are equal, the event is on the critical path. Dummy arrows (dotted lines) do not represent activities but rather connect related events in the network. Typically, a *double line* in a network represents the longest time path through the PERT network, the *critical path;* any delays in starting or completing times on this path will delay the end completion date. Initial consideration should be given to working personnel overtime or reallocating qualified personnel to the critical activities. If activities not on the critical path exceed their expected time, it is possible they may be moved to the critical path. In essence, all noncritical activities have the potential to become critical if not carefully managed.

Because the MIS manager is concerned with weekly performance, a typical weekly project report includes such information as (1) description of each activity; (2) start and due schedule dates; (3) total planned, cumulative planned-to-date, and cumulative actual-to-date; (4) percentage complete (calculated by dividing cumulated actual-to-date by total planned); and (5) days ahead and days behind in terms of the total project time (calculated by summing all days ahead or behind schedule from the lowest to the highest level). Regarding the last item, the weekly project report may indicate one hundred days ahead of schedule for certain activities, but fifty days behind schedule for others. From this information, the MIS project manager might assume that the project is ahead of schedule by fifty days. However, if a critical activity is behind schedule, action must be undertaken immediately to solve the problem. Obviously, an MIS project can appear ahead of schedule right to the completion date and still be in trouble.

The MIS manager determines the cost of each project by assigning various skill classifications and the pay rates appropriate to each, and multiplying the actual hours charged to a project by the applicable rates. The dollar cost is summarized by project, showing project costs from the start to the finish. These procedures for planning and controlling a PERT network should not be applied to relatively simple and straightforward projects. Rather, the cutoff point might be at least fifty detailed activities with a certain degree of interaction.

PERT Software Packages

Currently, there are a large number of project management software packages available for tracking MIS projects. As just indicated, the MIS manager may want to get a real handle on what is happening in terms of each MIS project. Such an approach can be handled easily by MacSchedule PLUS. This software package starts with all of the capability of MacSchedule and adds Earned Value Analysis: that is, projects can be managed graphically, and their resulting productivity can be evaluated with Earned Value Analysis.

Fundamentally, Earned Value Analysis is a method of relating three project factors: planned value, earned value, and actual cost. This provides a simple indication of a project's financial and schedule status. Typically, company accounting systems will collect cost information and tell how much has been spent to date on the project. This is the actual cost, which is then compared with the planned budget value. The MIS manager knows only that the project is over or under budget. However, what about tasks that are behind schedule and under budget?

To know where the project stands, there is need to relate cost to the actual completion of various tasks within the schedule. This is where MacSchedule PLUS comes into play. MacSchedule PLUS allows planned numerical values to be assigned to task bars. By clicking on a bar and entering the estimated planned value, these values are automatically summed to form a financial plan. As progress is reported, MacSchedule PLUS automatically calculates the earned value. Schedule slips mean that value can be earned later. MacSchedule automatically displays the variances between planned and actual budgets as they happen. This gives the MIS manager a quick and easy overview of the project's status. Finally, in order to analyze the real progress of an MIS project, it becomes necessary to compare estimates with reality. Using the three factors mentioned, MacSchedule PLUS calculates the difference between the estimate and reality in two ways: time and money. That is, it calculates "Cost Variance" (money) and "Schedule Variance" (time). For presentations, MacSchedule PLUS also allows the user to graph the variances for presentations and meetings as well as view project trends.

Select Appropriate PERT Software Package

Too often, MIS managers select and implement project management software on the basis of the following scenario. They review all trade publications and vendor sales literature to compile a list of desired features. Next, they make a short list of possible vendors, then try out their systems, using the features list as a basis for analysis. Finally, they select the winner. However, this features-oriented approach is generally not appropriate for selecting project management software. Essentially, project management is a business application and not a software tool per se. Consequently, features of project management software are only as important as the contribution they make to managing projects. Superfluous features can be more of a hindrance than a help. Relational databases, for example, are of little assistance in managing a project, availability of resource histograms does not affect business functions, and pull-down menus do not make the job of learning project management software easier. In total, only features that aid in business processes should be used as evaluation criteria.

Like any business application, PERT management consists of many business processes that correlate with the functions of an MIS project manager. They include creating the initial project plan, creating alternative plans, refining the initial plan, tracking the progress of the project in following the plan, replanning the project when necessary, communicating with the project team, reporting to management, and supporting departmental management, including the total project management environment. In turn, these business processes can be rephrased as questions (refer to Figure 6.6) to develop PERT software package evaluation criteria. In summary, the PERT software package should meet these objectives: (1) provide an easy-to-use personal tool for the MIS project manager, (2) satisfy the reporting needs of the MIS project manager's manager, and (3) satisfy the broader needs of the MIS department by capturing the appropriate information and providing user-friendly interfaces to the department's other management information systems.

GUIDELINES TO ASSIST MIS MANAGEMENT IN MAINTAINING EFFECTIVE INFORMAL MIS STRUCTURES AND SYSTEM PROJECTS

As a starting point, the *first* guideline centers on the human element. Although applying the appropriate information technology is important, the human element must not be overlooked. A foremost obstacle to successful MIS implementation is the resistance to change. Basically, it is difficult to bring a common discipline

Figure 6.6
PERT Software Package Evaluation Criteria in the Form of Questions

- How easily can the initial project plan be created?
- How easily can the initial project plan be revised?
- How easily can alternative plans be developed?
- How fully does the software track the project's progress?
- If changes are made, is it easy to replan the remainder of the project?
- Is the software package easy-to-use throughout the entire life cycle of the project?
- How well is information provided to MIS management?
- How well is information about the project communicated to the MIS project team leader and team?
- How well does the software package support the project management environment?
- How well does the software package support the company's business processes?

into existence when end users are used to doing it their way. It is bound to meet resistance. Sometimes it takes the form of loud and bitter complaints; other times it is a case of turning a deaf ear. This is particularly true in the case of short-term additional costs—which must be incurred to reach a desired long-term benefit—without immediate payback, which run counter to the modus operandi of a bottom-line-oriented unit. Reading between the lines indicates that there are a number of problems of working with and through people. In effect, a critical initial guideline is the proper utilization of the informal structure to interact with—complement or supplant—the formal structure. MIS management should use the informal structure to further its objectives and goals.

A *second* guideline is to feed accurate and timely information via the grapevine to the informal structure. As noted previously, the informal organization consists of myriad relationships, unofficial and unauthorized, created by individuals and groups within the formal organization. It is a by-product of human nature and is affected by the formal structure. Since much of the work performed within an organization is performed informally, intelligent MIS management will learn how the informal structure operates in order to use it for accomplishing its goals and objectives. As an example, an MIS manager should feed the grapevine accurate information, since it can spread rumors and false information as rapidly as it can spread facts. In fact, it tends to outstrip formal channels on speed, enabling MIS employees to secure information long before their supervisors do.

Related to the prior guideline is a *third* one focusing on the informal structure's taking over when decisions coming from the management information systems are in conflict with reality. Although it is possible for computerized systems to run the factory, in reality, the computer is only formally "running the factory," while informally production personnel are doing things for which the computer has never been programmed. For example, the supervisor on the floor will look around and see that the materials on hand are not where they are supposed to be or that the workers are not available. Because of these errors, the individual will tend to ignore the system. The first step to overcome production control problems is to identify the desired results; that is, the computerized system should not try to tell production personnel what jobs to do today; rather the system should tell how long the jobs will take, what materials will be needed, and where to get them. Next, the system should supply a daily worksheet that is a flexible, prioritized, and projected workload list. The information it provides is meant to be suggestive; if there is a problem with materials, for instance, plant personnel must adapt to what is actually on hand. The worksheet can serve as a turnaround document on which the department head can report progress. The integration of the foremen with the manufacturing control system, then, fully utilizes the resources of an organization. If the computer production decisions are in conflict with reality, the informal structure takes over.

A *fourth* guideline relates to the inclusion of a number of personnel who represent the "four corners of the organization" in the MIS organizationwide committee. There should be included as many diverse interests as possible in its members. Needless to say, the number should be kept small so that the real benefits of the committee can be realized. Thus, MIS department managers, PC and LAN managers, and important end users should compose this illustrious group that will give overall direction to an organization's computing needs. Such an approach will tie together MIS strategic plans that were implemented separately throughout the organization.

In the area of project management, a *fifth* guideline centers on establishing a project management methodology. Inasmuch as the systems development process has become increasingly complex as a result of advances in information technology and the ever-broadening scope of systems development efforts, a sound project management methodology is essential to maintaining control and ensuring that projects are completed on time and within budget. To help MIS management review and evaluate their systems development process, the basic elements of effective project management must be an integral part of a project management methodology.

A *sixth* guideline relating to project management is the proper selection of the appropriate PERT software package. Just as the importance of project management software increases in organizations today, so does the choice of project management software packages. Unfortunately, many organizations select a PERT package according to how many features it has rather than how well it serves their own business functions. A proper approach, then, for selecting and implementing a project management software package centers on how it meets the needs of the organization's business processes.

NOTES

1. William E. Reif, Robert M. Monczka, and John W. Newstrom, "Perceptions of the Formal and the Informal Organizations: Objective Measurement Through the Semantic Differential Technique," *Academy of Management Journal*, September 1973, pp. 389–403.

2. Rollie Tillman, Jr., "Problems in Review: Committees on Trial," *Harvard Business Review*, May–June, 1960, p. 12.

3. M. Kriesberg, "Executives Evaluate Administrative Conferences," *Advanced Management 15*, March 1950, p. 15.

4. Alan C. Filley, "Committee Management Guidelines from Social Science Research," *California Management Review*, Fall 1970, pp. 13–20.

PART IV

EFFECTIVE INFORMATION TECHNOLOGY

7

Computer Hardware and Software

OUTLINE

INTRODUCTION TO EFFECTIVE INFORMATION TECHNOLOGY

Today businesses reach outside their boundaries to other organizations. This trend will continue in the future. This was stressed in Chapter 1, where current management information systems were discussed along with the latest directions in leveraging information technology. More specifically, electronic data interchange among organizations for all types of information will be the norm. Point-of-sale and electronic payments will be an integral part of every electronic transactional processing system. Similarly, imaging technology will be the only way to process transactions within an organization. Essentially, internal image processing will allow direct linkage to external customers and suppliers for electronic partnerships of all types whether it be in engineering, marketing, manufacturing, finance, or accounting. It is from this enlarged perspective that material in this chapter is developed.

Although the essential hardware and software components of effective management information systems are the main theme of this chapter, an important aspect is underlying information technology. Management information systems must be tailored to meet the needs of end users, that is, managers and operating personnel, rather than tailored to the capabilities of the hardware and/or software. End-user considerations must always come first. This important point was partially ignored in previous information systems. However, this consideration for information technology constitutes a most important factor of effective MIS.

PRINCIPLES OF EFFECTIVE INFORMATION TECHNOLOGY

From an overview standpoint, there is need to view information technology as an important resource of a typical organization. With this view in mind, an organization's information technology platform is a major determinant of its success in the short to long run. This platform is shared information service delivery. Hence, an important principle is the *Principle of Shared Information Technology Platform,* where information in one part of the organization is shared electronically with other organization units to meet its needs. This electronic interconnection allows for a free flow of information among those who have need of such information. Related to this principle is another one, namely, the *Principle of Open Systems Architecture.* That is, no matter where users are located and regardless of the hardware and software platforms utilized, they can access the needed information. Later in the chapter, the important topic of open systems architecture will be explored.

Although the foregoing is a desired goal to be reached, currently many hardware platforms will not run software packages offered by vendors. For example, software written for a MacIntosh will not run on an IBM PC, and vice versa. Also, there are different operating systems (i.e., DOS, O/S 2, and Unix) which can be run on certain hardware and software platforms only. Needless to say, the *Principle of Compatible Hardware and Software* is needed to bring order to the MIS and functional end-user departments; that is, the MIS department should take the lead in standardizing of hardware and software platforms as well as operating systems.

Even if there is standardization among the hardware and software platforms, including operating systems, there are still potential problems since vendors have interpreted standards in these areas differently. This is also true of data communications and networking standards. Thus, what was thought to be compatible because the same standards were followed is not necessarily so. The *Principle of Compatible Hardware and Software Standards, Including Data Communications,* comes into play. There is need for MIS management and their staff to review the detailed standards followed before the organization commits itself to any expenditures. Failure at this point to do an adequate review can bring untold headaches to MIS management for a long time.

Linked to the prior principle is the *Principle of Evaluation Criteria of Vendors*. Before any type of hardware, software, or data communications equipment is acquired, competing vendors should be evaluated thoroughly. Usually, this takes the form of a decision table that centers on the important criterion of vendor evaluation. In a later section of this chapter, this important subject will be treated. At this point, it is important to note that poor or incorrect evaluation of vendors can jeopardize an organization's information technology direction for years to come.

The *Principle of the Equipment Selection Process* recognizes that there are a right way and a wrong way to undertake the acquisition of new equipment. The proper approach is outlined later in the chapter, where a methodical approach is advocated. The main thrust is having the MIS department in charge of the selection process. On the other hand, an improper approach is to have the vendors undertake their evaluation and present their final results to MIS management. The net result is that equipment proposals are quite different from one another and it is impossible or close to impossible to make an intelligent choice among widely divergent proposals.

RELATIONSHIP OF CURRENT RESEARCH TO INFORMATION TECHNOLOGY

Although there are no research results per se that tie in directly with problems of acquiring hardware and software platforms, several problems are related indirectly. They are:

- Lack of control over data center operations (rated no. 11)
- Lack of adherence to established methods and procedures (rated no. 13)
- Lack of control over information centers (rated no. 15)

Lack of control over data center operations can be related directly or indirectly (depending on the situation) to lack of control over information technology by the MIS manager. That is, inefficient hardware and inappropriate software are being utilized to develop a company's numerous MIS applications. In turn, the data center suffers in terms of slow production runs as well as reports that are not meeting end-user needs. This problem can also be related to the next, *lack of adherence to established methods and procedures*. Since established methods and procedures are not followed by systems analysts, programmers, and data-entry operators, the net result is inefficient information technology from the very beginning of the development process to the implementation of production runs. As an example, there is need for methods and procedures that are useful in acquiring the proper hardware and software. Such an approach is found in the chapter.

Typically, lack of control in the foregoing two areas spills over to the information centers. *Lack of control over information centers* relates to poorly run information centers that try to assist end users. Not only are end users turned off by such centers, but their computing needs are not met. The ultimate results are chaos and confusion about computer hardware and software. In this textbook, suggested approaches and guidelines to reap the benefits of information technology will be offered.

OPEN SYSTEMS ARCHITECTURE

Because MIS managers are being asked continually to manage more and more of the information technology (i.e., hardware, software, and networks) in their organizations, they must develop the ability to reach beyond the mainframe-oriented data center, into an end-user domain filled with a diversity of microcomputers, departmental systems, and networks as well as a mélange of software tools and applications. And they must be prepared to make the elements of this mixture work together. No longer can MIS managers think in terms of a single vendor or hardware or a single operating system. Currently, they need to find ways to integrate an expanding assortment of computing products and services to meet the demands of enterprisewide and even interenterprise information in a competitive environment that has expanded to a global scale. Such an approach is found in an open systems environment.

Open systems implement specifications for interfaces, services, and supporting formats that enable properly engineered application software to be ported across systems, interoperate with other applications, and interact with users in a consistent manner. To place open systems in perspective, large retailers, such as

Wal-Mart, J.C. Penney, Kmart, Dayton Hudson, and Sears, manage inventory by linking them to manufacturers as if in a single network. While this open systems approach eliminates the advantages of a supplier's proprietary network, it also gives manufacturers valuable information. These retailers provide manufacturers with updated sales and inventory information electronically so they can plan production. With such data arriving in a standard format from so many customers, a manufacturer like Levi Strauss or Vanity Fair can easily estimate aggregate demand weeks in advance. Newer systems have begun turning out six-month forecasts to help manufacturers plan production even further in advance.

From another perspective, systems vendors previously dictated how the pieces were put together in a data communications and networking structure. However, open systems change the power relationship between the user and the vendor. In open systems users control their destinies, being in charge of what gets purchased and installed and mandating that the vendors make sure it works together well. Thus, MIS managers are in the driver's seat more often in an open systems environment.

CLIENT/SERVER TECHNOLOGY

A client/server architecture is a logical evolution, the next step in the way computer and network technologies are applied. A client/server is a computing architecture in which any device in a network can request information or processing services from any other. When a device is asking for data or processing power, it is a *client*. When it is supplying information or services, it is a *server*. As such, client/server architectures provide users transparent access to file servers, database servers, print servers, and other devices, thereby maximizing user options and network throughput while minimizing operating costs and response time over the network. The client/server model is a powerful method for writing applications that partition the program into pieces installed in two or more separate network stations. Tools built for implementing applications in this way allow program parts developed independently to interoperate over a network.

In reference to improving payoff for information technology, client/server makes sense because it helps organizations maximize their extensive investments in processing power—from the desktop to the mainframe. Client/server architecture only makes sense if it is appropriate for all organizational applications. There are a number of factors in the shift to client/server computing. The most important are networks, standards, and the tremendous power and versatility of today's desktop devices.

Currently, no single vendor can supply all the pieces to make client/server computing a reality in the MIS organization. The MIS manager should beware of suppliers that claim to have it all. A good test of how well a vendor is positioned to meet an organization's client/server needs is to examine how open that company's product line is. Open computing, software, and network tools are the plug-and-play components that are the foundation of client/server architecture.

An Approach to Implement Client/Server Technology Successfully

All successful organizationwide client/server implementors begin with a small pilot project and a handful of volunteers from the in-house programming staff. The first project is completed in weeks or a few months and largely pays for the learning-curve costs. Subsequent projects are chosen from the organization's most mission-critical applications. These applications are reengineered around the client/server model, resulting in more modern and efficient work flow. Cost justification is relatively easy, regardless of the project size, and based on the organization's own return on investment cutoff.

Typically, the expectations of organization implementors are exceeded in the major categories of cost reduction, time to complete, and economic payoff. That is, expectations are met in gaining user productivity improvement and the ability of MIS to climb the learning curve. The author, along with others, believes that most MIS organizations and their companies are best served by first reengineering mission-critical operations using the client/server architecture for applications. Then they should functionally stabilize computer mainframe applications that are not to be reengineered soon, while adding client/server front-end applications that submit and retrieve data from the current application flow. This logical approach bodes well for successful implementation of a client/server architecture.

EFFECTIVE MIS MANAGEMENT OF COMPUTER HARDWARE

Effective MIS management of computer hardware begins with a good understanding of current computer hardware and their operating systems. Today, this means reference to newer developments in computer hardware. In contrast, a knowledgeable MIS manager would have a good grasp of computer mainframes. It is from this perspective that newer information technology for microcomputers and computer mainframes is set forth in the discussion that follows. In addition, effective MIS management of computer hardware relates to having in place not only key questions to evaluate hardware vendors, but also an equipment selection process to determine what vendors should be selected for large equipment contracts. Equally important is having a good relationship with end users who are purchasing large volumes of computing equipment to meet their operating needs. All of these areas are discussed later.

Computer Hardware for MIS Personnel and End Users

Computer hardware technology to satisfy the needs of MIS personnel and end users is truly remarkable today; it is expected to be even more so in the future.

In addition to the microcomputers (personal computers), minicomputers, and computer mainframes that abound these days, other important hardware developments are as follows:

- *Workstations*—sometimes called desktops, they are universally used and now are an important part of business computing. For less than $2,000, users can acquire one to run thousands of off-the-shelf applications.
- *Portable PCs*—complementary to personal computers are palmtops and notebook PCs. Looking like expanded calculators, palmtop computers have their own calendars, spreadsheets, and communications programs. In contrast, notebook PCs can do almost anything that a regular personal computer can do.
- *Pen-based PCs*—have the potential to be a convenient tool for data entry, manipulation, and retrieval. With pen-based systems, organizations can empower office and blue-collar workers, reduce paper, and speed the flow of information back to the home office.
- *Windows in a PC environment*—are currently widely used by organizations for a multitude of processing tasks. Windows NT is seen not as a replacement for Windows 3.1, but rather as the newest member of the "scalable Windows family."
- *Multimedia*—is a combination of audio, video, and graphic capabilities. From a broad viewpoint, multimedia is a set of tools that allow the user to create and view information from various perspectives.
- *Superservers*—allow for placing massive databases on a server to handle ad hoc queries while leaving critical corporate applications on the computer mainframe. They can have a meaningful relationship with almost any network, operating system, or database.
- *Multiprocessors*—are gaining acceptance as application servers. They are a step up from PCs and help in rightsizing from a computer mainframe environment.

Essentially, the MIS manager should have a good grasp of these hardware developments since they impact an organization's mission-critical applications daily.

Key Questions to Evaluate Vendors

As a starting point, the MIS manager and assistant should visit the vendor's office, talk with their personnel, and get a feel for the organization. Next, there is need for vendor evaluation criteria to assist MIS management in analyzing vendors in some detail. The criteria also help MIS management examine the vendor's background, support, and plans for the future. Key questions to evaluate vendors include those found in Figure 7.1

An incorrect evaluation of the key questions (Figure 7.1) could harm the systems function for years to come. What are the savings from improved planning, control, and accountability? What are the benefits of being associated with users using the same approach to design and management? What are the savings in training and good communications, to name but two areas? There are no clear-

Figure 7.1
Key Questions to Evaluate Vendors

- Does the vendor possess long-range plans for support of the product?
- Does the vendor have a good corporate reputation for reliability?
- Does the vendor demonstrate financial stability?
- Does the vendor possess a high credibility rating in the industry?
- Does the vendor provide a staff with in-depth industrial knowledge and experience?
- Does the vendor possess an intimate knowledge of their product?
- Is the vendor totally committed to the support of the product?
- Is the vendor easily accessible and available to clientele?
- Does the vendor provide an effective implementation program?
- Does the vendor provide additional services as needed to support the product?
- Does the vendor maintain effective communication with users?
- Does the vendor encourage user interaction and involvement?
- Does the vendor provide a well-designed maintenance plan?

cut answers to these questions since each installation is unique. What benefits one installation may not benefit another. Hence, the MIS manager must be actively involved in the vendor evaluation process for best results, for both hardware and software.

Gaining Support of End Users

Although the foregoing key factors have been the mainstay in vendor evaluation, the days when the MIS department had the first, last, and only word in acquiring equipment are long gone. As end users discovered the personal computer and departmental computing, vendors found they could sell around MIS. When end users became aware of the importance of information, vendors found opportunities to sell over MIS. However, the MIS department needs to act as a business-oriented architect of information policy. The job of MIS managers is much easier if vendors understand and support the goal of a rational, corporatewide approach to information management and office automation. For one thing, vendors can be MIS allies in gaining support from impatient departments. For another, vendors can concentrate on the hardware, software, and communications tools that provide the long-term, integrated solutions that MIS seeks.

EQUIPMENT SELECTION PROCESS

For large MIS projects, there can be a need to acquire various types of computer equipment that run into the millions of dollars. A methodical approach to equipment selection is given in this section. Generally, the equipment selection process is undertaken by the MIS project team after systems design is complete. Basic steps are the following: (1) determine equipment manufacturers, (2) submit bid invitations to manufacturers, (3) evaluate manufacturers' proposals, and (4) select equipment manufacturer(s).

1. Determine Equipment Manufacturers

Before submitting necessary data to equipment manufacturers, their representatives should be contacted and invited to an orientation meeting on the proposed new system. During the meeting, they should be instructed about the areas to be converted, general problems that will be encountered, approximate present and future volumes, and other pertinent data. Each manufacturer should indicate in writing whether it wishes to receive a bid invitation so that the preparation of a packet of specifications, data flow diagrams, program flowcharts, and comparable material will not be wasted on a company with no interest in bidding on the system.

Most organizations undertaking a management information systems project have some type of computer equipment based on the exploratory survey report under consideration. Since they have computer and related peripheral equipment salespersons calling at various times, they have had previous contact with most of the manufacturers. Hence, the determination of appropriate equipment manufacturers generally presents no problem to the MIS project team.

2. Submit Bid Invitations to Manufacturers

After letters of intent from equipment manufacturers are on file, the organization submits bid invitations to interested suppliers. The preferred approach is to mail the same set of data to all competing manufacturers. This permits bids to be placed on an unbiased basis, informs the manufacturers what requirements they must meet, minimizes questions, and allows a valid basis for comparison of equipment. The manufacturers will probably need additional information and assistance from the prospective customer as they progress with the preparation of their proposals. Generally, one person from the MIS project team will perform this consultative function for a specific manufacturer. With this approach, the respective manufacturers should have ample information to familiarize themselves with the company and its peculiar MIS problems.

Much of the material needed for the bid invitation can be taken directly from the exploratory survey report and developed during systems design. The contents of the bid invitation include the following sections:

1. General company information
2. Future management information systems plans
3. New system specifications

4. New data flow diagrams
5. Data requested of each manufacturer

Sections 1 and 2 should be brief to focus attention on the remaining parts of the invitation. Data necessary for a thorough study are contained in Sections 3 and 4 and will form the basis of the manufacturer's proposal. Section 3 contains five essential parts: planned inputs, methods and procedures for handling data, files to be maintained, output needs, and other requirements and considerations for the new MIS. Material developed for Section 4 can be taken from the final systems design phase. If the design was properly documented, most material can be used without change. Data flow diagrams will provide an overview of the system and its subsystems. Data to be stated in each manufacturer's proposal are listed in Section 5 of the bid invitation. Specifying in advance what the proposals should contain ensures that comparable information for a final evaluation will be forthcoming.

Even though bid invitations specify the numerous details of the new MIS, legitimate questions will be raised by the various equipment manufacturers. Many will reflect possible modification of some areas to take advantage of the equipment's special features. Conferences between the manufacturer and the potential customer, then, can prove beneficial to both parties.

3. Evaluate Manufacturers' Proposals

The manufacturers should be given a reasonable amount of time to prepare their proposals; sixty days is often adequate, although large and advanced systems may take longer. The customer receives several copies for review, followed by an oral presentation. After this procedure has been followed by all competing manufacturers, the MIS project team, in conjunction with the MIS manager, is prepared to evaluate the information in the various proposals.

Many general criteria can be developed for evaluating a manufacturer's proposal. They include the following:

- *Extent of automation proposed* refers to the amount of new MIS equipment proposed for the new MIS, ranging from microcomputers to large-scale mainframes. This criterion gives the group an overview of what is being advocated by each equipment manufacturer.
- *Throughput performance* relates to the amount of data that can be processed by the computer system within a specific time period. In view of the difficulties with running computer programs—malfunctions of the computer's components, paper jams, error stops, input/output errors, and so on—most experienced MIS managers add 50 percent to the manufacturer's time estimates. To test the validity of time estimates, a *benchmark* problem approach can be employed; this consists of selecting a representative job or group of jobs to be performed by the new MIS, and then requesting results from the vendor.
- *Type of equipment* addresses the make, model, and quantity of basic and related pe-

ripheral equipment, as well as their capabilities, operating characteristics, and technical features. Data on internal memory, operating speeds, storage capacity, and hardware controls are a part of the manufacturer's proposals on computers and related equipment.

- *Rental, purchase, or other basis* refers to the methods of acquiring MIS equipment. They currently include outright purchase, option to buy, rental, third-party leasing, and financial lessor (leased with borrowed money). Generally, total rental charges are high since manufacturers write off the costs of equipment over relatively short periods so that the capital recovery portion of the monthly lease is high. They also have to include cost factors to cover the possibility of having to lease the equipment to others. For these reasons, third-party leases and financial lessors are widely used today. Overall, the decision to purchase or lease is based on many factors, such as the availability of capital funds, obsolescence of equipment, and usage factor.
- *Delivery of equipment* relates to the delivery date. It must allow ample time to test the equipment on the user's premises. Delivery dates run from several weeks to several years. This is normally contingent upon the manufacturer, the type of hardware, and the order date.
- *Manufacturer's assistance* is the amount and type of assistance expected from the equipment manufacturers. Assistance includes programmers, systems analysts, and engineers to implement the new MIS; training schools for the client's managers, programmers, and operators; software packages to simplify programming; and equipment for program testing prior to the installation.
- *Availability and quality of software* concerns software to support the hardware. Software includes current-generation languages for programming business and scientific applications; program packages for reading and writing magnetic tapes and disks, sort and merge routines, and others; compilers to assist in writing the final programs' routines, to aid the computer operator during program debugging, and to handle successive programs during production runs; and routine programs for handling specialized problems. The availability of reliable software reduces the user's time and expense, since the MIS staff can work at a reasonably high level of programming efficiency.
- *Maintenance contracts* are normally provided free under a rental contract, but not when the equipment is purchased. For small equipment installations, the maintenance function will be performed from the manufacturer's sales office. For large machine systems, the manufacturer may assign maintenance personnel to one or more systems.
- *Other considerations* include the ability to handle exceptions and unusual items, nearness to compatible machines for processing data on an emergency basis, overtime costs, and similar items.

In addition to these general criteria for evaluating equipment proposed by a manufacturer, specific equipment criteria that are peculiar to the MIS being implemented must be identified. Because of space limitations, they are not covered. Hence, reference can be made to another publication by the author, where specific equipment criteria are given for a number of management information systems set forth in Chapter 1.[1]

One last consideration is how well each manufacturer (or software vendor, if applicable) has complied with the terms of the bid invitation. This involves completeness, clarity, accuracy, and responsiveness. Does each proposal cover all points set forth in the bid invitation? Is the proposal clear in every respect? Are all estimates of time and cost for peak, medium, and low workloads accurate? Does the proposal reflect a proper understanding of the bid? The manufacturer's failure in any one of these points could indicate a weakness and potential problems in the future. Final equipment evaluation, then, should include compliance with the original bid terms.

4. Select Equipment Manufacturer(s)

Selection of the equipment manufacturer(s) is a difficult task for the MIS project team. The selection process is much easier if the equipment proposed is virtually identical; the choice is normally based on the cost. But this is generally not possible since equipment features will vary. Various methods have been developed for evaluating and selecting from among dissimilar equipment. Often discussion with other customers of the vendor and/or consultants will yield useful information. Other methods include the decision table and the weighting method, which are discussed in the following sections.

One method of evaluation is the use of a *decision table,* as shown in Figure 7.2. Essentially, this decision table defines the important criteria in compact notation and permits an objective evaluation, since the values have been determined before receipt of the manufacturers' proposals. In the illustration, the highest possible score is 100 points for each of the five competing manufacturers. A value of 10 points is deducted for each "no" answer of a major criterion, and 5 points is deducted for each minor criterion. Each major criterion has long-range effects on profits and return on investment, so the deduction of 10 points indicates greater importance attached to this particular item. Values for another organization might be different. For the study currently under evaluation, this is a realistic approach in making this final decision for an interactive MIS. Thus, equipment manufacturer 3 with the highest score of 90 should be selected to receive the equipment contract.

Another approach is the *weighting method.* It consists of assigning different weighting factors to each criterion and giving each manufacturer a score for each weighting factor. In most cases, the score is lower than the absolute value of the weighting factor. The values of all criteria are totaled for each manufacturer. As with the decision table approach, the competitor with the highest score is selected.

BARGAINING ON EQUIPMENT CONTRACTS

Bargaining on equipment contracts is an important activity of MIS management. When sitting down at the bargaining table, the MIS manager should recognize that his or her objectives are to maximize contractual protection and minimize total systems expense. On the basis of these objectives, several guidelines apply.

Figure 7.2
Criteria to Select Equipment Manufacturer

Selection of Equipment

Manufacturer Table

Decision Table

Date: July 25, 199-
Preparer: R. J. Thierauf

	Alternative 1	2	3	4	5
Major Criteria for Evaluation					
Low-cost throughput performance	Y	Y	Y	Y	N
Expandability of equipment	Y	Y	Y	N	Y
Low monthly rental	N	Y	Y	Y	Y
Dependable and efficient software	Y	Y	Y	Y	Y
Equipment backup in local area	N	N	Y	Y	Y
Availability of operating personnel	Y	Y	Y	Y	Y
Minor Criteria for Evaluation					
High degree of automation proposed	Y	Y	Y	N	Y
Availability of equipment when needed	Y	N	Y	Y	Y
Capable of meeting installation requirements	Y	Y	Y	Y	Y
Adequate programming assistance	N	Y	N	Y	N
Good quality training offered	Y	Y	Y	Y	N
Equipment for initial compiling and testing	N	Y	Y	Y	N
Adequate equipment maintenance	Y	Y	N	Y	Y
Compliance with terms of bid invitation	Y	Y	Y	N	Y

Other information

Subtract 10 points for each no (N) answer of a major criterion
Subtract 5 points for each no (N) answer of a minor criterion

Total points = 100 (6 major criteria x 10 points + 8 minor criteria x 5 points)
Competitor's total points: 1 — 70, 2— 85, 3 — 90, 4 — 80, 5 —75

First, even if the MIS manager and the vendor have established a personal relationship—and the MIS manager may be friendly with the vendor personnel after years of working together—all the points agreed upon should be stipulated in the written contract. Only the terms of the written contract can be upheld in court. *Second,* the MIS manager should make it clear that the vendor's promised performance, software specifications, and other specific claims will be included in the contract. This approach has added benefit during the equipment selection phase, since vendors tend to submit accurate proposals when they know these will be reflected in the contract. The contract should also call for disaster backup, including any security and safeguard specifications to be provided.

Third, this kind of "nuts and bolts" contractual checklist should be augmented by larger protective considerations. If the vendor suddenly introduces a new and more powerful system than the one the user has purchased, the user should be able to switch over to it or upgrade without having to revise software or change peripheral devices. Similarly, the user should benefit from any price cuts the manufacturer announces within a specified period. *Fourth,* financial bargaining is a far more complicated matter and requires the MIS manager to be very careful. The unsuspecting MIS manager can be burned, particularly if the individual opts to acquire the vendor's whole package—everything from hardware and peripherals to maintenance and software—or accepts pricing figures at face value. Purchasing everything in one package is appealing because it is the easiest way to buy a system. But the user who is more concerned with cost than convenience might well break the package down and analyze each component to determine whether everything the vendor offers is really needed. Overall, each part of the package should be made to stand on its own merit against competitive bids. By shopping around for elements of a package that can be found elsewhere in the market—items like peripherals, programming and systems support, software, and financing—the MIS manager can often cut costs. In fact, a vendor sometimes charges more for an item that is tied into a package than if sold independently.

Signing of Equipment Contract

Signing the equipment contract by a top-level executive who has been the guiding force brings the equipment selection process to a formal close, which is then followed by systems implementation. However, before the official signing, the executive is well advised to submit the contract to a lawyer for interpretation and the inclusion of user-protecting addendums.

LAYOUT PLANNING FOR NEW EQUIPMENT

Because computer mainframes and a number of microcomputers can be hard to accommodate physically, the following areas must be considered by the MIS manager in the layout planning process: first is the floor area needed and the subsequent floor and ceiling requirements; power supplies and air conditioning come next, followed by a fire protection system. Also, when all physical requirements have been provided for, some thought must be given to the actual installation of the computer equipment. Generally, in large installations of mainframe and PC platforms, equipment manufacturers provide help with layout planning and installation. Some manufacturers develop a checklist for the installation and all manufacturers give a list of recommendations for the on-site installation. The manufacturer will want to assure that the site is adequate for the proper functioning of its system. Thus, the MIS manager should solicit the manufacturer's representatives for help during the layout planning and installation phases.

INSTALLATION OF NEW EQUIPMENT

When the new computer, microcomputers, and peripheral equipment arrive, they must be uncovered from their dust-proof bags. The manufacturer's representative should be contacted for assistance in unloading and uncrating the equipment; appropriate lifting equipment and employees for unloading and uncrating will be needed. Entryways into the computer area should be large enough so that a forklift or similar carrier can be used during the initial installation of the equipment. Unusual rigging problems should be discussed with the manufacturer's representative before the equipment arrives.

Installation, maintenance, and operation documentation will accompany the computer equipment. This documentation must initially be used by the customer's engineers and will then be made available for future access by operating personnel. Getting the computer platform up and running is another subject. However, observance of the foregoing guidelines assures that the equipment is in hospitable surroundings.

MAINTENANCE OF COMPUTER EQUIPMENT

Once the selected computer equipment and related parts have been placed in operation, it is necessary for the MIS manager to maintain this equipment along with the present computer equipment. One approach to maintain the equipment is to hire full-time maintenance personnel. This can be a difficult way to go for a number of reasons, chief among them the high costs and problems of hiring and keeping skilled maintenance personnel. The other approach is to employ maintenance providers; this is the current recommended approach for MIS management to follow. Services are now available that MIS managers only dreamed about a few years ago. Manufacturers and independent service organizations that once offered maintenance-only contracts are now introducing programs for site planning, network management, and disaster recovery. In fact, MIS managers can contract with a maintenance provider to do almost anything they would rather not do in-house, including applications programming, training, and systems integration.

Maintenance Providers

Maintenance providers are eager to find out what MIS managers want and are moving quickly to bring it to market. A number of factors have put the customer in the driver's seat. First are the profitability considerations. Hardware maintenance, once a cash cow for both manufacturers and independent service organizations, is not generating the revenue it once did. More and more computer companies have entered the market over the past few years, and many hardware manufacturers that used to service only their own equipment have begun to compete aggressively for third-party business in hopes of both establishing new profit areas and extending their contacts with both current and potential hardware customers.

MIS managers know that a computer hardware mechanic can walk in and fix a computer mainframe. However, they want a maintenance provider who can be responsible for the total system, including sales, installation, maintenance, software support, and education. Interest in total system coverage is attributed to the increased burden of supporting distributed computing and the complex amalgamations of equipment it entails. Essentially, utilizing a primary maintenance provider reduces the stress of MIS managers dealing with multiple service providers. Simplicity is the main attraction of a primary contractor arrangement. Not only does it minimize the number of people with whom MIS managers must communicate, but also it limits the amount of paperwork. It is recommended that only companies with very complex distributed system environments take this path since, in most cases, MIS managers are better off economically contracting for each individual service.

SOFTWARE TO ASSESS MACHINE PERFORMANCE

In order to determine whether or not computer equipment is properly employed, there is need for the MIS manager to assess machine performance. If the equipment is properly employed, there should be a high level of machine performance. Conversely, if the equipment is underutilized, desired performance is not obtained. To determine whether or not equipment is being effectively employed, periodic evaluation of equipment use beyond that shown on the machine-load schedules is necessary. More specifically, computer performance management software packages provide a typical MIS manager with the information needed to supervise data processing activities on a day-to-day basis. In turn, this information can be used to plan long-term system upgrades to meet the changing needs of end users.

Not only does performance management software identify existing or imminent problems; it can also pave the way to efficient use of existing resources, proper balance of the applications work load, effective task prioritization, improved system throughput, and improved service to end users. Traditionally, these packages have been used by large organizations with substantial MIS budgets, an arena predominantly populated by high-level IBM MVS systems in centralized environments. However, as organizations have downsized their operations, there has been increasing demand for performance management software in midsized organizations with significantly smaller MIS installations and budgets. This demand, coupled with the growth of departmental and distributed MIS, has resulted in performance management products for the midrange environment, most notably for DEC's VAX environment and IBM's VM- and VSE-based configurations.

Even though performance management software products are improving over the years, there is still a gap between organizations' requirements for effective performance analysis and the capabilities of current products. Vendors have yet to address a number of crucial trends in the evolution of corporate data processing. That is, most performance management products are still designed to operate in a single-site, single-function environment, an orientation that does not allow them to interface with the multiple operating systems and multivendor hardware platforms that are found in distributed environments. In addition, most products still focus on monitoring database management systems and on-line transaction-processing applications for large-scale IBM installations. But this situation is unlikely to continue since most major software developers are writing new programs or modifying existing ones for distributed and network environments.

EFFECTIVE MIS MANAGEMENT OF COMPUTER SOFTWARE

Effective MIS management of computer software is directly related to the number of requests for new applications throughout the organization. Today's MIS manager is indeed facing almost daily the problem of having many more requests and requirements from the organization's end-user community that can be met by his or her capability. Typically, the most frequent requests are for single-use, complex analysis reports. Certainly, a part of the problem may be due to gaps in software technology or state of the art. However, for the most part, it is simply a lack of available manpower within a given time frame for solution. In my experience, the majority of MIS departments are simply operating below budgeted staff and have been for several years because of a shortage of qualified personnel.

To overcome this difficulty, newer software packages, such as financial planning languages and statistical packages, can now give end users the ability to satisfy a significant percentage of their own requests. They provide a means of lessening a high proportion of end-user requests for computer mainframe time and of encouraging functional end-unit managers to reconsider the microcomputer as a solution to needs that might have been considered inappropriate in the past. With a flexible, human-oriented command structure permitting instantaneous reporting, answers to "what if" questions and such options as goal seeking and risk analysis capabilities using financial planning languages and statistical packages allow end users to operate at a higher level of service with minimal investments in software resources. Hence, effective MIS management of computer software centers on providing end users with the appropriate software and training to meet their information processing needs in lieu of developing the applications for them. A brief discussion of purchased versus custom-made software is given later along with the sources of purchased computer software for MIS and end users. Also, key questions to evaluate purchased software are set forth. Initially, however, the evolution of more recent computer software is explored.

Evolving Computer Software

Much has been written about the evolving stages of computer software by leading computer authors. For example, James Martin in 1982 published *Application Development Without Programming,* a widely read and influential work. He coined the term fourth-generation language (4GL) to describe a new, simplified type of software development language. Compared to third-generation languages (3GLs), such as COBOL and FORTRAN, fourth-generation languages promised higher developer productivity (by a factor of 10), greater user involvement in the development cycle, and code that is easier to maintain. Since then, the state of the art in 4GLs has advanced dramatically with a wide variety of products now falling under the 4GL label, from end-user query languages to forms-oriented report generators to complete application development environments. On the other hand, programmers are currently facing the challenges of the client/server world and application development using object-oriented programming.

In the years since Martin's book first appeared, it has become clear that it is not likely 4GL technology will ever replace the old standby 3GLs, such as COBOL. The reason is that according to a recent CSC Index report in which hundreds of MIS officials from throughout Europe and North America expressed their views, less than a third of the companies surveyed reported that any stages in the software development life cycle were automated. Generally, COBOL continues to dominate with approximately 70 percent of all applications written in this language.

The popularity of 4GLs is still growing, but not as quickly as Martin has predicted. Typically, 4GLs deliver very good cost and time savings in any tool category, better than CASE tools. This is due primarily to the superiority of 4GLs for prototyping and rapid application development. Also, 4GLs are the most frequently cited tools for reducing costs over the lifetime of a system. Another important advantage of 4GLs is that they are extensible: that is, functional extensions added to these evolving products enable existing applications to take advantage of new technologies, such as relational databases, document management, report writing, and graphics. Essentially, extensions aid in portability.

Currently, there is increasing use of graphical user interface (GUI) systems, that have brought change to the computing world. Powerful desktop systems and standardized user interfaces have hastened the distribution of processing power throughout the information enterprise. There is a migration from centralized computer mainframe and mini-based software applications to more cost-effective client/server configurations where front-end processing is transferred to the desktop. In some cases, the computer mainframe can be offloaded by moving front-end processing to a GUI workstation, with the mainframe staying in the picture as a data server. A typical scenario today is to develop applications on LANs and workstations, right up through unit testing and technical testing. They are then sent to the computer mainframe for final integration and testing. This is an approach that even a traditional computer mainframe environment can adopt readily.

Purchased Versus Custom-Made Software

Today, the amount spent on computer software in an MIS environment is inversely related to hardware purchases. As hardware costs continue to fall, software costs—as a component of the total cost equation—tend to increase. Equipping computers with flexible, easy-to-use application software is the wave of the future for two reasons. Applications are becoming more complex and application software must be truly easy for the unschooled end user to employ.

Many organizations, especially the small-system users, do not have the capabilities to develop their own software programs. Even companies that have such capability may find that the costs involved in the internal development of software programs are prohibitive. This is partially due to the shortage of trained software development personnel, which is forcing organizations to pay very high salaries to qualified people. As a result of this problem, demand increases for "off-the-shelf" software. The move to buy or use software developed by specialized software and service firms will accelerate. It will be wasteful, even impractical in terms of dollars and lead time, for organizations to develop software that already exists and can be easily tailored to specific organization needs. Hence, the decision to buy software centers on time, cost, off-the-shelf suitability, and necessary expertise.

When software is purchased off the shelf, the user receives several benefits. These include (1) the choice of a variety of offerings, (2) reduced risk by buying the expertise and experience of the vendor, and (3) curtailment of expenses by buying a software package that includes maintenance. In the future, business users will reap even more benefits from packaged software because many vendors are beginning to direct more attention as well as research and development expenditures to this area. Because users are computerizing more and more applications, as the cost of hardware comes down, more and more sophisticated software products are in demand. Currently, a virtual flood of packages is offered by a wide range of vendors.

SOURCES OF PURCHASED COMPUTER SOFTWARE

Today, there are five sources of computer software packages: (1) computer manufacturers, (2) software houses, (3) software brokers, (4) third-party vendors, and (5) user groups and individual users. IBM and other manufacturers until the 1970s provided software free in order to sell machines. When IBM unbundled and began to charge for its software, the whole software industry received a boost. Now a large part of a computer manufacturer's revenue comes from software designed for specific applications by internal employees, by field employees, and by customers.

Sources in the second category, software houses, are moving away from contract programming, which was once their lifeblood, to the development and mass distribution of packages. The best-selling packages have been extremely profitable. Some of these packages were created by small companies formed by people with a good deal of knowledge of a particular application area. These small organizations generally have excellent products. In contrast, because creating software is a cottage industry, software brokers have found a place in the market. Moreover, most new small software corporations cannot handle worldwide marketing and do not want to be bothered with the administrative chores that success can bring. A software broker, like a book publisher, handles sales, service, and administration and pays royalties to the software creators.

Third-party vendors, such as those in the area of electronic data interchange, are a fourth source of software packages. Such third-party EDI network service providers have the software to connect customers and their trading partners not only nationally but internationally. Finally, user groups are playing an important role in facilitating information exchange and making programs available to members. Since user groups vary considerably, when a company obtains a package or program from a user group or individual user, it should research such details as support, documentation, quality of product, and characteristics that affect maintenance. Also, some individual users who have developed an excellent application keep it proprietary; others sell it.

Computer Software for MIS Personnel and End Users

Today, the software that is available for use by MIS personnel and end users is overwhelming. From an overall viewpoint, software falls into the following categories:

- *Natural language query systems* employ the technology of artificial intelligence to understand the complex pronoun references and incomplete sentences that one uses in conversational English. One such system is INTELLECT—a true English-language query system—from the Artificial Intelligence Corporation.
- *Electronic spreadsheets* represent a popular software approach to transform a CRT screen into a large ledger sheet. By simulating the rows and columns of a ledger sheet, the program lets a user work with a large number of interrelated values. When a user changes a given value on the spreadsheet, the program automatically recalculates any affected value in seconds. Two such spreadsheets are Lotus 1-2-3 and Excel.
- *Financial planning languages* are high-level financial generators designed to excel in a certain class of applications that includes financial planning and analysis, strategic planning, budgeting, modeling, and business simulation. Two popular financial planning languages are FCS and EXPRESS.

- *Statistical analysis packages* are used in a business situation in which a series of data is used to see what the results are with a certain set of conditions. Interactively, the set of conditions can be changed and new output plotted. Typical business problems that benefit from graphic solutions are project planning, break-even curves, learning curves, and so forth. Two well-known statistical analysis packages are SAS and SPSS.
- *Business graphics packages* give the user the ability to simplify complex data relationships in a way that captures attention. In effect, graphics are an exciting and viable means of communicating numerical and financial data. A wide range of business graphics packages is available.
- *Image processing software* is available from many equipment manufacturers and software vendors. Some offer specialized platforms and highly developed software that provide a major performance advantage over the generalized applications of such vendors as IBM and DEC.
- *Electronic data interchange software* is available from major computer mainframe manufacturers like IBM and DEC. In addition, a number of software vendors along with third-party EDI network vendors are marketing a number of software products for tying in with an organization's trading partners.
- *Decision support system software* offered by a number of vendors can be used individually or by a group of people to support their decision-making efforts. A newer type of software called "groupware" takes advantage of the networks that connect groups of personal computers to each other and to printers and disks. Typical groupware packages are Notes (Lotus Development Corporation) and WordPerfect Office (WordPerfect Corporation).
- *Executive information systems software* gives executives the capability to drill down to the appropriate level of detail to answer important questions about a company's problems. It can distill data into useful managerial information. Popular EIS packages are Commander EIS (Comshare) and Command Center (Pilot Executive Software).
- *Expert system shells* are designed to help systems analysts mimic the problem-solving abilities of experts in a particular domain. The net result of using these shells is that expert systems are produced that work almost exactly the way humans do. A wide range of expert system shells is available from a large number of vendors.
- *Neural network software* is currently making its way into the mainstream of MIS departments. Large equipment vendors offer software products for developing neural networking. IBM, for example, offers its Neural Network Utility (NNU) Family, which is an interactive environment for the development of neural-net applications.
- *Idea generators* are a newer form of software that provides for an active exchange of ideas among participants. The software is the centerpiece of the exchange of ideas as well as the finalization of ideas for the problem under study. Effective idea generators are IdeaFisher 4.0 (Fisher Idea Systems, Inc.) and Idea Generator Plus 3.1 (Experience in Software Inc.).
- *Virtual reality software* is one of the latest software developments available for use by business organizations. One software package is Virtus WalkThrough (Virtus Corporation), which is a modeling and visualization package that takes the concept of virtual reality from esoteric experiment to practical terms. Virtual reality makes it possible to explore worlds and interiors that exist only in the minds of their creators.

In addition to these, software found in database management systems plus data communications and networking systems is discussed in the next chapter. In Chapter 9, CASE tools are set forth. Overall, the typical MIS manager should have a fundamental understanding of the wide range of software products. The rationale is that software has a dramatic impact on how the organization processes its data and derives its essential information to run the organization on a day-to-day basis.

Key Questions to Evaluate Purchased Software

The preceding material on equipment criteria for management information systems discussed the availability and quality of software. Although software can be purchased from equipment manufacturers, sometimes it does not meet the needs of the new MIS. Hence, it is necessary to inquire about software available from other sources.

No matter what sources are used to acquire purchased software, several questions must be asked:

- *How much does the fully operational product cost?* What options are offered, at what cost, and how are they installed? Getting a clear statement initially on the options, particularly on the cost of desirable options if they are incorporated into the delivered package versus how much the same options would cost if tacked on after installation, is important, to say the least.
- *Is there a trial period?* Some vendors customarily allow their software to be installed at a prospective purchaser's site for trial use. A nominal preacquisition investment can short-circuit many future problems by helping the user to decide on options, training, and other costly variables.
- *What are the costs for installation assistance and training?* Costs tend to vary from one vendor to another.
- *Is there adequate documentation?* Documentation can be a key issue when many end users are involved.
- *How are updates covered?* Update costs are usually bundled into the maintenance fee, although updates can often be purchased separately if the purchaser does not take a maintenance contract.
- *What is the cost of a maintenance* contract? The fee is generally about 10 percent of the then-current one-time license fee of the package, beginning in the second year. Because fees are being pressured upward toward the 15 percent level, a fixed rate at the front end of an agreement—rather than letting the rate float at the vendor's discretion—should be contracted.
- *How are the enhancements handled?* The difference between a genuine enhancement and a "fix" should be clarified. Enhancements for a fee are optional; fixes are usually free as long as the user has not tampered with the package. Also, the user should make sure that the full price of the package can be credited against the next major version of the package.

Answers to the preceding questions provide the potential purchaser with a good idea of software acquisition costs. However, many other factors can influence both the acquisition and the ongoing costs of software. Some selected questions that can be asked are the following:

- *Is the package flexible and easy to use?* The package should provide the capability to meet the company's changing requirements. In a similar manner, the package should be easy to use.
- *Does the package have the performance capabilities needed?* If the package can only handle the current work load, then the MIS manager should beware.
- *What is the operational status of the package?* The focus here is on when it was written, by whom, and for what users.
- *Is the source code available?* Given the source code and perhaps a couple of other listings, the purchaser knows as much about a package as the vendor. The vendor invariably charges a one-time fee for the code, and the purchaser usually then assumes all maintenance responsibilities.
- *What arrangements have been made for ongoing maintenance if the vendor goes out of business?* The answer to this question and the next one should be tied back to the availability of the source code.
- *What are the charges for custom modifications?* These are invariably expensive, but possibly beneficial in the long run if the modifications substantially improve the package's utility to the purchaser.
- *What penalties can be levied on the vendor for late delivery?* The same comment can be made of nonperformance.
- *What support will be provided?* Support should be received during the installation phase.

As with the first set of questions, answers to this second set help the purchaser determine the feasibility of acquiring the appropriate software.

CUSTOM-MADE COMPUTER PROGRAM DEVELOPMENT

Even though the main thrust of programming activities is somewhat away from the development of complex, custom-made computer programs, there is still need for such programs today. This is particularly true when periodic managerial and operational reports are needed to plan and control ongoing organizational activities. Because custom-made programs provide the essential framework for effective MIS, they are discussed in some detail in Chapter 9, using a structured approach and an object-oriented approach.

GUIDELINES TO ASSIST MIS MANAGEMENT IN OVERSEEING HARDWARE AND SOFTWARE

A *first* guideline to assist MIS management in getting a handle on hardware and software is to look at both from an overall standpoint. A successful strategy for a typical MIS manager, in addition to full participation in the company's strategic-planning process (as stressed in Chapter 3), includes the adoption of new application development methodologies, client/server architecture, and open systems and the revamping of business functions within a distributed computing environment. It is from this investment in new hardware and software that the organization will have a chance to meet and possibly beat competition.

A *second* guideline relates to undertaking a comprehensive search for new hardware before signing on the dotted line. Too often, initially one vendor offers a very attractive new system that will meet and possibly exceed what the MIS project calls for. However, the temptation to sign now must be viewed in terms of the very best cost/benefit ratio to the organization. Generally, a more extensive search will reveal other promising alternatives, such as using some of the company's present equipment which is current and add-ons from selected hardware vendors. The net result of an intensive review of a costly hardware outlay can result in substantial savings for the organization today and tomorrow.

A *third* guideline is the replacement of aging hardware with new hardware as a matter of policy so that increasing levels of productivity can be realized by organization personnel. The rapid introduction of new and more powerful microprocessing technologies, in particular, has shortened the life cycles of PCs. The MIS manager must stay abreast of the latest technology and give users sophisticated tools to do their jobs in a more productive manner. In doing so, the manager needs to redistribute or even dispose of outmoded equipment. This includes recycling older machines within the organization, selling them to equipment dealers, selling or giving them to employees for home use, and donating them to schools as well as to charitable organizations.

Because software continues to lag behind advances in hardware, the *fourth* guideline centers on MIS management's rethinking its position on software. This means treating software as a business asset, applying more advanced technologies whenever possible in software development, and training its MIS professionals in these latest technologies. Although spending money on improvements in software development may seem a dubious endeavor, many organizations have learned that creating a high-quality product saves money in the long run.

To assist the typical MIS manager in utilizing software effectively, a *fifth* guideline centers on a commonsense approach to managing developed software. That is, in addition to defining the software job to be accomplished, there is need to break down the software project into eighty-hour or two-week segments as well as set up a change procedure for unexpected problems accomplishing the tasks. The need for a short time frame, that is, 80 hours, is that MIS personnel can be rewarded on a more frequent basis. In addition, there is need to agree on an acceptance criteria that fulfill TQM requirements for these software tasks.

The *sixth* guideline relates to the productivity of MIS personnel. Increased productivity of systems analysts, programmers, operations personnel, and other MIS personnel just does not happen on its own. MIS management must provide both the environment and the tools so that increased productivity is the order of the day. Emphasis on TQM requirements can also be helpful to MIS management for improving productivity so that things are done right the first time around. Thus, the message is that MIS management is the key to getting the desired level of productivity out of the MIS organization whether people are within or outside the MIS department.

NOTE

1. Robert J. Thierauf, *Effective Management Information Systems,* second edition, Columbus, Ohio: Charles E. Merrill Publishing Company, 1987, pp. 305–307.

8

Databases and Data Communications

OUTLINE

INTRODUCTION TO EFFECTIVE DATABASES AND DATA COMMUNICATIONS

The proliferation of microcomputers connected in local area networks and the emergence of metropolitan networks and wide area networks necessitate an enlarged perspective of the MIS organization among its management. The earlier approach of centralized control has given rise to a decentralized approach that centers on distributed computing throughout the organization not only for the MIS department, but also for end users. This distributed processing mode also means that databases are to be found throughout the organization. It is from this decentralized perspective that databases and data communications are presented in this chapter.

Initially, a database management system (DBMS) approach to coordinating and controlling on-line data elements is described. The relational and object-oriented models are advocated for reaping the full benefits of widely dispersed databases. Then, the linkage between PCs and workstations and one or more computer systems with attached databases, called data communications networks, is discussed. There is a great accent on local area networks and their relationship with wide area networks. This presentation is tied in with an organizationwide networking architecture: that is, integrated services digital networks (ISDNs). This architecture is a means of integrating voice, data, and video into a total communications network.

PRINCIPLES OF EFFECTIVE DATABASES AND DATA COMMUNICATIONS

Successful management of databases and data communications does not just happen. There is need for a master plan to oversee the growth and installation of appropriate databases, local area networks, and organizationwide networks. Thus, the *Principle of Utilizing a Long-Range Strategy for Databases and Data Communications* is necessary. The strategy for databases and data communications centers on providing current databases and data communications throughout the organization not only now but over the long term, say the next five-plus years. The rationale is that movement from one strategy that centers on data and voice to one that includes data, voice, and video involves substantial outlays.

In turn, such outlays need to be budgeted over a number of years for their implementation.

In the area of databases, there is the *Principle of Utilizing an Appropriate Database Organization Model*. As will be seen, there are various models for creating, accessing, and maintaining a database. Essentially, the method will be determined by what an organization is trying to do with its data. In addition, these organization models are related to database management systems which refer to the current software offered by vendors to manage an organization's data needs.

In the past and today, the *Principle of Integrating Distributed Databases* has been ignored by MIS management. Unfortunately, this failure has come back to haunt them. With distributed databases throughout the typical organization, there is need to bring these widely scattered databases together so that management from the top to the bottom of an organization can get an overview of what is happening in their respective area. This is particularly the case when installation of a comprehensive system, such as an executive information system (refer to Chapter 1), is being contemplated.

The *Principle of Employing a Database Administrator (DBA)* on a part-time or a full-time basis is necessary to ensure proper placement of an organization's data on centralized or decentralized databases. Too often, new systems have been developed whereby two or more new systems have utilized the same storage space only to discover this problem in the systems implementation stage. Needless to say, this is much too late. Hence, the MIS manager needs to make one senior MIS professional responsible and accountable for overseeing what is stored where in the organization's total databases.

Today, since computers are designed to be used by virtually everyone in a typical organization, the result has been unprecedented access to and use of the wealth of data stored in computer systems, too often with little or no controls. While computer-abetted fraud, criminal mischief, and theft are the most visible threats of an organization's computer resources, the unintentional and improper use of data remains the largest, most basic data security issue. Hence, the *Principle of Data Security over Operations* is a major concern not only for databases, but also for data communications regardless of the source of the security problem. Essentially, this principle centers on securing or protecting data against theft, malicious manipulation, or unintentional manipulation.

Related to data security is the need for the *Principle of Data Integrity over Operations*. This principle relates to the fact that valuable data can be erroneously changed and altered. Data integrity also entails ensuring that data are processed correctly and do not become distorted or lost through information system mistakes. Hence, this principle applies to both databases and data communications.

Underlying the area of data communications is the *Principle of Integrating Computer Mainframe and LAN-Based Networks*. Today, the major challenge facing MIS management is the integration of existing computer mainframe applications and equipment with emerging LAN-based networks of all kinds. Carefully laid out networking plans need to be initiated by MIS management to complement the markets that the organization is serving. Appropriate corporate networks for the times do not just happen: they must be planned for so that computer mainframe and LAN-based networks serve the best interests of the organization today and tomorrow.

In the process of integrating computer mainframe and LAN-based networks, there is need for the *Principle of Making LANs Robust Enough to Handle Mission-Critical Applications.* LANs have traditionally been installed and managed at the department level with little concern for the organizationwide network. They often do not meet the standards necessary for mission-critical applications, commonly referred to as transactional processing. Thus, MIS management must find a way to make already installed LANs robust enough to handle these applications. This requires internetworking devices that emphasize reliability, availability, and serviceability, in addition to connectivity. Such MIS networking tools of the trade as problem resolution databases and traffic accounting capabilities need to be applied to LANs and LAN internetworking devices.

A most important networking principle is the *Principle of Integrating Different Computing Platforms.* A fundamental challenge for MIS management and their network builders is to create a single computing environment that seamlessly integrates diverse computing platforms. A typical organization might use SNA, NetBIOS, LAN Server, NetWare, DLC, and TCP/IP. A network builder has to combine all of these on the same wire at the same time while maintaining network performance, reliability, and ease of use. The fundamental building block of a successful corporate network is the internetworking device. This is the device that ties LANs, MANs, and WANs together in a coherent fashion.

Complementary to the prior principle is the *Principle of Utilizing Appropriate Security Procedures over Personnel.* Although operations may be optimal or near-optimal, the same cannot always be assumed for personnel whether MIS personnel or end users. In fact, what may appear to be a well-run operation on the surface may be undercut badly by the attitude and conduct of organization personnel. Hence, a typical well-run organization includes personnel who are challenged by or, at least, content with their jobs so that security procedures will be accomplished without too much difficulty.

RELATIONSHIP OF CURRENT RESEARCH TO DATABASES AND DATA COMMUNICATIONS

As in previous chapters, reference again is made to Chapter 2 (Figure 2.4) for current research results. An examination of the major problems identifies two that are directly applicable here, namely,

- Lack of or poor database administration (rated no. 6)
- Lack of a strategy and methods for network communications management and control (rated no. 14)

Many times, these two problems become intertwined in a typical organization.

The *lack of or poor database administration* can be detrimental to completing MIS projects successfully. If no one is totally in charge, disputes that must be settled by the MIS manager arise. His or her time could be better served overseeing operations rather than becoming involved in the day-to-day operations of database development and maintenance. It is highly recommended that a part-time or full-time database administrator be put in charge and given the full backing of the MIS manager to resolve the proper placement of data on centralized or decentralized databases. On the other hand, if there is poor database administration, it is recommended that the MIS manager assign a senior MIS professional who is respected by his or her peers. In this manner, disputes as to where the data are to be placed along with an appropriate means to retrieve the data (generally including some type of data communications network) can be resolved to serve the users of the MIS better.

In terms of the second problem, the *lack of a strategy and methods for network communications management and control,* the MIS manager needs to develop a specific strategy for the specific data communications methods that the organization will follow today as well as into the future. In the latter part of the chapter, current and newer directions in data communications will be stressed. While current data communications technologies emphasize data and/or voice, newer directions will focus on combining data, voice, and video. It is recommended that MIS managers follow a year-by-year course that will finally get the organization where it wants to be in the distant future, say in ten or more years. To try to undertake a crash course to a desired data communications technology would generally be too costly. Hence, a piecemeal approach is highly recommended for the MIS manager.

EFFECTIVE MIS MANAGEMENT OF DATABASE MANAGEMENT SYSTEMS (DBMSs)

Because data are of great importance to a typical organization, there is need to provide on-line access to database elements for immediate processing using direct access file storage devices. One method of maintaining a large, complex database and managing relationships among the database elements is to employ a database management system. Thus, MIS managers should employ DBMSs to their fullest capacity to satisfy present and future needs of users whether they are within or outside the MIS department.

Typically, the reach of a database management system extends beyond the individual file management systems, such as inventory files and accounts receivable files of the past, to an entire database (or databases), consisting of corporate planning, marketing, manufacturing, accounting, personnel, and other data elements. Furthermore, a DBMS allows *procedure independence* of the database for a large number of data elements. This means that the programmer does not have to describe the data file in detail, as is the case with procedure-oriented languages like COBOL, but rather specify only what is to be done in a *data management language*.

ADVANTAGES AND DISADVANTAGES OF A DBMS

Inasmuch as a typical MIS normally includes a database management system, its advantages should be considered. *First,* DBMS is not only effective for generating and maintaining a wide variety of routine management and operating reports, but also adaptable to meeting the new requirements of management to answer myriad "what if" questions. The latter capability means database management systems will be important aids to managers and their staffs seeking to explore and understand new relationships among various data elements.

Second, data elements can be structured in a manner more suitable to their application, thereby allowing retrieval with a minimum of effort. *Third,* DBMS keeps redundancy of data elements to a minimum since one data file serves many users. As a result of this "single-record" concept, a transaction is entered once for all users. The DBMS also allows two or more files to be updated with the entry of a single transaction. *Fourth,* application programs are independent of the changes in the database, so that their maintenance is kept to a minimum. *Fifth,* DBMS provides data protection not only for accessing one database record at a time, but also for preventing database access by unauthorized personnel.

Although the foregoing provide excellent advantages to DBMS users, the initial investment of system personnel time as well as software and equipment costs can be high; however, increasing experience with database management systems is reducing these costs. Another disadvantage of DBMS is that incorrect transaction data tend to precipitate additional problems and errors throughout the system. Therefore, various tests, such as limit checks and reasonableness tests, should be incorporated to catch errors before information is stored. Overall, these disadvantages of DBMS can be greatly minimized if the MIS is designed properly using the appropriate database organization model.

FOUR ORGANIZATION MODELS FOR DBMS

Although vendors offer a variety of database management systems, programs that provide for the creation, access, and maintenance of data to aid organizations in the effective management of databases fall into four categories:

1. Hierarchical
2. Network
3. Relational
4. Object

The first three organizational models for DBMS are discussed later, while the fourth model is discussed under the latest database management systems.

A *hierarchical* database system uses a tree structure to distinguish relationships among records in a file. Every data item or field is ''owned'' by a higher-ranking item, and access to it must be routed through that hierarchy. In other words, items are arranged according to a parent/child relationship whereby each parent may have many children, but each child may have only one parent. A fixed relationship between the data elements in the hierarchy is established, and data are retrieved by the database management system moving along the hierarchy in a manner dependent on the request from the user.

A *network* database system establishes individual files for each major element of data. ''Pointers'' in the records are used to link these elements together. Pointers are the disk addresses where each record in a file is stored. In effect, the network model allows ''children'' to be related to many ''parents,'' and very general interdependencies can be expressed. As such, a network database tends to be more flexible than a hierarchical database.

A *relational* database management system is simply a collection of two-dimensional tables (called relations) with no repeating group. In the tables, the rows constitute records and columns constitute fields. The term ''relational'' comes from the clearly defined relations of data within a field, which order the records in the database. For example, numeric fields can be ordered from least to greatest, alphabetic fields can be in alphabetical order, and so forth.

Advantages of the Relational Model

The relational model, which is found currently in DBMS models, offers many advantages over hierarchical and network models. It is based on a logical rather than a physical structure and shows the relationships among various items. Data are represented in tabular form and new relations can be created. Searching is generally faster than within the other schemes, modification is more straightforward, and the clarity and visibility of the database are improved.

Because the relational database management system (RDBMS) is based on a flexible row-and-table format, this approach is appropriate for all applications, from the simplest ones built by end users to high-volume applications involving millions of transactions per day built by MIS personnel. In addition, because software developers and programmers find a RDBMS far easier to use, they are using it to reduce the monumental applications backlogs found in most MIS departments currently. In fact, relational database vendors have reported productivity improvements over prior systems. RDBMS is appealing because hierarchical and network systems require in-depth knowledge of how to navigate the database structure with programming languages and of how to use the system's indices. A relational system does not require this knowledge; it allows the user to access information without having to go through a particular program to find data entered for that program. The user does not need to understand how the data are arranged within the database. The query language itself contains all of that information; thus, a query, in effect, automatically searches out data.

A RDBMS also processes records one set at a time. The computer will search for and identify all members of the sought-after set, for example, all past due accounts. By contrast, hierarchical DBMSs examine each record and identify whether it is past due. If it is not, the system goes to the next record. If it is overdue, the system sends out a notice. In addition to these time- and money-saving attributes, the RDBMS has a formal theoretical foundation, which provides rules for structure, maintenance, and integrity (preserving the data against unauthorized changes). More important, organizations can add new data fields, build new access paths, and split tables without disturbing other programs or data stored in the database.

CURRENT RELATIONAL DATABASE MANAGEMENT SYSTEMS (RDBMSs)

RDBMSs, which were developed for use on computer mainframes, are now an integral part of PCs in a LAN environment. Because of their ability to store large amounts of information, computer mainframes allow their database management systems to become more powerful in terms of actually managing and processing data needed for producing information. For an example of a current RDBMS for a computer mainframe, reference can be made to IBM's relational DB2. The impact of DB2 can be summarized in four main areas: (1) fostering broad acceptance of relational database management systems, (2) reinforcing the value of a data architecture, (3) demonstrating the performance possibilities of relational technology, and (4) standardizing on structured query language (SQL). DB2 is capable of supporting high-volume processing applications. Another relational database from IBM is SQL/DS. While DB2 is designed for use with MVS/XA, SQL/DS is designed for use under VM/CMS or DOS/USE. Typically, the DB2 is about twice as fast as SQL/DS. However, DB2 is more complicated to install and operate. It has more parameters to initialize and requires a master terminal operator to maintain constant monitoring and support. DB2 has more tools and utilizes more levels of security and control than SQL/DS. The database administrator under DB2 can grant access to certain records to users at certain levels in the organization. It is important to note that both DBMSs use SQL as a standard which is no longer an IBM issue. Both the American National Standards Institute (ANSI) and the International Standards Organization (ISO) have embraced it.

But DB2 and SQL/DS are not alone in the relational DBMS marketplace. There are a large number of RDBMS products from various vendors. Typical examples are Supra (Cincom Systems, Inc.) and IDMS/R and IDMS/SQL (Cullinet Software, Inc.). Another is Applied Data Research, Inc.; ADR's three-level AQL strategy includes support of SQL in the nucleus of the Datacom-DB DBMS; as a target protocol for its languages so that they generate SQL calls to the database; and embedded in the language themselves, thereby allowing the complete utilization of the supported SQL-based DBMS.

Distributed Database Management Systems (D-DBMSs)

RDBMSs increasingly are being pushed from corporate mainframes to department-level computers and local area networks as organizations evolve toward distributed database management systems (D-DBMSs). The advantages of a D-DBMS is its ability to present information in a transparent manner and in the most appropriate format. A D-DBMS manages data physically located on a number of networked computers, with the logical appearance to the user or applications programmer of a single database. Essentially, a distributed DBMS enables users to access information regardless of the hardware or application software used and without having to know where it resides or how to access it. A truly distributed DBMS allows users to split up data tables horizontally or vertically and put the fragments on different nodes at different sites. Queries are made exactly as if the information were local.

In a D-DBMS operating mode, integrity is maintained throughout the database during transactions and during recovery and backup. Control protocols such as two-phase commit provide locking mechanisms that assure data remain constant. Global query optimization features automatically select the best means of carrying out complex transactions over local- and wide-area networks, and on-line performance monitors give users a view into the distributed process to allow troubleshooting and system tuning. Vendor products that come closest to a true distributed DBMS are Informix On-Line (Informix Software, Inc.), Ingres Intelligent Database (Ingres Corporation), Oracle 7 (Oracle Corporation), and System 10 (Sybase, Inc.).

LATEST DATABASE MANAGEMENT SYSTEMS

As with databases of the past and present, the latest database management systems are the foundation of successful MIS architectures. Applications may come and go, but without a solid, stable data management environment, coherent enterprisewide systems cannot be developed. So essential are database management systems to organizationwide MIS efforts that vast sums of money are spent on this software. It is not unusual for a large organization to spend several hundred thousand dollars on a computer mainframe DBMS, such as DB2, Oracle, or RDB. When host hardware and applications are added, total database-related expenditures can run into the millions.

For several years, low-end, shared-file PC databases, such as dBase and Paradox, have mounted an important challenge to computer mainframe DBMS facilities. However, more recently, the second generation of distributed database products—which includes such client/server RDBMS packages as Sybase, Oracle, SQL Base, and Inter-Base—has mounted a much stronger challenge on the mainframe DBMS market, thereby displacing traditional mainframe DBMS software. Not only will this latest client/server database software be set forth, but also object-oriented DBMS will be presented here; both are related to local area networks. Initially, image processing RDBMS is included. An alternative approach for high-volume data storage, that is, database machines, is discussed later in this section.

Image Processing RDBMS

No matter how great the pictures are in image processing systems, there is a need for good performance. Some relational database management systems, including Informix's online RDBMS, can handle digitized images, video, or voice as part of the data-and-text RDBMS, storing these multimegabyte files as binary large objects (BLOBs). The BLOBs are strings of 1s and 0s, as digitized by document scanners. Designers of today's databases store labeling information separately as text. Other RDBMS vendors that support image retrieval are Ingres Corporation, Sybase, Inc., and Oracle Corporation. Nonrelational databases also can handle image retrieval through the use of pointers.

Even though scanned images are easily stored on optical disks and compact disk read-only memory as well as magnetic media, handling these multimegabyte images takes time. Users have to allow several seconds for an image to be painted on-screen. Often, transmitting such long files also takes more time than users expect. The challenge is to get multimedia working in a networked environment. Compression algorithms that shrink multimegabyte files into files of 100K bytes or less already exist, but RDBMS vendors have not offered them as standard features because demand for them has not been high. When storage problems have been resolved, imaging systems need to understand the images, even if the images are stored as BLOBs. The Ingres Corporation is working on defining new data types. It has built an infrastructure that can handle objects such as digitized images, but the RDBMS needs to understand the content of what has been stored. It is expected that such algorithms will be available by the mid-1990s.

Client/Server RDBMS

Currently, every major database vendor is staking its future on client/server computing that is tied in with its relational DBMS. As discussed in the prior chapter, client/server computing is a form of shared processing between a user's front-end, or *client,* machine and a back-end server machine. Basically, client/server is cooperative processing that occurs with a database engine acting as the back end, or *server*. Client applications formulate queries and communicate these to the database server by using structured SQL commands. Some consider client/server to be the process of breaking apart a monolithic application that previously resided on a computer mainframe or minicomputer. The client is responsible for the user interface and application programming logic, and the server is responsible for data management.

In the client/server paradigm, large databases such as those from Oracle,

Sybase, and Ingres generally act as the back-end engine while user-oriented databases such as Paradox and DataEase function as the front-end tool. Most large database management systems come with 4GL front-end development tools and do not require separate front-end systems. Conversely, databases commonly used as clients often run over a LAN, independent of a large database server, albeit not as a client/server system. The trend has been to use one package for front-end work and another as the engine actually controlling the data on the server. As a rule, these packages are not designed exclusively for one process or the other and can be used interchangeably. Overall, for a typical client/server situation, thc *server* focuses primarily on tasks that are compute-, disk-, or memory-intensive and that frequently involve managing large volumes of data. On the other hand, the *client* handles user interface and decision support functions, sends requests to the server using a SQL language, and displays or processes the results.

Object-Oriented DBMS

Typically, the simplicity of the relational model of data and the acceptance of the relational Structured Query Language as an industry standard have contributed to significant productivity enhancement in application development. Even as the acceptance of relational database management systems has spread, their limitations have been exposed by the emergence of various classes of new applications: multimedia, statistical and scientific, modeling and analysis, geographic information, and engineering and design. These limitations of relational database management systems helped fuel the emergence of object-oriented database management systems (OODBMSs).

Currently, object orientation is a term whose meaning changes in different situations. End users encounter *objects* in their graphical user interfaces in the form of icons or other graphical representations of parts of an application. Programmers use object-oriented programming (OOP) languages to write highly modular applications. In an object-oriented database management system, developers use *objects* to store complex data, say for CAD/CAM or geographic information systems. Object-oriented analysis and design (OOAD) allows programmers to apply design methodologies and use CASE tools to create object-oriented programs. In addition, Distributed Object Management provides a way for distributed, heterogenous applications spread across a wide area network to communicate and share data. Hence, OODBMS is intertwined with object technology in the total MIS organization, which will be discussed in the next chapter.

The first users of OODBMSs tended to be engineers who found that relational databases were unable to handle the storage requirements of complex scientific data or Computer-Aided Design (CAD) drawings. While RDBM systems can store straightforward, predefined alphanumeric data types, a system for storing scientific data might require the use of a variable-dimension array. A database for CAD drawings would need to preserve the relationships between the lines and angles of the vector graphics within each file.

In a somewhat similar manner, businesses have begun to consider OODBMS to centralize and simplify the storage of a wide range of complex data, such as text files and mapping data. Some of this information is stored in file systems with the applications that created them; much is still on paper. Business organizations are also expressing interest in OODBMS products for their capability to cut application development backlogs by reducing development time through the reuse of code. As organizations move more toward a unified, organization-wide system, they will be able to take a lot of disjointed systems that have been built on an application-by-application basis and create a single, local perspective on customers or products and services using object-oriented DBMS.

Database Machines

An alternative approach to database management systems are database machines. For business users who want information processed in the most cost-effective way, the database machine might well be a remedy for everyday processing disguised as a software tool. The two full-fledged database machines currently on the market free central processing unit (CPU) cycles for duties more kinetic than maintaining a database. Both the DBC/1012 from Teradata Corporation and the BL8000 from Britton Lee, Inc., are boxes scarcely distinguishable from the basic DASD devices. Essentially, Teradata is identified with computer mainframes while Britton Lee is associated more with minicomputers and microcomputers.

With parallel processing, the Teradata DBC/1012 machine can query an entire series of microprocessors. Further flexibility is gained from its ability to interface with a variety of fourth-generation languages. Essentially, the DBC/1012 is a database computer which has a microprocessor-based system that combines software running on IBM hosts and its own hardware. The hardware contains three basic modules: an interface module processor (IMP), an access module processor (AMP), and high-speed Winchester disk storage units (DSUs). As user requests increase, IMPs are added, and as data volume increases, AMPs and DSUs are added. Increasing the number of processors has an almost linear effect on the transaction rate. The DBC/1012 is not transaction-oriented, but uses set-at-a-time processing. However, it does not deal with small sets of data because it simply is not worth it. The sets should include at least 20,000 rows of data, maybe as many as 20 million, depending on the number of processors being used. Hence, database machines are designed for handling large volumes of data and their subsequent processing.

DATABASE PURCHASE STRATEGIES

In light of the foregoing discussion on database management systems, there are a number of database purchase strategies that the MIS manager should follow.

First, the individual should keep in mind potential price reductions. Hence, the MIS manager should avoid signing large contracts for client/server database site licenses. If the MIS manager must complete a large purchase agreement, the individual should negotiate protection against future price declines. *Second,* the MIS manager should make sure that database interface standards play a key part in the organization's application development strategy. This allows greater latitude in exploiting price differences among competing database packages. Similarly, front-end development tools that operate with a variety of database packages should be selected. *Third,* the MIS manager should deemphasize projects based on high-cost mainframe database platforms. That is, the more the price of distributed database software declines, the more difficult it is to justify expanding the use of traditional computer mainframe databases.

In conjunction with these price considerations, *fourth,* the MIS manager should buy unlimited user versions of client/server database packages. Although more costly than limited-user licenses, unlimited-user licenses offer the potential for future savings if the license can be transferred to a more powerful server without added cost. *Fifth,* the MIS manager should buy servers with multiprocessing capabilities and upgradable processor designs. These platforms will maximize the return on the database software investment by allowing the MIS organization to expand server power without spending more on database software. *Sixth,* and last, the MIS manager should revise the organization's application development strategy to reflect lower future costs for database software. Lower database pricing will open up new possibilities for client/server applications. Overall, these database purchase strategies can be financially rewarding to the MIS organization.

CRITICAL DATABASE PROBLEMS AND WAYS TO OVERCOME THEM

There are a number of problems that relate to a database in an MIS environment. *First,* the availability of appropriate image processing data is most important so that when data are moved electronically, they are what they should be when stored on the database. *Second* is the problem of the databases' being flexible enough to meet the needs of EDI processing. *Third,* the difficulty of integrating dispersed databases is a major problem facing corporations. Migrating to a single system is generally too costly and writing a company's own interface or using gateways can be extraordinarily complex. *Fourth,* data security and integrity problems tend to come into play when databases are distributed. *Fifth* is the problem of how databases fit into architectures for interoperability and open client/server computing. Because of the importance of the last three problems, they are explored here.

Lack of Integrated Distributed Databases

In many organizations, databases are not integrated throughout: that is, the centralized site processes data for its usage, but data are not forwarded to decentralized sites until later. Hence, the records at the centralized and decentralized sites are not in agreement at all times. To overcome this problem of lack of integration in an organization's databases, the move has been and continues to be to distributed computing. Distributed computing gives an organization's decentralized systems greater control over the data they need most and for which they are most responsible. Keeping data at sites where they are used most helps cut communication costs and prevent major disasters that can occur in centralized systems: that is, a failure at the central site can shut down an entire operation. With a distributed DBMS, however, an organization can manage its dispersed information as if it were in a single database, affording central control over MIS operations. Users at remote sites can gain easier access to any data on the corporate network. But more important, a distributed DBMS will help an organization ensure that database changes made at one remote site are automatically reflected at all other sites, a task left up to users and programmers in distributed processing systems.

Executing such simply stated concepts, however, requires solving a number of technological problems. Communications standards must be developed to allow different machines and different DBMSs to communicate. Means must be found to ensure the security and integrity of distributed data. And D-DBMSs must be structured to provide the most efficient use of computer resources. The success of a distributed network depends on the ability of all machines on the network to exchange information. Standards and architectures that provide the level of compatibility needed have been refined in recent years. IBM has extended its Systems Network Architecture (SNA) to allow communications among a wide range of its machines as well as other manufacturers' models that comply with the architecture. The International Standards Organization (ISO) has also progressed with its Open Systems Interconnection model and is coming closer to completion on the processor-to-processor communications part of the model.

Lack of Data Security and Data Integrity

Within an MIS, data control involves data security and data integrity. While data security is the securing or protecting of data against theft or malicious manipulation, data integrity involves assuring that the input data are accurate and complete. As will be seen later in the text (Chapters 14 and 15), processing controls are established through the actual software to determine whether data have been lost or invalid data have been entered. There are such programming checks as record counts, range and limit checks, and sequence checks. The amount of processing controls that can be established is limited only by the cost trade-offs of doing so. Output controls are final checks that establish the accuracy and ownership of the processed data. It should be noted, however, that all data integrity controls must have procedures associated with them to establish responsibility for correction and accountability for reporting all necessary infractions to the information flow.

Applying the foregoing comments to end users, data security and data integrity also need to be an integral part of their operations. Where will end users learn and understand the need for both data security and data integrity? Needless to say, these important facts on data security and data integrity should be an essential part of their training by the information centers in the functional end-user departments. Otherwise, a whole host of end-user control and security problems will abound in a typical organization.

Lack of Interoperability and Open Client/Server Computing

Today, vendors, such as Borland and Microsoft, talk persuasively about how their PC databases fit into architectures for interoperability and open client/server computing. But the reality is that multivendor database connectivity is still not easy at any level. In effect, Borland and Microsoft are asking their users to buy into their own worldview. For users that are weaning themselves away from proprietary solutions, this could be a step backward. What is needed, then, is a set of standard application programming interfaces. Borland has joined with IBM, Novell Inc., and others to propose a database interface standard called Integrated Database API. MIS managers should not be passive observers: they need to require vendors to be specific about what standards they will support, why, and when. Above all, MIS managers need to start thinking now about how PC databases will fit into the client/server model. In addition, the problem of interoperability among computer systems and networks of different vendors is an important consideration related to organizational databases. As discussed previously, the center of these control areas is related to the extent of open systems operating throughout the MIS organization.

EFFECTIVE MIS MANAGEMENT OF DATA COMMUNICATIONS AND NETWORKING

As information technology is moving in the direction of networks to support mission-critical applications and reach new markets globally, it has raised the importance of data communications and networking management. The complexity of tools, information, people, and processes needed to build, operate, and monitor networks has become visible to more and more users throughout the organization. The way an organization approaches the design, implementation, and operation of data communications and networking management can make or break the quality of its network service and, ultimately, its ability to compete both domestically and internationally. More importantly, data communications and networking strategies need to be more tightly linked to strategic corporate business plans. More than ever, networks of all types, whether they be LANs, MANs, WANs, or a combination of these, are at the very heart of business strategies, and they must be managed with greater levels of reliability and service quality. In the future, rapid network deployment, instantaneous moves and changes, dynamic on-demand capacity provision, high security and privacy, and accurate cost and TQM program monitoring will be necessities.

An integral part of the design, implementation, and operation of data communications and networking is the need to develop an open systems architecture. As discussed previously throughout the text, the MIS organization should make it possible to access any of the organization's platforms (whether they be computer mainframe, minicomputer, PC, or workstation platforms) and attached databases with a single easy-to-use interface. Thus data accessibility is assured no matter where it is located in the MIS organization. In the accomplishment of such a desirable goal that ties in with the strategic corporate business plans (mentioned earlier), MIS managers must have at least an overall knowledge of a number of areas in data communications and networking in order to give direction to the implementation of an open systems architecture. This is the main thrust of the second half of the chapter.

LOCAL AREA NETWORKS (LANs)

Local area networks (LANs) meet the increasingly vital need to interconnect computers, terminals, word processors, facsimile, and other office machines within a building, campus, or very small geographic area. A local area network may be designed to support only one vendor's terminal equipment, or it may be designed for multivendor support. Network logic may be embedded in the terminal equipment, in bus/network interface units, or in central controllers. Overall, when compared to computer mainframes, LANs are flexible and cost-effective tools that greatly expand the variety of services that can be performed by microcomputers and workstations. A model based on the International Standards Organization's Open Systems Interconnection (OSI) helps explain the software and hardware characteristics of LANs. Fundamentally, the OSI model describes the seven layers of activity for typical LAN communications.

Wiring of LANs

Underlying any local area network is the physical wire connecting computing devices. Some LANs use either coaxial cable or twisted-pair wire. Each has advantages and disadvantages, depending on the particular application. A LAN that uses coaxial cable—Ethernet, for example—can link more than 1,000 devices in a single network. It can carry data transmission with a bandwidth of up to 100 megabits per second (Mbps). Generally, the greater the bandwidth, the more information that can be sent through a system in a given amount of time. The high bandwidth offered by coaxial cable, therefore, is a safe choice for a LAN that may be required to perform many transmission functions among many users. A high bandwidth is also needed to accommodate video signals or to transfer very large files, such as extensive spreadsheets.

For some applications, the high bandwidth provided by coaxial cable is overkill. For instance, a rate of 1Mbps is sufficient for a number of PC networks. That rate is available with unshielded twisted-pair wire—the kind normally used for telephones. Twisted-pair wire is also available in forms other than standard phone wire; for example, IBM's cabling system—specified for its Token-Ring LAN—is twisted pair. However, it is specially shielded and is larger than telephone wire. Nevertheless, networked PCs can exchange data over common, unshielded twisted-pair wire. In fact, twisted pair is often promoted as a viable alternative to coax for linking PCs and peripherals in a work-group cluster or department. An advance in transmission technology now allows the use of adapters in linked PCs and servers to increase the performance of twisted-pair PC nets. This allows networked PCs to exchange large data files at 10Mbps over unshielded twisted-pair wire.

Fiber-optic cable is a somewhat newer alternative to both coaxial and twisted pair. It offers higher bandwidth than both. Not only is the fiber-optic cable used for LANs; it also is often used to connect separate LANs that are located at some distance from each other. Also, fiber optics are useful for LAN situations where there are data security problems with electromagnetic interference. Compared with copper wire and coaxial cable, fiber cable is relatively immune from tampering and interference from electromagnetic radiation.

Fiber-optic networks are typically used as backbone links connecting islands of office networks, minicomputers, or shared peripherals. Fiber links are also employed as point-to-point data highways connecting computer mainframes to distributed systems or other LANs. In such applications, high bandwidth and distance—fiber links can stretch as far as four kilometers unrepeated—are the prime considerations. Even in office applications, fiber is preferable to copper wire because it suffers no bandwidth degradation due to signal reflection and is easier to maintain.

Wireless LANs

Today, wireless LANs are emerging as an important addition to present-day offerings of wired LANs because of cost, compatibility, and ease-of-use issues. Although wireless networks are unlikely to replace wire-based systems (as discussed earlier), they offer an attractive alternative to MIS managers looking to add new users to corporate LANs and support mobile workers who telecommute from far-flung locations. Within a wireless network operating mode, there are two kinds. Wide-area wireless networks, like cellular and public packet-switching wireless networks, cover relatively long distances (metropolitan areas) with modest data communications performance. On the other hand, local-area wireless networks cover a shorter distance (a floor of a building or a corporate campus), but offer a much higher bandwidth.

The wireless LAN market actually comprises several segments. The *first* segment positions wireless LANs as a wire replacement for desktop computing, and most of the current wireless products fall into this category. However, the opportunities for wireless as a wire replacement for this first segment are not as great as for the second segment: flexible LANs. This *second* segment can do everything that wire replacement LANs do but also can provide support for adds, moves, and changes in small and large dynamic networks. Flexible LANs can also be used for temporary networks that must be set up in remote locations and with time constraints. Flexible LANs represent a larger market opportunity than wire replacement. The *third* and final market segment is wireless LANs that provide all the capabilities of wire replacement and flexible LANs and add the crucial missing ingredient—mobility—for nomadic computing. These are designed to operate with the growing number of laptops, pen-based PCs, notebooks, and the like, and allow users to move around while remaining attached to the LAN. This represents the largest and most important segment of the wireless market.

As examples of wireless LAN, consider the following. A marketing manager travels with a pen-based PC to several of her company's customers and vendors, gathering data and taking notes on new market opportunities. A wireless network connection to the corporate LAN allows the results to be published and made instantly available to other managers. Or an accounting firm's audit team sets up a temporary wireless network at a client's location using portable PCs and a printer. As the audit proceeds, a team member takes a portable PC and tours the facility to update the physical inventory. Without interference with the client's network configuration, the audit is completed and the results are distributed on the wireless network for an oral review with the client. Essentially, these applications demonstrate certain benefits, namely, mobility and convenience. Another important attribute is that each scenario can be accomplished using today's software applications. Wireless can be a powerful, effective tool without requiring a massive investment in a new application. In the future, as was the case in the development of portable PCs, new applications will be developed that capitalize on the unique capabilities of nomadic LANs as well as those of the new generation of handheld and pen-based PCs.

Selection of a LAN Architecture

In a LAN layout, network topology refers to physical and logical layout. There are four basic LAN topology configurations:

- *Star*—a star configuration connects end-users' workstations point-to-point to a master computer or controller. The end points can be intelligent or nonintelligent terminals/devices and can be data-, text-, or even voice-oriented. Since all end-user devices must be connected to it, the central control unit requires a great deal of cable. All transmissions must pass through the central control area to be passed along to a receiving device. The star configuration is the least effective option for a LAN, since failure of the central control area knocks out the system.
- *Bus*—this configuration is not centralized like a star, since the system has defined end

points that can be added to. All devices are connected directly to the main bus line. A signal originating at a terminal or processor propagates away in both directions along the bus line. Each connected device "listens" for its address on the bus. Recognizing its address, it accepts the data transmitted; otherwise, it ignores it. Control of a bus network resides in each individual terminal.

- *Tree*—the tree configuration offers an expanded version of the bus configuration. By turning the bus to a vertical position and extending its branches, there is now a tree. End-user terminals are spaced along a central "line." Workstations communicate with devices called servers that provide electronic mail, disk storage, and printer facilities.
- *Ring*—also known as "round robin," this approach is based on token passing (a slot in the communications program) logically implemented on a bus. Essentially, the ring is a continuous path without defined ends. Signals pass around the ring and are pushed along by each device as they pass.

When developing new LANs, the evaluation of these topologies is a complex task related to other aspects of LAN architecture.

As a starting point in the evaluation process, *latency* or *cross-network delay,* which is the time information takes to traverse the network, is one such architectural factor. In most office applications, excessive delay is only an inconvenience. But in a factory process-control environment, information must arrive at precise times or product quality will be affected. *Data throughput* is another factor that affects overall performance. It is usually much lower than the advertised speed, which is achieved only under ideal conditions. The reasons for this discrepancy have to do with how information accesses the LAN. *Reliability* is also an important architectural factor. An occasional failure is tolerable in a general office environment but not in a telemarketing operation. In today's era of downsizing, *cost* is usually the most important factor. Generally, installation and operating costs for each LAN architecture vary greatly. Although both must be considered, operating cost factors usually dominate.

EFFECTIVE MIS MANAGEMENT OF LANs

Running a local area network requires more technical know-how than using the typical PC. Despite the sales hype to the contrary, LANs are intricate computer systems that require supervision which must be administered by someone who is motivated and supported by management. From this perspective, MIS management needs to place a competent LAN administrator in charge. Generally, small, stable LANs (twenty or so users) should not need a full-time administrator. If the organization is not ready to invest in a network administrator, networking is not recommended. It should be noted that there will be more involvement with LAN vendors than with PC vendors. The rationale is that LAN vendors offer a high level of technical knowledge that the LAN administrator will need from time to time for efficient and effective operations.

Devise an Efficient and Effective LAN

As a way of getting started on the development and implementation of a local area network, *first* there is need for a plan by MIS management. The plan should start with people and move on to technology. MIS management should learn how people are using their stand-alone PCs and what their workflow is. Emphasis should be placed on observing the source of input and the destination of output. Also, MIS management should solicit end users about their current and future needs. *Second,* MIS management needs to review current software and hardware being used. Accent should be placed on the effectiveness of both. It is imperative that a list of software applications be identified before proceeding with any concrete network planning. Similarly, precise technical specifications on hardware need to be determined since a well-designed LAN must incorporate all of this hardware. The bulk of MIS management's time will be spent on software selection since hardware is mostly in place.

Third, MIS management must determine what level of downtime is permissible. Many network-operating systems support disk mirroring (duplicate writing of data files on separate disk drives) and backup file servers. The question is, How long can the organization afford to be down? Those systems that must always work are called mission-critical. As such, MIS management must determine what they are and where. *Fourth,* MIS management must determine whether there is need to communicate with other systems. If so, communication protocols that these systems support must be specified. Is it necessary to communicate with other locations? If so, will dial-up lines suffice or is a faster, leased line needed? *Fifth,* and last, there is need to decide where workstations, printers, and other devices will be located. This is a very important question—one that has stopped well-intended network plans dead in their tracks. End users' feelings may be hurt since some think that they deserve their own color laser printers and individual workstations. Deciding who gets a certain type of workstation, who shares which printer with whom can be very stressful, to say the least, for MIS management. Nevertheless, answers to these questions will dictate what type of cable scheme should be installed.

After the preceding five steps in the planning phase, the next focus is on the technical aspects of the LAN. *First,* MIS management should forget about cost by allowing network designers to design a most desirable local area network. Depending on this most desirable LAN, the *second* step is that the designers should then scale it back to what is really needed for efficient and effective operations whose cost the organization can legitimately justify. In the process of doing so, several technical decisions must be made. Hence, the *third* step is to select the network operating system. This selection can be determined by asking whether a client/server network or peer-to-peer network is needed. A *client/server LAN* revolves around a centralized server for operations, such as user log-in, file sharing, and E-mail, as well as the storage of applications. All networked PCs function as clients to the server. In contrast, *peer LANs* allow networked users to share each other's disks, printers, and other resources without requiring a dedicated server. Each user's workstation functions as both a client and a server. To illustrate, an office small in terms of people and floor space that needs basic office-automation applications may find a simple peer-to-peer network ideal. On the other hand, a large company running diverse applications over an entire multistory building should probably consider a client/server environment.

A *fourth* step is the determination of the best access methods. On the basis of what has been learned about workstation/printer location and the data flow, MIS management picks that topology which offers the best performance at an acceptable cost. Hence, it is important to learn the basics of LANs, like Ethernet and Token Ring. *Fifth,* MIS management must decide on the workstation. On a network, the program executes at the workstation; all the file servers and topologies in the world are not going to change this. If the software vendor recommends 4MB of random-access memory (RAM), 640KB workstations should not be purchased. Hence, select the workstation that supports the software applications with the lowest cost. Color monitors, RAM, number of slots, disk and diskette drives, clock speed, and bus architecture are all important considerations that need to be determined at this point. *Sixth* and last, MIS management must determine the file server. File server selection in a client/server environment is subject to more parameters than in a peer-to-peer network. The file server is going to hold all data and programs while actually running the network operating system. When specifying it, main memory and hard-disk expansion, clock speed, and caching must be considered. Nondedicated file servers in a client/server network, such as file servers that can pull double duty as user workstations, should be avoided.

It is highly recommended that external or internal MIS consultants be employed to review the final LAN project for appropriateness to the situation before asking vendors for bids. Once the proposal is approved by some independent third party, it is necessary to send the configuration to vendors with the clear understanding that the MIS manager is only requesting a cost proposal. In turn, this information will be used to arrive at a decision to network or not to network.

Ensure Reliability of LANs

In the process of developing and implementing a LAN, it is recommended that MIS management and its LAN administrator choose the simplest and most reliable solutions that get the job done. Research has indicated that a large percentage of LAN failures are due to cabling problems. Cable failures occur far more often than necessary. Organizations buy the cheapest cable they can find and give the job to the lowest bidder because, after all, it is just cable. However, LAN cable is not just cable. In a similar manner, one installer is not like another. It is recommended that MIS management find an organization who uses the same type of cable—somebody who has not had a cabling problem in a year. In turn,

MIS management should hire those cable installers who have a proven track record.

It is highly recommended that MIS management avoid the ''bleeding edge'' of new LAN technology. While some products fail to deliver on their promise, others disappear from view. Still others require several generations of improvements before they are reliable. By all means, the MIS manager should investigate new technology up to a reasonable point of feasibility. The MIS manager should recognize that once in a while, a bleeding-edge solution is the only one available, but more often older and more traditional solutions will get the job done. Additionally, production and test environments should be separated physically if necessary. Users should be notified well in advance and by all possible means (E-mail messages, system broadcasts, signs, and memorandums) of times when the network or certain services on the network will be unavailable. The MIS manager should not assume that because it is a Sunday afternoon, nobody will be in the office. System changes, even menu changes, should be very carefully made. Changes should not be made in the middle of a workday, nor should a new version of a spreadsheet be switched over the day the annual report is due.

The MIS manager should be aware of buying the least expensive hardware. Although prices in the mail-order catalog look great, a network full of mail-order machines each containing a different BIOS, different motherboard, and different vendors' components is destined to become a maintenance nightmare. There is no need to pay top dollar for reliable products, but the MIS manager need not fall into the no-name clone trap. If certain desktop machines gain a reputation for breaking down or not running software properly, this difficulty will transfer to the LAN itself.

Last, the MIS manager needs to establish a service-level agreement (SLA) with users. This is a very common document in computer mainframe environments since it specifies the level of service users can expect. Perhaps more important, it defines what constitutes up time and who is responsible for what. SLAs can become rather formal and technical in large environments. But a less formal, less structured SLA can be valuable, even on a small network. These agreements can make an unreliable network reliable, and they cannot prevent users from blaming the LAN administrator for everything that goes wrong. They can, however, help users understand what can and cannot be expected.

Overall, the local area network should be designed for reliability. However, it is the MIS manager's responsibility to plan for failure. Sooner or later, even in the most well run network, something will go wrong. For example, a server will crash. Hence, it is necessary to build in redundancy by planning how to handle or to compensate for intermittent errors that may take days or weeks to identify. When something does go wrong, MIS management and their LAN administrators will be evaluated on how fast they can get the LAN up and running again.

Use LAN Management Tools

Currently, vendors are now providing LAN management tools which can be of great help to LAN administrators. LAN administrators are finding that they can employ three tools that will help them make trekking the LAN wilderness less arduous: (1) LAN inventory packages, also known as asset managers, which monitor all software and hardware on the LAN; (2) software packages that are capable of metering the software used on the LAN for license compliance; and (3) file access and management packages, which collect information on the files and directories on the system. While no packages offer a universal panacea, they are intended to handle many common user requirements in the areas of inventory management, software metering, and file access and management.

One important comment regarding software inventory management should be made. No one product can determine all the software being used on a local area network because no single comprehensive list of software exists. Vendors have built databases of software applications that they know about into their products, many of which rely on a list from the Software Publishers Association (SPA). This list is updated twice yearly and contains the software of vendors that have paid to have their applications included on the list. Hence, when a local area network administrator uses a package for software inventory, it only identifies applications on the list. However, some vendors are supplementing the SPA list by adding applications to their products' databases that their users have let them know about.

FORGING LANs, MANs, AND WANs INTO A GLOBAL NETWORK

Going beyond the confines of a LAN existing within a building or several buildings in close proximity to one another, there are metropolitan area networks (MANs). A MAN is of limited geographic range, generally defined as within a fifty-mile radius. In the past, a number of small companies have begun businesses by installing fiber-optical cable in metropolitan business areas. Their primary customers are companies of all sizes that need to communicate within the metropolitan area. The customer is usually responsible for providing equipment. The primary market is the customer that needs a lot of high-speed digital service. The MAN providers typically offer lower prices than the telephone companies and offer diverse routing as well as backup in emergency conditions. As a result of the pressing need to link a typical organization with other organizations locally, nationally, or internationally, the following discussion takes this important direction into account. Needless to say, if there is a need to tie in with one of these MAN providers, a LAN-MAN-WAN link can be provided for a typical organization.

Today, wide area networks (WANs) are generally considered to be those that cover a large geographic area, require the crossing of public rights-of-way, and use circuits provided by a common carrier. WANs may be made up of a combination of switched and leased, terrestrial and satellite, and private microwave circuits. The WAN for a large multinational company may be global, whereas the WAN for a small company may cover only several cities or counties. General Electric, for example, has a private global network to transmit voice, data, and video signals to GE offices in twenty-five countries.

To overcome difficulties experienced by users in wide area networks, there is need for a new approach: that is, the farther the computer is from the data, the harder it is for the user to get to it. This is especially true if it is found in another city or across the nation. Trading the security and relative speed of a LAN for the sluggishness and uncertainty of a wide area network creates unforeseen data bottlenecks and administrative headaches. A new universal network transport mechanism, called asynchronous transfer mode (ATM), gives the user easier access between a Token Ring or Ethernet local area network and wide-area mechanisms, such as T1 and X.25. By providing a common infrastructure that is suitable for everything from desktop and LAN applications to campus, metropolitan, and global networks, ATM offers a new direction in network technology.

Until recently, LAN and WAN technologies have approached data transmission differently. The driving force behind ATM is a new class of applications involving voice, video, multimedia, imaging, and client/server functions. These broadband applications demand much higher network capacity than the traditional personal productivity, on-line transaction processing, and database programs. The disparity between LAN and WAN transport protocols makes it difficult to create broad-band enterprise networks. Regarded as a universal protocol for high-speed networking, ATM has been chosen by the CCITT (the international data communications standards organization) as the transport layer protocol for emerging broadband integrated services digital networks (BISDNs). Basic ISDN will be discussed later in the chapter.

Wireless WANs

Wireless WANs are being put to use in a variety of applications, although current technology limitations make wireless WANs unsuitable for many applications now common on LANs and internetworks. That is, wireless services are well suited mainly for applications that involve short, bursty messages. Wireless data networks already have provided a critical advantage in many industries. An example is the courier industry; in the late 1970s, Federal Express Corporation revolutionized the overnight delivery business by building a private wireless network to track its packages. The Federal Express network was not low in cost. It cost the courier hundreds of millions of dollars but helped propel the company to the front of a very competitive industry.

In the transportation industry, a large Northeast rail carrier now uses wireless WANs to transmit pickup and delivery information between its national customer service center and railyard and locomotive employees. In addition, several long-haul trucking companies have implemented wireless WANs to improve the efficiency of their fleet operations. A few insurance carriers now use wireless networks to enable claims adjusters to exchange data directly from accident or disaster sites, speeding the claims process and reducing paperwork. Typical of major corporations now using wireless WAN services are General Electric, Mastercard International, National Car Rental, Pitney Bowes Inc., and United Airlines.

Although wireless WAN services are found in organizations of varying sizes, the next few years will be critical in deciding how important they become in corporate networks. One of the most important issues that must be resolved is the matter of standards. Today's wireless WANs are based on proprietary technology even though several carriers have thrown open their systems to third-party developers. Until standards are in place, many organizations are reluctant to make major commitments to wireless WANs. As is the usual case with all standards, progress toward the development of standards for wireless WAN systems and equipment is slow.

Maintaining a WAN

Any wide area network manager who has the responsibility for developing and maintaining links to a wide area network is in for a major challenge. Once users come to rely on WAN link service, any link failure becomes a major problem for operations. Since most of a WAN circuit is beyond the WAN manager's control, good testing procedures are needed to track down problems when a remote link fails. Because a WAN link is actually a collection of dozens of cables, electronics, and circuits under the domain of multiple parties, each piece is critical to link-up time. Not only is there no way to see or monitor traffic directly on the WAN link, but three or more phone companies and distant user sites are often involved when a problem occurs.

The first indications of a problem developing on the WAN link may occur all at once, or slowly over a period of time. If the link fails completely, all users whose traffic crosses the link will be calling with abort/retry or read/write errors. A more intermittent problem will manifest itself as a traffic slowdown or an occasional network error. Even the slightest sign or suspicion of an intermittent problem between two WAN sites requires immediate attention. The network manager should start with the bridges and routers on site and check all premise links with great care. The individual should look at their traffic statistics and know what they mean. If send or receive errors are being racked up or a clear node failure is indicated, the manager should check the configurations. Proper setting of all bridge/router parameters is a complicated process and must be precise. Physical cabling to and from the routers also must be correct. If the problem persists, the next step is to determine whether the link itself is failing or whether the interface electronics or cable is to blame. Many times, this phase is related to the telephone companies, who are responsible for quick resolution of problems in their domain. In turn, the network manager is responsible for all premise problems on both the local and remote ends of the link. Needless to say, the specific details of the step-by-step activities are beyond the scope of this text. It should be noted that although reference can be made to a recent article,[1] there are consultants who specialize in assisting the network manager who cannot resolve difficult WAN-link problems.

Utilizing Network Analyzers

Related to the prior discussion of maintaining links to WANs are network analyzers that aim to keep large, complex networks trouble-free and to debug them quickly when trouble strikes. The communications test equipment industry continues to address expanding user needs, which are more complex than ever. Driven by emerging technologies (such as frame relay) and carrier services (such as SMDS), the industry is rapidly developing analysis tools. Today, products that support FDDI have become available and LAN internetworking has taken off, thereby creating other needs for analyzers. The complexity of these different types of analyzers that satisfy different troubleshooting needs can be confusing to users. Despite all the attention focused on LANs, WAN analyzers remain a vital tool for network troubleshooters because LAN interconnection depends on the availability and performance of WANs. With WANs supporting LAN traffic, a network manager needs to be able to determine WAN utilization by the interconnected LANs and to trouble-shoot multiple protocols within WAN data streams. Essentially, WAN analyzers have not changed much, but they have become more versatile by supporting additional applications and easier to use with point-and-click GUIs. Also, they support an ever increasing range of transmission protocols and an extensive and growing list of protocol decode suites. For more information on network analyzers, reference can be made to a current article on this important topic.[2]

ORGANIZATIONWIDE NETWORKING ARCHITECTURES

Related to the utilization of LANs, MANs, and WANs in a typical organization is the need for an organizationwide networking architecture. These architectures which have been traditionally computer mainframe-based are available from hardware vendors, such as IBM and DEC. Generally, a feasibility study is needed to determine not only what networking architecture is best, but also what type of hardware and software may be needed to fit in with the architecture. Additionally, the types and speeds of communication lines need to be evaluated and selected for a tie-in with the organizationwide networking architecture. From another perspective, local area networks can predominate throughout the organization. Vendors, such as Novell Inc. and Banyan Systems Inc., are leaders in this fast growing segment of networking architectures. In the material, the focus is on the two major mainframe-based firms (IBM and DEC) and two LAN vendors (Novell and Banyan).

From an *IBM perspective,* the System Network Architecture or SNA is clearly a de facto networking standard. With that has come expansion. No longer is the networking software just a tool for mainframe communications. Today, even medium-sized users take advantage of SNA's management and control facilities without putting an undue strain on their MIS budgets. Although SNA is a de facto networking standard, the spread of non-IBM computers and protocols has changed that. A mélange of DECnet, Appletalk, and Apollo Computer Inc.'s Domain protocols now handle the role previously exclusive to SNA. It should be noted that one problem programmers faced just after the advent of SNA was the challenge of writing networked applications for different types of hardware. Initially, each machine had its own set of system calls for communications, making programs difficult to write and nonportable. To solve this problem, IBM developed its Systems Application Architecture (SAA)—a set of application program interfaces (APIs), protocols, and user interface conventions that will allow programs to work consistently on multiple hardware platforms.

More recently, IBM considers its Advanced Peer-to-Peer Networking (APPN) scheme the key to its Systems Network Architecture networking strategy. With APPN, IBM provides interoperability between SAA and AIX systems over SNA, Transmission Control Protocol/Internet Protocol (TCP/IP), and Open Systems Interconnection protocols. In this era of increasingly open networking, IBM needs the APPN protocol stack to become universally accepted for high-speed enterprisewide networks, that is, to become a kind of universal architecture that wraps itself around SNA, TCP/IP, and OSI to provide node-to-node and server-to-server peer communications. APPN is being challenged by Advanced Peer-to-Peer Internetworking (APPI), a TCP/IP-based routing protocol (developed by Cisco Systems Inc.) that is likely to attract users not aligned with IBM who want to reduce or contain the number of protocols they support in their organizations. Basically, APPI lets users take advantage of the benefits it has over traditional SNA environments, but within the context of an open backbone. In addition, rather than using predeveloped NN (Network Node) code, third-party vendors can develop code optimized to their own router platforms.

Typically, the integration today of IBM computer mainframes and local area networks that exist side by side has been difficult. When SNA gear is linked to interconnected LANs, two network management systems must coexist: IBM's mainframe-based Netview and simple network management protocol (SNMP) that use TCP/IP protocols and typically run under Unix. In many organizations, the two management systems have an equal share in handling equipment, yet they function in separate worlds, and even in separate locations. Fortunately, new products and standardization effort promise to help relieve the headaches that arise from maintaining two management systems. Among the recent developments are software gateways that translate efforts between Netview and SNMP systems; more sophisticated applications that act as agents, converting

Netview data to a format compatible with a specific net management platform; and multiprotocol management systems that handle both Netview and SNMP information. In addition to these general trends, several vendors, such as Novell Inc., plan to put conversion utilities directly into their operating systems.

From an *DEC perspective,* Advantage Networks, which is DEC's latest iteration of DECnet, is the key component of DEC's multivendor enterprise networking strategy to interconnect desktops, local area networks, and legacy networks, such as IBM's SNA, and provide integrated management of the environment. Advantage Networks, previously referred to as DECnet Phase V, merges the proprietary protocols of DECnet Phase IV with OSI and TCP/IP. The protocol suites are configured as "towers," meaning they share the same physical- and data-link control layers but then split off into their respective network, transport, session, presentation, and application layers. The tower approach is designed to allow applications such as file transfer and terminal emulation to communicate using any one of the three protocols. While Advantage Networks is attractive to DECnet users with large nets, some DEC users see little benefit in moving unless they plan to migrate to OSI. However, some users are migrating to this latest iteration of DECnet because it has run out of address and routing space with the previous DECnet Phase IV.

From another perspective, DEC is addressing user needs for SNA connectivity by providing enhancements to its DECnet/SNA gateways. The company provides software for its gateways that allows IBM 3270 terminal users to access DECnet resources through transport protocol translation. DEC also has software that allows users to develop VMS applications that can communicate through a DECnet/SNA gateway with 3270 applications in an SNA network using the 3270 data stream. The software fosters tighter integration between DECnet and SNA environments by making an attached DECnet network look like an SNA subarea to the IBM host. This allows 3270 users to establish sessions with systems in the DEC environment as if they were on the SNA network.

From a *Novell perspective,* NetWare Version 4.0 reaches beyond mere LAN functionality. The main enhancements that make NetWare 4.0 different from earlier versions all revolve around the goal of providing enhanced server and management capabilities across WANs. Essentially, NetWare 4.0 embodies a new strategy for Novell since it has concentrated previously on providing file and print functions in local environments. But with NetWare 4.0, the company is demonstrating a new direction for the requirements of large, enterprisewide networks that have hundreds of servers and potentially thousands of users spread around the world.

An important feature in Version 4.0 called NetWare Directory Services (NDS) is a global-naming scheme and distributed directory of users, files, and services located not merely on the local server, but on all NDS-compatible servers attached to the network. NDS can automatically synchronize the information in local directory databases with information maintained in relevant files elsewhere on the WAN. This creates the logical equivalent of a single database. In reality, there are really multiple databases physically, usually maintained on local servers. Thus, this is a distributed directory, which should be distinguished from other schemes that require a single centralized directory. Centralized directories require long-distance communications just to obtain information about where information is lodged.

As a global directory, NDS has strategic importance to NetWare users. For example, a finance manager logs onto a departmental LAN located in New York, where the individual seeks information located outside the department, outside even New York, but does not know where the desired information is stored. The manager is able to use an application on NetWare 4.0 that can find the information anywhere in the world by locating its file in NDS and automatically establishing a connection with that file across the WAN. Such NDS-searching applications are expected to emerge in time, as NDS and other global directories become popular.

From a *Banyan perspective,* its new Enterprise Network Services (ENS) products make StreetTalk, Banyan's global naming and directory service, available not only on VINES networks, but on NetWare and other popular network environments as well. The benefit is a single-system view for the user, facilitating ease of use and ease of management of the network, lower costs, and enhanced business effectiveness. In addition, these network services are a platform for enterprise applications that increase network efficiency and, in turn, corporate competitiveness.

INTEGRATED SERVICES DIGITAL NETWORKS (ISDNs)

One way of bringing together the preceding discussion on data communications and networking is to think in terms of total communications for a typical organization. Although this can take many directions, only one is discussed here because of space limitations. The focus is on integrated services digital networks (ISDNs) which can provide users with a total network in which compatible voice, data, and video configurations will be transported on a single pair of wires, eliminating leased line and digital circuits for data, voice lines for telecommunications, and cable services for video. It can offer users a multifaceted communications network to transmit and receive information worldwide. The concept of ISDN is that of a standard protocol that is used to link private and public networks to receive and transmit digital information. Compatibility stems from predetermined standards, allowing all types of equipment to interface provided that they are manufactured to accepted standards.

The ultimate goal of ISDN is to combine all of the telecommunications services that are currently being provided by different networks into one large-scale network. Services to be offered through ISDN include telephone services (call forwarding, transferring, conference calling, automatic wake-up calling), data services (closed user groups, called and calling line identification, multiaddress calling), teletext services (delayed messages, multiple addressing, Telex access, and a graphic mode), facsimile services (delayed delivery and multiple designations), and video-text services (transactions, such as reservations and shopping, and special character sets). In preparing for ISDN, companies need to consider whether their current data communications decisions are compatible with an evolution to ISDN-based communications. In addition, companies should examine their internal structure for planning voice, data, and office facilities to ensure that internal conflicts between separate voice and data departments are minimized.

In summary, ISDN is an international network architecture that offers a standard universal interface for voice, data, and video, thereby allowing highly efficient, interactive use of the public telephone network. In contrast, Open Network Architecture (ONA) is a regulatory development that will allow specialty information services, such as messaging, electronic mail, security, and answering services, to take place over a local telephone network. Although the implementation time of ISDN and ONA technologies is uncertain, it would depend in large part on public demand. But their impact on the microcomputer user throughout the 1990s will be felt. One probable effect of this implementation will be increasing numbers of at-home workers, including executives. Without immediate access to the workplace, *telecommunicating* on a widespread basis was not possible before now, but this will change as network communication from the home, without special cabling or transmission facilities, will enable it to function like the company-owned office. Thus, a home computer will begin to assume the importance of an essential storage and communications device, much like the telephone. The public telephone network will be asked to transport this information.

GUIDELINES TO ASSIST MIS MANAGEMENT IN OVERSEEING DATABASES AND DATA COMMUNICATIONS

As organizations move to distributed computing that revolves around distributed databases and data communications to get at the data, a *first* guideline centers on an effective LAN management strategy that incorporates multiple vendors, topologies, operating systems, and applications as well as the changing organizations they support. It must also go beyond the traditional functions developed in the past, such as fault management, accounting, configuration management, performance evaluation, and system security. LAN strategies must tie in with MANs and WANs where there is need for a global network. In this manner, the "right hand knows what the left hand is doing" in the area of networks that crisscross within and outside the organization.

A *second* guideline centers on undertaking appropriate security measures over data and their systems. Currently, network administrators are discovering that security is a major problem for two reasons. First, net administrators need to set security policies that balance end users' needs for information access with their own needs to protect resources. Second, they then must find products capable of implementing those policies. The key to a successful implementation is to utilize end-user-directed corporate security policies. That is, giving end users a say in setting policies ensures that access to specific information is appropriately limited. After defining effective security policies, the next step is to establish a management organization that keeps the policies up-to-date. This can be accomplished by utilizing the MIS organizationwide committee set forth previously (refer to Chapter 5).

A related *third* guideline is the use of a client/server environment to equal the security found in a typical host mainframe environment. In a host environment, the MIS manager generally has to contend with a single operating system, with all users subject to a central security function. Although MIS has to maintain separate security procedures for different databases, it is not difficult. However, in the client/server world of multiple databases, there is a potential administrative nightmare since companies exponentially increase their security exposure every time they expand a network. In the client/server environment, there are acute security concerns because of the level of expertise of client/server users and their higher ability to interface with data. Hence, MIS management must balance this exposure against the competitive advantages afforded by the technology. Dealing with this issue demands a concerted management effort and an understanding of the value of information.

Related to the previous two guidelines is a *fourth* that centers on protection against computer viruses. The growth in network computing challenges the MIS manager as well as LAN, MAN, and WAN administrators to protect the organization's data without restricting information accessibility. Today, network security can be defined on several different levels. Traditionally, password protection and a locked door were enough to prevent unauthorized access to data. But the most serious and potentially damaging security threat to local area networks in recent years is the computer virus. A comprehensive strategy should include the use of commercially available hardware and software plus inclusion of proprietary protection measures as deemed necessary.

For best results, a *fifth* guideline stresses the need for a total quality management program that needs to be included in the strategies set forth. A TQM program under the direction of the MIS manager focuses on appropriate procedures to ensure the safety and integrity of data. Similarly, there is need for MIS management to have a TQM program in place for computer viruses because there have been virus epidemics in shrink-wrapped commercial software. The virus got there because of poor quality control. More and more software manufacturers are including virus detection as a required step in their total quality management programs, thereby reducing the number of these outbreaks.

A *sixth* guideline centers on a proper backup program, especially for LANs where everyday processing is performed. The range of LAN backup options has expanded dramatically in the past few years, as has the complexity of the backup process. Users now have new storage subsystems as well as the ability to back up remote nodes and local units. Designing an effective backup system is more than just attaching a tape drive to the server. Hardware, such as tape drives, and procedures, such as off-site backup, are still critical components of LAN backup strategies. But increasingly, it is the LAN backup software that determines what hardware is usable and what procedures are possible. Surprisingly, even the best LAN backup software costs only a few hundred dollars. The future of backup software will be driven by the growth of LANs. Greater on-line storage requirements, more mission-critical applications, more heterogeneous environments, and more users will place new demands on backup systems as well as on network administrators.

NOTES

1. Barry Quiat, "What to Do When Your Wide Area Link Goes Down," *Network Computing,* June 1992, pp. 120–125.

2. David H. Axner, "Analyzers Target LAN/WAN Internetworks," *Networking Management,* August 1992, pp. 52–61.

PART V

EFFECTIVE SYSTEMS DEVELOPMENT PROCESS AND END-USER COMPUTING

9

Systems Development

OUTLINE

INTRODUCTION TO EFFECTIVE SYSTEMS DEVELOPMENT

The ability of computer manufacturers to produce low-cost and highly reliable hardware has helped fuel the dramatic rise of personal computers and workstations. However, the production of systems has not kept pace. The development of new systems and maintenance of present systems in terms of cost and quality has improved at a barely discernible rate. Attention is now focused on systems development, programming, and maintenance. Ways are being sought to position software technology such that application solutions can be produced more rapidly, at less cost, and with higher quality. Such technology supports the use and reuse of standard software building blocks. Although a modular or building block approach for a structured systems methodology and an object-oriented systems methodology is set forth in the chapter, the latter is gaining in popularity.

Initially, the chapter centers on an approach to get started on an MIS project, followed by the utilization of computer-assisted systems engineering tools in a typical MIS project. This background provides a basis for systems analysis using a structured methodology. The feasibility or infeasibility of applying newer systems equipment and procedures is established. In turn, systems design is explored. An important part of the design process is making sure that the new MIS is being tailored to meet the needs of users rather than the capabilities of the hardware. Next, alternative systems development approaches are presented, followed by object technology and how it can be implemented in organizations. Finally, an alternative approach to systems development and operations, that is, outsourcing, is discussed.

PRINCIPLES OF EFFECTIVE SYSTEMS DEVELOPMENT

There are many principles underlying an effective systems development process. The first of these is the *Principle of a Phased Approach*. Each phase of the development process must have well-defined objectives, and at the end of each phase, progress toward meeting the objectives must be evaluated. The development process should not continue until the objectives of all prior phases have been met. A logical way of separating the entire development process into distinct phases is as follows: systems analysis, systems design, equipment selection (all found in this chapter), and systems implementation (found in the next chapter).

Another principle is the *Principle of Scope of the System.* For effective systems development, the scope of the new MIS must be broad enough to ensure that the desired results are achieved in an effective manner. It should be recognized that every system is a subsystem of some larger system and the computer is not "the center of the universe." Too narrow a focus on just one of the subsystems will not lead to the best results in leveraging information technology.

For effective systems development, there is need for the *Principle of End-User Involvement.* Because end users need to be involved in an MIS project, they can assist in defining what the new MIS will do and what end users will have to do to get the desired results. Failure to involve end users can be fatal to the success of the systems development process. In fact, three commonly stated reasons for MIS project failure are (1) the system does not work the way the end user wants, (2) the system does not do all that the end user wants, and (3) the end user is unclear what the system will do and what it will not do.

Related to these principles are those leading to the development of a well-designed system that ensures that the right *information* will go to the right *person* at the right *time* in the right *format* and at the right (lowest) *cost.* If any element is faulty, it is doubtful that the system will be accepted by organization personnel who are to operate it. In the process of doing so, systems analysts must consider the fact that the human factor comes first and the equipment comes second. Systems analysts must consider the capabilities and limitations of organization personnel first. Comparable factors for the equipment itself can then be considered. Hence, there is need for the *Principle of Placing the Human Factor First.*

The *Principle of Acceptability* of the new MIS to end users is of utmost importance. If end users are convinced that the new MIS will not benefit them, it is a poor one, it does not follow established company policies, or it has some other legitimate shortcoming, the new MIS is in serious trouble. To overcome this resistance, participation by end users, from the functional areas, particularly during the systems analysis and systems design phases, is necessary.

An effective MIS employs the *Principle of Enhancing the Decision-Making Process.* A new system's output should be pertinent and timely at the lowest possible cost for making decisions. Not only should the MIS be designed to meet the information needs and requirements of an organization and its managers, but it also should help define the decision-making process and ensure that it is performed by the appropriate personnel. Those decisions which can be handled best by the system should be relegated to it.

Another important principle is the *Principle of Economy* of the new MIS. For economic operations, data should be captured and edited as near to the source of information as possible. Functional organization groups responsible for activities that must be performed in sequence should be located as close to each other as possible. Eliminating duplicate information files, reducing the provision for every possible contingency, and eliminating small empires in an organization's functional areas are other examples of improving operations in an economic manner.

To be effective, the new MIS cannot be rigid. The *Principle of Flexibility* of the new MIS refers to the capability to adapt to changing conditions. There will always be variations of products, manufacturing processes, and accounting procedures, to name a few. Without the capability to absorb changes within the MIS, an organization may lose customer goodwill and encounter problems with end users. Thus, a well-designed system must be flexible to continue to meet its desired objectives. It should be able to operate in a changing environment.

The *Principle of Reliability* of the new MIS refers to consistency of operations. In other words, are data input, processing methods and procedures, and output information consistent over an extended period of operation? The degree of reliability can range from a constant and predictable mode of operation to a complete breakdown of the system. A high degree of reliability can be designed into the system by including good internal controls, that is, numerous control points where variances from established norms and practices can be detected and corrected before processing continues.

An important trademark of any effective system centers on the *Principle of Simplicity* of the new MIS. Another name is the *KISS Principle:* Keep It Simple, Stupid. Simplicity can be effected by providing a straight-line flow from one step to the next, avoiding needless backtracking. Input data should be recorded at their source or as close to the source as possible to reduce or eliminate the need for recopying. Functions should be assigned to organizational units to reduce the need for coordination, communication, and paperwork.

RELATIONSHIP OF CURRENT RESEARCH TO SYSTEMS DEVELOPMENT

There are fifteen current major problems—as noted in Chapter 2—that are related directly to some area of MIS. In terms of their relationship to the entire systems development process, there are the following:

- Lack of proper documentation over standards and procedures (rated no. 2)
- Lack of security protection measures over the management information system (rated no. 3)

In addition, there is an indirect linkage to other problems found in developing management information systems of all types. Typical ones include the lack of or poor database administration and the lack of communication in the MIS area as well as the lack of short- to long-range plans for management information systems. Effective systems development should also overcome the lack of training programs for new and experienced MIS personnel in the new computer-oriented system methodologies and code generators.

In the process of developing the new system, the documentation step may be overlooked or poorly undertaken. Hence, the *lack of proper documentation over standards and procedures* may be a major problem not only throughout the systems development process, but also when the system must be maintained. What was originally intended can be forgotten in a matter of weeks, not to mention years later when the personnel who developed the system are no longer with the organization.

The *lack of security protection measures over management information systems* relates to failure to build in appropriate security measures as the system is developed. This can be caused by lack of training by systems analysts or by the external rush to get a system designed and up and running as soon as possible. Also, internal auditors are not consulted at the appropriate times in the systems development process. That is, security protection measures are not designed at strategic control points to control ongoing operations. Typically, the net result is that the system must be redesigned to include adequate security, which can be a costly situation.

GETTING STARTED ON AN MIS PROJECT

To understand what activities need to be undertaken by the MIS manager and personnel on a new MIS project, it is helpful to examine these topical areas: (1) organization for a successful MIS project, (2) scope of the MIS project, and (3) time to be spent on the MIS project. Each of these areas is explored after a brief introduction to creativity in an MIS project.

Creativity is not only helpful in systems analysis, but also in systems design for any MIS project. More specifically, creativity assists systems analysts (i.e., systems designers) in uncovering poor designs found in present systems that should not be duplicated in new systems. Also, a creative mind can help trigger better methods and procedures that should be incorporated into the new systems. In essence, creativity is a starting point in the entire systems development process such that, in the final analysis, the best management information systems are forthcoming from the joint efforts of the executive steering committee, the end-user review group, and the MIS project team.

A most important approach to creativity is *brainstorming,* which is a method of generating as many solutions as possible in a relatively short time. During the session, any idea is recorded no matter how ridiculous it may appear; no criticism is allowed. Generally, one idea is useful in suggesting others. The session continues until the group has exhausted its ideas. Once the session has adjourned, those whose problem areas were discussed will evaluate the ideas presented. Most of the ideas will be rejected; perhaps none will be a potential solution. However, the creative faculty of systems analysts may provide the necessary impetus to modify one or more ideas as workable solutions to the system under study. Uninhibited and unrestricted free association can help solve system problems where the proposed solutions are different from the existing ones.

Organization for a Successful MIS Project

A highly successful organization model for a new MIS project consists of three groups: (1) the executive steering committee, (2) the end-user review group, and (3) the MIS project team. For small- to medium-sized projects without inter-organization issues, the executive steering committee may be unnecessary and the end-user review group may consist of only one or two others besides the MIS project manager.

Members of the *executive steering committee* include middle- to high-level managers of any organization groups that will use or be affected by the new MIS. The chairperson of the committee might be the highest level manager from the organization that will achieve the major benefits of the new MIS. For example, if a new inventory system is to be examined, the vice president of physical distribution might be the chairperson; other members might be the vice presidents of manufacturing, marketing, and accounting. As will all committees, the effectiveness is inversely proportional to the number of members. In other words, it is advisable to keep the committee small.

The executive steering committee typically has these responsibilities:

- To ensure appropriate personnel are assigned to the end-user review group and the MIS project team
- To resolve issues that cut across organizational units
- To review key decisions of the end-user review group and the MIS project team to ensure that they are consistent with long-range organization objectives and goals
- To ensure that the scope of the study is broad enough to allow accomplishment of organization objectives and goals in an effective manner
- To enhance credibility and support the end-user review group and the MIS project team

The *end-user review group* typically has the following responsibilities:

- To participate in developing system specifications, with final approval/rejection responsibility
- To identify benefits associated with the new MIS
- To identify tasks for people from the functional units that will use or be affected by the new MIS
- To prioritize this work and schedule it into the ongoing daily work load associated with the current operation
- To assign personnel and manage the work

The *MIS project team* includes the computer technical experts (systems analysts and programmers), current system users, and end users who will be interacting with the new MIS. End users on the MIS project team should bring a background of in-depth experience, an interest in working on details, and a desire to help implement the new system. The MIS project manager must be able to bring such a group of people together and help them to work together productively. The MIS project manager is often chosen from the computer area because the individual has previous experience in leading such groups, but many successful projects have been led by end users.

Scope of the MIS Project

Typically, the executive steering committee initially defines the scope of the new MIS. This top-level group might ask the MIS project team and end-user review group to restrict their activities to a single functional area or to include the entire organization. Or the scope might be somewhere between these two extremes. An outside consultant(s) may be engaged to help in this initial stage. As the MIS project team and the end-user review group get into the details of the study, it may be necessary for the consultant to suggest modification to the scope of the MIS project.

Once the overall scope has been set by the executive steering committee, the next step is to identify specific objectives to be met. The formulation of these objectives is a joint effort among the executive steering committee, the end-user review group, and the MIS project team. Selecting objectives forces management to think seriously about the organization's future and brings to light problems that might be overlooked. It provides the MIS project team with a framework from which to operate, since the constraints and limitations under which the system must function are clear. Experience has indicated that a new MIS project will go much more smoothly when it begins with a formal statement of objectives.

Objectives desired by management can take several directions. An important objective is to beat competition by offering faster service to customers. Other objectives can be improved profitability, increased sales, or decreased costs, in which case both tangible and intangible benefits must be considered for the evaluation to be complete and realistic. Another objective can emphasize faster and more timely information for supporting management decisions—an approach that really aims at cost reduction as well as faster customer service. Still other objectives can focus on meeting new corporate or government requirements, ensuring adequate internal control, and utilizing information from external databases to improve operational effectiveness. Ideally, a new system will meet as many objectives as possible and, at the same time, leverage information technology.

It is advisable to state the objectives in writing. A written memorandum by the executive steering committee ensures the accomplishment of what was originally intended and reduces the risk of going off on a tangent. A carefully laid-out plan indicates where the study will cut across organizational lines and where authority is needed for changes in systems, methods, procedures, forms, reports, or organization.

Time to Be Spent on the MIS Project

An important item for a new MIS project is the preparation of a time schedule. A long time frame, say, several years, may be necessary. Experience has shown that the tendency is to underestimate the time element of the new MIS project as well as other succeeding steps. The time factor is a function of the objectives to be met and the resources to be committed. For a successful project, depth and thoroughness are important; the time factor is secondary.

Another question to consider is, What is the potential payoff? If the potential payoff is small, it is unwise to spend a considerable amount of time on a new MIS project. When developing a time schedule, the end-user review group and the MIS project team determine the amount of work in each step of the systems change and what personnel and skills will be needed. Consideration must also be given to the following steps: training, programming, program testing, delivery of equipment, physical requirements and installation of the equipment, files development, delivery of new forms and supplies, and conversion activities. The foregoing includes the major items that must be included in a realistic schedule.

COMPUTER-AIDED SOFTWARE ENGINEERING (CASE) TOOLS

In the traditional life cycle methodology of an MIS project, the focus has been and continues to be on the manual preparation of system flowcharts and related charts to develop a new MIS. In contrast, structured and object-oriented methodologies center more on the utilization of computer-aided software engineering (CASE) tools. This orientation toward CASE tools is not only useful to improve the speed and ease of producing new systems, but also to take advantage of the power of the computer to assist systems analysts and programmers in performing their everyday tasks. The net result is that the productivity of systems analysts and programmers can be improved dramatically. To assist the typical MIS manager in gaining a better understanding of CASE tools, their essential components and their relationship with the central repository are given here along with their benefits and limitations. Initially, however, a way of classifying CASE tools is given.

Classification of CASE Tools

Currently, there are different ways of classifying CASE tools, that is, of viewing CASE environments. A first classification refers to a set of integrated tools that define CASE and address the whole software development process. For example,

CASE systems can be divided into (1) single components or tools, (2) integrated frameworks, and (3) integrated toolkits. Single components or tools, also known as stand-alone tools, address only single steps in the life cycle. Design Machine from Optima Inc. is an example of this type. Integrated frameworks combine separate CASE tools to address more than one phase in the systems development process. Examples of these toolsets include the Developer from ASYSTT Technologies and Excelerator from Index Technology. On the other hand, integrated toolkits combine a wide range of CASE tools to form an integrated CASE environment to address the full systems development process. Examples include Life-Cycle Productivity System from American Management Systems and Software Backplane from Atherton Technology.

Another popular way of classifying CASE tools is to think in terms of their life-cycle span, into upper CASE tools, middle CASE tools, and lower CASE tools. Upper CASE tools support the strategic planning portion of systems development while middle CASE tools support the systems analysis and design portions. In contrast, lower CASE tools are the components that support systems development. Upper CASE and middle CASE are thus front-end tools while lower CASE comprises back-end tools.

Another method of classification relates to separating CASE tools into two basic categories: toolkits and workbenches. Per this classification, a CASE toolkit is a collection of integrated software tools that provide automated support for a single activity or phase in the systems development process. A workbench, on the other hand, is a collection of integrated software tools that provide automated support for the entire systems development life cycle.

Functional Components of CASE Tools

No matter what classification is used, there are a number of functional components for an integrated CASE environment. They include the following:

- A central repository represents the very essence of a CASE environment, and its function is to accumulate information relating to planning, analysis, design, development, and maintenance of the new MIS.
- Design tools are the diagramming tools that focus on drawing, manipulating, and storing structured diagrams, such as data-flow diagrams and data-structure diagrams. Their function is to represent pictorially the models and system specifications for the entire development process.
- Specification tools are used to create minispecifications and convert logical design to physical design.
- Prototyping tools include such tools as screen painters, report painters, and menu builders. These tools are interactive in nature and their principal purpose is to help determine system requirements and predict performance beforehand.
- Syntax verifiers help enforce consistency in the design process by performing consistency- and error-checking.

Figure 9.1
Information Sharing During Each Phase of Systems Development via the Repository Manager

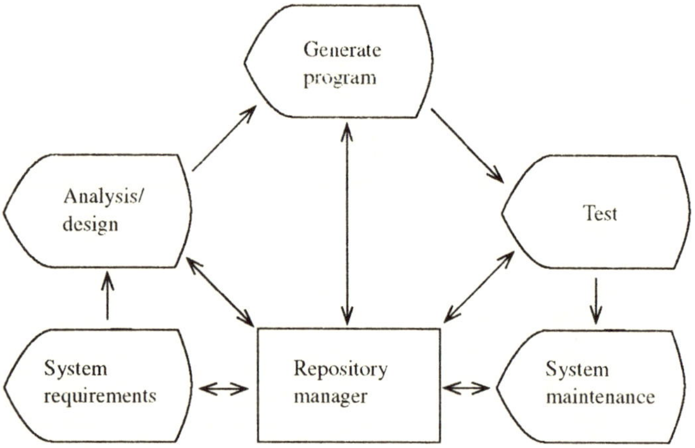

- Code generators generate program code from physical specifications. The more advanced code generators automatically generate code as physical specifications are fed to them.
- Documentation generators automatically generate adequate documentation as the systems development process progresses.
- Project management tools are useful to MIS project team leaders to monitor, manage, and track the progress of the project.

This wide range of functional components is central to a complete CASE environment.

Repository Manager's Importance in a CASE Environment

In a complete CASE environment, the central repository is a means of tying together all of its functional components. Its software is commonly called a repository manager, which is basically an interface to tie together CASE tools that share the same information during systems development. As shown in Figure 9.1, information is shared with the repository manager when utilizing one of the functional components of CASE tools. Within a complete CASE environment, there should be a complete integration not only through a common access to data (through the central repository), but also through a direct interface between any tool and another. These interfaces, as shown in Figure 9.1, allow design information to be passed from one tool to another. For flexibility and efficiency, these interfaces should be bidirectional and should allow communication between any tool and another in the integrated environment.

Currently, there is a major shortcoming with using repositories to tie CASE tools together. There are approximately 300 CASE tool vendors. Attempts to tie together their products often lead to two sources of problems: incompatible data and incompatible systems. As an example, IBM ran into trouble with the repository manager in its AD/Cycle (AD/Cycle is IBM's mainframe CASE product). The reason is that it tried to open the repository to a large number of CASE vendors. In doing so, IBM found that its repository spent the major part of the time doing translations between models. Users are also caught in the differences among vendors, some of which are repositories based on traditional DBMSs and others that are using object-oriented technology. Today, vendors such as IBM, DEC, Hewlett-Packard, and Texas Instruments typify the profusion of repository strategies and tools available to MIS organizations.

Client/Server CASE Tools

A very important current direction is client/server CASE tools. With interest in client/server computing at a very high level, organizations want flexible CASE products for developing applications capable of interoperating with a variety of different vendors' client and server computers. With client/server CASE, many graphic user interfaces, network products, operating systems, and application programming interfaces are supported.

Today, there are vendors of CASE tools who are expanding the number of operating systems and environments their products support to help users build applications that run on multivendor client/server systems. For example, one company selected Foundation (from Andersen Consulting) to add client/server capabilities to a customer service application because it needed a tool that runs on Unix (Microsoft Corporation's) Windows NT, and (IBM's) OS/2. Another company uses Application Development Workstation/Construction Workstation GUI (from Knowledge Ware), which it uses to build graphical user interfaces for client/server applications. It is expected that in the near future all vendors will be offering comprehensive client/server CASE tools of some type.

Selection of an Appropriate CASE Environment

To assist MIS managers to determine which CASE tools (one or more) should be acquired, they need to start with trying to understand what their developers' (i.e., systems analysts and programmers) needs are. After a careful analysis of developers' needs, the next step is a CASE tool evaluation, with the goal of finding a compatible match. Typically, there are a number of key areas of importance to systems analysts and programmers when it comes to CASE tools. These are (1) systems specifications, (2) systems design environment, (3) computer programming, (4) database management, (5) program testing, (6) run-time performance, (7) computing environment, (8) documentation capability, and (9) change management. In terms of the first area, for example, it is important to know how CASE tools produce definitions of business processes and data. Some CASE tools interface to prototyping tools, while others provide their own prototyping tools to define systems requirements. The same type of comments can be made regarding the other items.

Underlying all of these areas is *ease of use*. Many system development tools have impediments built into the human interface. Developers want CASE tools that support and accelerate their natural thought processes. Screen and command clarity, for instance, has become a particularly important feature with the advent of graphical user interfaces.

Next, MIS managers must consider qualifications specific to a certain environment. They need to weigh each area in terms of importance to their developers and then judge individual CASE tools on how well they meet these requirements. For example, if systems are typically installed with significant errors that affect customers and staff personnel, developers will need a CASE tool strong in the areas of analysis and testing. Also, MIS managers need to justify the cost of investment in a new CASE environment.

Benefits and Limitations of CASE Tools

Like any computer software, CASE tools have benefits and limitations. Current studies indicate that the use of CASE tools increases system developers' productivity and system quality. Additionally, there are improved documentation and communications among systems analysts and among consecutive phases of the development cycle. Standardized development techniques and discipline allow for consistency throughout systems development, thereby resulting in cost savings and less development time. A by-product of these benefits is higher system developer morale.

Presently, a typical CASE environment is far from the ideal even though there is a fully integrated CASE environment loaded with all possible automated tools and in which standardization and interfaces are complete. The present state of CASE technology falls short of this ideal and has these specific problems. Some complex CASE tools entail lengthy training requirements, and the learning curve is typically long. Other problems are poor compatibility, lack or awkward nature of interfaces between different tools, and a lack of a facility to forecast performance of the developed system.

Because CASE technology is still somewhat in its infancy, more development and sophistication need to be introduced in its tools to reap its promised benefits. A move to artificial intelligence and expert systems is a likely future development. The capabilities of knowledge-based systems will undoubtedly give the CASE technology significant leverage to move in the right direction. Overall, CASE technology that has made and continues to make great strides toward fundamentally changing the way systems are developed, maintained, and managed will be in great demand by the MIS organization.

Figure 9.2
Major Activities of an MIS Project Stated as a Percentage of Total Effort

Systems Development Activities	Traditional Systems Development	Structured or Object-Oriented Systems Development
Systems analysis (including MIS exploratory survey report)	10%	15%
Systems design	15	20
Equipment selection	10	10
Subtotal	35%	45%
Systems Implementation Activities		
Training personnel (programmers and all others)	10%	10%
Flowcharting and data flow diagrams	10	10
Programming and desk checking	15	10
Program compiling and testing	15	10
Parallel operations for checking new system	5	5
Final conversion to new system	10	10
Subtotal	65%	55%
Total	100%	100%

MAJOR PHASES OF AN MIS PROJECT

The percentage of total effort required for each of the various phases in an MIS project is given in Figure 9.2. These values are for a traditional systems development approach and a structured or object-oriented systems development approach and should not be construed as absolute values, but rather as a general guide for a typical large-scale project of two years or more. Depending on the complexity of the MIS project, a PERT/time schedule is generally used, although for very straightforward projects a Gantt chart can be used.

Normally for the traditional systems development approach, the period for systems development comprises about one-third of the total project time. In contrast, the period required for systems implementation comprises about two-thirds of the total effort. For a structured or object-oriented systems development approach, the values for systems development and systems implementation are about one-half each. The rationale is that more time is needed up front to develop the logical flow of the present and new systems for a structured approach; this is not the case with traditional systems development. Similarly, the same is true for an object-oriented approach since more time is needed to identify and structure objects in the new system.

Typically, the executive steering committee is very active throughout systems development. However, the same cannot be said for systems implementation. It is unfortunate that many on the executive steering committee feel that the real work has been completed when the systems development work is over, when, in reality, the reverse is true. This attitude among top-level managers explains the hurry to get the equipment installed and running during the systems implementation phase.

SYSTEMS ANALYSIS PROCESS FOR EFFECTIVE MIS

Since the purpose of systems analysis is to define what the new MIS must do, there are several steps performed during the systems analysis phase. Essentially, the strengths, weaknesses, and costs associated with the current system must be defined to serve as a benchmark for evaluation of feasible MIS alternatives. A very careful evaluation of these feasible MIS alternatives results in selecting the best alternative on the basis of a cost/benefit analysis. Finally, an MIS exploratory report by the MIS project team that states the conclusion of the systems analysis phase and recommends what should be performed during the rest of systems development is issued. Each of these steps is discussed next for a medium- to large-scale MIS project within a *structured* environment.

1. Analyze the Present System

Systems analysts, organization personnel from the functional end-user departments, and other appropriate personnel are usually split into teams to investigate each area under study. The study should concentrate on identifying the strengths, weaknesses, and costs associated with the current system. No area should be excluded unless it is unrelated to the desired objectives. The *physical* systems analysis should be comprehensive and include the following areas:

- *A review of historical facts* to identify the major turning points and milestones that have influenced the organization over time
- *An analysis of inputs* to identify where source documents are used to capture originating data
- *A review of methods and procedures* to understand the relationships among inputs, files, and outputs
- *A review of files maintained* to understand the number and size of files maintained by departments, where they are located, who uses them, the amount of time it takes to refer to a file, and the number of times they are referenced
- *An analysis of outputs* to determine how well present reports are meeting the organization's needs

- *A review of internal controls* to indicate control points critical to maintaining efficient MIS operations
- *An analysis of present personnel requirements* to classify present personnel by type, skill, and pay scale
- *A review of present work volumes* to identify average and peak work loads as well as periodic totals
- *A review of other requirements and considerations* to help locate important items that may be critical to the present system

Once the physical system has been documented, the next step in the structured approach is to develop the *logical* system. This entails using data flow diagrams to trace the origin of input data through each phase of processing and communication, into files, and finally out of files for desired outputs—many in the form of reports. The diagramming of the present operations not only organizes the facts, but also helps disclose gaps and duplication in the data gathered. It allows a thorough logical comprehension of the numerous details and related problems in the present operation. In essence, the knowledge gathered to date is brought altogether in a logical and meaningful relationship for the MIS project team and the end-user review group.

An important reason for reviewing the present system is to determine its costs. Present system benefits can also be identified. Benefits include the present level of service to customers, value of reports, return on investment, rate of profit, ability of the present system to grow with the organization, and increased inventory turnover. Many of these benefits can be measured precisely, while others are intangible and require subjective evaluation. Costs and benefits of the present system will provide a basis for comparison with feasible MIS alternatives.

2. Define Proposed System Specifications

Before feasible MIS alternatives are developed and evaluated, proposed system specifications (i.e., user requirements) must be clearly defined. These specifications, which pertain to each functional area under study in an MIS project, are determined from the desired objectives set forth initially in the project and information gained during the study of the current system. Likewise, consideration is given to the strengths and shortcomings of the existing system. Required system specifications, which must be clearly defined and in conformity with the project's objectives, might include such items as the following:

- Input data from original source documents for processing by the management information system
- Methods and procedures that show the relationship of input data to files and files to outputs of the management information system
- Files to be maintained with automated MIS equipment or otherwise

- Outputs to be produced, with emphasis on managerial reports that utilize the "exception principle"
- Work volumes and timing considerations for present and future periods, including peak periods

A starting point for compiling these system specifications is a clear statement of the cause of the current system weaknesses, after which it is possible to infer appropriate solutions—what outputs, inputs, and files are required and what methods and procedures must be utilized for each alternative. Future work loads of the new system must be defined for inputs, files, and outputs in terms of average and peak loads, cycles, and trends. This information is developed for each MIS alternative, but not to the same depth as was undertaken to understand the present system. Otherwise, such an effort would increase the time and personnel requirements of the study beyond its intended scope and budget.

3. Develop Feasible MIS Alternatives

The requirements of the new management information system may appear on the surface to be fixed; a closer examination often reveals their flexibility. For example, the original objectives set forth in the MIS project may state that certain computer files or a common database must be updated once a day, whereas the best solution may be an interactive computer system where files or common databases are updated as actual transactions occur. This approach is within the constraints initially set forth and introduces a new way of maintaining files. With this in mind, it is possible to design a number of different systems with varying features, costs, and benefits. In many cases, additional MIS alternatives can be investigated and analyzed when flexible system requirements are considered. The MIS project team must clearly communicate with the end-user review group any time it seems appropriate to modify an original requirement. Changes must be clearly documented and approved. It should be noted that outside consultants can be of great value to the MIS project team. The consultant's knowledge can narrow down the number of promising solutions. Too often, an MIS project team focuses on a specific system alternative that should have been discarded initially as infeasible. The consultant's objectivity can enhance the organization's chances of developing viable MIS alternatives and selecting the best choice.

4. Select the Best MIS Alternative

The next step after developing feasible MIS alternatives is to select the best one. The best MIS alternative can be determined by examining the anticipated savings and incremental costs for each. The difference between the estimated savings and estimated incremental costs represents the estimated net savings (losses) to the organization before federal income taxes. It should be noted that when computing the estimated savings and incremental costs, the trend of growth or

Figure 9.3
Intangible Benefits or Qualitative Factors to Consider for a New Management Information System

- Improved customer service through better techniques to anticipate customer requirements, resulting in fewer lost sales, less overtime in the plant for rush orders, and so forth.
- Better support of decision-making capability in the areas of marketing, manufacturing, finance, purchasing, personnel, engineering, and research and development through more timely and informative reports.
- More effective use of management time for planning, organizing, directing, and controlling because of the availability of timely data and information.
- Ability to handle more customers faster with automatic processing equipment.
- Closer control over capital investments and expenses through comparisons with budgets, standards, or forecasts.
- Improved scheduling and production control, resulting in more efficient employment of personnel and machines.
- Greater accuracy, speed, and control in information handling and MIS operations.
- Better control of credit through more frequent aging of accounts receivables and analyses of credit data.
- Reversal of trend to higher hiring and training costs arising from the difficulties in filling clerical jobs.
- Improved promotional efforts to attract new customers and retain present ones.
- Enhanced stature in the business community as a progressive and forward-looking organization.

cutback in the organization's work load should be analyzed and projected. These data can then be used to project savings and costs, similar to the cost/benefit analysis set forth in Chapter 3 (refer to Figure 3.5). Since projected savings and costs are in the future, the difference between the two sums after federal income taxes should be discounted back to the present time to account for the time value of money. Such an analysis was also found in Chapter 3 (refer to Figure 3.6).

In addition, a number of intangible benefits or qualitative factors may be uncovered by studying the potential contributions of the new MIS to the organization's activities and problems. A listing of such factors is found in Figure 9.3. These factors may ultimately lead to an increase in revenues or a decrease in operating costs. There is not a strong, directly traceable relationship between achieving these benefits and improved profitability.

The study of implementing a new management information system is difficult when numerous alternatives are available. Comparing only the tangible benefits shown in Figure 9.4, only alternatives 1 and 2 appear attractive. However, when

Figure 9.4
Decision Table for Appraising Feasible MIS Alternatives

Feasible MIS Alternatives

Exploratory Survey Table

Decision Table

Date: **July 1, 199-**
Preparer: **R. J. Thierauf**

Criteria for Evaluation	**Alternative 1**	**2**	**3**	**4**	**5**
Tangible Benefits					
Meets return on investment criteria — 20% after taxes*	Y	Y	N	N	N
Reduced order processing costs	Y	Y	Y	Y	Y
Lower investment in inventory	Y	Y	Y	Y	Y
Lower future cash requirements	N	N	Y	Y	Y
Intangible Benefits					
Improved customer service	N	N	Y	Y	Y
Improved promotional efforts	N	N	N	Y	Y
Ability to handle more customers faster	N	N	N	Y	Y
Better decision-making ability	Y	Y	Y	Y	Y
Better use of management's time	N	N	N	Y	Y
Improved scheduling and production control	Y	Y	Y	Y	Y
Closer control over capital investments	N	N	Y	Y	Y
Handle more volume at lower costs	N	N	Y	Y	Y
More accuracy and reliability of data	Y	Y	Y	Y	Y
System Features					
Uses a batch processing system	X	-	-	-	-
Uses an interactive system	-	X	X	X	X
Substantial changes of inputs and outputs	X	X	X	X	X
Need for new files	X	X	X	X	X
Moderate revision of methods and procedures	X	X	X	-	-
Major revision of methods and procedures	-	-	-	X	X
Employ outside consultants	-	-	-	X	X
Recruit new MIS personnel	-	-	X	X	X

Other Information

*1 — 22%, 2 — 21%, 3 — 19%, 4 — 19%, 5 — 18%

the intangible benefits are included, the remaining alternatives become more promising. Thus, the feasibility of implementing a new MIS has been established. The question, then, is to determine which alternative is best when all critical factors are appraised.

Since the MIS project team's primary job is to recommend the best alternative, it must weigh quantitative and qualitative factors with emphasis on the organization's growth pattern and future problems. A specific organization's circumstances must be analyzed for an accurate conclusion. In the example, an examination of Figure 9.4 indicates that alternatives 4 and 5 are best. In terms of tangible and intangible benefits, more affirmative answers for an image processing system exist than for a newer interactive MIS (alternative 2 or 3). The returns on investment are generally comparable. Which alternative should be implemented? In terms of alternative 5, imaging equipment can be tied in with electronic data interchange processing. Conversion today to imaging terminals will mean no or minimal conversion costs in the future for EDI. With this added advantage in mind, the MIS project team believes that future cost savings justify accepting a lower return. Its recommendation to the executive steering committee is now clear.

5. Submit MIS Exploratory Survey Report to the Executive Steering Committee

At the conclusion of the studies just mentioned, ample information has been accumulated for the final recommendation. The exploratory survey report should be prepared by the MIS project team, approved by the end-user review group, and directed to the executive steering committee. It may be financially oriented since large sums of money may be involved. Generally, the approval of the recommendation must come from the executive steering committee before any further steps are taken.

The contents of this report must be as objective as possible so that the best MIS alternative is selected. Consideration must be given to a fundamental principle underlying management information systems, which is that a computer-oriented system is in a far better position to absorb growth in volume with a slight increase in operating costs than are other systems. Comparable principles should be embodied in the system recommended for a constructive report to management.

A suggested format for the final exploratory survey report to the executive steering committee is depicted in Figure 9.5. The report gives management an opportunity to examine the data and appraise the validity and merit of the recommendation and provides a sound basis for constructive criticism of the MIS project. It should be noted that although considerable time, effort, and cost have been expended during systems analysis, the infeasibility of newer computer and peripheral equipment and newer methods and procedures may be the final result. Sometimes this conclusion may be caused by inappropriately limiting the initial

Figure 9.5
Suggested Format for a Final Exploratory Survey Report to the Executive Steering Committee

---

1. Scope and objective of the MIS project
2. Overview of the existing system, noting its weaknesses and problems
3. Adequate description of the recommended MIS alternative, indicating its tangible and intangible benefits, its superiority in eliminating or reducing the deficiencies of the present system, and its general impact on the organization
4. Financial data on the recommended MIS alternative (refer to Figures 3.5 and 3.6)
5. Reference to other feasible MIS alternatives which were investigated, giving reasons for their financial rejection; a decision table (refer to Figure 9.4) should be included
6. Financial data on system alternatives that were not selected (refer to Figures 3.5 and 3.6)
7. Schedule of funds required for specific periods of time during system implementation
8. List of additional personnel needed to implement the new system and personnel requirements during conversion
9. Accurate time schedule for the remainder of the MIS project
10. Other special factors and considerations

scope of the study to areas where technological progress has been slow or nonexistent or areas that do not lend themselves to newer equipment. When an opportunity exists for implementing information technology, a broader approach is usually desirable. Generally, infeasibility can be minimized with the help of one or more outside consultants or experienced end users in setting the initial scope of the MIS project.

SYSTEMS DESIGN PROCESS FOR EFFECTIVE MIS

The MIS project manager and the participants who draw up the exploratory survey report generally undertake the design of the recommended MIS alternative. If additional systems personnel are required, they should be enlisted. The participation and cooperation of the appropriate functional areas, represented by end-user departmental personnel, are the key to successful development. It is much easier to design the system to accommodate their constructive suggestions than to redesign it at a later date. Too many installations have faced this embarrassing situation, only because appropriate personnel were not given an opportunity to evaluate the systems design as it progressed. As will be seen, there are a number of steps involved in systems design within a *structured* environment.

1. Establish TQM Requirements

In order to have an effectively designed system, MIS management must insist that a total quality management program for MIS development include life-cycle quality metrics starting with preventing defects in system specifications. Previously, quality improvement programs used techniques employing metrics for quality assurance (QA) during the design and prototyping stages of the development process. Unfortunately, these QA techniques are applied too late in the process to affect the overall quality of the system when viewed from an organizationwide perspective. To design and implement TQM programs, MIS management must ensure that systems specifications include organizationwide business rules that are communicated to both systems analysts and programmers. Most system specifications are too narrowly focused on the specifics of a system to reflect concerns for sharing data adequately. This is the primary reason why systems are inflexible and unacceptably expensive to maintain in the face of changing business conditions.

Studies have shown that many of the errors reported during system testing and production can be traced to the initial stages of development. The most common cause of these errors are specifications that are missing, erroneous, ambiguous, or conflicting. Only a small percentage of errors have to do with code that does not meet specifications. Even CASE tools provide only limited help in identifying defects in the initial stages. Hence, MIS management, working with project managers and end users, need to establish TQM requirements for MIS projects.

As a way of ensuring that the TQM requirements are met, the organization's internal auditors can carry out this function at periodic intervals during systems development. At the same time, the internal auditors can review and comment on the auditability of the system being developed. The responsibility for the auditability of new systems lies jointly with the end-user departments, systems analysts, and programmers. The functional end-user departments are responsible for specifying the application system controls. Implementing these controls is the responsibility of the systems analysts and programmers. The auditors need to interact with each of these groups during systems development to determine the adequacy of auditability provisions. By becoming involved at strategic points, the auditors can, with a limited amount of effort, ensure adequate internal control when the system becomes operational.

2. Review Information on Selected MIS Alternative

Going beyond establishing TQM requirements, the MIS project team needs to review all information collected on the selected MIS alternative. Essentially, key information on the new MIS, especially its systems requirements, should be contained in the exploratory survey report to the executive steering committee. Similarly, detailed information is generally found in the documentation that was used in preparing the report. This combined information should be sufficient to get started on determining the new MIS requirements.

3. Determine the New MIS Requirements

Before the logical design of the new MIS can be started using a structured methodology and a CASE tool, it is necessary that the MIS project team, working with end users, determine the new MIS requirements. This means starting with policies and outputs since the concept of *minimal systems* will be used in the logical design process. That is, only data needed for output will be collected by the new MIS based on simplified organization policies. This approach results in a low-cost processing basis. Also, it simplifies the whole design process since only selected data are captured and used in outputs from the new MIS. Once outputs have been determined, data files along with related methods and procedures can be inferred as they relate to inputs. In the process, appropriate internal controls can be incorporated at strategic control points by working with the internal auditors. Hence, new MIS requirements of the new logical system that must be determined include the following:

- *New policies consistent with organization objectives* to reduce the complexity and the number of exceptions in the new system. Examples are simplifying pricing and discount policies to conform to organization objectives.
- *Output needs* as determined by end-users' requirements. End users should work with systems analysts so that the format, detail and degree of accuracy, and frequency of the report can be specified.
- *Data files maintained* or the amount of data to be contained in on-line and off-line files. Efficient systems design dictates keeping storage data at a minimum.
- *Planned inputs* to capture source data initially in a processible form. Time constraints on the inputs and variations in input volume are important considerations.
- *New methods and procedures* to produce output given certain inputs and data files. Operational procedures should be tested for practicality. In addition methods and procedures must be compatible among functional areas or activities.
- *Internal controls* or checks established at control points to ensure that what has been processed is accurate. Likewise, established internal controls focus on making certain that no one person has full responsibility over an entire operation. This should be apparent in such areas as cash and payroll since one person with complete responsibility can too easily defraud an organization.

4. Design the New MIS and Determine Data Requirements

Basically, determining the preceding requirements is concurrent with designing the *logical* flow of the new MIS using a CASE tool. The structured design of a system involves many decisions about each of its parts—outputs desired, files to be maintained, planned inputs, and methods and procedures that link inputs with outputs. An integral part of logical systems design work is answering questions about new reports and procedures.

Within a structured framework, the logical design of the new MIS centers on modularity using a CASE tool. All system requirements are incorporated into a functional block diagram. Starting with the highest, each function is broken down into individual subfunctions, applying the process iteratively from the top down. The resulting analysis can be represented by an inverted tree diagram in which major functions at the top are successively broken into separate functions in the lower branches.

As the breakdown continues, two important phenomena can be observed: some branches are beginning to terminate (they do not lend themselves to further breakdown), and some of the functions are turning up in more than one place (duplicated modules). When the breakdown is complete, a thorough functional analysis is obtained even though the system has not been fully designed. A systems analyst often finds alternative ways to break down a function into its component parts. Much time is spent on changing and filling in details considered unimportant on an earlier pass. Time spent here now is worthwhile, however, since this step forms the heart of the new system. When the functional analysis using a CASE tool is complete, the systems analyst creates a logical system structure for the functional modules that will operate under whatever constraints are imposed. This modular approach allows the complexity of an overall system to be reduced, since many of the duplicated modules are eliminated. It also provides excellent documentation that will facilitate modification or updating of the system in the future.

As discussed earlier, a CASE tool assists systems analysts in designing the various levels of data flow diagrams—from the highest level to the lowest level for the functional modules. In addition, the CASE tool has the capability of developing a data dictionary of data items found in the new MIS. As changes are made throughout the system, changes are made to the data dictionary so that it is always up-to-date. In this manner, the systems analysts have a current listing of all data to be found in the new system.

When using this technology, some CASE tools allow users to build systems using graphical representations of functions that the CASE tool then translates into code. But the graphical representations CASE users are bringing together are not objects. Hence, the code underlying the pictures is created according to structured programming techniques. (In the section on object technology, there will be a further discussion of this important topic.) At this point in the structured approach, there may be no need to create the code because the system as designed may need to undergo a number of changes recommended by users. Hence, there is need to proceed to the next step—prototyping.

5. Utilize Prototyping to Finalize the New MIS

To finalize the new MIS and determine exact data requirements, prototyping is employed: that is, prototyping using a fourth-generation language is used to produce sample output, which the end users can judge for system requirements satisfaction. Through the use of prototyping, systems analysts and end users discover new refinements that can be incorporated in the next version. Quite often during development, end users will require new output. In essence, prototyping is a trial-and-error process in which a version of the system is built, used, evaluated, and revised or new output functions are added. Each new prototype performs more of the required functions in an increasingly efficient manner. The end result is that the new system's output is defined in the utmost detail.

Prototyping can also help in programming. Because a software prototype is a scaled-down version of the final program that focuses on the functions end users require, it is studied by end users and programmers to see whether it meets specified system requirements, needs additional options, and can be modified to meet future business changes. The real software package built is then modeled on this prototype. Although this prototype may cost thousands, users will save hundreds of thousands of dollars since the major cost in software development begins after the initial software is completed. This is particularly true where a large part of the cost of software (i.e., at least 60 percent) is in the area of program maintenance. In other words, after the new system is delivered, a large percentage of the code must be rewritten to fit requirements that were never specified properly. In addition, still more code must be rewritten as end-users' needs change. Typically, the cost of changing a software system after building it is many times the cost of developing it. Thus, prototyping can save considerable time and expense over the traditional approach to programming.

6. Fulfill TQM Requirements

Once the design of the new MIS has been finalized by the prototyping process or otherwise, there is need to review the system for adherence to quality standards. CASE technology which automates structured design and programming activities can obviously improve quality within its own automated operations. However, there is still need for a comprehensive test program overseen by the TQM group that is a useful complement to the CASE tool. That is, each module for every level of design needs to undergo ample pretesting such that it is error-free before it is integrated with other modules of a higher, equal, or lower level. In turn, these modules need to be tested thoroughly with a set of test data before acceptance.

Modular testing is only part of the total testing process. A broader view of testing includes defining requirements in such a way that it can be demonstrated that they have been met, planning the testing activities, reviewing the software design and program code, defining and generating test data, defining expected results of program execution, and executing programs. However, an even broader view for TQM includes comparing actual with expected test results and consequent retesting if the software must be modified. Typically, the functions constituting this definition include an important portion of the total systems development effort. From this broadened view, the TQM group participates in all phases of systems development, from requirements review to walkthroughs to final systems acceptance. Unless the group is continuously involved, its effect is minimal. Occasionally, even end users become a test because if end users run a completed system and it fails to work, that system becomes a test system instead of a production system.

One of the major problems inherent in testing software stems from the difficulty of determining what constitutes high-quality software that will fulfill TQM requirements. To determine whether all requirements have been met, they must be *first* stated in terms that will be interpreted in the same way by both the requesters and the developers of the software. *Second,* the requirements must be complete: that is, they must include not only a definition of the function to be performed, but also such factors as response time, reliability, and ease of use. *Third,* requirements must be measurable. *Fourth,* requirements must be traceable so as to show how the requirements at implementation are derived from those agreed to at the project's inception. This is important because of the changes that are inevitably made. These requirements, then, represent a practical, results-oriented approach to software quality improvement, one that strives toward "zero-defects" software in a TQM environment.

The essential focus of establishing TQM requirements (refer to the first step) and the sixth step of fulfilling them is a positive one of preventing errors rather than a negative one of finding errors. To determine quality, appropriate measurements must be established and documented. That is, quality metrics should be kept on those measures that determine the degree of quality for systems development. Initial efforts of the TQM group should be directed toward those areas of systems development in which the most immediate improvement can be shown. This is usually at the beginning stages of systems development. As positive results are achieved, attention to quality assurance can be extended into the latter phases of the life cycle. The benefits of the TQM program will become widely apparent when it is seen that systems implemented under the total quality management program require less maintenance than older systems. Their benefits will be broadened when the quality procedures applied to new systems development are extended to systems maintenance. Additional benefits of this approach include the improved credibility and morale of systems analysts and programmers as well as the TQM group.

7. Document the New MIS

An important part of the structured systems design is preparing diagrams and flowcharts for the physical flow of the recommended management information system, without specifying the actual equipment. Accuracy, simplicity, and ease of understanding are the essential components since nontechnical personnel may be reviewing and evaluating them. All data compiled on the new MIS will be needed for submitting bid invitations to equipment manufacturers and preparing program flowcharts.

To prepare program flowcharts for later coding, appropriate logic must be developed. Block diagrams or program flowcharts can be prepared to document the new system that show the details of the programming effort required during systems implementation. However, if a CASE tool performed part or all of the programming effort, the program flowcharts are generally prepared as a by-product of programming. The development of system documentation should be supervised by MIS management throughout the entire MIS project to ensure accuracy, completeness, and ease of understanding.

EQUIPMENT CONSIDERATIONS

In the last step of the systems design process, documentation is undertaken. The detailed documentation is the basis for preparing bid invitations to equipment manufacturers. Equipment for the new MIS should be identified in general terms. However, to design a system with only one equipment manufacturer in mind is restrictive, reduces the potential of the system, and often reduces the ultimate success of the systems project. Equipment is important at this stage, but only in terms of class and type. This area is covered in Chapter 7.

Once the entire systems development process is completed, any significant deviations from the findings of the exploratory survey report must be reported to the executive steering committee by the MIS project team. It is the function of these top-level managers to make a final decision on the feasibility of applying the recommended MIS under changed conditions. In this manner, the systems design evolves from the system proposed in the exploratory survey report.

ALTERNATIVE SYSTEMS DEVELOPMENT APPROACHES

In addition to the structured methodology set forth previously that makes use of CASE tools, there are alternative systems development approaches that may be appropriate for the situation. For example, the involvement of end users in the systems development process is necessary so that applications which are really needed by their organizations are designed and implemented. Techniques like joint application development (JAD) and rapid application development (RAD) are useful from this standpoint. In a similar manner, windows-based application development can be undertaken. Each of the foregoing approaches is discussed later, followed by a newer approach to systems development and maintenance—object technology.

Joint Application Development

Joint application development, which is basically a systems design technique, has as its goal to improve the quality of project specifications by engaging users in the requirements definition process. JAD is performed in structured workshops driven by a JAD leader and documented by a scribe. Over time, a quality systems specification evolves and becomes a blueprint for project development. Typically, MIS projects are prone to delays, errors, and failure for a number of reasons. Poor communications, a protracted systems development process, a "we-they" environment, and massive, incomprehensible, and inconsistent documentation are some of the symptoms.

To be responsive to organizational needs, MIS projects must be completed before the problem parameters change. By having MIS professionals and a group of users work together in a nonthreatening series of analysis and design sessions, the total time to understand and document the requirements for a new MIS can be greatly reduced. The goals of JAD are to accelerate the development process, increase productivity, improve quality, and build better developer-client relationships. Overall, joint application development facilitates the interaction between systems analysts and users.

Rapid Application Development

Rapid application development represents the body of development approaches that use CASE tools, JAD, and 4GLs to build systems faster. RAD is a systems development approach currently gaining acceptance in the MIS development community. It combines elements of JAD and automated prototyping techniques with a stringent time limit to create an environment which fosters rapid systems development and maintenance. RAD employs small teams with specialized skills. Unlike other development approaches, it has no interim deliverables. Each RAD team simply builds a piece of a larger prototype and refines it until it becomes a working system.

Currently, many software vendors are offering their own RAD products and services. While vendors offer widely differing products, their approaches to RAD are characterized by some key common elements: an iterative development approach; great emphasis on enterprise and data modeling; use of automated tools for rapid prototyping and code generation; active end-user involvement throughout systems development; and reliance on reusable code, forms, and modules. Since most businesses revolve around a few critical success factors, the reason for centering on data modeling is to identify just what those success factors are and how the pieces fit together. In turn, this foundation can be utilized for building and prototyping system applications.

A most important distinguishing factor of RAD is its time limit—projects typically run from 60 to 120 days. While this short time limit can be a motivator, it can also become the single greatest reason for employee dissatisfaction and turnover. Careful planning and execution are needed to make RAD projects work. Rapid application development calls for leaders who are forward in their thinking and confident enough in their staffs to empower them to get the job done.

Windows-Based Application Development

Currently, there is a new set of development tools available to systems analysts and programmers: windows-based application development. The most popular representatives of this new breed of high-level development languages and/or frameworks include Borland Turbo C++ for Windows, Microsoft Visual Basic with Professional Toolkit, Asymetrix Toolbook, the Whitewater Group's Actor 3.0, and Microsoft C/C++ 7.0. These products and many more have sprung up to assist systems developers in making the change to developing for, and sometimes within, a graphical environment. Many Windows programs are graphically based versions of existing text-based applications. But as Windows 3.X has gained unprecedented market penetration along with the next generation of Windows (NT), there has been and continues to be more interest in developing new types of applications geared to the operating environment.

Because Windows is event-driven, Windows programmers are freed from thinking in the traditional logical and sequential manner of DOS programming. Windows programmers construct applications in that environment which allows them to think in a much less linear fashion. Since events can be invoked from all parts of the screen (menu, toolbar, dialog box, etc.), a Windows programmer needs to anticipate all the actions a user might like to do and take into account any order that the user decides. To this fact must be added that other programs may be running and interacting with the program under development. One of Windows's greatest strengths is its multitasking capability. Overall, windows-based application development gives programmers an easy way to get up to speed.

A NEWER APPROACH TO SYSTEMS DEVELOPMENT AND MAINTENANCE—OBJECT TECHNOLOGY

Object-oriented technology is an approach to software engineering that can increase the productivity of systems analysts and programmers by giving them a single construct with which to address analysis, design, and related activities. The fundamental construct is the object, which combines both data structure and behavior in a single entity. Object models are particularly valuable for communication and documentation. And they serve well as the framework for program code and database schemas. With object-oriented methodology, the end results are a much better understanding of requirements, cleaner designs, and more maintainable and reliable systems.

Object technology is sometimes considered to be a subset of CASE because the two share the characteristic of reusable programming modules. However, there are important differences. While CASE is a semiautomated form of structured programming in which each function is broken down into sets of instructions, object-oriented programming is based on modeling the physical aspects of the business rather than the procedures themselves. Objects contain programming and data so the object knows what it is and how it behaves. While a CASE module could be reused in a similar application with a little extra coding, a well-designed object could be used in any application, regardless of its type. Object modularity also means that a designer need only make changes to a single object in order to modify a program, rather than having to modify hundreds or even thousands of lines of code, because one change causes a chain reaction. Such modularity is a primary reason why many organizations are moving to this latest direction in systems development and maintenance.

Making the Transition to Object Technology

When making the transition to object technology, it is wise to do so in an evolutionary fashion and be aware that there is a steep learning curve. Learning to think in terms of objects may take some time. Typically, it takes close to a year to make the shift. It should be recognized that class construction or the building of objects is a complex business. Every object can have hundreds of relationships with other objects, and its creation requires strong analysis and design skills. Object proponents have high hopes for object-oriented COBOL extension that makes the technology available in an environment familiar to mainframe programmers.

To ensure a successful transition to object technology, there are several initial steps that the MIS manager should follow. First, there is need to secure a financial commitment from senior corporate management. These top-level managers should realize that savings will occur in subsequent MIS projects. To gain acceptance, a new project should be picked, rather than a partially completed one. If applications are being downsized or moved to a client/server environment, systems analysts and programmers are likely to be more open to object technology. If deemed appropriate, external training and consulting organizations should be used for the transition to object technology. The MIS manager needs to address the shift in skills mix that must accompany the corresponding shift of activities toward the front end of the software development process. Also, the individual needs to encourage systems analysts to use object-oriented analysis and design methods that concentrate on modeling their businesses. Similarly, programmers should be encouraged to create and use reusable object-oriented code. Putting the preceding steps into action will signify to MIS personnel that this new technology is to be taken seriously.

Object-Oriented Analysis and Design

Because the logical way to design any system is to break it down subsystem by subsystem (i.e, decomposition), structured design methodologies have been taking this approach for a long time. In object-oriented analysis and design, on the other hand, the primary emphasis is on classes and objects. Typically, CASE tools provide support for diagramming in one or more methodologies. This means that they allow a systems analyst to draw the diagram and enter the descriptions according to the definition of the method. It should be noted that this is not enough. The tools must also implement the various rules and evaluation criteria to perform design checking and ensure the method is being properly followed. Also, the tool should allow systems analysts to follow the step-by-step process of the method naturally. Most of these tools have some sort of repository associated with them. Only a few were developed specifically to be optimized for OOAD. Their repositories are structured with the idea of storing the object-oriented design in a canonical form appropriate to the paradigm. When this is the case, the tool can often support more than one OOAD method, storing the essence and details of the design in its repository and displaying it more than one way. A tool with this capability generally lends itself to customization. Another important aspect of the tool is whether and how another tool vendor can interface its tool (e.g., a project management package) to the repository.

Object-Oriented Programming

The basic building block of an object-oriented program is an object. *Objects* are software entities: that is, they may model something physical, such as a person, or they may model something virtual, such as a checking account. An object normally has one or more attributes (fields) that collectively define the state of the object. Some objects may be transient, existing temporarily during the execution of a program. Others may be persistent, existing on some form of permanent storage after the program finishes. In contrast, a *class* is a description of a number of objects which have certain likenesses or common traits.

Related to classes and objects is *inheritance*. It means that when a programmer makes a change to one class of object, say an insurance policy, every subclass within that class is automatically changed accordingly. In order to make a change in an insurance rate or regulation that will affect many different types of policies, a programmer need only make the change to the one policy upon which all the others are based. Overall, object-oriented programming languages are characterized by features that support (1) the definition of *objects* encapsulating state and behavior as a set of services, (2) *classes* for instantiating new objects, and (3) *inheritance* as a mechanism for defining new (sub)classes. These features provide the means to model applications as collections of cooperating objects (i.e., for decomposition) and the potential to derive new specifications of objects from existing ones (i.e., composition). Currently, there are OOP languages with special libraries of reusable components.

Underlying object-oriented program development is a *bottom-up* approach. Its basic premise is that during the life of an application, data structures remain relatively stable while the operations on those data structures change, depending on particular situations. Essentially, the procedure is first to identify data structures that write small programs (procedures) for the operations on each data structure and combine those into the objects that encapsulate the data structures with the procedures. At the end, programmers combine the objects into working programs in which work is accomplished by objects passing messages to each other. An object is activated by receiving a message specifying a behavior and parameters to describe the behavior. After an object executes the behavior, it sends a message to another object. In contrast, this approach is the antithesis of structured programming, where the focus is on a *top-down* approach.

From an enterprisewide view, object technology promises to be the gateway to the distributed, client/server computing that MIS groups have been hard pressed to realize using structured programming systems. Objects that have a characteristic called dynamic binding allow programmers to design distributed applications without specifying ahead of time which systems will be communicating with which for any given application. Dynamic binding allows the system to decide which objects on which servers to access at the time of the request. In summary, client/server computing is expected to be object-based because object-oriented programming generates code that is reusable and modular, making it easier, faster, and more cost-effective to develop complex client/server applications.

Object-Oriented Database Management Systems

Because objects must continue to exist after the program has been completed, object-oriented database management systems have become very helpful to MIS personnel to provide permanent storage for objects. Their data model has objects with the same characteristics as objects in object-oriented programming. OODBMSs are also helpful for other reasons, including handling complex data structures and abstract data types, and supporting long-duration transactions. OODBMS vendors provide both the capabilities and features of traditional DBMSs, that is, backup and recovery, transaction management, security, and performance, but also support object orientation, that is, object identity, encapsulation, types or classes, and inheritance.

AN ALTERNATIVE APPROACH TO SYSTEMS DEVELOPMENT AND OPERATIONS—OUTSOURCING

Outsourcing, which is an alternative approach to developing systems internally and operating them, is not new. Electronic Data Systems, for example, thrived decades ago by managing a client's in-house data processing facilities. Under an outsourcing arrangement, a client takes advantage of the expertise of others who are more effective at specialized tasks, while the client concentrates on its core business. The outsourcing firm provides the people, equipment, supplies, management, and systems needed to do the work in a variety of areas.

Contributing to the growing popularity of outsourcing is its endorsement by many respected business consultants. In his book *Liberation Management,* management expert Tom Peters advises organizations to outsource all possible support services, excluding the very few services that represent the core business of an organization. Alternately referring to outsources as subcontractors, networkers, outsiders, partners, and internal associates, Mr. Peters includes efficiency, innovation, and information among the many benefits possible through outsourcing. Other benefits include those that focus on cost savings, more critical business issues, leveraging of information resources, and consolidation of operations.

GUIDELINES TO ASSIST MIS MANAGEMENT IN SYSTEMS DEVELOPMENT

A *first* and foremost guideline on systems development centers on the human element. There is need initially to get the backing of senior corporate management who are tied in with the MIS project organizationally. This can be accomplished via the executive steering committee. Also, this high level of management should be involved in the overall planning phase as well as in the succeeding phases of an MIS project. Similarly, the MIS department needs the assistance of appropriate managers from the functional end-user departments and their support personnel in the detailed aspects of the MIS project. Overall, all parties in the project should be employed in a productive manner and should sincerely believe that it is in their best interest to achieve the goals of the new MIS.

Although qualified personnel have been recruited from within or outside the organization to undertake the MIS project, there is need for an important *second* guideline, that is, that the management information system being built is truly molded to meet end-user objectives, not just self-serving interests of the MIS staff. Hence, the MIS staff should not assume full responsibility for building the system by themselves; rather there must be meaningful involvement of senior corporate management, functional end-user management, and end users. This is particularly true when the system extends to multiple functional areas.

A *third* guideline is that the MIS manager needs to assign priorities to MIS projects. Those projects that give a competitive advantage should be considered first, followed by those that yield the highest cost/benefit ratio and the least risk. Next, those projects that offer a high cost/benefit ratio and provide average risk for the organization should be undertaken. When implemented, these projects need to be broken down into manageable parts. Depending on the type of MIS project, the sizes of the manageable parts may vary. However, each part should allow the MIS project manager to have complete control over the project and its members. It is recommended that the project be divided into eighty-hour tasks. This time limitation divides the jobs into more manageable tasks, making it easier to define user requirements and maintain team members' enthusiasm.

A *fourth* guideline is directed toward selecting appropriate systems development technologies and methods for a coordinated systems development and implementation effort. Because there are different ways to analyze, design, program, and implement a new MIS, one or more system methods may be necessary to enhance the productivity of MIS personnel and end users in order to produce an effective system. No matter what methods are employed, it is helpful to think in terms of modularity of methods and procedures. The capability of bringing together different procedural modules or building blocks that can stand alone greatly reduces the complexity of a system. Modularity will facilitate any system modification or update that may be necessary in the future.

In the development of new MIS, systems analysts and end users must think in terms of establishing control points, a *fifth* guideline. The determination of how such standards as flexible budgets and production tolerances are to be controlled is vital to the effective management of a system and the quality of the final output. The timing for comparing actual results with standards at control points should permit the process to be stopped or altered before serious damage can occur. The managers at the various operating levels who are accountable for the data flow being controlled must be identified. Accountability enhances the effective control of ongoing operations. Related to establishing control points is providing for corrective action. As incorrect data are detected, corrective methods and procedures are initiated before processing continues. In this manner, not only is the reliability of system methods and procedures maintained, but variances from established norms and standards are detected and corrected before processing can continue.

A *sixth* and last guideline is the involvement of end users in an MIS project. This involvement should be agreed upon before any work on the project takes place. It is necessary that end users both understand and accept full responsibility for and commitment to the ultimate success of the MIS project. End-user involvement needs to be active, not passive, and maintained throughout the development and implementation of the MIS. The dominant thrust in end-user involvement is that it must emanate from end users and not MIS staff. In addition, schedules of the MIS project should be realistic and accurately reflect not only the MIS staff's ability, but also that of end users to participate in developing the new MIS. But once the schedules are set, there is need to adhere to these commitments.

10

Systems Implementation and Maintenance

OUTLINE

Estimating Time for Program Maintenance
Guidelines to Assist MIS Management in Systems Implementation and Maintenance

INTRODUCTION TO EFFECTIVE SYSTEMS IMPLEMENTATION AND MAINTENANCE

The prior chapter focused on the effective management of the systems development process. In this chapter, the next phase of an effectively managed MIS project is studied. Systems implementation becomes more of a team effort since end users, systems analysts, and operations personnel are involved in a wide range of MIS activities. This group will not only schedule the new system, advise on personnel selection and training, and assist in the preparation of the new MIS, but also do whatever is necessary to assist in the operation of the new system. In the first half of the chapter the essentials of systems implementation are covered and the operation of the new MIS is set forth. Additionally, techniques to assist in scheduling MIS operations are given, and the need for a periodic review of new system approaches to replace existing information technology is discussed.

The second half of the chapter centers on effective management of systems and program maintenance. Typically, most organizations operate in a reactive maintenance mode: that is, the staff responds to a problem. In contrast, active maintenance is more controlled. The staff analyzes and updates applications in response to the changing needs of the enterprise, and changes are made while the system is stable. Such an approach is taken in the chapter. The tools enable an active maintenance approach to go hand in hand with one of today's most popular buzzwords—*reengineering*. Reengineering can refer to a wide range of tools, that is, approaches from the simple, such as those that restructure code for readability, to the complex, such as those that move existing applications onto a new platform. In addition to discussing these approaches to maintaining present systems and their programs, a method for developing accurate time estimates will be presented.

PRINCIPLES OF EFFECTIVE SYSTEMS IMPLEMENTATION AND MAINTENANCE

Effective systems implementation should include the *Principle of Modularity of Methods and Procedures*. Modularity or the building block approach is a way of breaking down a functional area into its component parts and of grouping methods and procedures that logically fit together. The capability of bringing together different procedural modules or building blocks that can stand alone greatly reduces the complexity of a system. In turn, modularity will facilitate any modification or updating of a system that may be necessary in the future. Complementary to this is the *Principle of Reliable Methods and Procedures*. Reliability concerns effective methods and procedures that allow for accuracy of data flow.

Integral to the reliability process is the *Principle of Establishing Control Points*. The determination of where standards, such as flexible budgets and production tolerances, are to be controlled is vital to the effective management of a system. The timing for comparing actual results with standards at control points should permit the process to be stopped or altered before serious damage can occur. Managers at the various functional end-user units, accountable for the data flow being controlled, must be identified. Accountability will enhance the effective control of ongoing operations. Tied in with this principle is the *Principle of Provision for Correction*. As incorrect data are detected, correcting methods and procedures are initiated before processing continues. In this manner, not only is the reliability of system methods and procedures maintained, but variances from established norms and standards are detected and corrected before processing can continue.

An important consideration for effective system scheduling is the *Principle of Flexible Schedules*. Because of the ever-changing business environment, it may be necessary to adjust MIS schedules; such changes may or may not be under the MIS manager's control. For example, an equipment malfunction means that alternative processing procedures must be initiated by the MIS manager, whereas unusual organizational growth will require the scheduling of additional processing time. Schedules must be flexible enough to handle expansion or contraction of MIS activities.

To assist in the development of an effective schedule, the *Principle of Eliminating or Reducing Bottlenecks* is required to reduce problems encountered in day-to-day MIS operations. Included is eliminating or minimizing duplication and unnecessary information so that lengthy processing steps are reduced. Use of operational flowcharts and machine load schedules can help disclose bottlenecks. In addition, Gantt charts and PERT/time networks can foresee potential trouble spots before they occur. Because of the importance of these effective scheduling techniques, they are discussed in the first half of the chapter. Related to this is the *Principle of Integrating Inputs Through Outputs*. Effective scheduling should integrate outputs from one functional area to another in a straightforward flow. Such a tie-in may give the MIS manager some insight into simplifying the information flow.

Once the new system is operating on a day-to-day basis, there is need to maintain it over time until it is replaced by a different system. Hence, the *Principle of Maintaining the Integrity of the System* comes into play. That is, the new system must be maintained in such a manner that the system is not compromised by any changes made to it throughout its life. In essence, the system is capable of processing data accurately from the time data are received as input until they are produced as output from the system. Closely tied in with this principle is the *Principle of Maintaining Security over the System*. Too often in the past, maintenance of the system has resulted in poor security which may or may not have been intended. The end result is that data being processed by the system are not as secure as they once were. Overall, the need for data integrity and data security underlies these last two principles, that are linked to maintenance.

RELATIONSHIP OF CURRENT RESEARCH TO SYSTEMS IMPLEMENTATION AND MAINTENANCE

In reference to Chapter 2, several current problems are related to systems implementation and maintenance:

- Lack of proper documentation over standards and procedures (rated no. 2)
- Lack of training programs for new and experienced MIS personnel (rated no. 5)
- Lack of a contingency recovery program (rated no. 7)
- Lack of control over input and/or output data (rated no. 8)
- Lack of control over data center operations (rated no. 11)
- Lack of adherence to established methods and procedures (rated no. 13)

Related to these problems is the fact that systems are repaired only when necessary, they are enhanced only when users clamor for changes, and they are totally replaced only when maintenance costs become prohibitive. Typically, MIS managers defend this maintenance strategy by stating that they want to devote as many resources as possible to new systems developmental projects. With recent tight budgets, this means devoting as little as possible to systems maintenance.

The *lack of proper documentation over standards and procedures* generally makes the systems implementation phase more difficult since last minute changes may be necessary. If the new system is not properly documented, MIS personnel are going to have a difficult time on the floor working with end users. In fact, the success or failure of new systems implementation may hinge on giving out the proper information based on what is perceived to be the proper documentation for everyday methods and procedures. Similarly, if documentation is not done or is poorly done, the task of maintaining the program and its related parts can be very difficult, to say the least. Hence, this important item of documentation impacts not only the implementation of the system, but also its maintenance over time.

Many times, the lack of proper documentation is caused by the *lack of training programs for new and experienced MIS personnel.* Since MIS personnel do not receive the proper training at certain points in their careers, the documentation issue is not given the proper emphasis. Hence, training on better methodologies to assist in better documentation is not given or, if it is given, the documentation issue is sidestepped. This sad state of affairs is caused largely by the fact that MIS managers are pressured by top management and end users to get systems up and running as quickly as possible.

The *lack of a contingency recovery program* is found in many new system installations for a number of reasons. No one thought that this could happen or that its probability was about zero. As will be seen later in the chapter, reference will be made to this problem. More precisely, there should be a provision for alternative plans in case of equipment failure.

Scheduling of MIS operations is related directly to the *lack of control over input and/or output data*. That is, schedules are being changed daily because of the problem of not having the input in the proper format or at the proper time when needed. Similarly, the same can be said about output. Since output for one processing unit becomes input for another, predetermined schedules are not being met. Related to this problem is the *lack of control over data center operations*. If there is poor or little control over day-to-day operations of the data center, production run schedules will not be met and users of selected data will not be receiving the data they need for their new operations. Hence, users will be operating in an inefficient manner.

Additionally, there can be a *lack of adherence to established methods and procedures*. This can be caused by the laziness of MIS personnel, insufficient time to do it properly, or a general disregard for established methods and procedures. This avoidance of following established methods and procedures shows up during systems implementation when end users are given different sets of instructions to follow. Needless to say, end users are confused and wonder about the capability of MIS personnel. In a similar manner, when the system is being maintained, maintenance personnel may interpret the present system to be performing a certain operation when, in reality, it is doing just the reverse. Overall, the general disregard for adhering to established methods and procedures so that MIS personnel can "do their own thing" can be very detrimental to the MIS organization not only in the short run for systems implementation, but also in the long run for systems and program maintenance.

Although none of these problems can be related directly to systems maintenance, each can be tied in indirectly. The lack of proper documentation, for example, leads to longer maintenance time since changes to programs require more time to understand what is currently going on. Similarly, the lack of training programs means that MIS personnel are not being given the proper instruction on new techniques to speed up the programming maintenance process.

EFFECTIVE MIS MANAGEMENT OF SYSTEMS IMPLEMENTATION

The task of systems implementation is generally a major undertaking, especially if a number of functional end-user units are involved. This results in a great need for implementation planning by the MIS manager. A logical starting point for this type of planning involves knowledge of the following areas: personnel needs, programming, documentation, controls, equipment selection, physical requirements, and conversion activities. An understanding of these areas establishes the specific tasks that must be undertaken and the relationship among them. Also, knowledge of the problems and exceptions is needed. This background permits detailed planning of the various tasks that must be incorporated into a schedule with specific deadlines. The scheduling method should follow the natural flow of work to be undertaken. The usual questions of who, what, where, how, and why must be answered in developing the schedule. Implementation planning should include a method for reviewing completed and uncompleted tasks so that it can be a control tool for the entire MIS project. The major steps for MIS management of systems implementation are preparatory work of new MIS and operation of new MIS. These basic elements and their related subcomponents are discussed in the following sections.

PREPARATORY WORK OF NEW MIS

The preparatory work that must be accomplished and managed before the new system can operate on a daily basis includes a number of activities:

- *Select qualified personnel* for systems implementation and the ongoing system operations. The MIS manager has the authority and responsibility for staffing the MIS project team. The management from the functional end-user units select the staff for system operations. If qualified personnel cannot be found within the organization, it may be necessary to train personnel or to look outside.
- *Schedule the installation* in sufficient detail that each important activity can be identified and assigned appropriate starting and completion dates. For complex installations, the use of a PERT network (refer to Chapter 6) is recommended to ensure that the relationships among activities are considered.
- *Train personnel* to operate the new system, complementing formal training with on-the-job training. Management too must have a good grasp of what the MIS is, who can use it, and how to control it. Otherwise, there is great potential for system misuse.
- *Realign personnel* by reassigning personnel prior to conversion to the new system. During systems implementation, both the new and old systems are running in parallel in order to check the new system. Hence, personnel realignment begins on a massive scale when converting the functional areas set forth in the MIS project.
- *Determine physical requirements and alterations* to implement the new system. Alterations may be needed to handle new inputs, data files, and outputs. New methods and procedures may require physical modifications to many departments.
- *Test and accept new equipment* by utilizing manufacturer-supplied diagnostic routines to test the major equipment components. A common method is to use field service programs capable of testing the various hardware components. This method should be supplemented with company-developed tests.
- *Program and test* the computer programs, equipment, methods, and procedures. Development of computer programs that include total quality management was discussed in Chapter 9.
- *Convert files* from one medium to another before programming and testing is completed. Typically, there is a great need for control over data files so that records are not lost.

Many of these activities can take months to complete before moving on to the conversion of the old system to the new one.

Managing Time of Software Development Projects

When referring to the program and test activities mentioned, MIS managers have made two incorrect assumptions about software development: (1) that people and time are interchangeable and (2) that productivity levels are relatively constant for all software projects within the same organization. The *first* assumption is that the development time can be determined arbitrarily by management simply by setting the number of people on the project. For large programs, people and time are not interchangeable. Fred Brooks (past manager of the IBM 360 operating system project) described this phenomenon so graphically that a variant of it has become known as *Brooks' law:* that is, adding people to a late project only makes it later. The reason should be clear. As the number of people on a project increases arithmetically, the number of human interactions increases geometrically. More and more time must be spent on human communication and less and less on productive work. The only way to avoid this inevitability is to reduce the number of people who must interact by stretching out the time. However, reduction should be limited because of risks of personnel turnover and system obsolescence.

MIS managers arrive at the *second* assumption by taking overall productivity figures from previous projects that they think are similar. However, they do not examine closely the precise characteristics of that similarity. An estimate of the total computer program lines of code to be written is divided by the productivity figures to give an effort-year estimate. For example, if a system of 100,000 lines of code is to be completed and that productivity is 2,000 lines of code per effort-year, the development effort is 50 effort-years (100,000 divided by 2,000). Experience shows that productivity is not constant. Rather, it is a complex function of the effort, time, and technology applied to the task. As noted in Chapter 4, function point analysis can be of great assistance to MIS management regarding this second assumption.

OPERATION OF A NEW MIS

Once the computer programs have been written and tested within a TQM environment, considerable work remains to integrate all the components into a successful MIS. Even though the programs have been systems tested, there is no way of knowing that the system will operate correctly without duplicating the actual flow of work with all its exceptions and timing considerations. The best way to ensure that the new system will work is to complete the following activities:

1. Run parallel operations
2. Convert to new MIS
3. Provide for necessary changes
4. Schedule equipment and personnel
5. Develop alternative plans in case of equipment failure

Each of these activities is now described.

1. Run Parallel Operations

Parallel operations consist of feeding both the old and new systems the same input data and comparing files and output results. Despite the fact that the best possible systems testing within a TQM environment was undertaken during the preparatory work phase, related conditions and combinations of conditions that were not envisioned are likely to occur. Last-minute computer program changes are generally necessary to accommodate these new conditions. The systems implementation project team must keep the entire organization informed about parallel operations and other conversion activities. This can be accomplished by a series of bulletins which start at the inception of the MIS project. Department personnel should be informed when systems implementation is to start and what specific activities will be required of them. Department heads should be informed before the actual date of conversion activities so that potential problems can be identified and corrected. The time spent instructing personnel on parallel operations or conversion activities is well worth it.

When implementing an interactive MIS, the process of running dual operations for both new and old systems is more difficult than for a comparable batch-processing system. The problem is that the new system has no true counterpart in the old system. One procedure for testing the new interactive system is to have several input/output terminals connected on-line and to have them operated by supervised personnel who are backed up by other personnel operating the old system. The outputs are checked for compatibility and appropriate corrections are made to the on-line computer programs. Once this segment of the new system has proved satisfactory, the entire terminal network can be placed into operation for this one area. Additional sections of the system can be added by testing in this manner until all programs are operational.

2. Convert to New MIS

After data files have been converted and the new system's reliability has been proved for a given functional area, daily processing can be shifted from the existing system to the new one. A *cutoff point* is established so that all files and other data requirements can be updated to the cutover point. All transactions initiated after this time are processed on the new system. The systems implementation team should be available to assist and answer any questions that might develop. The old system should be operated for a little longer in case of new system failure during conversion.

3. Provide for Necessary Changes

Both programming and operational procedures should be completely documented for the new system before any parallel or conversion activities can start. Information on inputs, files, methods, procedures, outputs, and internal controls must be set forth in clear, concise, and understandable terms for end users. Written operating procedures must be supplemented by oral communication during training sessions; many more questions will arise during the conversion activities. Having qualified MIS personnel in the conversion area to communicate and coordinate new developments as they occur is a must. Likewise, revisions to operating procedures should be issued as quickly as possible.

Once the new MIS has been completely converted, the systems implementation team should check with all supervisory personnel about their respective areas. As with every new installation, minor adjustments can be expected. The system as initially designed should be flexible enough to accommodate the changes. Channels of communication should be open between the systems implementation team and all supervisory personnel so that modifications can be initiated as conditions change. There is no need to get locked into a rigid system when it would be more beneficial to make necessary changes.

4. Schedule Equipment and Personnel

Schedules should be set up by the MIS manager in conjunction with the end-user department managers serviced by the equipment. The master schedule for next month should provide sufficient computer time to handle production runs that occur daily, weekly, semimonthly, monthly, or on some other periodic basis. Daily schedules should be prepared in accordance with the master schedule and should include time for reruns (if necessary), program compiling and testing, special nonrecurring reports, and other programs. In all cases, the schedules should be as realistic as possible.

Just as the equipment must be scheduled for maximum use, so must operators. It is imperative that personnel who enter input data and handle output data be included in the data processing schedule. Otherwise, data may not be available when the equipment needs them for processing. Effective supervision of personnel enhances compliance with established procedures and scheduled deadlines. This important area of scheduling and its techniques will be covered in the next section.

5. Develop Alternative Plans in Case of Equipment Failure

Alternative processing plans must be employed in case of equipment failure. It does not matter who or what caused it; the fact is that the system is down. Priority must be given to critical jobs, such as billing, payroll, and inventory. Critical jobs can be performed manually until the equipment is functioning again. For obvious reasons, the preferred method is using identical equipment at another location. The failure of an interactive system for any length of time may mean loss of data for certain areas, such as inventory and sales analysis. There is not sufficient time to enter all the information that is necessary to update the files, say for one week. This amounts to establishing a cutoff date and starting from there.

Documentation of alternative plans in case of equipment failure is the responsibility of the MIS manager and should be part of the organization's systems and procedures manual. It should state explicitly what the critical jobs are, how they are to be handled in case of equipment failure (use identical equipment at another location, manual methods, or some other data processing method), where compatible equipment (including service bureaus) is located, who will be responsible for each during downtime, and what deadlines must be met during the emergency. A written manual of procedures will help expedite the unfortunate situation. Otherwise, panic conditions will cause the least efficient method to be employed when time is of the essence.

TECHNIQUES TO ASSIST IN SCHEDULING MIS OPERATIONS

If the MIS manager is to have effective control over MIS processing, specialized scheduling techniques are greatly needed, specifically operational flowcharts detailing the essential on- and off-line processing operations. In turn, they provide a logical basis for preparing machine-load schedules. Both of these scheduling techniques are discussed.

Operational Flowchart

An operational flowchart breaks down a system into its required clerical and equipment steps. An estimated or standard time factor is affixed for each one. Figure 10.1 depicts the flow of cash receipts to the master accounts receivable file and includes the time element: that is, data-entry equipment time (0.8 hour), data verification time (0.3 hour), and computer time (0.2 hour). While data-entry and verification processing times are generally determined without much difficulty, computer processing time is more of a problem. Processing time by a computer is affected by the equipment features, input/output capabilities, database organization, and amount of multitasking between batch and interactive tasks. Additionally, elapsed processing is affected by the input/output channel

Figure 10.1
An Operational Flowchart Showing the Flow of Cash Receipts from Customer Through Subsequent Processing

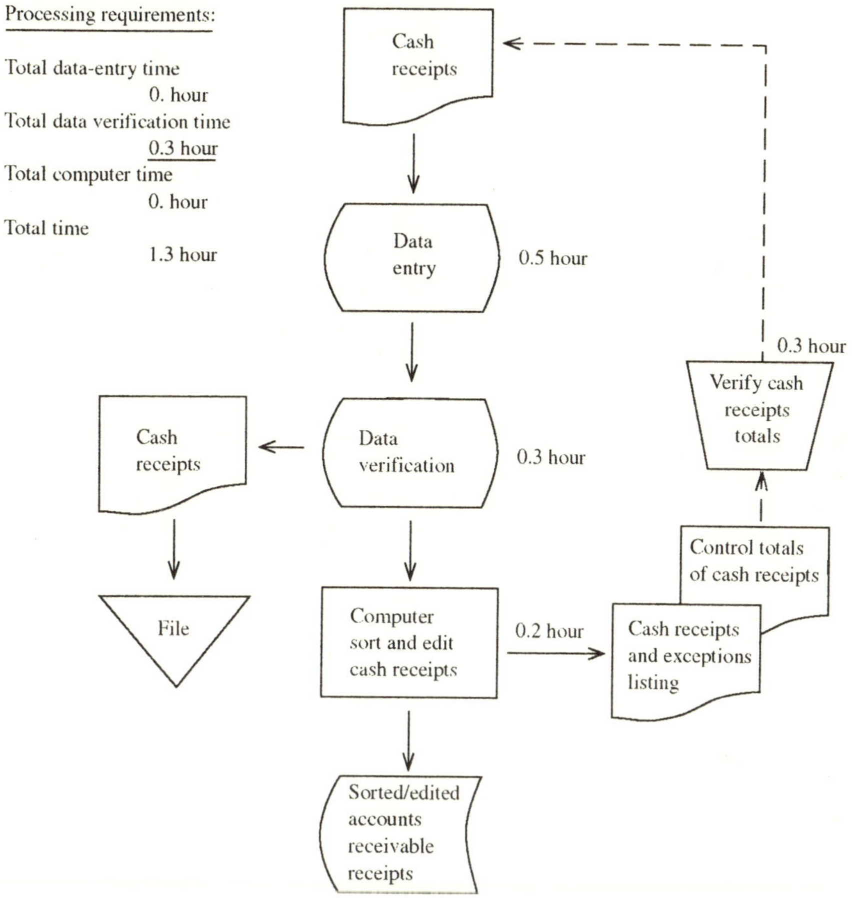

and controller delays, among other factors. Other delays can arise during processing; the printer may run out of paper or an incorrect tape or disk be mounted. Despite these problems, the operational flowchart does provide a method for relating steps and procedures logically, giving the MIS manager a means for analyzing and determining the required resource requirements in a specific MIS area.

Machine-Load Schedule

To assist in the scheduling of equipment operations, a machine-load schedule can be prepared (refer to Figure 10.2). For each category of equipment utilized,

Figure 10.2
A Typical Machine-Load Schedule Worksheet

Machine-Load Schedule Worksheet

MIS Appl. Number	Scheculed Operation	Oper. No.	Machine Used	Estimated Volume	Estimated Process Time	Due In		Due Out		Comment
						Day	Time	Day	Time	
A/R - 1	Posting sales	1	Computer	15,000	0.75 hr.	4/1	8:00	4/1	8:45	
I/C -3	Posting inventory	2	Computer	22,000	1.25 hr.	4/1	8:45	4/1	10:00	
A/R - 4	Editing cash	3	Computer	8,000	0.50 hr.	4/1	10:00	4/1	10:30	

a separate schedule must be developed. Although the illustrated example identifies the start of computer operations for a particular day, it can be expanded to cover more time. When developing a machine-load schedule, the MIS manager considers due-in and due-out requirements, priorities, and conflicts among the various processing runs. All equipment schedules must be reconciled before any can be finalized. Many times, there may be need to reschedule certain processing for more efficient operations.

FEEDBACK ON SCHEDULING

An important part of the scheduling process is *feedback* on the MIS manager's schedule. Once a system has been implemented, the operational flowchart and machine-load schedule approaches determine and schedule daily operations, respectively. Because environmental factors from inside and outside the organization do not remain static, feedback on scheduling MIS operations is needed. Work loads increase, current processing objectives cannot be met, priorities of scheduled activities change, and interaction of new systems with end-user activities, and the like, affect present MIS activities. Needless to say, these factors dramatically impact personnel and equipment scheduling over time. The effects of these changing conditions must be detected, identified, and analyzed before appropriate corrective action can be taken.

Feedback to the MIS manager can take several forms: oral, written, and statistical reports. The *oral* form of communication is widely used by operational personnel inside and outside the MIS structure. When report deadlines are missed, processing is behind schedule, and like items are causing difficulties, the MIS manager will hear about these problems immediately. In a somewhat different manner, most of the feedback on system activities, such as new system studies, development of systems, programming projects, and training of new personnel, is obtained from daily and/or weekly *written* reports.

Ultimately, oral and written reports become integral parts of *statistical* analyses. Some analyses summarize overall equipment use and breakdown by activities; these become the basis to account for total equipment utilization for charging the respective user departments. In addition, statistics can be compiled on computer reruns and productivity of computer mainframes. Overall, many statistical figures can be compiled as essential feedback to the MIS manager on critical clerical, personnel, systems, and equipment activities. The attendant circumstances will dictate which ones are best suited for effective feedback.

PERIODIC REVIEW OF NEW SYSTEM APPROACHES

After the new MIS is installed and operating as originally intended, the MIS manager and end users should review the tangible and intangible benefits set forth in the exploratory survey report. The purpose of such a review is to verify that these benefits are, in fact, being achieved. Discussions with managers of functional end-user departments will determine how well the new MIS is performing. Tangible benefits, such as clerical reduction and lower inventory, and intangible benefits of improved customer service and more managerial information are open to constructive criticism. Typical comments will be along the following lines: certain areas have been improved significantly, some are about the same, and others are not as good as before. The task of the MIS department, then, is to make the necessary adjustments to accomplish the quantitative and qualitative goals of the exploratory survey report. It may take from several months up to one year or more to effect the changes, which may include reprogramming the most frequently used programs for greater efficiency.

Over time, the work load of the MIS increases. Factors that were not previously problems can become significant. Can the equipment run longer hours or should additional equipment be obtained? Can methods and procedures be modified to reduce processing time and cost? Can noncritical processing be shifted to another time? How does the time differential affect the staffing of a system operating throughout the United States? Answers to these questions must be evaluated by the MIS manager and his or her staff through a periodic review of the system. The ultimate aim of such an investigation is system improvements. In essence, it may be necessary to undertake a new feasibility study periodically in order to devise a new system for changed operating conditions.

Future Direction in MIS Improvements

As discussed in Chapter 1, there are a number of newer approaches to management information systems. These include electronic data interchange systems, decision support systems (including a group perspective), and executive information systems, as well as the latest in MIS centers on expert systems, neural networks, and idea processing systems. In all cases, these MIS improvements are useful in leveraging information technology for the betterment of the total organization. Hence, MIS management should review periodically the need for these systems since end users may not take the lead in supporting a move to implement them. It is recommended that MIS management use the MIS organizationwide committee as a vehicle for moving to newer information technology and systems that will better meet the needs of the organization and its customers.

EFFECTIVE MIS MANAGEMENT OF SYSTEMS AND PROGRAM MAINTENANCE

In the past, MIS managers have felt trapped by a number of older systems and hundreds (or even thousands) of older application programs and data files that they would like to replace. But with a backlog of perhaps two or more years' worth of new MIS projects already in the queue, they see no way of replacing these systems and/or programs. Until recently, there have been few choices for dealing creatively with these systems and programs. In general, organizations could replace an older system with a package or totally rewrite it in a procedural language, such as COBOL. Today, there are several other alternatives, made possible by the new tools, new programming languages, and new development techniques. Fourth-generation languages, application and program generators, and application packages now make improvement or replacement of many older applications possible and practical.

In this section, specific approaches to reengineering for dealing with present systems, ranging from internal restructuring through complete replacement with new programs, are examined. This is particularly important since maintenance budgets have been slashed, the number of maintenance staffs has been reduced, and maintenance work loads remain about the same. Initially, there is a discussion of the important factors to consider when deciding whether to continue maintenance or to redesign.

Continue Maintenance Versus Redesign

A critical issue today in the area of reengineering are the costs and benefits of continuing to maintain software that has become error-prone, ineffective, and costly. Although there are no absolute rules for when to rebuild rather than maintain an existing system, some of the factors to consider are (1) code that is more than eight years old, (2) overly complex program structure and logic, (3) frequency of failures, (4) code written for outdated hardware, (5) a system that is run in an emulation mode, (6) very large modules or unit subroutines, (7) excessive resource requirements, (8) difficulty in keeping maintenance personnel, (9) missing or incomplete design specifications, and (10) poor documentation.

Today, it is generally recognized that the estimated life cycle of a major application is seven to ten years, although fifteen-year-old software systems are not uncommon. Software typically deteriorates with age since it is repeatedly fixed and patched. However, if a system is designed in a systematic manner and if maintenance is performed carefully and documented by established standards and guidelines, all of which utilize a TQM approach, the system may run efficiently and effectively for many years.

Currently, as in the past, COBOL is the world's most popular business programming language and is the primary or secondary language in most IBM and IBM-compatible mainframe sites. The rationale for its popularity is that it lets programmers express computational and business procedures in English-like statements. COBOL has a somewhat bad reputation because old COBOL programs are slow, difficult to maintain, inflexible, and nonportable. As of June 1994, IBM no longer supports older versions of ANSI 74 COBOL. Those older versions may be dying, but not without a fight. An organization can spend up to $1 million to upgrade thousands of old programs from ANSI 74 COBOL to ANSI 85 COBOL. Is the cost worth it? The answer is yes.

Most MIS departments have found that newer COBOL products are significantly better than the old. Replacing obsolete versions of COBOL is a business opportunity for most organizations, not just for IBM. Converting ANSI 74 applications to ANSI 85 actually primes the pump for reengineering. Generally, users report productivity gains and cost savings by moving COBOL application development to PCs and workstations. They found that while migration is difficult and expensive, in the long run it is worth it. Not only is COBOL development and testing cheaper on a workstation or a networked microcomputer, it is more productive.

Staffing the Maintenance Function

Typically, software maintenance is viewed as unappreciated work by the programming staff since the work produces little motivation or satisfaction. In the past, junior programmers have been placed in maintenance. Those with demonstrated ability are quickly promoted to new MIS developmental projects. From this perspective, maintenance programming is an undesirable task for programmers. In reality, it should be done by the more highly skilled programmers. It is the more skilled maintenance programmers who can give the most objective and thorough evaluation of a developmental effort. They are aware of the limitations and the errors in design and coding.

An effective software approach to program maintenance is to rotate assignments between development and maintenance. One approach in the rotation of programmers is the maintenance liaison. That is, at least one person accompanies a new system as it is transferred from development to maintenance. In effect, the developmental history is not lost. In addition, this allows one or more maintenance programmers to be rotated to new MIS development.

APPROACHES TO REENGINEERING

Approaches to maintaining present systems are often referred to as *reengineering software development:* that is, there is need to go back and redo what has been done previously. They are:

1. Rewrite the system
2. Restructure the system
3. Refurbish the system
4. Rejuvenate the system
5. Replace the system with a purchased package

All of these approaches to reengineering are now discussed.

1. Rewrite the System

The basic approach to reengineering is to change part or all of the system code to reflect changes that may be caused by changing governmental regulations, labor contracts, introduction of new products and services, and the like. In other cases, the current system may be too far gone to rescue. If the code is convoluted and patched, if the information technology is antiquated, and if the design is poor, it may be necessary to start anew. The thought of rewriting a large system in a traditional procedural language is often discouraging because of the large amount of resources it will require. However, the newer development approaches noted in the previous chapter offer some promise to minimize the task.

As set forth in Chapter 9, iterative systems development generally merges prototyping and newer development methods. Typically, prototyping is very helpful to finalize system requirements, end-user interfaces, and difficult modules. Once these portions of the system have been created and tested, the development life cycle is used to build the production version. In some cases, the prototype becomes the production system.

A very big problem facing maintenance programmers in rebuilding old applications arises when they try to deduce the business requirements embodied in the code. If the business requirements can be recovered from existing systems, albeit not perfectly, then an organization can leverage its existing software investment into new applications. Generally tools like Index Technology's Design Recovery can fulfill this need. However, if all these old applications are so inefficient and laden with redundant or inoperative code, what is the point in rebuilding them? There is need to start anew from scratch. Hence, applications that are analyzed are not always destined for reengineering but should be started again. The key is to help understand the current software investment and how to help adjust it to new requirements. While some old applications need only a few modifications, others must be replaced altogether once their underlying business functions are fully analyzed and understood.

2. Restructure the System

If a system or an application is doing the job it was intended to do, it may not need much change in input/output, function, or data handling. Yet it may run inefficiently or be unmaintainable by current maintenance personnel. In such cases, the system should be restructured. Several vendors have begun offering software products to aid in this process. Such a package restructures the code in the system, thereby making it easier to maintain. Essentially, the structured retrofit uses automated tools to turn running "spaghetti code" into more structured code.

Typically, the process involves several steps. The *first* is to evaluate the amount of structure in the current system (number of layers of nesting, degree of complexity, breakout of verb utilization, and failure analysis). It presents a trace of the program's control logic and represents the technical analysis of the code. A subjective evaluation of the code that is made by people and not by machines is then necessary. The *second* step is to compile the program, to be sure it is in working order. Structured retrofit will not make a nonoperational program run. *Third,* the program is run through a structuring engine which cleans up and restructures the code, following structured programming concepts. It should be noted that this automated process does not change the logic of the program, but rather replaces poor coding conventions with structured coding conventions. Basically, it reduces the number of GOTOs, removes dead code and ALTER statements, highlights looping conditions, isolates the control hierarchy, and so forth. Also, it uncovers structure that is hidden inside convoluted code.

In step *four,* a formatting package is used to reformat the listing to make it easier for programmers to understand. *Fifth,* a file-to-file comparator package is used to compare the old and new versions in order to be sure that they produce the same output. And *sixth,* an object code optimizer package is used to minimize overhead introduced by structured retrofitting. After optimization, vendors have reported that structured retrofitted programs require between 5 percent and 10 percent more run time than unstructured versions. A *seventh* step, which is optional, is to "rationalize" the data, by giving all uses of the same data one data name. In summary, restructuring can be an important option for improving systems when they need to be cleaned up without major revisions.

3. Refurbish the System

Although the present system is maintainable and causing no major problems, it may be worthwhile to add some extensions. Some valuable extensions would be those that make it easier to supply the necessary input, use the output, or allow the program to deal with data in a more comprehensive way. There are several ways that a system can be extended by using a fourth-generation language. They focus on (1) input, (2) data manipulation, (3) query, and (4) output processes.

In terms of the input process, a front end can be added by using a fourth-generation language. To accomplish this, a database is created with the new language's database management system, using fields from the present files as well as adding new ones. From that point on, all source data flow into the new database. This approach allows validation routines to be added to check on the input data. To integrate this new database with the present system and its data files, a routine is written to pass the necessary data to the original system in the format it requires. By adding this front end, users have a more convenient way to enter transactions into the present system. In a similar manner, data manipulation capabilities, on-line query capabilities, and report generation can be extended such that the system is refurbished. All of these extensions are based on the database management and programming capabilities of fourth-generation languages.

4. Rejuvenate the System

Typically, rejuvenating a system does more than just clean up the code or add features to enhance usability of the system. That is, rejuvenation adds enough function so that the system has more value to the organization. The process for achieving system rejuvenation has these distinct phases whereby each builds on the previous one. In the *first* phase, there is need to recognize the value of the present system. One or more present systems may provide the foundation for one or more future systems that have or had strategic value for the organization. For example, a company's payroll system could be upgraded to a human resource management system whereby the company could offer employees not one fixed set of fringe benefits, but a choice of several benefits options. Employees may then choose the benefits that they prefer. If the system were able to support this type of plan, it could have strategic value to the company in attracting and retaining high-quality employees. Another reason to consider rejuvenating present systems is to increase the organization's flexibility to change with the times. This capability increases the organization's ability to compete in a rapidly changing business world.

Once it has been determined to build new strategic systems around current systems, the existing systems need to be cleaned up so that they can provide a stable base for enhancements. Essentially, this is the *second* phase. Some systems are so unmaintainable that MIS management is afraid to touch them for fear that they will "blow up." A starting point in the cleanup effort is evaluating the maintainability of the system. One approach is to run the program through a code evaluator, similar to the software tool described for structured retrofitting.

In the *third* phase, the focus is on making the cleaned-up system not only more efficient, but more effective. There are several ways to improve system efficiency, such as moving it to a newer operating system; updating the file structure; redesigning parts of the system; rewriting some of the most often used, most inefficient, and most convoluted modules; and introducing newer information technologies. In the *fourth* and last phase, once the present system is maintainable and is operating more efficiently, it can be extended to perform the strategic functions stated for the first phase. At this point, the benefits of rejuvenation accrue to the entire organization and not just to the MIS department. Typically, executives find the idea of rejuvenating a system very appealing since it will make the system more responsive in meeting customer and organization needs. As noted previously in the text, the focus of strategic systems using newer information technology is to give an organization a competitive advantage as well as make its organization personnel more productive.

5. Replace the System with a Purchased Package

Another popular approach is to replace the system with a purchased package. One important reason for choosing a purchased package is to move a present application to a new operating environment. An organization might want to distribute an application work load among a host computer, a local area network, and a number of PCs. There are an increasing number of commercial packages that provide the links among the computers in such a hierarchy. These packages not only support communication among different types of machines, but permit downloading and uploading of files in many cases. Another reason to replace a present system with a commercial package is that these products are becoming more versatile. Many offer selectable features that allow purchasers to tailor the package to the way they operate their business. These options may be turned off or on by using control files so that little or no programming is necessary. Even end users have the capability to specify some of the operating instructions.

ESTIMATING TIME FOR PROGRAM MAINTENANCE

A most challenging task for the typical MIS manager is estimating the amount of time and money a program maintenance project will take. Project leaders often try to impress MIS managers by making intuitive estimates, that is, pulling numbers out of the air. Only when a project is still incomplete months later does anyone challenge the estimate. A project leader might blame a number of factors, ranging from the maintenance programmers, end users, and computer operations to the documentation, but certainly not himself or herself, for the project overrun. Hence, the task of estimating time requirements for maintenance projects seems to be especially troublesome. While MIS managers' estimates for the planned changes involved in new MIS projects are somewhat uneven, estimates for the unplanned changes of maintenance projects are generally poor.

Typically, in the past, MIS managers have used a historical approach in which they compared the current project to past projects and estimated the time and money required. But experience shows that MIS managers need more than historical evidence to estimate a maintenance project accurately; they need to know more about the program, the programmer, the user, and the nature of the request. Thus, a method is needed to assist MIS managers in doing a good job of estimation. Reference can be made to Chapter 4, where function point analysis was used in developing accurate times for new MIS projects. In a similar manner, appropriate values can be developed for basic maintenance elements along with complexity and familiarity factors to obtain total project manpower estimates. Needless to say, accuracy in estimating maintenance projects will improve over time.

GUIDELINES TO ASSIST MIS MANAGEMENT IN SYSTEMS IMPLEMENTATION AND MAINTENANCE

For successful systems implementation, a *first* guideline for MIS management to use revolves around detailed planning of all conversion activities. A high-quality project plan should include a description of the methodology, a functional description of conversion tools, schedules, checkpoints, hardware and software configurations, investments, user training, and staffing requirements. An effective plan should also identify potential problems posed by incompatibilities between the chosen conversion tools and the migrating material. These are the glitches that can cause nightmares in a conversion schedule if unanticipated, or worse, unrecognized at occurrence. With all its varied content, the systems implementation plan is a means for finding the glitches before they happen. Overall, the plan should represent a proactive approach to systems implementation.

A *second* guideline relates to the way MIS management supervises and rewards organization personnel involved in systems implementation. Typically, organization personnel involved in a systems conversion perceive their jobs as a set of duties and responsibilities, with job performance measured in terms of the effectiveness and efficiency with which those duties are carried out. However, within the confines of a management-by-objectives (MBO) program, they participate in the definition of the goals and objectives of the job while the how of achieving those objectives is left, for the most part, to their discretion. Job performance is measured by the progress made toward achieving those set goals. The emphasis shifts from functions to objectives. Fundamentally, management by objectives is a method by which organization members jointly establish the organization's goals. Each member, with assistance from his or her superior, defines his or her area of responsibility and sets objectives that state expected results clearly. The persons involved develop organization performance measures that are guides for managing and serve as standards for evaluation. MBO has four steps: (1) set objectives, (2) develop action plans, (3) conduct periodic reviews, and (4) appraise annual performance. The success of management by objectives, then, is due to the ability of MIS management and staff to convert organization objectives into personal goals.

In the area of maintenance, a *third* guideline for MIS management to follow is to develop a training program specifically for this area. Typically, training is thought of almost exclusively in terms of development of new systems. Also, though it is accepted that some sort of apprenticeship is a prerequisite to becoming a developer, there is an inexplicable assumption that MIS staff members become adept at maintenance as soon as they are assigned the title. The MIS trainer who is faced with creating a curriculum that addresses both development of new systems and their maintenance must acknowledge the differences between the two activities and understand their similarities as well. It is recommended that the MIS trainer not only customize development courses, but also create maintenance courses. In customizing development courses, it is feasible to break them down into parts and tailor the parts to reflect maintenance within the framework of standards, procedures, and existing systems. Thus, the MIS trainer, with the help of some experienced maintenance programmers, is capable of creating canned scenarios of authentic maintenance situations relating to existing systems. At a minimum, this approach would teach familiarity with tools and techniques and provide readiness training for the real situations.

A *fourth* guideline to ease the maintenance problem is the use of application generators and fourth-generation languages. Application generators/fourth-generation languages ease maintenance in several areas and help eliminate corrective modifications because their code generators produce error-free code. Enhancement modifications are much easier to perform on systems generated with application generators/fourth-generation languages. They are readily extensible because enhancements only involve changing the system specifications, not the source code. Adaptive maintenance will surely benefit from the use of application generators/fourth-generation languages. Because all of the environmentally dependent routines are in the application generators/fourth-generation languages, system specifications can be moved to other environments in which the unmodified application generators/fourth-generation languages also have been implemented. By using application generators/fourth-generation languages, systems analysts and programmers are forced to conform to a standard methodology, thereby making specifications easy to verify. Documentation which will provide further assistance toward enhancing the maintainer's ability to understand the system can also be automatically generated.

A *fifth* guideline refers to minimizing modifications by making quality corrections. The quick fix is a most structurally detrimental practice. The most prolific quick fixers are developers, who want to solve the problem as fast as possible so they can get back to developmental tasks. But patches, especially when they are piled on top of other patches, create unstable systems that can never be the bases for progress. There is a maintenance principle that bug fixes beget bugs. Every time there is a program modification, there is a good chance of introducing more bugs. Most often, this is because corrective modifications are made hastily and in no particular order. Thus, an effort needs to be made so that quality corrections are made. Thoughtfully implemented modifications are bound to have fewer errors. It is a widely acknowledged fact that by fixing the most troublesome problems first, many more future problems are prevented.

Some experts suggest that by correcting the worst 20 percent of any code, 80 percent of future problems are also corrected.

A *sixth* guideline for MIS management to employ is to improve existing documentation on existing systems for ease of maintenance. According to some estimates, maintenance programmers spend about half of their time attempting to understand the documentation and the logic of programs. This is such an overwhelming problem that most large organizations have applications supported by specialists because only they understand the applications' logic. Essentially, documentation is one of the most important tools to assist programmers in understanding and maintaining a system. Any effort by the MIS manager to improve system and program documentation can only yield benefits to the MIS department.

11

End-User Computing

OUTLINE

Introduction to Effective End-User Computing
Principles of Effective End-User Computing
Relationship of Current Research to End-User Computing
Effective MIS Management of End-User Computing
  Encourage End Users to Leverage Information Technology
An Effective End-User Approach to Acquire and Leverage Information Technology
  Hardware Considerations
  Software Considerations
  Database Considerations
  Data Communications Considerations
  Maintaining a Well-Equipped Help Desk
Training and Education of End Users in Leveraging Information Technology
  Standards Considerations
  Training Considerations
  Education Considerations
  Consulting Considerations
End-User Systems Development Life Cycle
  1. Define System Requirements
  2. Design System and Determine Data Requirements
  3. Prototype to Finalize System
  4. Fulfill TQM Requirements
  5. Document and Train End Users
Workflow Useful in Automating MIS
  Workflow Software
Document Management Found in Automating MIS
  Document Management Software
Guidelines to Assist MIS Management in End-User Computing

INTRODUCTION TO EFFECTIVE END-USER COMPUTING

The previous two chapters have focused on an effective MIS approach to developing, implementing, and maintaining all types of management information systems. This chapter expands these areas by referencing end-user activities when interfacing with information technology. Essentially, end-user computing is the direct, hands-on use of computers by end users. They include executives, functional managers, professional staff, secretaries, office workers, and salespeople. An integral part of end-user computing is end-user programming. Here, end users create procedures that they store and use over and over. For example, they can build a spreadsheet with Lotus 1-2-3 or Excel. End-user computing and the development of systems that include programming generally take place mostly at the lower levels of the organization, namely, the department, work group, and individual levels.

In light of these facts underlying end-user computing, this chapter ties in with the previous chapters, but there is also a thorough discussion of end-user activities and what influence MIS management has over these activities. If MIS management fails to exert some influence over end-user computing activities, many of the problems set forth in Chapter 2 will be cropping up again in the functional end-user units. As will be discussed in the chapter, the MIS department and functional end-user departments need to be "marching to the same beat." Failure of the MIS manager to exert some leadership could result in a massive misuse of organization dollars for information technology.

PRINCIPLES OF EFFECTIVE END-USER COMPUTING

The *Principle of Making Information Technology Readily Available to End Users* relates to ensuring a wide range of information technology is made available to them. Generally, this can be accomplished effectively through information centers set up in functional end-user departments. These centers (as noted in Chapter 5) are an integral part of end-user units and, as an integral part of such departments, are better equipped to meet specific end-user needs versus a generalized information center serving many functional end-user departments. Thus, the resources of MIS personnel are better utilized to serve specific end-user requirements.

Tied in with this first principle is the *Principle of Training and Educating End Users in Utilizing Information Technology*. End users cannot be expected to know about leading-edge information technology. Hence, it is up to the functional end-user information centers to disseminate such information to end users through formal or informal training and education. In turn, end users are expected to make requests to the information centers for implementing the latest information technology that impacts their functional areas. Essentially, there is a joint effort between the functional end-user information centers and end users for making operations more efficient and, if possible, making end users more effective. In other words, information technology is being leveraged for the benefit of the functional units as well as the entire organization.

Making specialized knowledge about information technology available to end users is related to the *Principle of Facilitating the End User's Work Flow*. Not only should such information make the end user's job easier, it should also encourage the individual to seek new and better work-related solutions. Because data are widely dispersed in a typical organization, end users may need to access specific information. In turn, the information facilitates the work flow of ongoing information processing operations.

To facilitate the end-user's work flow, the *Principle of the End-User Development Life Cycle* applies. That is, end users need to follow an established methodology. Typically, these steps of the methodology (refer to the five steps given later in the chapter) are contained in an MIS guidebook or manual which is found in the functional end-user information centers scattered throughout the organization. The following of these steps assures that the final system will be a high-quality one not only for the end user, but also for other possible end users.

An often overlooked principle is the *Principle of Facilitating the End User's Thought Processes*. Because end users are interested in more than processing data in an efficient manner, they have great interest in information technology that assists in facilitating their thought processes. That is, the focus is helping the typical end user in solving a wide range of problems that are readily solvable by the computer. Because each problem must be solved from a different perspective, appropriate software can be used to help the individual follow the problem logic for a solution.

A most important principle related to the end user is the *Principle of Holding the End User Responsible and Accountable for Using Information Technology*. Too often in the past, end users have employed information technology with little concern for the security and quality issues that are so important today. However, this situation can be overcome, as noted, by having information centers located in the functional end-user departments. That is, end users can be given adequate training about security and quality issues that govern the proper utilization of information technology. In turn, MIS personnel from these specialized information centers can make random checks to ensure that end users are taking full responsibility for control over their PCs and databases. This periodic audit function by the functional end-user information centers will highlight for end users where improvements can be made such that they will be fully accountable for breaches of security and lapses of quality in their applications.

RELATIONSHIP OF CURRENT RESEARCH TO END-USER COMPUTING

In the list of current problems facing MIS management (refer to Figure 2.4), three are tied in with end-user computing activities:

- Lack of proper documentation over standards and procedures (rated no. 2)
- Lack of adherence to established methods and procedures (rated no. 13)
- Lack of control over information centers (rated no. 15)

As noted later, many of these problems of the MIS department are now being found in end-user activities.

The problems of *lack of proper documentation over standards and procedures* and the *lack of adherence to established methods and procedures* are now showing up in the functional end-user departments. What has been going on over the years in terms of the MIS department is now appearing full force at all levels of end-user activities. In fact, these problems are now or are becoming pervasive throughout many organizations whether they be small, medium, or large. These problems are related to the *lack of control over information centers* by the MIS department. However, with the relocation of information centers in the functional end-user departments, the MIS department is in a better position to meet the specialized needs of a specific end-user department, versus using a generalized approach which has been around since the inception of information centers. Overall, functional end-user information centers have the capability of not only educating end users about the need for utilizing good documentation and established methods and procedures, but also evaluating end users in terms of the proper methodologies to develop and implement newer systems in their areas and ensure data security and data integrity when utilizing these systems.

EFFECTIVE MIS MANAGEMENT OF END-USER COMPUTING

The important message to be found in the following exposition on end-user activities is that end-user computing can easily overwhelm the MIS department unless the department is prepared for it. Essentially, end users' demand for services and support can far exceed what an MIS department can provide. Allocation of resources for management information systems and end-user activities has become a major question facing MIS management. Typically, end users of PCs are doing their own thing, thereby bypassing the MIS department. Because growth in number and use of PCs has been tremendous in most organizations, MIS management is scrambling to make this new PC environment work. From this perspective, the MIS manager is basically *reactive* to end users utilizing information technology.

Encourage End Users to Leverage Information Technology

From a more proactive and aggressive viewpoint, MIS management needs to identify high-value applications that can make a noticeable impact on the success of the organization. This can be accomplished by having functional end-user departmental information-center consultants work with end users not only to identify these key-impact applications, but also to be involved in their development, as described in the discussion of the end-user system systems development life cycle. Hence, a *proactive* approach is needed to assist end users in leveraging information technology that really impacts an organization not only in improving its competitiveness, but also in giving end users information they need to improve the effectiveness of their functional units. Typically, MIS management seems to be preoccupied with making end-user computing work smoothly. That is, they are more concerned with the proliferation of incompatible PCs and limiting access to corporate data by untrained end users. Much of their concern centers on how to control end-user computing. A more important objective is to get end users to seek high-leverage uses of computing. If end users accept this objective, then the problems of incompatible hardware and software, data integrity and security, and data communications and networking will be easier to solve. In order to leverage an organization's information technology to its fullest, end-user computing needs to be tied more closely to the needs of the business function. The high-leverage uses are then tied to activities that help functional managers and operating personnel perform their jobs more *efficiently*. In turn, MIS managers can expect over time that end users will develop more ways to use their PCs and access to computer mainframes for improving the *effectiveness* of the organization in reaching its objectives and goals since it will be a part of the organization's corporate culture. That is, this is how things are done around here to leverage information technology.

AN EFFECTIVE END-USER APPROACH TO ACQUIRE AND LEVERAGE INFORMATION TECHNOLOGY

A recurring theme throughout the text is that end-user computing continues to expand. Typically, the computing power concentrated in the hands of non-MIS professionals exceeds that of the MIS department. Ratios of 2:1, 3:1, and 4:1 are common. This is the rationale for establishing information centers in end-user functional units. However, in the process of this attempt to exercise more control over organizationwide computing activities, important hardware and software issues need to be addressed and resolved as far as possible by the MIS manager. Hence, the MIS manager needs to take a realistic approach to end users in acquiring and leveraging information technology. In addition, this includes considerations for databases and data communications. Each of these areas is explored here. It should be noted that hardware and software were the subject matter of Chapter 7, while databases and data communications were set forth in Chapter 8 from the standpoint of the MIS department and not from an end-user perspective.

Hardware Considerations

Regarding the hardware issue, MIS management in the past has often found that there were a variety of PCs in use. Prior to the IBM PC, there was little compatibility among the different brands of PCs for exchanging data, text, or programs. As a result, establishing suitable data communications between a variety of micros and an organization's mainframe computers was a serious problem. The emergence of the IBM PC, however, as the ad hoc standard helped in resolving the compatibility problem. The emergence of the Apple MacIntosh as a standard has also helped.

Currently, vendors are taking an interesting approach to assist both end users and software developers with some compatibility problems. They offer an intermediate level of software, between the operating system and application programs, called "window managers" or "operating environments." These packages allow users to run different application packages under them. When activated, each application is displayed in a different area of the screen (a window) and information can be moved among windows. Not only does window management software allow use of multiple packages simultaneously, but also it may alleviate some compatibility problems of PCs. If the window manager runs on a plug-compatible machine, then application software designed to run under it is likely to run on that machine also.

Many in MIS management see the IBM PC and its look-alikes along with the Apple MacIntosh as the workstations of the future. The IBM PC is a relatively "open" system that other suppliers can copy where innovative product development is stimulated. As long as there is an open environment in which competitors can maneuver, such de facto standards are healthy. The typical organization can reap benefits from these developments.

Software Considerations

A most important software consideration is who will develop the application. One criterion for deciding whether end users should develop certain applications is the sensitivity of the application. This refers to the potential exposure to fraud or the disclosure of important information to unauthorized persons. Auditors have traditionally recommended the separation of duties to reduce the risk of loss for accounting and financial transactions. This means separating those employees who authorize specific transactions from those who record them and from those who have responsibility and authority over the results. For example, an end-user department might want to develop its own application programs for keeping track of purchases, inventory, or assets. In such a case, both the MIS department and the internal audit group will want to investigate the sensitivity of the application. If it is to be developed, operated, and used by quite a few individuals, the company may be exposing itself to trouble. Typically, functional management may want both programming and operation of such applications to be undertaken by the MIS department under the direction of the MIS manager.

In addition, application programs that are used to advise clients or to generate reports for regulatory agencies should also be written by the MIS department. Organizations will need to determine which applications are sensitive to their business and how they should be handled. This same concern for potential loss also applies to systems that feed on centralized databases. In this case, not only the correctness but also the validity of the data are at risk. If an application has been written or could be rewritten by an end user, and if the data are also entered by that same end user, some data control procedures need to assure that the data is authentic.

For those applications that should be developed by end users, the appropriate software needs to be used. As was shown in Chapter 7, there is currently a wide range of software packages that can be purchased to meet most end-user computing needs. It is up to the end user working with his or her own functional end-user information center to decide what software package is best for the application under study. Typically, more than one purchased software package can be employed for the end-user application. Consultation with the functional end-user information center is advisable to resolve any problems of selection of the best software package.

Other important software considerations center on program change control and multiuser applications. Program change control is important for sensitive applications. Verification procedures are clearly needed, but if the end user wrote the program and can easily change it, a program change procedure cannot easily be enforced. Hence, sensitive applications should not be written by end users, and especially not for running on their PCs. Also, there is cause for concern about end users' creating multiuser applications for multiuser PCs. Hence, backup and recovery facilities on these machines are generally not the best when compared to those on computer mainframes and minicomputers (under the jurisdiction of the MIS department). There have been cases where users have accidentally destroyed the files or programs of others on multiuser PCs. Thus, end-user backup and recovery procedures for PCs must equal those of the MIS department for best results.

Although most organizations first implemented end-user computing policies by controlling the acquisition of PC hardware and software packages, today it is more important to control user-developed software, data, or usage of all of these. It is recommended that the MIS manager establish a policy that employee-developed applications belong to the company if they have been written on company time. Such a policy would be administered by functional end-user departmental information centers that are currently responsible for keeping track of proprietary company work. Because it is easy to copy floppy and hard disks, enforcement requires developing specific policies and guidelines for end-user management, along with an education program for these functional managers and end users. In addition, it would be helpful to keep copies of end-user-written applications in a software library. This resource will provide a central site for backup as well as for sharing of software by end users and informing them of software changes. End users should be taught to document their programs properly so they can, indeed, be understood and used by others, since they can be important company assets.

Database Considerations

In terms of database considerations, end-user computing activities give new concerns to MIS management about *data security* and *data integrity*. Typically, organizations employ security features when end users access data no matter where they are. Also, they restrict end users to extract data only from the organization's databases. Generally, end users cannot input new data or change existing databases. The most likely uses of PCs will be to extract data from the organization's databases, store it on a PC, and manipulate it locally. In terms of safeguarding the integrity of the data from a PC, this really does not differ from a computer terminal user.

However, files that end users create will, for the most part, be *personal files*, that is, files that MIS department members and other people do not really have a need to see or use. These files will generally include drafts of memos and reports, personal programs for analyzing data, and so forth. These files will be the user's responsibility and not that of the MIS department. In contrast, for departmental minicomputers or work group multiuser PCs, there is more chance that the data entered onto those computers might be of use to others within the organization. Here the question of data integrity comes into play. In essence, should data be put onto a corporate computer so that it can be used by other organization personnel? This question can be answered by allowing such end-user data to be uploaded to the organization's databases, where the MIS department has the proper validation programs in place. It should be noted that policies on end-user data exchange are often open ended. For example, employees who want access to data on a departmental computer must get permission from that department directly, not from the MIS department. This problem of data integrity can also be solved by requiring that reports generated by user-developed programs identify the name of the generating program or the responsible end user.

In reality, personal computers may be more secure than corporate computers. End users can lock up floppy disks that contain sensitive information. Knowing that there is only one copy of the data and that it cannot be accessed by anyone else electronically may make employees feel that their end-user systems are more secure than the corporate computers. However, without proper control, floppy disks and hard disks can be a greater security risk because they are so widely distributed and easily carried off. In addition, security becomes an even more important concern on multiuser systems. The small multiuser systems do not have the same quality of data security features as the larger computer systems.

The problem exists whenever there are data on, say, a hard disk unit that is shared by multiple users. Hence, the MIS manager must not only be aware of these problems, but also be willing to work with end users on feasible data security and data integrity solutions.

Data Communications Considerations

Data communication desired by end users will be somewhat different from that desired by the MIS department. While the MIS department's focus is on local as well as wide-area information processing, the end user typically is oriented more toward local processing than corporatewide processing. Typically, end users are likely to want (1) to utilize the capabilities of the local area network, (2) to download data from a local or central database to a PC, (3) to upload data to corporate mainframe databases, (4) to download reports to PCs, and (5) to send documents and graphic images between work stations. Each of these items is discussed.

First, end users want to utilize the capabilities of local area networks. That is, they want to utilize the capabilities of the equipment on the LAN which allow them to print reports, present data in graphic form, and the like. *Second,* end users will want to download data to their PCs from a local or central database. There are several ways organizations can handle this need. One approach is to extract portions of company production files to a database on another computer, thereby restructuring data into a more accessible format. Using this downloading approach also facilitates advising end users of the correct interpretation of the data, perhaps by providing footnotes to explain unusual data. The MIS manager needs to determine not only what data are allowed to be offloaded, but also what access policies and restrictions should be put on downloaded files.

Third, end users will also want to use their PCs as intelligent data-entry machines to upload data to a corporate mainframe database. Most organizations prefer to use memo posting with later batch processing, rather than allow end users to do direct interactive updating. In addition to data uploading, end users may want to upload programs for backup on another computer or to store them in a program library.

Fourth, rather than download data or programs, end users will sometimes want to have reports downloaded directly to PCs, where they can be reviewed and perhaps reformatted before printing. This displaces the physical distribution of reports. End users might receive an electronic message that the monthly departmental budget variance reports are available for review using their PCs. In turn, some end users may want to store the reports on a PC disk for later reference without even printing it. If reports are printed, there may be a problem getting the report into a text format that is consistent with the report-printing software on the PC. *Fifth,* this same compatibility problem occurs in the case when end users try to send documents and graphic images between two word processors. Text representations and formatting characters vary from product to product. Sending graphic images may also require broader bandwidths or longer transmission times than are required for only data or text transmission.

Maintaining a Well-Equipped Help Desk

In order to help leverage information technology more fully for end users in the areas discussed, it is necessary that MIS management establish a well-equipped help desk. Basically, a *help desk* is a centralized, reliable, and high-quality service that can be called upon by end users. Typically, most organizations start with basic needs which include the following: (1) logging incoming calls, (2) tracking requests through the help cycle, and (3) developing a problem management system or a comprehensive database of solutions. On a typical automated help desk, when a call comes in, an operator will log the name of the caller and record the kind of equipment being used along with the exact nature of the problem. This information is automatically stored in a database or logging system. In turn, this database forms the basis of a problem management system which operators use for background information, such as a history of the caller's problems or records of similar problems and how they were solved.

Most help-desk systems allow different types of searches, including key-word search and search retrieval. Hypertext capabilities are also available as part of some automated help-desk systems. What really sets off one help desk from another is what happens to the information once the operator logs it in. On one side are expert systems–based products. Most of them rely on either decision-tree logic or rules-based technology to automate problem resolution. Decision-tree logic often requires an intensive and time-consuming effort of programmers. They write a fixed series of questions that, in actual use, prompt operators for answers and lead them to a resolution. In contrast, rules-based technology is somewhat more flexible, but like decision-tree logic, it is not intended for novices.

These help-desk systems give programmers a start by supplying some built-in problem determination procedures geared toward a certain type of equipment or common problems that arise in a particular environment, such as a LAN operating mode. Other systems allow the problem resolution database to be built with free text. Instead of being prompted with preprogrammed questions, the operator searches the database via a variety of parameters, including problem status, machine serial number, and technician name. Somewhere in between are "case-based reasoning" products. Whereas traditional expert systems rely on structured logic to build a resolution database, case-based reasoning takes a "by example" approach to problem solving. One of the chief benefits of these available self-help products is that help-desk analysts can build the cases more cheaply than programmers developing them. Hence, a number of software products are commercially available today from a number of vendors to assist MIS management and their staff in maintaining a well-equipped help desk.

When buying these products, MIS management should consider the cost and time it may take to develop interfaces in-house as opposed to buying off-the-shelf interface solutions. Only after an organization has the basic help-desk tools installed and running smoothly should it begin to consider some of the useful add-on technologies. Add-ons include automatic call distributors, voice response units, and remote access software. In the future, some experts say the array of help-desk tools will only continue to broaden as end users' computing needs grow more and more complex. Just how many help desks are able to implement new systems quickly and effectively is still open to question.

TRAINING AND EDUCATION OF END USERS IN LEVERAGING INFORMATION TECHNOLOGY

Although end users may understand the usefulness of new offerings in software and hardware, database management systems, and data communications, they are generally poorly equipped to evaluate them in terms of an organization's information architecture of design features that will facilitate or inhibit their applications. The MIS department is better equipped to review the horizon of new information technology and to compare offerings in similar IT categories. This can create an opportunity for MIS management to forge closer relationships with the end-user community, perhaps by polling end users for interest in new types of information technology, including end users in the evaluation process, and informing end users about leading-edge applications. Within this framework, considerations for standards, training, education, and consulting activities need to be undertaken by MIS management at the appropriate level to facilitate further end-user involvement and, at the same time, assist in leveraging information technology.

Standards Considerations

Because the typical organization cannot support every variety and brand of equipment and software, database management systems, and data communications systems, standards are required. As noted previously, total quality management underlies standards whether they are directed to the MIS department or functional end-user departments. Standards allow the MIS department to deliver higher levels of support activities, such as training, education, consulting, and troubleshooting, because it is not diluting its efforts by offering numerous versions of the same application category. Additionally, the MIS department is better equipped than end users to evaluate vendors in terms of service levels, reliability, compatibility with existing systems, and other salient issues. Important factors to consider when acquiring hardware and software, database management systems, and data communications were discussed previously (Chapters 7 and 8). Because the MIS department can influence the tools used in an organization primarily through its functional end-user information centers, a heavy-handed approach is not necessary. If the MIS department has a proven track record of quality support, few end users will choose unsupported products. Rather than responding to end-user requests with a flat "no," the MIS department can gently but firmly inform end users that the product will not be supported. Saying "Sorry, but you are on your own" will usually deter inexperienced end users while more experienced end users will venture into new territory with their eyes open.

Training Considerations

To encourage end-user training, MIS management must emphasize a range of tools to serve various end-user needs. An effective training program is another way to bring together MIS personnel and end users. End users greatly appreciate anything that gets them up and running quickly. Functional end-user managers will also appreciate training programs because they do not want the attainment of computer literacy to deter essential functional department tasks. The training program can be used as an early opportunity to explain the reasons for standards or subtly to introduce standards. Thus, if MIS provides an appropriate level of training, it is sure to strengthen its relationship with end users.

Education Considerations

Education goes one step further than training because it helps end users to understand the implications of information technology. The MIS department can help stimulate discussion of how end users might migrate from the individual efficiency point of view to applications that improve their effectiveness or change their jobs to bring about this effectiveness. This ties in with the previous discussion on encouraging end users to leverage information technology. Instead of being top down, this approach is bottom up. Essentially, the education of end users is the means to broaden their perspective of employing information technology to its fullest.

Education can be delivered in various ways, from classroom instruction to individual consultation, newsletters, videotaped lessons, and programs in other media. One important educational practice is to disseminate information about other end-user applications. Typically, the MIS department is well positioned to undertake this important role. MIS educational programs can cover a wide range of topics, such as tool evaluation, security, backup, and documentation. In the area of *tool evaluation,* end users, in particular new ones, tend to build every new application with a familiar software package. MIS can tell end users about mainframe-based end-user computing and offer guidelines for determining when an application is pushing the limits of a PC. In the area of *security,* end users may not recognize that electronic data can be much more vulnerable to theft or unauthorized inspection than paper data. MIS can present them with a range of alternatives for ensuring the security of important materials. In terms of *backup,* MIS can help end users understand how backup procedures will save valuable time and prevent aggravation. Last, in the area of *documentation,* the exercise of rigorous documentation may be a waste of time if the application is a one-time use or so highly customized to the individual that it would be inappropriate to try to institutionalize it through documentation. MIS can be very helpful to end users by showing them that some individual applications require only a bare minimum of documentation while others require a more rigorous approach. All in all, education considerations are very important to help end users get a better handle on changing information technology.

Consulting Considerations

Training and education activities should be augmented by effective consulting. As noted previously in the text (refer to Chapter 5), the functional end-user information centers should include IT consultants who know not only the functional area where they are located, but also how to translate information technology into helpful applications that end users are interested in pursuing. Typically, a well-run consulting function in specific information centers can reduce the overall cost of end-user computing. While some end users need guidance on getting started, others need to have their difficult IT questions answered. Consulting can help the end user become more productive sooner, and it is another opportunity for the team building that may be necessary for future activities, especially those that will affect the organization, its customers, or its suppliers. The feedback from consulting end users will provide valuable direction for training and educational activities as well as help pinpoint end users who are stepping beyond their domain so that new levels of support can be provided. Linked with these consulting activities is the self-help desk that end users can call at any time for assistance. The availability of a quick response to questions will go a long way to help end users utilize and leverage information technology.

END-USER SYSTEMS DEVELOPMENT LIFE CYCLE

As discussed in Chapter 9, there are several ways that a system can be developed within the MIS department. However, it is highly recommended that end-user developmental activities be standardized on one approach for best results. Generally, if an end-user-developed system involves only ad hoc querying or extracting data from an existing local database, then the recommended end-user development life cycle approach is not mandatory. On the other hand, if an end-user application requires creation of a new database and the like, then the following systems development life cycle procedures need to be followed. If the application is to be used by others, or if it is to become an integral part of the end-user's job and supply information to others, then it also needs to follow the five steps given later.

The recommended five steps in the end-user systems development life cycle are as follows:

1. Define system requirements
2. Design system and determine data requirements
3. Prototype to finalize system
4. Fulfill TQM requirements
5. Document and train end users

Each of these steps is explained. These steps are somewhat like those described in Chapter 9 for MIS personnel.

1. Define System Requirements

The initial step of a project, defining system requirements, is normally done in its entirety by the end user. Assisted by the information center's systems development guidebook, the end user fills out a project request form where he or she describes the problem(s) with the current system, the scope and objectives of the new system, the known requirements or specifications of the proposed system, and the tangible and intangible benefits expected from the proposed system. The end user also needs the signature of his or her functional departmental manager. At this point, the end user generally has no idea of how much effort this project will take. Hence, the system development costs are not included on the request form. In signing this form, however, the functional departmental manager realizes that the end user must be given the time to develop the new system. Generally, this part of the project takes about 10 percent of the total project time. It ends with an agreement that a functional end-user information center consultant will help the end user develop the system.

2. Design System and Determine Data Requirements

The next step, designing the system and determining data requirements, involves not only designing the new system, but also identifying the data to be included in it. This step accounts for another 15 to 20 percent of the total system effort. Generally, the end user has some design already in mind and can proceed on this basis. However, the same cannot be said about data requirements. The programming guide from the functional end-user information center can be of help since it describes what types of data the end user should collect from the documents used in his or her department. It also describes the various attributes to be defined for each data item, various types of validation checks, and the different kinds of relationships among data elements that the end user must specify. In addition, end users are encouraged to use the information center's on-line data dictionary to locate and organize the data for their application. Since the functional end-user information center stores the data definitions for all end-user-developed systems, end users can borrow data definitions from other applications to shorten the data definition phase. More importantly, it increases the use of standard data definitions among end-user-developed systems.

During the process of designing the new system, the end user will draw heavily on the consultant's advice in the information center. Various approaches to systems design will normally be run past the consultant in order to help the end user select the best one. In a similar manner, the end user will draw upon the advice and expertise of the consultant in creating the data dictionary. Since data definitions are new to end users, it takes some handholding from the information center consultants to help end users correctly define the data that their systems will need. The programming guide mentioned earlier also helps by explaining the database definition process. With the proper guidance and help, most end users can pick up an understanding of the database quickly. This step concludes with a completed data dictionary for the new system application.

3. Prototype to Finalize System

The largest portion of the total systems development time occurs in the third step, creating a prototype. About 50 percent of the project effort goes into developing the details of the database and the application. Using the data definitions created by the end user, the information center consultant completes the design of the database. Using this database design, the end user creates the system logic. The end user is aided in his or her programming efforts by models created by the information center. Essentially, these models are skeleton screen layouts for the typical kinds of database maintenance functions most applications perform. In addition, there are models for adding or making changes to a database, inquiring into a database, and deleting records from a database.

Utilizing a *prototyping* process which is iterative, a first attempt at the database design leads from a general design to a first-round systems design. If the results are satisfactory, then the end user loads in test data and tests the system. This inevitably identifies needed changes, perhaps in both the database and the system; then there are more test runs and so forth. This step ends when the end user has a complete and running system that performs all the necessary functions.

4. Fulfill TQM Requirements

Although not noted in the previous steps, total quality management is an integral part of the entire end-user systems development life cycle. TQM starts at the beginning of the process by focusing on making the end user more effective and efficient in terms of day-to-day operations, that is, improving end-user satisfaction on the job and empowering the end user to make decisions about the work. The net result is that the end user is continually improving the system processes that affect the quality of the product or service delivered to the ultimate customer.

Typically, from the beginning to the end of the project, 20 to 30 percent of the project time is spent on total quality management. There is need to check the system throughout its development to make sure that it meets TQM standards. Generally, the information center consultants perform TQM functions by testing all system functions, looking for problems as well as incomplete options. One of the main purposes of the check is to increase the maintainability of the system. (TQM activities are discussed in Chapter 4.)

5. Document and Train End Users

Both documentation and training are the end user's responsibility. Documentation includes a paper-based user manual, embedded help screens and error messages, and application documentation. Typically, training is both developed and taught by end users. End users get a thrill teaching others to use a system they have developed. This step represents about 5 to 10 percent of total time.

It is suggested that there be a *feedback mechanism* to the developers about the pros and cons of the system. The net result is that this mechanism provides a means for maintaining and possibly upgrading the system. Although the developer can see room for improvement, a larger audience provides a better vehicle for system maintenance and possible improvements.

WORKFLOW USEFUL IN AUTOMATING MIS

Workflow, which is of great interest to MIS personnel and end users, is a relatively new approach to automating MIS. Needless to say, the movement of work throughout an organization is far from new. Information, forms, and documents have been flowing through organizations for decades, albeit on paper. Basically, workflow systems automate business processes that involve people working together. They are designed to automate business procedures using computers, networks, databases, and messaging systems. With workflow software, organizational employees can create and move data between individuals, departments, and organizations. User access is transparent and independent of geographic location or underlying computer platform.

Workflow technology builds upon and enhances the concept of groupware by introducing client/server computing and distributed processing to this technology. Groupware systems tend to work on departmental PC LANs. Workflow systems can span a wide range of computing platforms, including PCs, workstations, minicomputers, and computer mainframes, throughout an organization. These systems are capable of impressive productivity gains because they offer a new way of getting the job done. Current-generation applications, such as word processors and spreadsheets, automate business procedures but offer little in the way of measurable productivity gains. The net result is that the market for workflow automation is likely to grow rapidly.

There are several approaches that a workflow system can take: that is, some support document flow whereas others focus on task automation or process automation. For example, image processing systems tend to support document flow by automating paper-based systems and procedures. In some cases, these systems rely on costly proprietary hardware and software. The other category of workflow products tends to be more general purpose, using existing PC and computer mainframe technology. It tends to be more open and less expensive.

Overall, workflow automates the movement of documents and forms between end users and their work groups. Workflow systems provide end users with transparent access to data across a variety of computing platforms. They also support intelligent routing of documents between workers in a predetermined sequence. Typically, workflow software encompasses PCs, LANs, host computers, messaging systems, and databases.

Workflow Software

Currently, a number of vendors offer workflow software. Reach Software Corporation (Sunnyvale, California) and Action Technologies Inc. (ATI, Alameda, California) lead the field with PC LAN-based products that work with existing systems, such as Novell's NetWare and Banyan's Vines. AT&T's Rhapsody, an early workflow contender, tried to bring users into a full suite of AT&T hardware and software. NCR, now owned by AT&T, discontinued Rhapsody sales in favor of its own workflow approach. Digital Equipment Corporation (Maynard, Massachusetts) also offers a workflow package, TeamRoute, as part of its TeamLinks application suite. Although it supports Microsoft Windows clients, DEC's suite requires a VAX VMS server.

Instead of complete systems, users can install workflow as a component of their existing network. Such groupware products can be sorted into three categories: *user-centered, process-centered,* and *work-centered.* BeyondMail from Beyond Inc. and Notes from the Lotus Development Corporation are *user-centered* because the system is designed around the user. Beyond users can build their own workflow applications atop Beyond's E-mail platform by writing mail-handling macros. They can create forms, such as purchase orders, and rules to route the forms around the organization. Likewise, Notes users can construct data views, set up procedures to move work from one mailbox to another, or build process-oriented applications in the shared database. Notes is built on databases that are replicated across a network. Notes can compile related documents from different sources in a distributed environment.

Unlike user-centered Beyond and Notes, ATI's software is *process-centered* because it models users, data (files), applications, the cycle of work, and the state of the transaction. Though best known as the creator of Novell's Message Handling System (MHS), ATI was a groupware pioneer. Its first product, the Coordinator, broke down human interactions into units that could be carried on a network and tracked by computer. ATI's workflow is based on similar ideas. In the ATI model, all work can be defined by twelve basic transactions between performers (workers) and customers. These actions are based on people-to-people understanding and commitments.

In contrast, the workflow component of Keyfile, a product from Keyfile Corporation (Nashua, New Hampshire), is *work-centered* because users design their workflows as they go along. Also, Reach is work centered, that is, a Windows client-based product aimed at business users. Basically, workflows evolve from the middle out. If Beyond can be characterized as mail filtering and routing and ATI as organizational modeling, Reach is best seen as forms processing. That is, documents determine their own routes, displaying and updating themselves according to instructions that follow them around. Reach's WorkMan software tackles three information challenges: organization, routing, and processing. Information is organized by using object-oriented forms that present their fields in various views based on their stage in the process.

To understand this important new area, MIS management must learn all they can and choose with care. They should begin by studying the organization carefully and recognizing which approach best suits it. There is need for MIS managers to understand what they are trying to accomplish and include functional management and end users in designing the workflow. Workflow software is not an end in itself, but simply a means to that end.

DOCUMENT MANAGEMENT FOUND IN AUTOMATING MIS

Related to workflow is the area of document management. Essentially, if every document were printed immediately, without revision, then sent to someone and stored in a circular file right after review, document management would be unnecessary. However, in practice, documents—by which is meant revisable computer files that represent spreadsheets, database reports, images, program code, and other kinds of information plus files containing work processing documents—do not make their trip from keyboard to deletion without some type of distribution, editing, review, and revision. Typically, they are stored or archived for a time as well. When thousands and millions of documents are stored on today's increasingly large and complex networks, the problems associated with tracking, storing, retrieving, and generally managing the flow of documents can quickly become unmanageable without help. This is where document management software can help the typical MIS manager to address these problems.

Document Management Software

There are a number of document management software packages available. Among them are Keyfile (from Keyfile Corporation), PC Docs (from PC Docs Inc.), SoftSolutions (from SoftSolutions Technology Corporation), and Document Administrator (from Interpreter Inc.). Although they differ considerably from each other, they all address a number of common document tracking issues, including version control, viewing/previewing, indexing, archiving, and accounting/billing. Most of them are designed to work closely with one or more word processing programs.

As a result of the rapid growth of electronic imaging within and outside the typical organization today, many of the document management software packages focus on the management of scanned images of paper documents versus document management, which focuses on the management of revisable computer files that happen to be printable. Scanned images tend to flow from workstation to workstation for perusal, some kind of action, and finally archiving, much as the paper documents they replace would flow in a manual system. Revisable files, in contrast, tend to be located, edited, printed, and very often purged. Keyfile and Document Administrator are examples of electronic imaging packages.

Currently, document management software is undergoing redefinition and refinement. The movement into graphical user interfaces (GUIs) and the need to manage compound documents created with a variety of applications are impacting the software that once was a fairly straightforward category. It is expected that there will be a continued blurring of lines between document management and electronic imaging. While the character-based systems will still find a market among high-volume word processing operations, Windows applications are clearly gaining ground.

GUIDELINES TO ASSIST MIS MANAGEMENT IN END-USER COMPUTING

A *first* guideline for MIS management to employ for end-user computing is to develop short- and long-term goals for training programs. When setting these goals, it is common for MIS management to find the exercise filled with a conflicting relationship between time and money. In short, the faster the conversion to new information technology, the more expensive it will be for end users. Short- to long-term goals for training programs should be related to the acquisition of the skills identified as vital to maximum utilization of the new information technology. MIS management should not overestimate the power of training. It takes much more than a five-day end-user introductory class to train an individual thoroughly in a new IT product or service. Some organizations have had to pay the price of bringing in an army of consultants to fix problems that arose when end users were placed in command of different projects because it was perceived that, after a five-day course, they had the necessary skills.

A *second* guideline that is often ignored relates to training of end users at the top and middle management levels. A group of individuals often overlooked in many training plans is management. And, ironically, one of the best ways to secure support for training is to expose upper management to introductory courses for end users. Top management gains an awareness of the capabilities, limitations, and complexity of the new information technology. This exposure often helps top managers realize the long-term value of an investment in training.

Similarly, middle managers and supervisors should also participate in the introductory programs. As with top management, they need not become experts, but they should understand the environment in which end users operate. For example, a major aerospace manufacturer recently introduced a Windows-based system. Many of the managers felt that this meant the system could be mastered in one or two hours. Once these managers were trained on the system, this misconception disappeared very fast.

A particularly important *third* guideline for MIS management to follow is to have an effective two-way flow of communication between it and end users in the functional units. Typically, technical problems crop up during development of new systems by end users. If the end users planning the system are not fully aware of the capabilities of the technology used, they may sell a solution to their peers that cannot be developed. At other times, end users may find an easier or better way to accomplish a particular task in the written requirements without knowing that the original plan accomplished other undocumented goals. Essentially, both of these problems stem from a lack of communication between end users and the MIS department. Although both sides may think that they know what the other is talking about, they both lack a true understanding of the issues affecting each other's operations. Many times, according to organization experts, it is a problem that can only be solved through a cultural change in an organization.

A *fourth* guideline for MIS management to follow is training end users properly, in particular, using the systems development life cycle that includes fulfilling TQM requirements. Typically, this end-user training is undertaken by the information center in the functional units. To determine its effectiveness, the MIS manager can ask functional end-user managers and staff members what they thought of it. Also, the MIS manager can determine whether the learning objectives were achieved and discover whether employees are applying their new knowledge or skills on the job. Formal questionnaires or group discussions might be used for feedback. Or the MIS manager can observe employees on-the-job to get a firsthand impression, then look for changes in the key business indicators that generated the need for training and calculate the bottom-line effect on the organization's results.

A *fifth* guideline is the establishment of standards over PC-mainframe platforms and their security. MIS management must take the lead in this area. More specifically, it is essential that micro-mainframe standards be an integral part of the functional end-user departments. With a mandate by MIS management, functional end-user managers, working with MIS personnel, need to develop standards not only by which PCs and computer mainframes are purchased and used, but also by which security over them is controlled. These standards, if handled appropriately, will be perceived by end users as a way of improving their departmental work load. On the other hand, the risks are equally clear. If end users ignore the need for standards, a "Tower of Babel" will develop with limited or no ability for end users to deal with each other's data and applications or security over them. At this point, MIS management will probably take a considerable amount of heat for letting the organization "do this to itself." Thus, an organization needs not only to centralize the information end users are using on their PCs and mainframes, but also to have specific security measures in place over this information.

A *sixth* critical guideline centers on documentation by end users. Typically, the MIS department requires its own personnel to utilize some type of documentation approach or some kind of documentation software as described in the chapter. On the other hand, because end users do not always have MIS professionals looking over their shoulders, documentation does not get done or done properly. Hence, the responsibility of getting the proper documentation performed is often relegated to the information center of the functional end-user unit. This MIS unit, which works with end users on developing new systems, can recommend one software package (or a combination) that has documentation procedures built into the software. In this manner, the documentation process is facilitated for end users.

A *seventh* and last guideline relates to a proper approach to auditing of end-user systems whether by internal or external auditors. Auditors have reason for concern about end-user applications that primarily benefit the individual end user but have only a limited role to play in the total organization. If the organization audits certain manual procedures, it should continue to audit them after they are automated. Too often, end users of functional units are too willing to place blind faith in computer-generated output. The introduction of information technology should not automatically cause an organization to change its auditing policies unless they are already obsolete. A practical approach that can be followed by auditors and backed up by MIS management is to monitor systems that affect the functional unit. The specific approach taken will depend on the nature of the system. Low exposure to risk and low complexity require only minimal hardware, software, and data standards; also, documentation can be rudimentary. In contrast, high exposure to risk and high complexity require an adequate level of auditing. As systems become more important, more complex, and hence riskier, the auditors should become more involved. They can call on the same methods used for larger traditional systems, which provide for backup and recovery and guarantee the accuracy and security of results. Additionally, over time, end users will learn to recognize when systems require the close attention of the auditors.

PART VI

EFFECTIVE DIRECTION OF MIS PERSONNEL AND END USERS

12

Selection and Motivation of MIS Personnel

OUTLINE

- Introduction to Effective Selection and Motivation of MIS Personnel
- Principles of Effective MIS Selection and Motivation
- Relationship of Current Research to Selection and Motivation of MIS Personnel
- Effective MIS Management of the Selection Process
  - Sources of MIS Personnel
  - Basis for Evaluation of MIS Personnel
- Selection Process of MIS Personnel
  1. Development of a Job Description
  2. Initial Screening of Job Candidates
  3. Company Visit and Interview
  4. Final Selection
- Effective MIS Management of Motivating Employees
- Essential Nature of Motivation
  - High Growth Needs of MIS Personnel
- Ways for MIS Management to Measure Current Motivation
- Current Motivation Approaches and Theories
  - Motivation Approaches That Have Been Used Successfully
  - Maslow's Hierarchy of Needs Theory
  - Herzberg's Motivation-Hygiene Theory
- An Approach to Expand Maslow's Hierarchy of Needs
  - Mutual Actualization
  - Self-Donation
- Revised Hierarchy of Needs for MIS Personnel and End Users
- Job Stress of MIS Personnel and End Users
  - Living with Stress
- Effective Way to Reduce or Resolve Conflict and Stress in the MIS Organization
  - Confronting and Smoothing Versus Other Methods

INTRODUCTION TO EFFECTIVE SELECTION AND MOTIVATION OF MIS PERSONNEL

A logical starting point for staffing an MIS organization is their recruitment and selection. The chapter's first topic is devoted to the selection process of personnel by MIS management. This important topic is essential to maintain and expand an MIS organization. Hence, the MIS manager must establish the number and kinds of positions to be filled, determine the tasks and job requirements, and obtain the appropriate personnel to fill the positions.

An important job of the typical manager is working with and through people, including a large accent on motivation. Since individual behavior can be beneficial or detrimental to an organization, studying it will help the MIS manager reach desired organization goals. Desirable human behavior includes conformance with desired MIS organization objectives and goals; development of new technical skills, creativity, and ingenuity on assigned day-to-day tasks; adaptability to changing conditions; and loyalty to the organization during good and bad times. Observation of ongoing activities, however, often reveals undesirable behavior that is characterized by absenteeism, a high rate of turnover, needless confrontation, and restriction of output. The second topic of the chapter, then, focuses on the behavior of MIS personnel and the various theories that have been proposed to help understand and predict it. Related to the topic of motivation is the high level of job stress experienced by MIS personnel. Similarly, conflict in the MIS organization is typically found. Both of these topical areas (job stress and conflict) are covered at the very end of the chapter.

PRINCIPLES OF EFFECTIVE MIS SELECTION AND MOTIVATION

Several fundamental principles should be incorporated in selecting MIS personnel, beginning with the *Principle of an Effective Selection Process.* Because MIS management wants to bring qualified personnel into their organizations, the selection process must be effective. Furthermore, harsh penalties—in the form of relocation, training costs, and management time—result from mistakes in personnel selection.

The *Principle of Effective Interviewing Skills* refers to the interviewer's ability to ask questions essential to evaluate the candidate for a particular position. A typical question is, Does the combination of the individual's attitude, training, and experience quality him or her for the position? If there is a good fit between the candidate and the organization, an offer should be made.

The *Principle of Effective Human Communication* refers to an open and free two-way exchange. Not only should the MIS organization obtain pertinent information about the individual, but he or she should also learn enough about the MIS organization to evaluate an offer of employment. Beyond the particulars associated with a position, candidates are most interested in knowing the degree to which the organization invests in its employees, including professional development, training, salary, benefits, and career opportunities.

Another important principle is the *Principle of Expediting the Selection Process*. An MIS organization cannot afford the luxury of a long decision process when it comes to selecting a candidate and making an offer. Generally, a candidate quickly loses the good impressions and personal rapport developed during an interview. An effective interviewing organization that waits more than two weeks to extend an offer will have lost much of the competitive edge it had gained.

The *Principle of Changing the Selection Process* refers to the continual review and modification to conform to changing conditions, such as the Affirmative Action Program and the Equal Employment Opportunities regulation. Education and training in these new areas are required of those who interview prospective employees.

In the area of motivation, the *Principle of Self-Motivation* refers to an inner desire to do a job well; an individual must be self-motivated even when stripped of outside influence. Without inner motivation, the application of external motivators will have little effect on the individual. The enthusiasm one brings to the job is generally evidence of self-motivation.

As will be stressed in the chapter, there is a need for the *Principle of Satisfying the Needs of Each Individual*. Individual needs range from basic physiological requirements to self-actualization, or the realization of one's ambitions. In some cases, the individual's needs go beyond self-actualization and include mutual actualization and self donation. Essentially, once lower-level needs are satisfied, they fail to motivate; another higher-level need emerges and becomes the basis for satisfaction. Therefore, only unsatisfied needs can influence future behavior.

RELATIONSHIP OF CURRENT RESEARCH TO SELECTION AND MOTIVATION OF MIS PERSONNEL

As noted in Chapter 2, current research results have disclosed many problems in directing MIS personnel (see Figure 2.4) that need to be discussed further. In areas related to the selection and motivation of MIS personnel, several problems were noted:

- Lack of career pathing (rated no. 9)
- Lack of performance standards to evaluate MIS personnel (rated no. 10)
- Lack of an adequate performance appraisal program (rated no. 12)

Typically, the problems found in the MIS department are the same ones found in the functional end-user units of an organization.

Referring to the first problem, the *lack of career pathing* demonstrates to MIS personnel the lack of concern involving the individual and, in turn, the ability to work together so that the organization and the individual win in the long run, that is, a "win-win" situation. In fact, current research indicates that it is more of a "win-lose" situation. Hence, the individual's loyalty to the organization is minimal, thereby contributing to a high rate of turnover.

In terms of the second problem, *lack of performance standards to evaluate MIS personnel,* MIS personnel perceive this failure to set standards as a means to fire them if they are not liked by MIS management. In other words, any performance criteria can be used to dismiss MIS personnel. This arbitrary approach does not motivate personnel: in fact, it does just the opposite. Generally, the lack of performance standards adds to the insecurity of MIS personnel, resulting in even more turnover.

Related to both of these problems is the *lack of an adequate performance appraisal program.* Junior MIS personnel should be evaluated every six months while senior members can be placed on an annual basis. Many times, the performance appraisal is very superficial. The net result is that the person does not know whether current performance is adequate, much less being able to undertake new and more difficult assignments in the years to come. The person feels frustrated by these half-hearted attempts at his or her evaluation. Because of the poor performance appraisal programs, MIS personnel tend to leave after a period of time, hoping to get a better appraisal of their work at another company.

Underlying these problems is the basic one that MIS personnel feel isolated from MIS management; that is, there appears to be "a wall" between them. Even though many of their needs (per Maslow's hierarchy of needs) are met on the job, there is a sense of frustration that goes quite deep. Likewise, many of the other motivation approaches discussed previously tend to center on the individual and not on the joint efforts of MIS personnel and their managers. In light of these realities, there is need for a new direction that goes beyond the current motivation approaches and theories set forth in the chapter.

EFFECTIVE MIS MANAGEMENT OF THE SELECTION PROCESS

Over the years, attempts have been made to utilize specific methods that will minimize the MIS manager's risk in selecting from among job applicants as well as the applicant's risk in accepting. These have included previous experience; membership in a professional organization; completion of a standard apprenticeship, training program, or college curriculum; various types of written and performance tests; one-person and panel interviews of individuals and groups; references from previous employers; general character suitability investigations; mploymenttraining;andprobationaryortrialperiodsofemployment. Although no one method or combination of methods has proved completely foolproof, some are considered to be more satisfactory than others under different circumstances. One recommended approach that has been successfully used by a number of companies, regardless of size, is set forth here. Such an approach is helpful to MIS management in reducing a calculated risk that must be undertaken. However, first, the sources of MIS personnel and the basis for evaluation of MIS personnel are discussed.

Sources of MIS Personnel

Fundamentally, there are four main sources of entry-level MIS personnel: (1) colleges, universities, and business schools; (2) other departments in the organization; (3) other companies; and (4) personnel recruiting firms. Hundreds of community (junior) colleges, universities, and business schools offer academic programs in computer science and information systems. In addition to students who have specialized in computer disciplines, many organizations consider business administration, mathematics, and engineering majors for openings in MIS. Most large organizations have highly active campus recruiting programs and regularly send personnel recruiters or members of their professional staff to stimulate student interest in their organizations and to conduct an initial screening process for potential candidates.

MIS positions are also filled by people from the functional end-user units within the organization. These individuals have helped to develop a major new system or to complete a major feasibility study. Often, they were involved in the systems work either as end users who would receive the benefits of the new MIS or as operational or managerial persons whose activities would be directly affected by the system. Many times, these people become excited about a career in MIS because of their positive, direct experience with the MIS organization. If the organizational climate is such that these people can approach their management and/or that of the MIS group about their career aspirations, an excellent source of new MIS personnel becomes available. Not only is the organization saved the relocation expenses commonly associated with new hires, but the initial training time and cost are greatly reduced because of the individual's already existing knowledge of the organization.

As is true in most major career fields that are experiencing rapid growth, qualified MIS people for highly responsible positions will continue to be in short supply. There are two main sources of entry-level and experienced MIS professionals from outside the organization: other organizations and experienced personnel recruited through newspaper or computer science/MIS periodicals advertisements, which usually draw a good response. Some organizations will take a direct approach and tactfully inquire whether members of other organizations would be interested in changing jobs. Many of these direct contacts take place as a result of a casual conversation conducted at a meeting of some professional association, business seminar, or convention.

Specialized employment consultants can be effective in matching organizational needs with highly qualified individuals. Those consultants who are most effective have a nationwide source of prospective clients, adhere to a high standard of professional competence and integrity, and have demonstrated good skill at performing an initial screening of candidates. The consultants charge the hiring organization a commission of a certain rate, say 10 to 25 percent of the individual's starting salary. The resulting fee is typically in the $2,000 to $10,000 range; however, the fee is considerably lower for entry-level positions.

Basis for Evaluation of MIS Personnel

One of the most important criteria for evaluating MIS personnel is how well the individual relates to other people. Certainly no organization wants to hire someone who cannot work well with others. Occasionally, management may take a chance with an applicant who seems technically very strong, but has weak interpersonal skills. Such an individual could be considered for a position where he or she could operate as an individual contributor with little need for interaction. Management should guard against being overly optimistic about improving the individual's interpersonal skills. On the other hand, management may take a chance on an applicant who seems to lack the necessary technical training and experience, but who possesses extremely strong interpersonal skills, because technical skills can be learned. Overall, there is more likelihood of improving an individual's technical than interpersonal skills, a most important consideration for the typical MIS manager.

In addition to interpersonal skills, there are a number of other important traits used to evaluate MIS personnel. For one, the individual has the continuing desire to do what is necessary to become extra good at his or her chosen career. For activities that place a great emphasis upon mental abilities, like programming, excellence comes not only from "practicing," but also from keeping one's mind in sound condition. Another trait is the ability to keep one's cool, to operate under pressure. Some MIS personnel can work well under ordinary circumstances but not under adverse circumstances. Being able to produce under an adverse set of conditions is much more important.

There are other traits that separate the best from the mediocre. The individual has the desire to excel. Another quality is ambition, which can sometimes get in the way of excellence. The ability to communicate, including listening carefully and intelligently, is also important, as are interpersonal skills. Overall, the more important basis for evaluation of MIS personnel may be psychological, that is, the desire to excel, the willingness to work hard, the ability to concentrate, and the ability to produce in what may be an unsympathetic environment.

SELECTION PROCESS OF MIS PERSONNEL

Of all the resources available to MIS management, MIS personnel are by far the most important. It is essential to the organization's success that the appropriate number of good people be selected to staff the MIS organization. The costs associated with the selection and training of new personnel are extremely high. Travel expenses and management recruiting time for a single candidate can exceed several thousand dollars. Relocation expenses push the amount still higher. Total first-year training expenses, including formal and informal training and management time, can easily exceed $20,000. A hiring error is very expensive. In the material that follows, an approach to the hiring of personnel that has been widely used by small- to large-size organizations and has proved highly effective is set forth:

1. Development of a job description
2. Initial screening of job candidates
3. Company visit and interview
4. Final selection

1. Development of a Job Description

Development of a clear job description is the first step in the selection process. The job description should be written as a joint effort by both the MIS and personnel managers. It should discuss the work environment in which the individual will operate and the results the individual is expected to achieve. It should discuss the job's relationship to management, peers, and subordinates. The job description should then list those skills, personal attributes, and experiences that the ideal candidate should possess. These should be divided into three categories: absolutely required, highly desirable, and desirable.

2. Initial Screening of Job Candidates

An initial screening process is recommended to improve the effectiveness of the entire hiring process. The objective of the initial screening is to eliminate potential candidates who are obviously unsuited for the opening or who, on learning more about it, are not really interested in the job. The initial screening should seek information about the qualifications of the candidate as well as provide an overview of the organization and the particular position for which the individual is being considered. Upon conclusion of the initial screening, the candidate and the recruiter should have exchanged sufficient information that they can reach a decision on continuing with the hiring process. The initial screening will help ensure that further management time is spent only on interested and qualified candidates.

Employment application forms and résumés are the traditional tools used for initial screening. These tools are most effective for screening candidates for positions that require specific training and/or experience, but many do not have clearly defined requirements for previous training and experience. This is particularly true for entry-level and newly defined positions. Even the traditional role of systems analyst is sometimes filled by people without a computer background but who possess certain attributes that indicate they have excellent potential. A personal interview, then, between the candidate and a well-trained recruiter is often appropriate so that the candidate can be evaluated on a broad range of factors that cannot be easily quantified and documented on an application form or résumé. Specific desirable attributes for MIS personnel include a logical approach to problem solving, ability to work well with others, strong oral and written communication skills, assertive behavior when appropriate, confidence in making decisions, creativity in problem solving, strong desire to achieve good results, thoroughness in undertaking projects, curiosity about making improvements, intelligence in analyzing problems, ability to relate to the other person's situation, and tact when appropriate. It should be noted that most of these attributes cannot be evaluated without a personal interview.

The recruiter who performs the initial screening process needs to be well trained in the entire employee selection process, be enthusiastic and knowledgeable about the organization, possess some detailed knowledge of the position for which the individual is being considered, and have excellent oral communication skills (both talking and listening). This individual also needs training and a good understanding of the Equal Employment Opportunities regulations and the organization's Affirmative Action program.

Typically, the initial screening interview should last half an hour to an hour. It is important that the recruiter help the candidate feel at ease to facilitate the flow of information. The recruiter will probably need to ask several very direct questions in order to gather all of the pertinent information quickly; however, a few open-ended questions should be included, such as the following: Why is the individual interested in applying for this position? What are the individual's short- to long-term career goals? What specific courses have been taken or experiences been undertaken that would prepare the individual for the position? Can the individual describe a recent situation where he or she brought together a number of people to meet a common goal?

The recruiter should be prepared to provide candidates with information to help them assess the potential opportunity in terms of their interests, capabilities, and career plans. Basic information that should be provided includes an overview of the organization; a discussion of the position for which the candidate is being considered; career development opportunities within the organization; and an overview of the total compensation package—approximate salary range, benefits, training, and career development program.

On conclusion of the initial screening interview, the recruiter must attempt to provide some insights into the candidate's true character and motivation about the job position. Generally, the following questions can provide some important answers:

1. Does the combination of the individual's attitude, training, and experience qualify him or her for the position?

2. Would the individual's personality fit in with others inside and outside the MIS department with whom he or she must deal?
3. Does the individual possess a strong motivation to succeed?
4. Is the individual interested in a long career with the organization?

On the basis of the answers to these questions, the recruiter can then make an appropriate decision. If the decision is to continue the selection process, the candidate should be invited for a company visit. It is important at this point to make it clear to the candidate what the remaining steps are in the selection process and what is to be done next by whom.

3. Company Visit and Interview

The company visit and interview constitute the most important phase of the hiring process since the objective at this stage is to take a much closer look at the candidate and to provide him or her with detailed information about the organization. The company visit and the interview process must be carefully planned to allow this two-way exchange of information. It is essential that the candidate be given a specially prepared packet of information about the company well in advance of the visit. The packet should contain information about the company visit itself. This information will help put the candidate at ease, increase the exchange of meaningful information, and allow the candidate to prepare a carefully selected set of questions to help reach a decision on employment. Detailed information should be provided to the candidate prior to the company visit. Such information should focus on the visit, the location in which the candidate will live, and the organization itself.

For best results, it is important for all those involved in the company visit and the interview process to approach it in the right frame of mind. The candidate should be trying to make a fair, accurate, and favorable impression on the organization, and the organization must present itself honestly. Allowing the candidate to spend an hour or so with another recent hire can be highly effective. The same four key questions about the candidate noted in the initial screening can be used at this stage. It is important that more than one person interview a candidate so that several individuals have an opportunity to evaluate and form a collective opinion.

The most effective interviewers are able to put the candidate at ease and show genuine interest in him or her. Interviews that are routine or stressful to the candidate tend to reduce the exchange of useful data. The interviewer must prepare for the interview and design specific questions that are meaningful to the candidate. Some organizations use written tests. However, the use of written tests has been on the decline for some time. Equal Employment Opportunities regulations and rulings challenge these tests and require that a very strong correlation between test results and on-the-job performance be proved. Use of formal written tests should be reviewed carefully by an organization's personnel department and legal staff.

4. Final Selection

The final selection process involves deciding whether or not to offer employment to the candidate and, if so, the terms of that offer. This should be a careful and deliberate decision based on an exchange of information among all individuals who have been involved in any steps of the recruiting process. Included are those involved in the initial screening and in the day visit and interview. These individuals must discuss candidly their opinions of the candidate relative to the same four questions asked throughout the selection process. In other words, is there a good fit among the organization, the job, and the individual? Because the decision is seldom unanimous, it usually takes hours of discussion.

Once a decision has been reached, the candidate should be informed promptly—ideally within a week or less of the visit and interview—via telephone or letter. This promptness will ensure that the organization does not lose a candidate who decides to accept another offer. Candidates lose interest in and enthusiasm for the organization as time passes, especially after two weeks.

Once a decision is made to offer the candidate a position, the terms of the offer should be expressed in a letter discussing the following points: (1) a brief description of the position; (2) starting date and location of employment; (3) salary; (4) any conditions for acceptance, such as a physical examination or graduation from a specific program; (5) how relocation expenses will be handled; and (6) whom in the organization to contact with questions concerning the offer. On the other hand, if the decision is not to make an offer, common courtesy dictates promptly informing the candidate.

EFFECTIVE MIS MANAGEMENT OF MOTIVATING EMPLOYEES

Typically, MIS managers need to learn more about how to motivate their people. Many questions center on the issue of employee motivation. For example, do MIS personnel complete assigned projects or programs on schedule and within budget? Are the programs generally right the first time or is twice the budget spent correcting and debugging them? What about turnover? How many ten-year systems analysts are still on the job? The department that seemed to be running smoothly may not really be so great after all. Fundamentally, the problem may be a lack of motivation: that is, MIS personnel do not care enough to stay with the organization and put forth their best effort.

The implementation of appropriate motivation approaches can have a pronounced effect on the typical MIS manager. For one, motivated MIS personnel do more than just produce better work; they also make the manager's job a lot easier. They require less supervision. The MIS manager is not constantly "firefighting'' because there is less ''fire'' from motivated people. When people are motivated, work can be delegated and will be done as expected. And the manager will spend less time developing alibis about why the best-thought-out plan did not work. Simply stated, motivation is the key to turning responsible individuals into creative, productive, and loyal employees. Today, few people go to work just for a paycheck. Most people prefer to do a good job, but they must be provided the opportunity. Unfortunately, not all people can be motivated. Some employees do not want to compete with others; their interests in life are outside the organization. These people should be identified so that most of the MIS manager's energies can be concentrated on the rest.

ESSENTIAL NATURE OF MOTIVATION

Motivation can be defined as those inner drives that activate or move an individual to action. Since motivation in itself cannot be seen or heard directly through observable behavior of an individual, we can only measure or infer it from a person's actions. Hence, to measure motivation, MIS management must measure presumed effects of it, such as productivity level and turnover.

Most psychologists would agree that on-the-job behavior is not without some type of motivating factor. The usual explanation of human motivating factors on the job is based on human needs. For example, a young new employee is motivated by the desire to satisfy his or her basic needs. When this immediate goal has been satisfied, other motivators come into play. The listing of needs varies from one writer to another. However, the disagreement appears to be more one of terminology than of content. In any event, the common approach to establish individual need patterns is that of developing a hierarchy according to the individual's priorities. This is the approach taken in this chapter: Maslow's hierarchy of needs is stated and enlarged upon from the standpoint of meeting the individual's highest-level needs on the job. Herzberg's theory on motivation is also explored. The benefits of adding newer higher-level needs are discussed, followed by a revised hierarchy of needs for MIS personnel and end users.

High Growth Needs of MIS Personnel

To understand better what motivates MIS personnel, it is helpful to take a look at some basic factors that have been identified by MIS research. J. Daniel Couger and Robert A. Zawacki (professors at the University of Colorado, Colorado Springs campus) have conducted research in the area of motivating and managing MIS personnel. The results of their studies were published in book form where they measured the attitudes that MIS personnel have about their jobs.[1] For this study, they chose the Job Diagnostic Survey (JDS), developed by J. R. Hackman (University of Illinois) and G. R. Oldham (Yale University). Hackman and Oldham established the validity and accuracy of their instrument by testing more than 6,000 individuals who were performing more than 500 different jobs at more than fifty organizations. The JDS includes questions to assess some characteristics of the employee to aid in matching the employee to job types.

The first of the computed measures centered on *growth need strength.* A high growth need strength indicates that the people in the group have a high need for personal growth and development. In turn, the people in this group will become internally motivated if their jobs have a high motivating potential. The growth need strength score is determined by averaging employee answers for the questions related to personal growth and development. The second computed measure is *social need strength.* A high group score in this area indicates that the people in the group have a strong desire to interact with others; a low score indicates that they prefer to be ''loners.'' The social need strength measure is obtained from those questions having to do with interacting with other people. A third important computing measure is the *motivating potential score* of the job. It is computed from questions that measure the five core job dimensions, such as skill variety and task identity. Although there are other computed measures, these three are the most important items in their analysis.

In their study, Couger and Zawacki added some components to the JDS for probing certain aspects of MIS personnel problems. They obtained the cooperation of fifty organizations, thirty-four companies and sixteen government organizations. The computer staffs at these organizations ranged in size from twenty-five to more than three hundred. In all, they administered the JDS to approximately 1,000 systems analysts and programmers, and to some 1,500 MIS managers and their staff members. Their research uncovered the fact that systems analysts and programmers have the *highest* growth need strength of any job category that has been analyzed using the JDS. This may seem somewhat surprising, but MIS management has long known that MIS professionals want work that includes the use of the latest in hardware, operating systems, and languages. The fact that they rate the highest in this first computed measure means that they require special attention. If the systems analysts and programmers seek high personal development and their jobs do not provide it, they are generally going to change jobs.

Another survey finding that has important implications for MIS management is that systems analysts and programmers have the *lowest* social need strength of any of the more than 500 different jobs that have been measured by the JDS. On the other hand, most users have a *high* social need strength. Persons with a high social need utilize meetings as a prime device for fulfilling their social needs while systems analysts and programmers do not need meetings. This helps explain why users do not understand why MIS personnel show frustration at lengthy or frequent meetings. The same point applies to MIS project or departmental meetings. Systems analysts and programmers will participate actively in meetings that are meaningful to them. But their high growth need also causes intolerance for group activities that are not well organized and conducted efficiently. Subsequent research has verified these important implications for MIS management.

WAYS FOR MIS MANAGEMENT TO MEASURE CURRENT MOTIVATION

In terms of managing, motivating, and maximizing efficiency of MIS personnel, there are two distinct problems: how to perceive an existing motivational problem and how to motivate personnel on an ongoing basis to achieve maximum efficiency. In either case, there are not hard-and-fast rules to be laid down for use. There are, instead, only general guidelines that may be used in solving these two persistent problems.

The most obvious opportunity for motivational activities to be effective is to solve existing motivational problems. The most difficult portion of this is, in fact, the perception that a problem exists. In order to understand and to diagnose a motivational problem correctly, there are two types of information available to the MIS manager. These fall into the broad categories of structured and unstructured information. In terms of *structured* information, the MIS manager should organize and routinize as much crucial information as possible so that it is obtained through formal routes and can be monitored by activities for which the individual is responsible. Such items as turnover rates, grievances, weekly or periodic status reports, and reports of MIS supervisors should normally tell the MIS manager when something is amiss.

These pieces of structured information are signal systems set up in advance to warn the MIS manager when problems are about to occur or have occurred. The greatest practical danger is total reliance upon these pieces of structured information to the exclusion of other sources. In fact, much information may be gathered outside the formal organizational structure, and such information is necessary. Hence, the more frequent and more useful type of information is *unstructured.* The principal source of unstructured information is the social system of the organization. Off-hand comments, conflicting reports, unexpected news, and a general feeling that a motivational problem exists should all point to a potential problem among MIS personnel. These will very frequently point to potential or future problems as well as existing problems.

CURRENT MOTIVATION APPROACHES AND THEORIES

Currently, there are a number of motivation approaches available to MIS management. The more popular ones are discussed here. In turn, this analysis is followed by the basics of Maslow's hierarchy of needs and Herzberg's motivation-hygiene theory. Many of these approaches and theories are equally applicable to end users.

Motivation Approaches That Have Been Used Successfully

As a starting point, an important approach to motivation is to think in terms of *victories.* A systems analyst who has undertaken a long-term project assignment, perhaps two years, will someday get a victory if the system works. However, it is recommended that the MIS project be broken down into smaller segments of work no longer than two weeks each. The potential for several personal victories will have much greater motivational impact over time than for one victory at the very end.

A *reduction in tension* must be the order of the day. Tension is generally created externally, that is, outside the MIS department. However, it could be caused by a supervisor's failing to tell the MIS manager that the project cannot be completed in the allocated time and giving subordinates a deadline that cannot be reached. The result is tension, the very kind that breeds mistakes, costly rework, and considerable unhappiness.

Another way of motivating people is through *work variety*. How is this handled? Personnel can be rotated as well as cross-trained. If one person leaves, another can pick up the slack. It means that everyone has to learn more than one job. In learning a new job, the new person may often find a better way to do things. Additionally, project supervision can be rotated so that everybody gets to lead an assignment. This approach to motivation gives people an opportunity to set up a schedule, to plan an approach to a system problem, and so forth. The MIS manager can always veto this approach if it is not feasible for any valid reason.

One very important approach to motivation is the opportunity for personnel *to be innovative and creative* without fearing the manager's wrath. If an individual makes a mistake, he or she wants to learn from it and not be reprimanded or fired. The individual who lives in fear of losing his or her job certainly is not going to take a chance on trying something new. On the other side of the coin, personnel should be rewarded for a job well done. There are two types of such recognition. First, there are the *tangibles,* a promotion, a bigger job, more money, and the like. Equally important are the *intangibles*. These can take many directions: complimenting employees in front of their peers acknowledges their expertise; a written memorandum gives status among one's peers. By coupling every tangible reward with an intangible one, an MIS manager can accomplish a lot of motivation with little effort.

Another approach to improve motivation is to have *job titles accurately reflect employee efforts*. The emphasis should be on the high-level and important aspects of the job rather than on its mundane aspects. Rather than use common titles like systems analyst or programmer, the accent in the description should be on the real content of the job, such as senior systems analyst or lead systems programmer. In this manner, the individual is accorded the respect that he or she has coming from the true nature of the work.

Regarding *money as a motivator,* MIS people were the first to use the letter K as a designation for thousands of dollars and talk about how many K per year they make. The MIS manager should recognize that money has lost some of the motivational power it once had. It now seems to be more of a dissatisfier than a satisfier, in Herzberg's terms (to be discussed later). An individual who feels underpaid will be dissatisfied with his or her job, but one who feels overpaid still may not like it very much. In fact, there is evidence to suggest that giving someone less may actually cause him or her to enjoy a job more. At a time when most salaries are adequate and many are really quite high, the old practice of giving a K or two extra as both compensation and reward seems to have lost some of its effectiveness. On the other hand, the MIS manager who uses praise and concern to develop a sense of worth and achievement is the individual best suited to the task of motivating others.

In terms of motivating approaches *to reduce turnover,* several factors should be kept in mind by MIS management or functional end-user department managers. They are to keep employees informed on company matters, set up clear channels of communication between employees and management, encourage self-improvement and provide opportunities for advancement, and finally, never oversell a candidate in the employment interview. In addition, it is essential for management to define an employee's job and the expected results through both a written job description and frequent personal review sessions. Specific benchmarks for measuring success must be established so that both the employee and the supervisor will agree on what constitutes a good job.

Increasing motivation and reducing turnover are not difficult if management asks itself certain basic questions: What kinds of people leave the company? Is it only the marginal employees or is it really the top performers? What are the differences between those who survive in the company and those who do not? If the answers to these questions indicate that most often it is the talented employees who are leaving, it is time for an in-depth appraisal of the working climate. By paying attention to what it is that employees really want, instead of what MIS management thinks they want, managers can reduce turnover, improve morale, and create a more effective, productive working environment.

Maslow's Hierarchy of Needs Theory

A widely accepted need theory, set forth by Abraham Maslow, postulates that people are motivated by a desire to satisfy a hierarchy of needs. Those important determinants of human behavior known as *conative* (striving) needs appear in a specific ranking or hierarchy. Those needs which come first must be satisfied, at least to some extent, before higher, more abstract needs emerge and become determinants of behavior. Maslow's proposed classification of needs in their order of importance is as follows: (1) physiological, (2) security, (3) social, (4) esteem, and (5) self-actualization.[2] This classification of needs is set forth in Figure 12.1.

The first level, *basic physiological needs,* consists of the primary needs for sustaining the human body. A person must have food, water, clothing, shelter, sex, and air to maintain his or her existence. Physiological needs dominate when basic needs are unsatisfied. Since other needs do not serve as a basis for motivation, it is fruitless to consider any of a higher order. Management writers have

Figure 12.1
The Relationship of Maslow's and Herzberg's Motivation Models

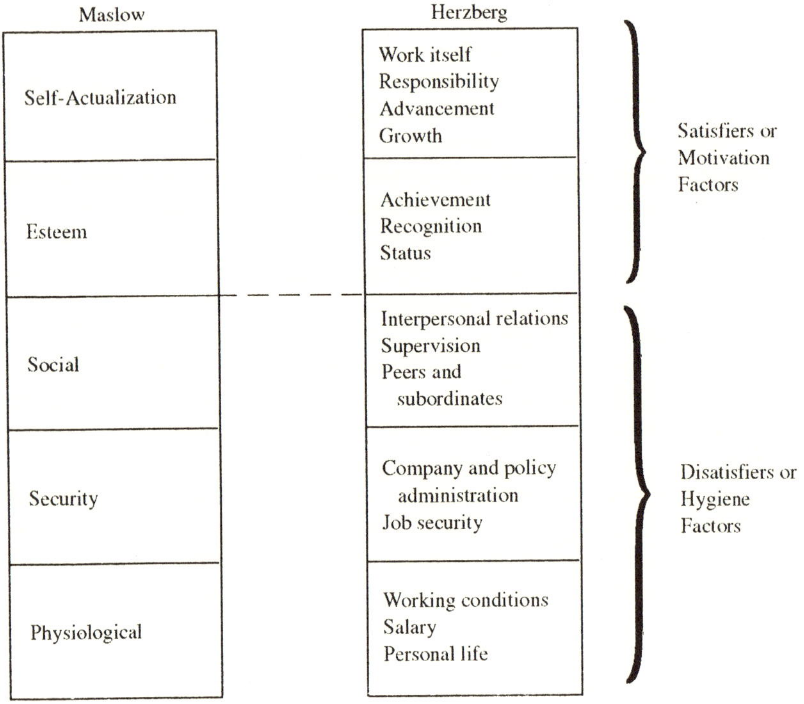

noted that these conditions probably do not arise often in business organizations in the United States.[3] Nevertheless, according to Maslow, when these first-level needs are satisfied to a reasonable degree, the next higher level assumes importance.

The second level, *security* (or safety) *needs,* is concerned with assuring the individual that satisfaction of his or her basic needs will continue. In essence, the individual desires protection against changes, economic disaster, and the like. From a management standpoint, security or safety needs are regarded as the motivation behind attempts to ensure job security and economic security. Many unions today are making demands on management for job security along with expanded fringe benefits. In a similar manner, the U.S. government has passed the Occupational Safety and Health Act (OSHA) of 1970 to reduce the number of safety and health hazards found in industrial environments. When the individual's physiological needs are satisfied and the individual is not fearful about his or her welfare, the next order of needs assumes importance.

The third level, *social needs,* centers on the individual's desire for affection and association with others. To state it another way, social needs are those that relate to being accepted. As before, once these needs are gratified to any acceptable degree, the individual is free to move onto the next level.

The fourth level, *esteem needs,* represents the need for both awareness of one's importance and recognition by others of the same. Based upon the respect of peers in and out of the work environment, satisfaction of one's esteem needs leads to a feeling of self-confidence and prestige. The satisfaction of this level to a reasonable degree permits one to move on to the last level.

The fifth and highest level per Maslow, *self-actualization needs,* is the "desire to become more and more what one is, to become everything that one is capable of becoming."[4] This is the ultimate need in Maslow's hierarchy. It is the need to realize one's capacities and potentialities by achieving some stated goal.

While Maslow recognizes that the individual is never completely satisfied on any need level, he contends that decreasing percentages of satisfaction are encountered as a lower-level need is replaced in predominance by a higher-level one. Maslow suggests a hypothetical example for an average person who is 85 percent satisfied in his or her basic physiological needs, 70 percent in his or her security needs, 50 percent in his or her social needs, 40 percent in the self-esteem category, and 10 percent in his or her self-actualization needs.[5] As can be seen from these percentages, self-actualization needs do not become activated until most of the prior-level needs are somewhat satisfied. The author, in conjunction with Robert C. Klekamp, has developed a management science (i.e., mathematical) approach to determine the probable level of needs sometime in the future.[6]

Considerable research has been undertaken and has been supportive of Maslow's hierarchy of needs. It should be noted, however, that a management researcher (Lyman W. Porter) altered the hierarchy by adding an autonomy need between the fourth and fifth levels and eliminating the physiological needs. The *autonomy need* measures the satisfaction with his or her ability to make decisions independently, participate in goal setting for his or her position, and utilize the authority connected with his or her position in the managerial hierarchy. The physiological need level was dropped since business and governmental organizations in the United States have largely satisfied this need.

Herzberg's Motivation-Hygiene Theory

Another widely known model of motivation is one proposed by Frederick Herzberg and his associates.[7] It grew out of research directed toward ascertaining those employee wants that lead to satisfaction on the job. The traditional approach is one of examining a multiplicity of factors, such as the work itself, pay, security of job, working conditions, congenial associates, opportunity to advance, effective leadership, and credit for work done. These factors are the determinants of particular locations on a single continuum that ranges from job dissatisfaction on one end to job satisfaction on the other.

In the study undertaken by Herzberg and his associates, the research approach was somewhat simplistic, since it was built around the questions "Can you describe, in detail, when you felt exceptionally *good* about your job?" and "Can you describe, in detail, when you felt exceptionally *bad* about your job?" An analysis of the responses indicated that employees seldom named the same kinds of job experiences with good and bad feelings.[8] For example, if responsibility produced good feelings about the individual's job, the lack of responsibility was seldom given as a cause of bad feelings. In fact, these factors appeared to be separate and distinct. This finding is the most important aspect of Herzberg's theory and led him to propose that there are, in reality, two significantly different classes of factors and therefore two different continuums.

The first class, referred to as "dissatisfiers" or "hygiene factors," consists of a continuum that ranges from *dissatisfaction* to *no dissatisfaction.* These factors operate primarily to dissatisfy employees when the factors are absent or are poorly or incorrectly managed. Their presence does not build strong motivation, but can only serve to eliminate dissatisfaction. The most important dissatisfiers identified by Herzberg are company policies, technical supervision, interpersonal relations, and working conditions. The entire range of hygiene factors (dissatisfiers) is related to Maslow's model of motivation in Figure 12.1.

The second class, referred to as "satisfiers" or "motivation factors," makes up a continuum ranging from *no satisfaction* to *satisfaction.* If these factors are present on the job, they operate to build a strong level of motivation, spurring on the individual to superior performance. On the other hand, if they are not present, they do not prove highly dissatisfying. Herzberg identified the following factors as satisfiers: achievement, recognition, status, work itself, responsibility, advancement, and the possibility of growth. The last item refers to the actual learning of new skills with a greater possibility of advancement. This range of motivation is illustrated in Figure 12.1 and, like the dissatisfiers, is related to Maslow's hierarchy of needs.

A comparison of the two classes of factors shows that the satisfiers are job centered and relate to the *nature* of the work; the job itself is the major source of motivation. On the other hand, the dissatisfiers are associated with the *context* of the work and their presence serves to "clean up" the environment and prevent dissatisfaction. If workers are inclined toward only satisfiers and no dissatisfiers, management has achieved an ideal condition. As might be expected, this is generally not the case.

When viewing Herzberg's theory in its totality (see Figure 12.1), one can see that an individual's *real* motivation results from his or her personal accomplishments through the challenge of work itself and not from the working conditions in the work environment. Herzberg recognizes that hygiene factors must be adequately provided if the individual is to become a superior performer. Thus, if the dissatisfiers are quite pronounced or increase, the individual becomes concerned about these factors instead of striving for superior performance; conversely, if there are no dissatisfiers in the work environment, the individual will be striving for superior performance.

Research results indicate that motivation factors were generally the primary cause of satisfaction, while hygiene factors were the primary cause of unhappiness on the job. However, in some cases, Herzberg's theory has not been upheld. In those studies critical of his theory, some researchers concluded that a given factor which caused satisfaction in one sample was the cause of dissatisfaction in another. Other research results have concluded that the job level affects the outcome for a given factor, while still others found that the age of the respondent was a determining element. Overall, the research results seem to be somewhat mixed.

AN APPROACH TO EXPAND MASLOW'S HIERARCHY OF NEEDS

As indicated in the previous discussion, the highest-level need, as postulated by Abraham Maslow, centers on self-actualization, that is, realizing one's ambitions. In other words, the focus is on self-fulfillment where the individual is the focal point. In reality, self-actualization is a stop on the way to meeting other higher-level needs. This is in contrast with Maslow's contention that once a person has become self-actualized, he or she will go back down the "hierarchy of needs ladder" and concentrate on lower-level needs that were never fully satisfied when working for meeting higher-level needs. The author contends that this may not be true. Hence, in light of the many problems facing MIS and functional end-user management, there is need to replace the self-actualization concept with a newer direction so that many of the problems set forth in Chapter 2 (see Figure 2.4) can be addressed and reduced to a tolerable level.

Mutual Actualization

The next step after self-actualization per Maslow must go beyond an inward-looking approach and is directed toward an outward-looking approach. This approach is called *mutual actualization.*[9] Mutual actualization is the process where two or more individuals enrich one another and, in doing so, grow both as individuals and as a group. The challenge of mutual actualization is to grow and to share. Each person grows individually. Each is further self-actualized by interacting with others in a positive manner. Each grows not only by interacting with others who have mutual interests, but by working out a problem with sympathy and understanding. Individuals also grow by sharing, that is, by sharing hurts and problems. Mutual actualization can also mean not being nice to one another. Although each tries to express his or her own feelings without charges and accusations against the other, he or she shares both bad feelings and good ones.

To put the foregoing concept of mutual actualization into focus within an MIS environment, consider a senior systems analyst who has realized her life's ambition: being an MIS project manager on the organization's largest project. The individual is not only looked upon as an important source of systems design expertise by other MIS project managers, but also is highly regarded by MIS and functional end-user departmental managers. In essence, this individual is a self-actualized person. In order for this person to be more productive and at the same time grow with the organization, mutual actualization is needed. In a mutual actualization state, she has the opportunity to acquire special friendships at different times. These friendships may be short- or long-term. They enhance her personal growth and others'. Overall, each person helps actualize the other by growing and sharing on the job.

Self-Donation

For many organizational personnel, mutual actualization may well be the highest level of fulfillment. Mutual actualization, however, is still not the final goal. It too is a stage wherein the "self" is learning to transcend itself. Donation is the goal that human beings strive for. Call it altruism or call it love. Like self-actualization and mutual actualization, it is a process of improving the self. *Self-donation* is the process where we give ourselves easily and regularly.[10] In the self-donation stage, a person is no longer afraid of being rejected or hurt. The image of self-donation is the "selfless saint." Persons like Mahatma Gandhi, Mother Teresa, and Martin Luther King come to mind. There is no jealousy, no need to balance the amount given against the amount received. Rather, in this ideal self-donation stage, the person gives himself or herself to other human beings, then gets himself or herself back, richer for the experience. What better way to find out who we are, to find ourselves, than to get feedback from the regular "gift" of ourselves to others.

It is possible to reach the self-donation stage without going through mutual actualization; however, it is much more difficult. Mutual actualization allows us to grow and share with other people in the organization. In turn, each person helps to actualize the other persons so that each develops his or her own potential.

To illustrate the concept of self-donation, reference can be made again to the senior systems analyst who is highly regarded as an expert on large MIS projects. She may not be internationally known as the people mentioned earlier are, but, nevertheless she too can engage in self-donation. More specifically, she can serve as an important *role model* for junior systems analysts who aspire to follow in her footsteps. She can donate some of her free time (such as during lunch and rest breaks) to talk to junior personnel and encourage them to aspire to higher-level positions. In effect, she is donating her time to encourage other junior members to aspire to higher levels in the MIS organization. At performance appraisal time, her name will be mentioned as the driving force for their efforts to do a better job. Feedback of this type can do more for her than a semiannual bonus paid for work performed. In effect, she is donating her time regularly to help struggling MIS personnel who need different assists at different stages of

Figure 12.2
The Relationship of Maslow's Hierarchy of Needs and the Revised Hierarchy of Needs

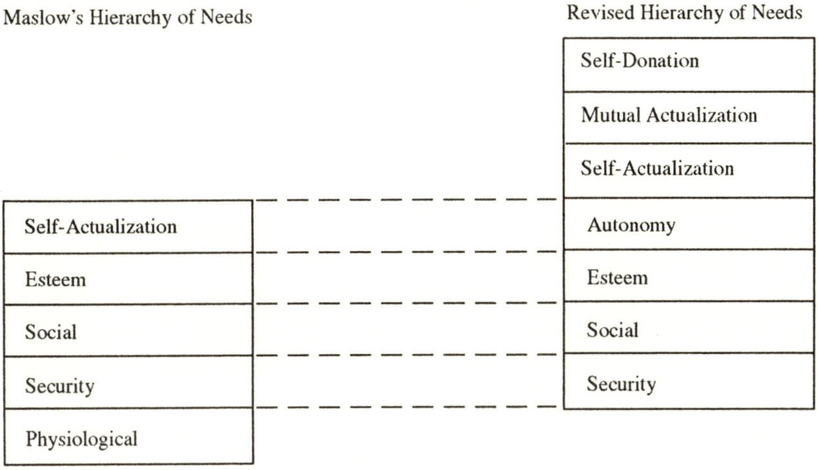

their careers. In turn, she is richer for the experience. Additionally, the organization is benefitting from this win-win approach of self-donation.

REVISED HIERARCHY OF NEEDS FOR MIS PERSONNEL AND END USERS

A way of bringing the preceding material together is to illustrate a revised hierarchy of needs. Such is the case in Figure 12.2, where Maslow's hierarchy of needs is shown first, followed by the revised hierarchy. There is a significant difference in need levels between the two hierarchies. Needless to say, the revised hierarchy represents the direction that MIS and functional end-user departmental managers should take today and in the future.

To reap benefits from the revised hierarchy of needs, a number of measures must be undertaken by MIS and functional end-user management to make the job environment as attractive as possible. Today, some of the options include shorter work weeks and improved hardware and software along with athletic memberships and "wellness" programs that teach employees how to balance their lives outside work as well as inside. Everyone benefits from a program that improves the employee's health and welfare. It cuts down on absenteeism, fatigue, and other forms of job burnout. In addition, MIS management and functional end-user management should capitalize on the inherent self-motivation of the workers and try to keep the "demotivators" out of the way. Some of the demotivating practices include burdening the individual with excessive red tape and paperwork, or leaving him or her alone without feedback. Employees who do not get feedback start to feel unimportant, and this can be the greatest de-motivator of all. Overall, treating human resources as some companies have treated their factories, as wasting assets, has the same price: failure. Adopting a longer-range view of investing in people, as some manufacturing companies do in factories, can have the same results: success and growth.

JOB STRESS OF MIS PERSONNEL AND END USERS

Generally, job stress of MIS personnel and end users manifests itself primarily in the formal structure, although it can be found in the informal structure. *Stress* results when people are under pressure or intense strain over time. Typical research results show that almost nine out of ten American adults experience high levels of stress at least once or twice a week. Seventy-five percent of all American workers describe their jobs as stressful and believe the problem is becoming more intense. Other studies indicate that five out of six workers feel that job stress was a major factor that had caused them to be ill.

Typical stress-related symptoms and disorders include headaches, fatigue, back pain, hypertension, heart disease, irritability, anger, depression, ulcers, apathy, anxiety, smoking, overeating, drug abuse, sleep disorders, worry, and hostility. Many researchers believe that job-related stress can lead to *burnout* when the stress goes on far too long and overwhelms a person's ability to cope with it. What constitutes too long depends on the individual. Burnout is a physical and emotional reaction to extensive periods of job-related stress that result in a feeling of apathy or hostility toward work, toward the organization, or toward the people with whom one works. Sometimes, the symptoms can mask other serious problems, such as alcoholism or marital problems. Job burnout is more likely in people who have had the same job for seven or more years. That can be a turning point at which they begin to question where they are and where they are going in an organization.

Living with Stress

Typically, MIS personnel and end users who think they control what happens to them are less likely to burn out than people who believe they are out of control in what is happening to them. The important factor is empowerment, as found in TQM. Basically, this means influencing as much of one's environment as possible so that one does make a difference. Many MIS personnel and end users feel behind the eight ball, perpetually feeling not caught up. That is a major stressor. The trend toward downsizing of the total organization, including MIS, is also placing more stress on people. Some employees are working longer hours because they are afraid of losing their jobs or their work load has increased. When a company downsizes, it is important to change the organizational structure, not just redistribute the work load. That is, organizations can help reduce stress by encouraging employees to balance their jobs with the rest of their lives.

If MIS personnel and end users cannot eliminate whatever is causing stress, the next best thing is to develop a resiliency to it. Some ways to do that are to balance work with other activities, eat a well-balanced diet, exercise, practice deep relaxation techniques, develop social relationships, foster a team environment, and define problems as manageable. When all else fails, MIS personnel and end users should try taking a short mental vacation by putting their feet up on their desks, leaning back in their chairs, and imagining that they are on a beach for a few minutes.

EFFECTIVE WAY TO REDUCE OR RESOLVE CONFLICT AND STRESS IN THE MIS ORGANIZATION

The formal as well as the informal structures provide a mechanism of reducing conflict between management and nonmanagement personnel. Also, the implementation of *job enrichment,* where the worker has control over the work environment and participates in the decision making that affects his or her work, and a participation system, where the worker has some say over working conditions and may participate in profit sharing, may resolve conflict in certain situations. But these are not the complete answer.

Because of the frequent incompatibility of organization objectives and employee needs, conflict between MIS managers and their personnel is inevitable. Any recommendation to resolve this conflict must recognize that employees and organizations need each other, even though their value systems are often different. Employees and organizations have conflicting values in many areas, such as security versus efficiency and self-realization versus control. In view of these realities, managers must be prepared not only to confront conflict when it arises, but also to reduce or resolve it insofar as possible. The same comment can be made regarding stress on the job: there is a need to confront stress on the job and try to reduce it.

Confronting and Smoothing Versus Other Methods

Recommendations for resolving or minimizing conflict (the same holds true for stress) by MIS management depend on the situation. Several generalized approaches to resolve or reduce conflict are (1) confronting the conflict with an open exchange of information and working through the differences so that both sides can win, (2) smoothing or playing down the differences and emphasizing common values, (3) compromising or bargaining to search for intermediate positions, (4) withdrawing from the conflict, and (5) forcing one party to accept the values of the other. The first approach is behaviorally oriented, with a win-win philosophy instead of the traditional win-lose philosophy. For this confrontation approach to be effective, it should operate in an open atmosphere of mutual trust and acceptance of the fact that conflict is inevitable and mistakes can be made on both sides. The admission of guilt by one of the parties should not be construed as a sign of weakness, but rather as acknowledgment that one is rarely completely right or wrong.

In a study of seventy-four managers (for one department) of a large organization, opinions concerning the efficacy of these five methods of dealing with conflict were obtained. Correlations were computed between these methods and their effectiveness of conflict resolution. The results are as follows:

Method	*Effectiveness Rating*
Confrontation	+0.26
Smoothing	+0.20
Compromising	−0.08
Withdrawal	−0.19
Forcing	−0.26

As the data show, the first approach (confrontation) results in the highest positive correlation, followed closely by the smoothing approach. In a second study, of fifty-three managers from various organizations, managers were asked to describe both effective and ineffective conflict resolutions they had experienced. Again using the five approaches, the study showed that 58.5 percent of the effective resolutions used the confrontation approach and 24.5 percent used forcing. None of the ineffective resolutions used confrontation, while 79.2 percent of them used forcing. The other three methods appeared to be used an insignificant portion of the time, except withdrawal, which was employed in 9.4 percent of the ineffective resolutions. In short, both studies indicate that the confrontation approach will usually effect better resolutions than the other four methods.[11]

Unresolved Conflict and Stress

If either confrontation or smoothing is not used, there is a tendency for conflict to be unresolved over a period of time. This can lead to a number of unfavorable reactions by MIS personnel. For one, they can leave the company or ask for a transfer to another department. Second, they can withdraw from the conflict and exert their energies in the direction of activities outside work, such as hobbies or preparation for a new career. Third, they can internalize the conflict and come up with a wide assortment of physical ailments over time. Although none of these approaches resolves the ongoing conflict, all of them help employees escape temporarily from the conflict. It is recommended that MIS management operate in an open atmosphere in which conflict is resolved as soon as possible. In this manner, a reduced conflict environment will allow MIS personnel to put forth their best efforts and operate in a win-win operating environment as opposed to being stifled by unresolved conflict in a win-lose mode. Essentially, the same approach can be applied to reducing stress.

GUIDELINES TO ASSIST MIS MANAGEMENT IN EFFECTIVE PERSONNEL SELECTION AND MOTIVATION

A *first* guideline to assist MIS management in the personnel selection process relates to being consistent when applying the steps for the selection process. The rationale is that information about the selection of MIS personnel finally makes the rounds via the informal structure, that is, the grapevine. What may have been expedient at the time to get a certain MIS professional by bypassing set selection procedures may come back to haunt the MIS manager at a later date. The essential message, then, is that recruiting certain MIS professionals can be disastrous unless MIS management can give a logical reason for their recruitment and why they did not follow the set procedures in the MIS selection process.

A *second* guideline recognizes that some MIS professionals who are recruited will have inclinations toward MIS management. On the other hand, it should be recognized that many prefer to be technicians all of their lives. Hence, MIS management should not only recruit MIS professionals who possess technical skills, but consider some in terms of their potential as future MIS managers and supervisors from the lowest level to the highest level. Typically, new MIS personnel are more concerned with the technical aspects of their jobs and may not be able to relate to management immediately. Furthermore, MIS purists have trouble leading and motivating subordinates to do a good job. In either case, MIS management is interested in recruiting people who can apply technology to business solutions.

In the area of motivation, a *third* guideline useful to MIS management that ties in with total quality management is the empowerment of MIS personnel and end users to permit their increased involvement in decisions that affect them. From this perspective, each person is genuinely valued as unique and worthwhile. In other words, the person feels that he or she is operating in a win-win environment. From another perspective, the empowerment of personnel in the MIS organization can have a pronounced effect on MIS management. For one, motivated employees do more than just produce better work; they also make the manager's job a lot easier. They require less supervision. When people are motivated, work can be delegated and will be done as expected. And the MIS manager will spend less time developing alibis about why the best plans did not work.

A *fourth* guideline related to motivation recognizes that the latest direction in motivation goes outside oneself. Since *motivation* is the key to turning responsible individuals into creative, productive, and loyal employees, MIS management must understand fully what motivation is. Maslow's hierarchy of needs does not represent the end state needed today to cope with changing organizationwide computing activities. However, the higher-level needs of MIS personnel, mutual actualization and self-donation, are a logical way of bringing together MIS personnel with end users for a more positive and productive way to meet their newer, higher-level needs.

Tied in with the topic of motivation is turnover. A *fifth* guideline on how to reduce turnover includes the following items set forth in the chapter: always keep employees informed on company matters, set up clear channels of communication between MIS management and personnel, encourage employee creativity and try to keep work as challenging as possible, encourage self-improvement and point out opportunities for advancement, and never oversell a candidate in the employment interview. In addition, it is essential for MIS management to define an employee's job and the expected results through a written job description and frequent personal review sessions. Specific benchmarks for measuring success must be established so that both employee and supervisor agree on what constitutes a good job.

A most desirable *sixth* guideline to assist MIS management in resolving or reducing conflict and stress centers on a confrontation approach that uses an open exchange of ideas. The confrontation approach results in a win-win situation such that both parties—the MIS manager and the MIS personnel—feel that they have won important points throughout the discussion. In essence, both hold their heads high and feel that something constructive has been accomplished.

NOTES

1. J. Daniel Couger and Robert A. Zawacki, *Motivating and Managing Computer Personnel,* New York: John Wiley & Sons, 1980.

2. Abraham Maslow, *Motivation and Personality,* New York: Harper & Brothers, 1954.

3. Lyman W. Porter, "A Study of Perceived Need Satisfaction in Bottom and Middle Management Jobs," *Journal of Applied Psychology,* vol. 45, 1961, pp. 1–10.

4. Abraham Maslow, *Motivation and Personality,* second edition, New York: Harper & Row, 1970, p. 46.

5. Abraham Maslow, *Motivation and Personality,* New York: Harper & Brothers, 1954, chapter 5.

6. Robert J. Thierauf and Robert C. Klekamp, "Behavioral Models," in *Decision Making Through Operations Research,* second edition, New York: John Wiley & Sons, 1975, pp. 541–565.

7. Frederick Herzberg, B. Mausner, and B. Snyderman, *The Motivation to Work,* New York: John Wiley & Sons, 1959.

8. Frederick Herzberg and William F. Dowling, "An Interview with Frederick Herzberg: Managers or Animal Trainers?" *Management Review,* July 1971, pp. 2–15.

9. Robert J. Thierauf, *New Directions in MIS Management: A Guide for the 1990s,* New York: Quorum Books, 1988, p. 181.

10. Ibid., pp. 181–182.

11. Rollie Tillman, Jr., "Problems in Review: Committees on Trial," *Harvard Business Review,* May–June 1960, pp. 6–12 and 162–172.

13

Training and Performance Evaluation of MIS Personnel

OUTLINE

INTRODUCTION TO EFFECTIVE TRAINING AND PERFORMANCE EVALUATION OF MIS PERSONNEL

Among the most pressing concerns of MIS management are the training, evaluation, and development of its personnel. In the past, MIS management has focused on the latest advances in equipment and software as the primary means to improve information processing services; major conversions to newer-generation computers, distributed data processing, and database management systems have all been justified on this basis. Today, however, MIS management must be aware that improved personnel productivity and creativity are the real keys to tapping the organization's potential to meet the challenges of tomorrow. After all, it is the organization's people who provide the information processing services, work with end users to identify opportunities for improvement, and help capitalize on these opportunities. Furthermore, personnel costs now exceed equipment costs in most organizations, and this difference continues to widen.

Because the training, evaluation, and development of MIS personnel are so important today, they are discussed in some detail. Key steps necessary for the development of an effective training program and the special training needs of new employees are highlighted. A recommended approach to the performance evaluation process will be outlined. In addition, a career planning process for the development of future MIS personnel will be presented. The importance of career planning and its relationship to performance evaluation will be emphasized.

PRINCIPLES OF EFFECTIVE MIS TRAINING AND PERFORMANCE EVALUATION

Basic principles underlying effective training start with the *Principle of MIS Training Objectives.* Management of the training process should be handled like that of an MIS project. Training objectives must be clearly defined and, along with associated schedules, costs, and benefits, approved by senior corporate management. The manager of MIS training must obtain data to track progress of these factors and be prepared to take appropriate corrective action to ensure that objectives are met. It should be noted that a training program, no matter how cleverly designed, is not the answer for everyone. Uniform training is a convenience for the MIS manager and the training group, but may be woefully inappropriate for certain individuals, especially new personnel.

Next, the *Principle of an Effective MIS Training Program* is mandatory. Too often, in many organizations, the MIS training program is a rehash of the prior year. That is, the emphasis is on repeating the prior year's training without an eye to providing training on new information technologies and methodologies that will improve productivity of MIS personnel as well as the quality of final production systems and their everyday operations. Hence, an effective training program not only delivers current training on new directions in MIS, but also anticipates the needs of MIS personnel. In addition, this same comment can be made in reference to end-user training.

Additionally, training relates to the *Principle of Improving On-the-Job Performance*. The primary goal of an effective training program must be to improve the on-the-job performance of MIS personnel. Any departure from this goal should be regarded as a decrease in the cost-effectiveness of training efforts. The MIS manager must be especially sensitive to the training needs of the new employees. Training must not only teach the new employee the fundamentals of the job, but also meet socialization and performance expectation needs. In essence, an effective program requires a carefully planned and cost-justifiable approach to training.

In the area of performance evaluation, there is initially need for the *Principle of Performance Evaluation Objectives*. Underlying this principle is the fact that an effective performance evaluation process is a continuous, ongoing process and should not be treated as a once-a-year activity that somehow or other must be undertaken. Typical performance evaluation objectives are to help MIS managers perform better in coaching and developing people, thereby leading eventually to improved performance; help MIS managers build and staff an organization founded on the strengths of its personnel; help motivate employees by providing fair, accurate, timely, and constructive feedback on their performance; and improve organizational development by identifying those employees with high potential for promotion. In addition, performance evaluation provides information for MIS management regarding decisions on merit increases, promotions, new assignments, and dismissals as well as identifies strengths and weaknesses of employees to provide input to training and improvement programs.

The *Principle of a Fair and Objective Performance Evaluation* relates an open atmosphere in which the MIS manager and the individual being evaluated can feel that they have won some of their major points. The open exchange is fair from both viewpoints as well as objective so that substantive issues can be discussed. In effect, both parties feel that there is a *win-win situation* at the completion of the performance evaluation process. This is particularly important when the person being evaluated must face his or her colleagues whatever the results of the performance evaluation.

The *Principle of Detection and Correction of Employee Shortcomings* applies to performance evaluation. An effective performance evaluation process focuses not only on recognizing and rewarding an individual's good performance, but also on identifying and correcting an individual's weaknesses. Weaknesses discussed in evaluation must meet the following conditions: the weakness can be substantiated by objective facts; the weakness detracts substantially from the results the individual is expected to achieve; and the weakness can be improved. Overall, an effective performance evaluation process must compare the quantity and quality of results actually achieved with that which the individual was expected to achieve.

An underlying principle in the area of career planning is the *Principle of*

Effective Career Direction. An effective MIS manager must do three things to aid the professional in career planning: (1) the manager and the organization must provide an environment most conducive to professional development; (2) the manager must provide support and encouragement for others to reach their full potential; and (3) the manager must judiciously supply direction necessary to help chart the individual's career path. In essence, career planning does not just happen: It must be developed, implemented, and supported by MIS management.

An integral part of this principle is the *Principle of Realizing an Individual's Short- to Long-Term Growth Objectives.* Essentially, this is tied in with an individual's total career plans: that is, a starting point is the employee's short-term objectives for the coming year and next year, followed by those for the long term over the next three to five years. As the individual experiences more time on the job, these growth objectives tend to widen and include moving into some position of management. But more importantly, they represent the realization of one's career path over the long term.

RELATIONSHIP OF CURRENT RESEARCH TO TRAINING AND PERFORMANCE EVALUATION OF MIS PERSONNEL

Current research results (refer to Chapter 2) have disclosed a number of major problems confronting the typical MIS manager. In the area of training, the following problem (refer to Figure 2.4) was noted:

- Lack of training programs for new and experienced MIS personnel (rated no. 5)

In addition, other problem areas (refer to Figure 2.4) that are related to the topical areas of this chapter were noted in Chapter 12 because they tie in directly or indirectly with motivation. By way of review, these included:

- Lack of career pathing (rated no. 9)
- Lack of performance standards to evaluate MIS personnel (rated no. 10)
- Lack of an adequate performance appraisal program (rated no. 12)

Since these have been discussed, they will not be treated again. However, it is appropriate to say that the lack of concern for MIS personnel shows up in these three problems. The same can be said of the *lack of training programs for new and experienced MIS personnel.*

To address this training problem, the MIS manager needs to start planning a training program by determining what he or she wants it to accomplish. The focus should be on what the MIS problems are and how training will help to overcome them. The manager also needs to think about what he or she wants employees to accomplish when their training is finished. On the basis of the objectives that have been set, the MIS manager must determine how effective the training was. An effective approach to training will be given here. In addition, this chapter will focus on an effective performance evaluation process and offer some comments on career planning for MIS professionals.

EFFECTIVE MIS MANAGEMENT OF THE TRAINING PROGRAM

The primary goal of any training program must be to improve the on-the-job performance of MIS personnel. An effective MIS training program has two very worthwhile side benefits. First, it strongly influences the quality and quantity of individuals attracted by the recruiting effort. Potential employees carefully evaluate the willingness of a company to invest in its employees, and the presence of an effective training program provides clear evidence of this. Second, it helps the MIS organization retain experienced personnel by enabling them to continue their professional growth, thus meeting their higher-level needs (as set forth in Chapter 12). An effective training program will help make work more interesting, motivate employees, and cut down on personnel turnover.

Despite the many benefits of a sound training program, many organizations approach training in a haphazard manner. The training budget is usually determined as some increase or decrease of last year's budget with no relationship to the real training needs of the organization. Total training costs are seldom known, nor are training results measured in a way that determines their benefits. Individual training is rarely planned and justified on an objective basis. It is not at all unusual for an organization to set a training goal, say, two weeks of training per employee per year, but not plan the training to meet the needs of MIS personnel or the MIS organization.

Unfortunately, in many MIS organizations the training of MIS personnel is poorly managed. Common symptoms of an ineffective training program are as follows. First, the total training effort is outside the range of 1.5 to 2.5 percent of the total MIS budget. Second, MIS personnel performance does not consistently meet user expectations, although the personnel seem highly motivated. Third, extraordinary measures must be employed frequently to meet totally unanticipated training needs. Fourth, end users of information services frequently complain that MIS personnel lack a basic understanding of the company's fundamental business, priorities, and objectives. Fifth, it is extremely difficult to free up qualified MIS personnel to deliver in-house training. Sixth, MIS management does not support the training effort. Seventh and last, there is no attempt to cost justify or evaluate the effectiveness of training.

AN EFFECTIVE TRAINING PROGRAM OF MIS PERSONNEL

Overcoming this bad situation and developing an effective MIS training program require a carefully planned and cost-justifiable approach. The following is an effective way to obtain such results:

1. Identify the training needs of the MIS organization
2. Define the appropriate means to deliver the training
3. Screen for potential trainees
4. Deliver the training
5. Evaluate the training, trainer, and trainees
6. Manage the training program

These steps are illustrated as process blocks in Figure 13.1. The inputs necessary to perform each process and the resulting outputs are also shown. The steps are explained in detail later. In addition, this section will highlight the special needs of new employees.

1. Identify the Training Needs of the MIS Organization

An effective MIS training program must be sensitive to current training needs and be able to anticipate future needs. Those responsible for the training program must seek out key individuals in the MIS organization and other functional end-user units served by it to identify these needs. Anticipated hardware/software installations, changes to databases and data communications, a change in the relationship of MIS to end-user departments, or a change in the operations of the company all signal a need for training. An analysis of current MIS projects and an evaluation of the reasons for their success or failure provide another perspective on training needs. Furthermore, needs can be evaluated by paying attention to the requests for training.

These perceived needs must then be carefully evaluated to decide whether they really can or should be met. Will delivery of the desired training lead to improved performance of personnel in an activity consistent with the goals and long-range direction of the company? Is the importance of meeting the need sufficient to justify management attention and the required training effort? Can the need be fulfilled through training?

As shown in Figure 13.1, the output of this step consists of defined training needs, an estimate of the number of people needing the training, and a rough schedule of when and how often the training should be offered. The basic training needs description provides an overview of the training and its purpose. The estimate of the number of people who need the training should consider future employment and recruiting plans because of the heavy participation of new employees in training.

2. Define the Appropriate Means to Deliver the Training

Once the training needs have been determined, the next step is to define the appropriate means to deliver the training. One way to define the means clearly is to specify the following items:

Figure 13.1
Steps in the Development of an Effective Training Program for MIS Personnel

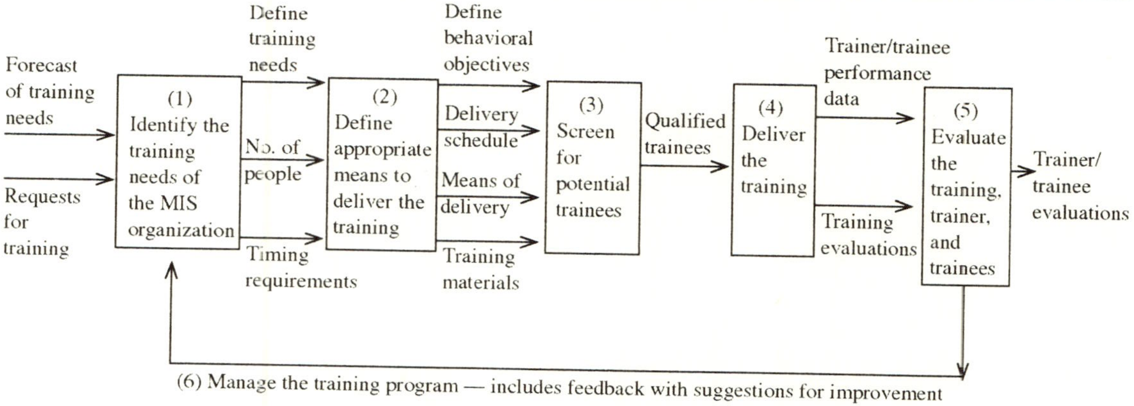

- *Behavioral objectives*—describe a measurable behavior that the trainer will be expected to perform on successful completion of the training.
- *Delivery schedule*—defines when and how frequently training will be offered. The schedule should state how many people need the training and when they must have it.
- *Means of delivery*—refers to training by on-the-job experiences or formal courses.
- *Training materials*—commonly includes software, texts, case-study notebooks, workbooks, audio-visual films and equipment, and computer-related equipment for hands-on experience.

These items are helpful to the MIS manager in specifying how the training needs will be met. They are also illustrated in Figure 13.1.

3. Screen for Potential Trainees

An effective MIS training program must have a screening process to ensure that the participants are enrolled in the appropriate parts of the program. Prerequisites for each part of the program should be defined. Potential trainees and their managers should be encouraged to make a careful and deliberate decision on participation in any training by answering the following questions: Can the individual meet the behavioral objectives of the course now, before training? Is there a more effective way to prepare the individual to meet the behavioral objectives of the course? Does the individual meet all of the prerequisites for the course? Does the individual need this training to improve on-the-job performance? Would the individual be better prepared for or receive greater value from the training if it were taken in the future? Answering these questions will go a long way to determining that potential trainees are enrolled in the appropriate training program. As before, reference can be made to Figure 13.1.

4. Deliver the Training

For training to be successful, it must be presented in a well-organized and interesting manner. All trainees must receive the appropriate training material in advance and complete any necessary prework. The behavioral objectives for each portion of the training must be highlighted before, during, and after. A clear connection must be made between major topics in the training and real, job-connected activities of the trainees. It is recommended that daily quizzes based on course material be designed to reinforce learning, provide trainees with feedback on their understanding of key concepts, and evaluate trainees' progress.

To maintain a high degree of trainee interest, the delivery must be carefully planned. A high-interest level will motivate the trainees and greatly improve their ability to meet the behavioral objectives of the course. The use of audio-visual materials, case studies, and team exercises is an excellent means of keeping the interest level high and reinforcing the training. Careful selection of the trainer also can help to ensure a high degree of interest. The trainer must be capable of taking a responsible position toward improving organizational and individual performance, have a solid background in the subject, possess a high degree of instructional talent, and empathize with trainees. Such an approach is an integral part of Figure 13.1.

5. Evaluate the Training, Trainer, and Trainees

On completion of the training, the trainees should be evaluated to see whether they can now meet the behavioral objectives of the course. This evaluation could be performed by having the trainees take a written test or pass an oral exam given by their trainer and/or manager or by closely observing their on-the-job performance. The trainees must be given feedback on the degree of success that they have in meeting the behavioral objectives. If there are behavioral objectives that the trainees cannot meet, and this failure lowers the on-the-job performance, the trainee, manager, and trainer must work together to eliminate this weakness.

Trainees should be encouraged to fill out training/trainer evaluation forms for use by the trainer and the manager in charge of training. Trainees can thus provide feedback valuable for improving training the next time it is given. It is helpful for trainee feedback on the following areas to be solicited:

- Are there any behavioral objectives that you feel were not met? If so, which ones are they and why?
- Are there any behavioral objectives which you feel should be added to this course? If so, what are they and why?
- Are there any behavioral objectives which you feel should be eliminated from this course? If so, which ones are they and why?
- What feedback would you like to provide about the course screening process and course prerequisites?
- What feedback would you like to provide about the training materials (text, case study, audio-visuals, etc.)?
- What feedback would you like to provide about the instructor (knowledge of material, organization, delivery, style, empathy with trainees, ability to maintain interest level, etc.)?
- What specific suggestions would you offer to improve this course?

As shown in Figure 13.1, the end result of answering these questions is trainer/trainee evaluations.

6. Manage the Training Program

Typically, a specific person should be responsible for the management of the training program. The training manager must clearly define objectives for the program, analyze the costs and benefits associated with it, and obtain approval to meet these objectives from the highest-level MIS management. An attempt to quantify the benefits of a strong training program in terms of improved on-the-job performance, an enhanced recruiting effort, and reduced turnover of experienced employees is suggested.

For each major phase of the training program, it is necessary to prepare a timetable and budget. The training manager must periodically review and report progress relative to these milestones and take appropriate corrective action if progress deviates too widely from the plan (refer to Figure 13.1). The individual must obtain the resources necessary to meet the objectives—training facilities, equipment, materials, and trainers, as well as regular feedback. This information can then be used by the training manager to identify and justify appropriate changes to the training program.

SPECIAL TRAINING NEEDS OF NEW EMPLOYEES

New MIS employees have three areas of special training needs, that is, socialization, performance expectations, and job fundamentals. The training program must be carefully assigned to meet their special needs. The *socialization* training needs of new employees include gaining a basic understanding of the goals and norms of the organization and learning to work effectively with others. These needs must be met before new employees can feel a part of the organization and function at their full effectiveness. Some organizations address these needs in a company policy manual and by introducing new employees to their immediate work associates. The new employees are then left on their own with the assumption that they will learn what they need to learn to survive in the organization. Significant improvement can be made in the socialization process by preparing a checklist of the most common new employee questions and having new employees discuss the items on that list with their managers. Typical socialization questions include the following: Where does my job end and someone else's begin? What type of relationship should I have with my manager? What type of relationship should I have with my peers? How do I know whether I am doing a good or a bad job? Where can I get information to help me manage my career?

In the area of *performance expectations,* new employees are eager to learn what their MIS manager expects of them. The new employees should be encouraged to ask for clarification of the manager's expectations, and the manager should be willing to discuss what they can expect of him or her. The sharing of mutual expectations within the first few days should be a goal of both manager and new employee. Common questions include: How do I find out what is really expected of me? When should I go to my manager for help? What kind of help can I expect from my manager? What should I do if I do not like or cannot complete an assignment? How will I find out what my manager thinks of my performance? Will my manager help with my training and career planning and in what ways? What kinds of mistakes are acceptable and what kinds are not?

Regarding the third item, *job fundamentals* relates to training in terms of the employee's first assignment. The areas and levels of necessary training, when and how the training is to be delivered, and specific training materials and experiences needed to acquire the desired skills must be a very careful and deliberate decision involving the new employee, the new employee's manager, and the training manager. The model in Figure 13.1 may be used. However, the emphasis is now on developing a customized program for a specific individual. The forecast of training needs is constructed from a statement by the MIS manager of the individual's current job and most likely near-future assignments, an analysis of the new employee's training and experiences relative to the requirements of the current job, and suggestions by the training manager of some possibly overlooked training needs.

AN EXAMPLE OF AN EFFECTIVE MIS TRAINING PROGRAM

To place the foregoing activities into perspective, reference can be made to the MIS department of a large manufacturer of consumer products that consists of nearly 120 MIS professionals and management personnel. For its training program, it has designed the following practices. An MIS training committee (which reports to the MIS organizationwide committee) meets once a month to identify and define training needs of the organization. Formal requests for training (stated in terms of behavioral objectives) are submitted to the committee; these, as well as ideas of the committee, are discussed. The committee consists of two high-level managers from the functional end-user units served by the MIS organization to ensure that training about the business is considered in addition to pure MIS training. From within the MIS department, there are two high-level managers, two first-level managers, two technical specialists, and the training manager.

The appropriate means to deliver the training is worked out by the training manager and the individuals with the training requests. The behavioral objectives for the training are reviewed. Frequently, most of the objectives may be met through an existing course with only minor changes in scope and content. If not, then the individuals within the organization who are qualified to develop and/or teach the course are identified. If no one can be found, the recommendation is to take the course from an outside source.

A calendar of courses and instructors is prepared quarterly for six-month periods. The calendar is broadly distributed to all managers and professionals. For each course, there is a written testimonial from a student who has taken the course, along with a summary of the course and instructor rating by students from the course. Since there are no full-time instructors, instructors are contacted at least three months in advance to teach a single course. The instructor's commitment to teach a course is taken seriously; if one is unable to teach a course, a qualified replacement must be found.

The instructors are chosen on the basis of their knowledge of the subject matter, their ability to communicate well, and their ability to relate well to others. New instructors are given two days of training on effective teaching—stressing behavioral objectives, motivation of students, and use of various training aids. Also, the capability to serve as an effective instructor is strongly considered in promotions. No one is eligible for promotion to the first-level management position unless he or she has either successfully developed or taught at least one course.

Managers are strongly encouraged to review the course behavioral objectives with potential trainees and to handle the course registration activities. This serves as a screening device to minimize trainees' taking an unnecessary course, allows a discussion on how the course matches the individual's short- and long-term professional growth objectives, and allows the manager to review the course in terms of the individual's current responsibilities.

The training manager publishes a quarterly report that highlights the on-the-job impact of newly developed courses. This is done by communicating the results achieved by trainees as they attempt to apply the skills and knowledge provided by the course. This requires that the training manager follow up closely on the work of these individuals and solicit their opinions on the effectiveness of the training. This effort has paid for itself many times over by identifying and eliminating poor courses and instructors and by providing strong justification to continue offering other courses.

EFFECTIVE MIS MANAGEMENT OF PERFORMANCE EVALUATION

Because a most important role of an MIS manager is to direct others to achieve organizational goals, the individual must develop MIS personnel who are highly motivated and have the ability to meet these goals. Handled correctly, performance evaluation is an excellent motivational and personal development tool. The ability to formulate and communicate a fair, accurate, and constructive performance evaluation, then, is a highly important skill for the MIS manager to master. It should be noted that an effective performance evaluation process is a continual one. The MIS manager provides frequent feedback to all of his or her employees, letting them know how their performance measures up to the manager's and the organization's expectations. In this manner, the MIS manager coaches, motivates, and helps others to gain the ability to meet the goals of the organization.

For best results, the evaluation process does not focus on the identification and the correction of weaknesses of the individual unless those weaknesses can be substantiated by objective facts, detract substantially from the results that the individual is expected to achieve, and can be improved. A concentration on minor or uncorrectable weaknesses serves only to demotivate and frustrate the individual. Rather, the performance evaluation should concentrate on the quantity and quality of the results the individual actually achieved compared to the results that he or she was expected to achieve.

Even for the highly effective MIS manager, personnel performance evaluation is clearly an activity full of pitfalls. Probably no other activity can cause a manager so much anxiety and discomfort as preparing for and conducting an honest and constructive evaluation for an employee who is failing miserably. But what greater personal satisfaction can a manager feel than to see such an employee execute a complete turnaround and begin to perform effectively?

Performance evaluation seems like such a natural thing for a manager to do, that is, letting people know how they stand, identifying areas for improvement, and providing constructive criticism in a manner intended to improve effectiveness. What could be more natural? Unfortunately, results frequently fall short of good intentions. This section identifies some of the main objectives for the performance evaluation and a recommended approach for an effective performance evaluation.

Objectives of Performance Evaluation

An effective performance evaluation process should be capable of meeting many objectives. Some of the most common are the following: Initially, it helps MIS managers perform a better job of coaching and developing their people, thereby leading eventually to improved performance. In the long run, it should help MIS managers build and staff an organization founded on the strengths of its personnel. Performance evaluation, if done properly, can improve organizational development by identifying those employees with high potential for promotion. Also, it can help motivate employees by providing fair, accurate, timely, and constructive feedback on their performance. Another important objective of performance evaluation is to provide data for management decisions on merit increases, promotions, new assignments, and dismissals. In the final analysis, performance evaluation can help identify strengths and weaknesses of employees in order to provide input to training and improvement programs.

From another perspective, a legal objective for conducting regular and formal performance appraisal of MIS personnel is that both the Equal Employment Opportunity Commission (EEOC) and Affirmative Action (AA) require that a company be able to demonstrate a direct and traceable relationship between a job description and its performance criteria and the appraisal of performance against the description and criteria. The direct involvement of the individual in setting, monitoring, and measuring objectives must also be shown.

AN EFFECTIVE PERFORMANCE EVALUATION PROCESS

An effective performance evaluation program, as just noted, must be an ongoing process rather than a once-a-year activity. It focuses not only on recognizing and rewarding good performance but also on identifying and correcting weaknesses of the individual. The performance evaluation process, if carefully designed and carried out, can help the MIS manager to meet organization goals as well as the goals of his or her employees. A recommended approach consists of the following steps:

1. Define the results the individual is expected to achieve
2. Gather data to evaluate the individual
3. Prepare for the evaluation
4. Schedule a date for the evaluation
5. Share the performance data
6. Develop a joint action plan

Before employees can be fairly evaluated on their performance, it is obvious that they must know what is expected of them. To ensure that the expectations are understood, the MIS manager and employee should discuss what specifically constitutes acceptable performance. Per the last step, the joint action plan stands a much better chance of being carried out if the employee develops the specific goals. The action plan should be discussed and reviewed at least three or four times a year to maintain its effectiveness.

1. Define the Results the Individual Is Expected to Achieve

In the first step of performance evaluation, there is a clear communication to the employee of what is expected. To ensure that the expectations are understood, the MIS manager and employee should discuss specifically what is to be accomplished and what constitutes acceptable performance. For a new employee, the MIS manager may develop the expectations and, in turn, discuss them with the individual. On the other hand, for an experienced employee, the manager and employee may jointly develop performance expectations. Either way, the results that the individual is expected to achieve should be documented for future use at performance evaluation time. Performance expectations should not be thought of as frozen, but as flexible. If the nature of an individual's assignment changes, the expectations should be jointly reviewed and revised as appropriate.

2. Gather Data to Evaluate the Individual

Typically, an effective MIS manager is continually receiving a wealth of formal and informal information about the performance of employees. He or she should seek specifics and understand the situation surrounding the performance in order to share the data constructively with the subordinate. Frequent discussions with the employee on work-related matters, professional growth, and career planning provide the means of obtaining this information. Formal and informal discussions are an effective way to gather performance data. One hour per week for each employee is not an excessive amount of time. The old standby, a weekly manager/employee meeting, can become too routine and automatic, with no really meaningful matters being discussed. The MIS manager must guard against this possibility and find creative new ways to open the communication channels. A common practice of many effective MIS managers is to take one employee to lunch periodically and just listen.

In addition, close observation and review of the work of employees will yield much detailed information. Thorough review of written reports, user documentation, and even program code written by the employee will give the manager first-hand knowledge of the individual's ability. Formal and informal discussions with peers of the employee, other managers who have recently worked with the employee, and people to whom the employee has delivered recent results can provide excellent data. Data gathering interviews with these people must be handled in a very professional manner. It must be clear that the purpose is to obtain data that will be shared constructively with the individual. Nothing will cut off the flow of communication more quickly than to formalize the process with questionnaires and checklists. Two questions are generally sufficient. What specific aspects of this individual's performance are worthy of comment? What specific things could the individual do to be more effective?

3. Prepare for the Evaluation

Once the data have been gathered, considerable effort must go into the analysis, filtering out insignificant data, summarizing the significant data into key points, and preparing what to say to the employee. It is not unusual to spend several hours in the preparation stage if it has been six to twelve months since the employee's last performance evaluation. This small investment in time is repaid many times over by the impact of an effective performance evaluation.

Much preparation time should be spent relating the data back to specific performance expectations defined at the first step in this process. The relationship between the data that the manager shares with the employee and the results expected to be achieved must be very close. These standards of acceptable performance must continue as the basis of evaluation.

It is very important that the MIS manager anticipate questions and develop well thought out responses to the most likely questions. The one appraising must be prepared for the employee to challenge key points discussed. It is best to have specific objective facts and examples to back up and reinforce the MIS manager's points. Having the answers to questions shows the manager's concern for the employee. How soon can I expect a promotion? What specific things can I do to improve? When is my next job assignment? When is my next raise? Also, notes from several previous performance evaluation sessions with this employee should be reviewed, in particular areas of both improved and deteriorated performance.

4. Schedule a Date for the Evaluation

The MIS manager should contact the employee and schedule a one- to two-hour time for the performance evaluation. A two- or five-day advance notice should be provided to allow the employee time to prepare for the evaluation as well. However, setting the date and time too far in advance can tend to build anxiety and pressure. Hence, the time frame should be approximately one week from schedule to completion.

5. Share the Performance Data

Before the performance data can be shared, there is need for standard forms and procedures to be specified by the organization so that they can be used consistently. This requirement is especially important for conforming with EEOC and AA guidelines. Standardization also helps prevent government audits that often occur when individuals feel that shifting standards are being applied.

The MIS manager and employee should attempt to share data on the employee's performance in a relaxed, open, and objective manner. It is essential to a good performance evaluation that two-way communication be established and that the employee feel free to add his or her viewpoint and perspective. Communication feedback from the employee will ensure that more data are brought out and discussed and that the employee's feelings and opinions are heard. Furthermore, by carefully listening to the responses of the employee, the manager can determine whether his or her points are being understood and accepted by the individual.

As an effective starting point, the MIS manager should begin with a restatement of the specific results the individual is expected to achieve. These expectations were documented in the first step. Next, each key point should be presented in an honest, open-for-discussion, and straightforward manner. Sufficient background and detail data must be presented to put the key points into perspective. Each key point must be supported by solid objective facts and illustrated by at least one good example. The evaluation should not be a monologue, but a discussion between the manager and the employee. The manager should encourage responses from the employee and listen with an open mind. Specific areas of strength and weakness noted in previous evaluations that have exhibited a change for the better or worse should be discussed. It is suggested that the areas of strength be addressed first since this represents an attempt by the MIS manager to put forward his or her best for a fair and an objective evaluation.

For the poor performer, the MIS manager should not dwell on the minor weaknesses, but rather stress those that seriously detract from effectiveness and which can be corrected with effort. Every attempt should be made initially to identify those strengths the individual may have that are worth improving. If a poor performer can be motivated to improve just one weak area each review period, eventually performance will reach acceptability and the individual will no longer be a weak link in the organization. Before completing the evaluation, the MIS manager must review and highlight the key points that were made. It must be made clear whether overall performance has been strong, average, or weak.

Whether the employee is a strong, average, or weak performer, the MIS manager should ask the individual questions concerning sexual harassment. Today, federal and state courts have ruled that sexual harassment covers conduct ranging from blatant grabbing and touching to subtle hints and suggestions. The U.S. Supreme Court ruled several years ago that a hostile environment exists when these actions unreasonably interfere with an employee's performance or create an intimidating work environment. Judges have recognized the following allegations as grounds for suits: unwelcome sexual advances, coercion, favoritism, indirect harassment, physical conduct, and visual harassment. Since expensive lawsuits can be filed against the organization, this important topic must be discussed, and, if there are allegations, they must be documented. After the performance evaluation process, the MIS manager needs to pursue the sexual harassment problem as a separate issue immediately.

At this point in the performance evaluation process, the MIS manager should move to set the stage for the next phase—develop a joint action plan for the next evaluation period. The manager and employee should discuss what types of actions would be appropriate. For example, there may be need for specific training or on-the-job experience. Perhaps more frequent counseling and coaching by the manager are necessary. The manager should then ask the employee to set a specific date for them to review a written joint action plan and discuss the results the individual is expected to achieve before the next evaluation period. It is recommended that the date not exceed one week from step 5 to step 6.

6. Develop a Joint Action Plan

The sixth step provides the MIS manager and the individual with an opportunity to have a second meaningful discussion about the individual's performance. It demonstrates the high level of continuing interest of the manager, thereby building further on the mutual confidence and trust established during the previous steps. Most importantly, it defines specific steps to be taken by both to improve the individual's effectiveness and to help the individual meet his or her career goals.

It is important that the joint action plan be strongly influenced by the career and development objectives of the individual. An effective MIS manager must work hard at matching the needs of the organization with those of the individual. The ideal match occurs when the needs of the organization can be met by the strengths of the individual and in an area in which the individual has career and professional aspirations. An individual with the right abilities that are highly developed and who is very highly motivated to achieve will produce outstanding results.

During the development of the joint action plan, the MIS manager should attempt to have the MIS professional develop a set of personally challenging career and development objectives. It is certainly important that these objectives be consistent with improving goals; it is of the utmost importance that they be developed with a very high degree of participation by the one being appraised. Goals that seem to be set arbitrarily by the manager will likely not be accepted as meaningful by the individual. Consequently, motivation to meet the goals will be lessened and the likelihood of their being met will be reduced. There is one word of caution—the goals must be reviewed carefully for realism: too many goals or goals of too high a level will set the individual up for inevitable failure, lead to demotivation, and undo all the efforts to improve effectiveness.

Specific actionable steps could include any or all of the following:

- *Work-related experiences*—The MIS manager and the professional must identify the types of appropriate experiences and the manager must attempt to provide a job assignment providing the experience.
- *Training*—The specific behavioral objectives to be met should be defined. The appropriate course(s) and date(s) for training should then be scheduled.
- *Upgrading an area of performance*—Objectives must be set for this area of performance, an acceptable level of performance defined, and progress must be reviewed on a regular basis by the MIS manager and the professional.
- *Eliminating factors that impede performance*—Barriers to good performance, such as racism and sexism, should be discussed with the MIS manager, the professional, and Affirmative Action program members. The same comment can be made about sexual harassment.

The joint action plan should be reviewed and approved by both the MIS manager and the individual being appraised. It should then be documented for use in ongoing progress review sessions with the professional. It is suggested that the action plan be discussed and reviewed at least three or four times a year to maintain its effectiveness.

From the MIS manager's viewpoint, there is need to rank all the members of the department by general categories: above average, average, and below average. This ranking can be used to determine fairly who is most deserving of a merit increase, promotion, new assignment, or dismissal.

AN EXAMPLE OF A WRITTEN PERFORMANCE EVALUATION

An example of a written performance evaluation is found in Figure 13.2 for a junior programmer who has been on the job for about one year. The performance evaluation process begins with a clear statement of the results the individual is expected to achieve. In this example, the MIS department conducts a formal evaluation with new employees (less than three years with the organization)

Figure 13.2
Sample Performance Evaluation

Performance Evaluation for Robert Waller (name) Date of This Evaluation 6/16/93

Current Job: Junior Programmer Date of Employment 7/1/92

Current Assignment: Accounts Receivables and Payables Systems (approximately 12 months on this project and on the job)

1. *Describe the results the individual is expected to achieve:*
   a. Display the ability to get good results by applying techniques and skills learned in the computer-aided software engineering program.
   b. Complete at least 90 perenct of all assigned programming projects within the estimated time and budget.
   c. Improve his ability to work on multiple programming projects at the same time.
   d. Participate with his manager in the preparation of a personal training and development program that will direct his professional growth.
   e. Begin to manage himself more autonomously by partially defining his own work load and setting programming deadlines.
2. *Effectiveness in current assignment:*
   Robert has completed several difficult programming modifications to the Accounts Receivables and Payable Systems. The modifications were made carefully, tested thoroughly, and when installed for the users, worked correctly the first time. The systems users were very impressed with the professionalism and quality of Robert's work. Unfortunately, Robert was unable to complete programming modifications to either system on time. He did keep the clients well informed of the status of the modifications so that they were able to adjust to the delay with no problems.
   Robert has developed quickly and completed the company's 12-month training program goals for new employees in 9 months. He has worked well with his manager in developing a personal training program and in keeping his manager well informed on the status of all projects.
3. *Overall strengths and limitations:*
   Strengths: Robert not only is enthusiastic about his work, but also has a strong motivation to succeed. He has a good working and friendly relationship with those he meets. He has good programming skills and makes good use of others as resources. Also, he possesses good written communication skills.n
   Limitations: Robert needs to become more assertive and forceful in preseting his ideas and viewpoints. Although he communicates well, his use of technical jargon with end users should be minimized. Typically, he has a tendency to become overly detailed which slows down his communication of key points.
4. *Emphasis needed to improve job mastery:*
   Robert needs to improve his ability to work on multiple programming projects at the same time: planning work details in advance, setting milestones, estimating time required, and setting priorities.

Figure 13.2 continued

5. *Other comments:*

____________ (manger) (date) ____________

Date of next evaluation: 6 months

6. I have had the opportunity to discuss this performance evaluation.
Comments:

____________ (name) ____________ (date)

every six months. For this evaluation in June, Robert and his manager jointly developed and agreed to the results Robert is expected to achieve by January. His manager gathered performance data from the users of the Accounts Receivables and Payables Systems with whom Robert had worked most closely. Two of his peers in the systems department were also interviewed to obtain data. And, of course, the observations and conclusions of his direct manager were included. The manager spent roughly four hours summarizing and analyzing the data and another couple of hours writing the formal evaluation. The manager and Robert then met and discussed his performance using the points made in the performance evaluation as a guideline. The joint action plan was developed by Robert and approved by his manager.

TIE-IN OF CAREER PLANNING WITH THE PERFORMANCE EVALUATION PROCESS

A most important role of an MIS manager is counseling in the area of career planning. Some MIS managers avoid this responsibility, causing career frustration among their employees and a consequently high turnover. On the other hand, the MIS manager who is actively involved in career planning can help the professional reach his or her full potential while meeting the goals of the organization. Active involvement in career planning enables the manager to influence and develop personnel to meet the future staffing needs of the organization.

To give a better understanding of the career planning process, reference can be made to Figure 13.3. As illustrated, performance evaluation data are used as input to the process to provide the professional with an objective viewpoint relative to achievement of full potential. In addition, specific action steps defined in the joint action plan are used to help define a part of the career action plan. The MIS manager can provide a perspective on the needs of the organization to help the professional set short- to long-range career objectives. That is, the MIS manager can provide information about training opportunities and potential next assignments for the individual. The professional then matches this information with his or her personal assessments of strengths, needs, and interests. The output of the process consists of a documented career plan clearly stating the individual's short- to long-term growth objectives, a list of desired action steps for the MIS manager, and a list of specification steps to be undertaken by the individual.

GUIDELINES TO ASSIST MIS MANAGEMENT IN TRAINING AND PERFORMANCE EVALUATION

A *first* guideline in the area of MIS training focuses on a presentation that is brief, simple, and direct. For the most part, training in the past for users has relied on well-prepared, printed materials. However, these materials may be less effective than personal instruction by a trained teacher, especially for an interactive system. Many organizations have experimented with various training alternatives and have generally found that personalized one-to-one instruction, with considerable hands-on terminal operation, is the most effective teaching mode. Personalized instruction is probably the most satisfactory to the learner and will quite likely produce rapid results. Typically, the approach includes some type of orientation including possible reading assignments. However, it is the exceptional user who does not require the assistance of a trained teacher. Many organizations are using presentations thirty minutes long, incorporating color slides and a taped narrative, for orientation. These "canned" presentations are followed by on-line demonstrations.

A *second* guideline is the need to manage the training program by MIS management. Training programs do not come about by themselves. It is necessary that they be planned as any other MIS activity is. Typically, this area requires a lot of forward thinking by MIS management since new analysis, design, and programming tools must be presented to appropriate MIS personnel months in advance of application. Hence, a typical training committee must anticipate the needs of the MIS organization approximately one year in advance of imple-

Figure 13.3
The Career Planning Process for an MIS Professional

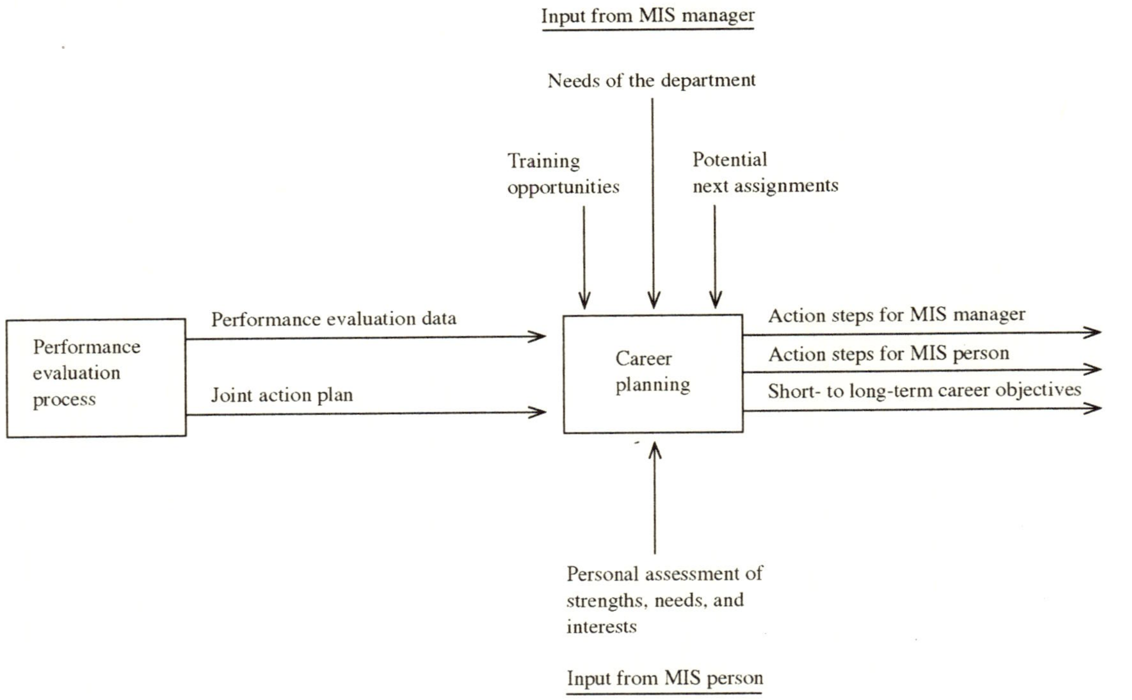

mentation. This important guideline was noted previously in the chapter as step 6 of an effective training program of MIS personnel.

A *third* guideline that centers on performance evaluation allows MIS management to talk about good points as well as bad points of MIS professionals in an open atmosphere. Performance evaluation gives MIS management an excellent opportunity to communicate to its MIS professionals precisely what the organization wants them to do. If an MIS manager wants to talk about a specific point where he or she can exert leverage, this is an opportune time for it. However, in order to realize the full managerial potential of performance appraisal, the MIS manager must think of it not as an event, but as a process that goes on year-round. The process consists as much of coaching and counseling as it does of evaluation. And to work, it must be a two-way exercise, with the MIS manager listening as much as he or she talks. In this manner, a free exchange of information about the individual can result in the development of an effective joint action plan that can be viewed from a win-win standpoint.

Another performance evaluation guideline, the *fourth,* is centered on developing an action plan that is tied in with career pathing. More to the point, both the MIS manager and the individual must agree on what are the goals for this coming year, what are the standards by which he or she will be measured, and what constitutes superior performance. The individual being evaluated should be given time beforehand to think about what he or she hopes to get out of another year on the job. Also, the MIS manager should do some homework. What will the organization require of the individual, that is, anything new or different? How did the person perform last year? What areas of performance does the individual particularly need to apply to himself or herself? Because MIS professionals are interested in their careers, and in talking about their careers, action plans for discussion can also be related to this important topic. Hence, the MIS manager and the individual being evaluated can tie career pathing with appropriate action plans for the coming year so that the individual feels progress is being made toward his or her long-term goals.

A *fifth* important guideline for MIS management is assuring new and experienced MIS personnel that a career-pathing program is in place. That is, it is an actual program whereby MIS professionals can relate to the program on an ongoing basis. Such a program demonstrates to these professionals that MIS management is sincere about their employment with the organization today and tomorrow.

Related to this guideline is a *sixth* one, namely, the tie-in of a career-path program with realization of the individual's higher-level needs over his or her total career, as opposed to staying at one specific need level over an extended period. Essentially, this guideline relates to satisfying lower-level needs first, before moving on to self-actualization, mutual actualization, and, ideally, self-donation. MIS management can help MIS professionals achieve these high-level needs with a career path that is well defined for the MIS organization. And, at the same time, it is well promoted and supported wholeheartedly by MIS management as well as senior corporate management.

PART VII

EFFECTIVE CONTROL OVER THE MIS ORGANIZATION

14

MIS Controls

OUTLINE

INTRODUCTION TO EFFECTIVE MIS CONTROLS

In this last part of the text, many of the essential elements of the prior chapters are brought together under the umbrella of MIS controls. More specifically, MIS management not only needs to oversee short- to long-range MIS strategic plans, new MIS organization structures, and new motivation techniques, but also to manage those MIS activities that center on control over the MIS organization. It is from this perspective that effective MIS controls are developed in this chapter and the final one. Additionally, the text has centered on relating effectively with end users. Currently, MIS management is gaining a better understanding of end-user environments, needs, and applications, primarily through the functional end-user information centers. This growing awareness, the applications backlog, and the need to reduce end-user ''reinvention of the wheel'' on common applications are forcing MIS management to take a second look not only at the planning, organizing, and directing aspects of their jobs, but also at the area of controlling. The need for greater control of MIS resources (i.e., people and machines) from a positive viewpoint is a serious prod for change, as are swiftly developing information technological advancements. MIS management needs to take a new direction to MIS control over organizationwide computing activities, that is, a *soft controls approach.*

In the opening part of the chapter, the linkage of MIS strategic plans and organization structures is related to control over the MIS department and functional end-user departments. Next, the nature of the internal control structure is discussed along with a soft controls approach and the importance of education, especially from an end-user perspective. Also, an effective MIS approach to data security and data integrity is set forth. An important part of the chapter is to define the general and application controls which are under the jurisdiction of the MIS manager. In turn, this background is helpful in developing a detailed two-part MIS questionnaire to evaluate the entire MIS organization (discussed in Chapter 15).

LINKAGE OF MIS STRATEGIC PLANS AND ORGANIZATION STRUCTURE WITH CONTROL

In the past, the concern of MIS management was effective control over MIS operations whether they were centralized or decentralized. Because the typical organization had only computer mainframes, including minicomputers, the linkage of control with MIS strategic plans and organization structure was readily visible to the MIS manager as well as those looking from the outside in. A number of control problems proliferated, as indicated in Chapter 2. However, with the proliferation of microcomputers throughout a typical organization today, there is a "dark side" to the area of control. While obvious problems such as potential fraud get much publicity, more subtle problems are just beginning to receive their share of attention. The microcomputer allows one to make errors with more confidence. Hence, there is need to change the GIGO principle, from "Garbage-In, Garbage-Out" to "Garbage-In, Gospel-Out." With the assistance of information centers in the functional end-user departments, end users can choose from many figures and information in their personal databases. They can enter their own data and keep them on their own floppies and hard disks. And no one can guarantee the accuracy or pertinence of those data to the corporate scheme. On the other hand, the one thing that the organization should care about is the accuracy of the data from which business decisions are made. The data are what it bases its business on, not on pieces of data here that differ from pieces of data there.

Currently, microcomputers are connected with other office automation equipment through local area networks which may or may not be linked to host computers. Typically, this approach causes major changes in the way microcomputers are purchased in large organizations. This is in sharp contrast to past practices wherein the MIS department purchased the micros and applications software. Because of the rise of functional end-user departments, end users have greater control over these purchases as well as purchases of other types of office automation equipment. End users through the MIS unit attached to their functional departments need to assure adequate control over their databases and assure compatibility among the various types of equipment.

In light of the concern about better control over the microcomputers of end users, there is even a greater need to link important control factors with MIS strategic plans and organization structures. That is, when appropriate MIS strategic plans along with its organization structures are developed for the coming year, there is a need to establish an appropriate control mechanism to ensure that what was planned has been accomplished. The basic control mechanism is the MIS annual budget, which is broken down on a monthly basis for comparison to actual expenditures. In this manner, financial results can be compared to the original plan to determine the proper accomplishment of stated MIS short-term goals. This approach was noted in Chapter 4. However, there are other mechanisms that center on control over MIS operations and end-user computing on a day-to-day basis, which are covered in this chapter.

PRINCIPLES OF EFFECTIVE MIS CONTROLS

Foremost of all the MIS principles is the *Principle of Acceptability of Controls,* stating that system controls should be acceptable to organization personnel and assist MIS management in accomplishing assigned tasks. Controls should help management develop confidence in the system to perform daily operations and meet desired organization objectives. The acceptability of system controls involves the human element. Needless to say as indicated previously in this text, organization personnel can make or break any MIS project. The nonacceptance of system controls may result in out-of-control conditions leading to a system failure.

Although controls may be accepted by end users, there is need for other principles, including those dealing with data integrity and data security. The *Principle of Data Integrity,* which centers on controls applied to data during the input, processing, and output phases, involves assuring that the input data are accurate and complete. Data integrity also involves assuring that data are processed correctly and do not become distorted, or lost, through system mistakes. In contrast, the *Principle of Data Security* is the securing, or protection, of data against theft, malicious manipulation, or unintentional manipulation. This includes the protection of the stored data and the physical protection of the computer involvement. It should be noted that data integrity and data security also need to be integral parts of end-user operations. Where will end users learn and understand the need for both data integrity and data security? For the most part, these important facts on data should be an essential part of end-user training. Otherwise, a whole host of control and security problems will abound in a typical organization. It should be noted that these two principles were set forth previously in Chapter 8. However, because of their great importance, they are highlighted here again.

An important question in systems development is: Where are actual results to be compared to system standards? This involves an important principle—the *Principle of Strategic Control Points*—referring to check points established for key operations or events to permit the computer operations to be stopped or altered before serious damage is done or a mistake is compounded. For example, a count of checks and total payment amount may be compared to computer control totals prior to mailing the checks produced by a computerized accounts payable system. In essence, control points should enable management to retain the degree of control necessary for efficient operations.

A last important principle relating to system controls is the *Principle of Control Accountability.* As various strategic control points are established, the managers at the appropriate operating level must be held accountable for the process being controlled. The fact that an individual is accountable for results enhances the chances of more effective control over ongoing operations. It should be noted that control accountability utilizes both quantitative and qualitative measurements, depending on the circumstances.

RELATIONSHIP OF CURRENT RESEARCH TO MIS CONTROLS

Although a number of internal controls and procedures are in place in a typical MIS organization, there are quite a number of control problems, as indicated by the research results reported in Chapter 2 (see Figure 2.4). They are as follows:

- Lack of an independent third party to review MIS operations (rated no. 1)
- Lack of proper documentation over standards and procedures (rated no. 2)
- Lack of security protection measures over the management information system (rated no. 3)
- Lack of a contingency recovery program (rated no. 7)
- Lack of control over input and/or output data (rated no. 8)
- Lack of control over data center operations (rated no. 11)

It should be noted that some of these problems have been discussed in previous chapters since they are related to planning and control.

The first problem, the *lack of an independent third party to review MIS operations,* is the principal reason why the listing is so long. If MIS personnel know that their operations are not evaluated thoroughly on a periodic basis, there will be a tendency to be lax on control over day-to-day organizationwide computing activities. Thus, the major problem of not scrutinizing MIS operations periodically eventually leads to a number of related problems. In terms of the number two rated problem, the *lack of proper documentation over standards and procedures,* this means that controls are nonexistent or lax where MIS personnel are concerned. There is the tendency of MIS personnel to keep all of the important details of a system or a program in their heads rather than commit them to some form of documentation. The old excuse "There isn't time" comes into play to the detriment of the organization, especially when MIS personnel leave.

The number three rated problem, the *lack of security protection measures over the management information system,* means that MIS management and their staff do not enforce security protection measures over MIS operations whether within the MIS department or functional end-user departments. In a similar manner, there is a *lack of a contingency recovery program,* the seventh rated problem, which can be caused by any number of factors. These problems are related to the *lack of control over input and/or output data,* the number eight rated problem. Essentially, end users fail to provide the proper level of data integrity needed to assure that the data center receives accurate information. In turn, the *lack of control over data center operations,* the number eleven rated problem, can be related (to a large degree) to this prior problem. The message here is that the lack of control in one area spills over to another, thereby resulting in a chain reaction that is detrimental to MIS control over daily operations within or outside the MIS department.

INTERNAL CONTROL STRUCTURE

Before discussing effective MIS management of controls and procedures, it is helpful to look at a typical internal control structure. Issued in 1988 by the American Institute of Certified Public Accountants (AICPAs), SAS (Statement on Auditing Standards) No. 55 covers audits of financial statements for periods beginning on or after January 1, 1990. It requires the auditor, in every audit, to gain an understanding of each element of the internal control structure (control environment, accounting system, and control procedures) sufficient to plan the audit and to assess control risk for assertions related to significant account balances and transaction classes. In order to plan the audit, the auditor needs to know enough about the three elements of the internal control structure to recognize the potential for material misstatements that can occur in an assertion and to be able to use that information in designing an effective audit plan.[1]

In addition, an effective internal control structure includes legal requirements for computer security. Although computer security is a critical nationwide concern, Congress has been relatively slow to formulate computer security laws and regulations, perhaps because of the issue's technical and rapidly changing nature. The major federal computer security laws and regulations include the Privacy and Security Act of 1974, the Foreign Corrupt Practices Act of 1977, the Electronic Fund Transfer Act of 1978, the Right to Financial Privacy Act of 1978, and the Counterfeit Access Device and Computer and Abuse Act of 1984. At this time, some states have enacted computer security laws.

Control Environment

First, the auditor must understand the client's control environment. This centers on management's philosophy and operating style as well as the method of assigning authority and delegating responsibility. These factors can have a major effect on elements of the control structure. For example, in a small organization, the owner determines the level of care given to executing and recording transactions. In a large organization, management's attitude determines the care with which lower management carries out the organization's plans.

When consideration is given to the computer aspects of the control environment, the auditor should focus on such factors as management's involvement in setting and monitoring computer operations policies, testing program changes, or controlling access to programs and data files. Obtaining an understanding of these control environment factors may involve inspecting accounting and computer operations manuals and reports, and making inquiries about implementation of policies and procedures.

Accounting System

Second, the auditor must understand how the computerized accounting system processes significant classes of transactions. This includes which computer reports are produced, which computer files are accessed and updated, and the nature of computer processing from initiation of a transaction to its posting to the general ledger. Because different processing methods are used, they are subject to different risks of error. In addition, the auditor must understand how the data are summarized in the financial reporting process and how transactions are converted to machine-readable form. Inasmuch as computers are used to summarize information for financial statements, the auditor must understand whether the client has a set-up program that specifies how accounts processed by the computer are summarized and included in the financial statements.

Control Procedures

Third, the auditor must learn about control procedures. The auditor often learns about certain control procedures while gaining an understanding of the control environment and accounting system. For example, it is difficult not to learn about such basic control procedures as reconciliation of subsidiary records to general ledger accounts. When an auditor plans to follow a specific approach to audit a particular assertion, the knowledge of control procedures obtained when examining the control environment and accounting system is usually adequate to determine specific procedures. When an auditor plans to assess control risk at a lower level than would be obtained by following a primarily substantive approach, the individual will place more emphasis on understanding and testing control procedures. Although such decisions are a function of strategy, there are circumstances in which an auditor must understand and test control procedures.

While the auditor seeks an understanding of the three internal control structure elements for a client, it is a matter of judgment. SAS No. 55 states that the auditor cannot, because of a decision to assess control risk at the maximum, ignore the control structure. Such knowledge is needed to identify the types of potential misstatements and related risks and to design effective substantive tests. Hence, substantive tests are not designed in a vacuum, but are based on a certain knowledge of the organization's control structure.[2]

EFFECTIVE MIS MANAGEMENT OF MIS CONTROLS

As a result of the importance of the internal control structure and problems related to it, MIS management must take charge. It must lead its own personnel and end users by developing a strategy for implementing MIS controls throughout the organization. If MIS management does not give direction early in the game for this important area, "periodic crises" may be the order of the day rather than rare exceptions, especially in the functional end-user departments.

Although these aspects tend to focus on the technical areas of responsibility and control, MIS management must not forget the *human element*. In actuality, the typical MIS organization is driven much more by the human element than the actual information technology. Hence, if MIS management wants end users to be a part of the total MIS, there is need to give them ownership and let them participate. Overall, MIS management must have a goal to develop a partnership between MIS personnel and end users that results in responsibility and effective control over organizationwide MIS activities. Lack of an MIS management goal in this area may have far-reaching effects over the short run to the long run. In turn, this goal must be backed by general and application MIS controls. An approach to improve MIS controls and the importance of education to improve MIS controls precede a more detailed discussion of general and application controls.

Soft Controls Approach

Currently, there is a gap between "what is" and "what should be." To overcome or, at least, reduce these problems to manageable levels, there is need for a new direction to improve MIS controls and, at the same time, to be compatible with the newer directions for planning, organizing, and directing discussed earlier in the text. Such an approach is not rigid and inflexible, but rather is helpful and flexible for both MIS managers and end users. For our purposes, a most useful approach is one that uses a *soft controls approach*. Such an approach is explained later and incorporated into the controls over the MIS organization that are set forth in the next section.

Typically, many MIS managers have lost or are losing control over their operations as a result of their modus operandi. This refers to the fact that they practice management by exception rather than management by perception. As discussed previously, the first approach refers to fixing what has gone wrong after the fact; it is a *reactive* one. In contrast, the second approach looks out into the future and determines what is wrong and proceeds to plan so that these problems are minimized when they become the current situation. The end result is that MIS managers are always in control; they are *proactive* rather than reactive. This is the underlying framework for a soft controls approach.

Essentially, a soft controls approach provides incentives for both MIS personnel and end users to adhere to MIS standards and procedures. Such freedom replaces the *rigid controls approach* and generates an environment that encourages them to experiment. In turn, important breakthroughs can happen. To illustrate the use of soft controls that yield subtle but important results for the organization, consider end users who develop their own applications. The functional end-user information center has provided them with the necessary training on data integrity and data security measures. The need to adhere to the organization's rigid controls (contained in a PC standards and procedures manual) in their development of new applications tends to stifle the most creative end users. In essence, the adherence to very strict methods of development and the incorporation of data integrity and data security controls over their applications restrict end users in their microcomputer activities.

In order to overcome this "straitjacket" approach, end users should be allowed to develop their own applications where they can drift naturally toward another approach to application development, such as prototyping. In the prototyping process, end users can develop a simple model that can be computerized, tested, improved, retested, and so forth. Despite its "roughness," the model often produces useful results very quickly. This is in contrast with standard MIS procedures in which end users spend months developing a sophisticated program using strict controls in the process. The goal of end users is to install an operational computer system that may require little or no change for one or more years.

Going beyond this example, a number of other areas can benefit from the soft controls approach. For microcomputers, the functional end-user information center can support the purchase of selected hardware and software. In this manner, many of the problems of *incompatibility* of equipment and *inconsistencies* of using one software package over others are resolved. In addition, a soft controls approach in these important areas will pay important dividends: that is, quantity discounts on hardware and software through centralized purchasing can be passed on to the functional end-user departments.

Another area that can benefit from a soft controls approach is standards, that is, software that meets the company's standards for data integrity and data security. Any software package that fails to meet these standards is not supported by the organization's information centers and, in turn, is not a part of the functional end-user information center's upcoming training schedule. Overall, a soft controls approach is a subtle way for MIS management to get what it wants in the first place in terms of effective MIS controls whether it be from the organization's end users or members of the MIS department, including its functional end-user information centers.

Data Security Procedures

Going beyond the soft controls approach, MIS management needs to institute appropriate procedures for MIS personnel to utilize that, in turn, are picked up by end users. Recognizing the vulnerability of the data stored on and accessible by microcomputers, MIS management has come up with various control procedures to deal with these problems. One primary way is to protect microcomputers, software, and data physically by making unauthorized access more difficult. A starting point in controlling who can use computers and data is to restrict physical access to the equipment. This includes locking rooms that contain microcomputers or terminals when they are not in use, using locks to prevent unauthorized people from accessing a keyboard, and instituting sign-on logs to provide a record of who has used the system. Going beyond this first step, other control procedures are covered next along with newer security directions.

In reference to *sign-on logs,* all users must sign a log sheet showing when and for what purposes they are accessing the computer. This approach is best suited to environments in which microcomputers or terminals are centrally located, making it easier to control who uses them and when. It does not adequately address the assignment of micros to desktops scattered throughout an organization. Unfortunately, the proliferation of microcomputers and communications equipment both inside and outside the organization has made it harder to restrict physical access to these systems. For this reason, organizations are putting an increased emphasis on controlling access to data and software programs, instead of restricting access to the hardware.

One way to control physical access to sensitive information and software programs is by creating *a data and program library*. Users must formally request the data and software applications they wish to use from the library. Again, this approach may not be productive where microcomputers are dispersed because users typically will have their own programs and data files. Because of the shortcomings of access-control methods, *password systems* are used in situations in which stand-alone microcomputers can access host computers or where microcomputers are linked in a local area network. Any user who wants to access data on the central computer must first key in his or her password before the connection can take place.

Because users need data from locations other than their own, they must first key in a password before a connection can take place for accessing desired data. Solutions to computer security, in many cases, hinge on a single secret password, a word known only by the legitimate user of the system or the information. The major problem with this type of user authentication is that if the password for an account is compromised, then the entire security base is at risk. Most computer-security software protects the system and the information by defining who can access what, at what time, and under what circumstances, rather than permitting unrestricted access. The password is a form of a more generic solution subclass of computer-security techniques known as user authentication. *User authentication* is the specific task of verifying that users are who they claim to be. If the security manager is completely assured of the users' identities, security is enhanced and the manager can more easily define what each user can access.

Passwords should be customized so that they apply to individual users, locations of terminals, specific applications, or any combination of these. Password routines should also be written so that a person attempting to enter the system is automatically disconnected after a limited number of unsuccessful tries. These routines are generally controlled by a program in the central computer. Password systems can be further enhanced by implementing a *call-back routine*. With this, a user requests access to the central computer by supplying an approved password. After determining the authenticity of the request, the host computer then calls back the user's microcomputer at a predetermined, approved phone number. Only at that point can the user gain access to data and programs. This type of system goes a long way toward resolving the problem of unauthorized users accessing and changing data, whether they are on or off the organization's premises.

In addition to password systems, user-authentication techniques include *token devices*. A token device consists of a physical key, much like a key to a house or automobile, that permits access to specific computer systems. The keys now on the market vary in design and appearance but all accomplish the same thing: they open access to a computer system. One token device consists of a dominosized key that includes an input end and an output LCD. The input consists of pulses of light from a computer terminal. The key interprets the streams as electronic bits of data. An algorithm in the key uses this challenge bit-stream (a prompt issued by the system in the form of a stream of bits to determine whether the device is the correct one) and, with information that was embedded in the key when it was initialized, displays a six-character code on the LCD display. When the user types in the appropriate code, host software accepts the key code, drives the same algorithm contained in the key, and checks that the token device is the correct one. Using the algorithm, the system issues a prompt to the device to verify its validity, based on information that has been previously entered or initialized into the system. If the host-software result matches the entered key code, access is granted.

For an even greater level of assurance, users can rely on a *biometric device.* A biometric user-authentication device relies on a physical attribute of the user. Biometric systems also have different approaches: fingerprint systems, signature-recognition systems, and retinal scans. One such system includes a fingerprint-reader device that is as long as a shoe box but only one-and-a-half inches in width. A user places a finger on a glass plate on the front of the unit. An optical scan is performed and the gray-scale variation of light and dark places on the optical scan is digitally mapped. Once a digital representation is available, unique points of the print, called minutiae points, are searched for and plotted in relation to one another. This mapping is then transferred to the host for a comparison against a mapping that was made when the user enrolled onto the system. If the points of the mapping are close enough to the original, a match is made. Except in rare cases, the overlay map will not be a 100 percent match. Therefore, the degree of exactness that constitutes an acceptable match must be determined. Normally, this range can be adjusted to suit individual preference.

In terms of the other biometric devices, there are devices that scan the blood-vessel pattern of a user's retina. The scan is performed by using a low-intensity laser beam. The blood-vessel pattern is digitized much as a fingerprint would be and is then compared with a stored template for this user. Still other devices accept a signature written on a pad with a special pen, which becomes digitized and is compared with a known sample of that user's signature. Fundamentally, biometric user-authentication devices are judged according to two important factors: the false-rejection rate, or the frequency with which valid users present the proper physical attributes such as fingerprints or signatures, and are denied access; and the false-acceptance rate, or the frequency with which imposters gain access.

In today's management information systems, *data encryption* is particularly helpful since it protects data in several ways. It protects against unauthorized access and eavesdropping, prevents alteration, and authenticates users. Although encryption will not protect against viruses that enter the system through authorized channels such as disk media, it can prevent unauthorized callers from gaining access and using the system. The most commonly used encryption technique is

DES (Data Encryption Standard), which scrambles data by using a complex nonlinear ciphering algorithm. The key used to perform this operation is a 56-bit binary word, usually a random number. If the user on the receiving end has an encryptor with the same key, that user can decrypt the ciphertext to produce the original data. If the sender's key does not match the receiver's key, the data will not be destroyed. To make it even more difficult, the cipher can also be fed back to the encryptor in one of several approved modes of operation to make the ciphertext dependent upon the characters preceding it. This makes repeated messages and blank fill (in which even the spaces between messages and message elements are encrypted) produce a different stream of ciphertext each time they are sent, thereby frustrating attempts at data substitution or an eavesdropper's attempted analysis. As a result, commercial networks have a high degree of protection. It should be noted that a 56-bit key has 72 quadrillion possible combinations.

Going beyond the current data security procedures, the next generation of security technology will include the use of artificial intelligence (i.e., expert systems), fiber optics, satellite communication, and advancements in biometrics. Prototype systems are being developed by innovative startup companies and are being tested by a small but rapidly growing group of pioneer users, such as government agencies and private development laboratories. *Expert system–based security systems* consist of software and hardware that monitor essential data within an information system twenty-four hours a day. Monitoring handles stored or active information and provides an audit trail of the data. Artificial intelligence technology can also be used to monitor user activity on the system and to alert system managers to actions which are extremely different from day-to-day routines. It is predicted that in the distant future artificial intelligence will be used in the design of all new management information systems. Its use will enable computer manufacturers to embed monitoring and other security measures in the initial design of a system. These analysts also see that a major benefit of *fiber optics* is its use in deterring computer crime. Light pulses traveling over optical fibers do not emit electromagnetic radiation and therefore are less vulnerable to remote monitoring devices. It is almost impossible to detect signals on a fiber-optic cable without cutting and splicing the cable.

While not foolproof, *satellite technology* may prove to be more secure than traditional networks. To get information from a satellite network, one first must locate the code and than crack it. On satellite networks, signal channels are assigned to each user, and that makes it difficult to locate the code. Even if a hacker found the correct frequency, a special demodulation device would be required to convert the microwave signals into telephone transmissions. The modulators and demodulators used by RCA, for example, are highly sophisticated machines sold in matched pairs, so the likelihood that anyone will obtain a workable demodulator is low. If a demodulator is acquired, the person then has to deal with two levels of actual data coding. For competitive reasons, only the manufacturers know the coding and ensure that encoders and decoders used are proprietary.

Data Integrity Procedures

Once the data security procedures are in place to make sure that only authorized users are utilizing their computing facilities, they must then ensure that the data input into the system are, and remain, accurate. The importance of inputting data correctly cannot be overestimated. This is because inaccuracies tend to multiply. If undetected, a single error can have wide-ranging effects, as the same data are often used in many different ways in different programs. Furthermore, once entered into a system, erroneous data become more difficult to locate. Even if successfully spotted in one part of the system, they may remain undetected elsewhere. For example, if the stock number of an item to be shipped to a customer is miskeyed, the inventory or records will be incorrect because the wrong item will be removed from stock to fill the order. In addition, the invoice will charge the customer for the wrong item. If the erroneously keyed item has a different price from the correct item, the customer's accounts receivable will also be wrong. And if the organization uses an automatic inventory replenishment system, the input error will cause the wrong item to be reordered. Thus, the best time to catch mistakes is when data are first entered into a system. But managing data-entry operations is complicated by the variety of ways in which data can be created and entered. Typical data integrity procedures are discussed later.

In the area of *data-entry controls,* data can be created and entered by the user; or they can be created by the user and entered into the system by a clerical staff member. Also, new data can be created by using all or part of a user's existing microcomputer data; they can be obtained from an internal central computer or database; or they can be obtained from an external database. Each input or data creation method has advantages and disadvantages.

In microcomputer applications, for example, the user often has the best idea of what the data mean and how they will be used. Thus, the user may want to create and enter the data. Also, it is often faster and easier to enter the data personally, rather than wait for someone else to do it. But having a manager enter data may be an inefficient use of that person's time, and a person who is unfamiliar with keyboarding or data-entry procedures can easily input errors without realizing it. A user who creates data but has someone else enter it can personalize and control the data, while avoiding the drudgery of inputting it. Nevertheless, the data-entry person may lack sufficient understanding of what the data mean and this can lead to errors. The advantages of creating new data from a user's previously input PC data files include significant time and cost savings in data creation as well as elimination of keyboarding errors. On the other hand, if errors lie undetected in the source data, they will be transferred to the new data files.

In the area of *error reduction,* the process of revising and correcting data may itself introduce new keyboarding errors. For this reason, the revision and correction process must be monitored as vigilantly as initial data entry. Error-reduction procedures need not be complex to be effective. The adoption of a few basic practices can go a long way toward protecting the integrity of data. These include using write/protect tabs on diskettes (disks) to prevent the accidental alteration of information, erasing files that are no longer needed, establishing logical file-naming rules, and labeling the diskette (disk).

Sometimes, the initial data may be error free, but the user's application of them may lead to flawed results. The most common mistake of this type is the unintentional use of outdated and inapplicable data. For example, a strategic planner may be asked to evaluate the potential return on investment if her company acquires one of its suppliers. Because she has performed similar evaluations in the past, the planner uses data already stored in her microcomputer. The planner is unaware, however, that a recent change in the way her company processes financial investment data has made the information stored in her microcomputer obsolete. She performs the evaluation and recommends that her superiors proceed with the deal. A year later, the company is losing money on what originally looked like a profitable venture. And management is mystified about why its projections were so wrong. Beyond implementing data integrity controls, managers can resolve this type of problem by stressing the critical importance of safeguarding the accuracy and timeliness of data. This can be done by developing a corporate policy outlining responsibility and accountability for the use of data.

Another procedure to ensure data integrity is the *self-checking digit,* which is a special type of verification for reference numbers, such as account and inventory numbers. This method employs information in the form of an extra digit that is mathematically designed to provide detection of transposition or substitution of digits within a number. Most data-entry equipment currently has the capability to perform this checking of critical data.

Computer Virus Procedures

Basically, a computer virus is a program that "infects" other programs by modifying them to include a copy of itself. Considerable press time and space have been given lately to computer viruses. In December 1987, for example, the world's largest computer company (IBM) had to shut down its entire worldwide computer network for two hours. Thousands of computer mainframes were brought to a halt by a 20-line "virus" program written by a novice student in a German university. One-half million instances of the program appeared in only two hours, and for eight weeks afterward, there were "aftershocks" where individual computers had to be shut down. With this "infection," a virus can spread from one program to others, one user to other users, one computer to other computers, and one network to other networks, thereby corrupting programs and data. In just six months, beginning in September 1987, about 100,000 computer systems sustained some form of damage from computer viruses. Microcomputers, computer mainframes, engineering workstations, and worldwide computer networks have all been affected. Viruses have hit every major computer manufacturer, and they have even begun to enter commercial software distribution channels. Over 100,000 legitimate software packages from major software vendors have been distributed with viruses in them, and viruses have been found in beta test software delivered to distributors.

There are some important differences between computer viruses and other known attack techniques (generality, persistence, and extent). Because a virus can carry other program codes along with it, the nature of the damage it can do is only limited by the creativity of the attacker (generality). Viruses have been found that delete files, prevent saving of edited files, and slow operations. Viruses have been directed against individuals, specific organizational activities, companies, and even entire classes of computers. Because viruses can reinfect programs that have been "cleaned up," they can survive many generations of program changes and upgrades (persistence). Even the most thoroughly verified program might become infected in its executable form, and typical change control mechanisms do not stop or detect this. Backup tapes cannot protect a company from computer viruses. Rather than being a safety net, they can act as a safe harbor for infections. Some viruses lie dormant for months, even years, thus corrupting backups made over a long period. Because a virus can spread far and wide, a single programmer with a microcomputer can cause worldwide computer problems (extent). Many known viruses have spread to thousands of computer systems, crossing both national and geographical boundaries. From a risk assessment viewpoint, this changes the very nature of the threat. Even a highly improbable attack can have globally catastrophic effects.

In view of these comments on viruses, it is recommended that the MIS manager and his staff plus end users follow these guidelines. *First,* software disks should be scanned for viruses before installing the software; this includes shrink-wrapped commercial software packages. *Second,* users' disks should be scanned before they use public computer facilities. Some sites have dedicated virus scanning stations for this. *Third,* locked (write-protected) backup copies of master software disks should be used and the master disks should be kept in a safe place. *Fourth,* important data should be backed up frequently. A rule of thumb is that if one would not want to redo all the work done since the last backup, the next backup is overdue. *Fifth* and last, if a virus warning appears, the user should know whom to contact for assistance or what to do to remove the virus independently. If these guidelines are followed, it is very likely that virus infections can be prevented or, at least, reduced drastically.

Currently, there are products on the market designed to provide limited protection against computer viruses. Generally, most offer little more than a false sense of security. Recent studies, however, have stimulated a new generation of products which are expected to offer better protection and greater convenience than their predecessors. These "integrity shells" will likely be improved over time to provide extensive services, such as integrated backups and restores, integrated networking capabilities, and high-integrity information exchange between computer mainframes and microcomputers.

Importance of End-User Training and Education

Although MIS personnel are typically knowledgeable about what MIS controls are and their place in the MIS organization, the same cannot be said for end users. Therefore, it is important that the MIS manager explore the need for end-user training and education to improve MIS controls. As a starting point, it is recommended that the functional end-user information centers teach end users about good systems development methodology that includes the fundamentals of data security and data integrity plus information about computer viruses. If end-user applications are developed using built-in system controls, not only will the applications be producing the desired results for end users, but less time will be spent to maintain the programs since proper controls have been built in initially. Essentially, end-user training and education is the responsibility of MIS management so that the potential pitfalls of MIS controls can be disseminated. In contrast, the accuracy of the final data is the responsibility of end users.

Going one step further, the MIS department has an obligation to make sure that functional end-user department managers understand the consequences of the improper handling of data, including computer crime (explored in the next chapter), and that end users know what is and is not acceptable in terms of MIS controls. The end result is that MIS managers should see themselves not only as the enforcers of policy, but as encouragers who guide policy formulation, offer alternative solutions, act as devil's advocates, and interpret final policy for end users. Hence, MIS managers need to see themselves less as technocrats and more as facilitators for integrating end users and computers.

These comments, in turn, are related to training and education. From the first days of work, employees need to hear what their technological responsibilities are, and these should be reinforced every step of the way. It is an MIS responsibility to indoctrinate new employees who will become end users in the very near future. This should not be left to a personnel representative. Hence, a few suggested rules on MIS education are necessary. *First,* the functional end-user information center needs to get involved with employee orientation sessions; *second,* it needs to keep end users current with updates, synopses of events or trends, and warnings about impending issues.

Third, the functional end-user information center needs to be observant: that is, MIS managers need to walk around and observe how end users employ microcomputers. Many organizations might be surprised to discover how much money they have spent to buy what amounts to a "fancy" word processor. Is the technology being used to its full potential or is it being abused? Remember, abuse of the technology is not limited to dishonest end users; it can also come from end users who are not using it as it was intended or who have no idea of how it can be used. Walking around may also point to someone who does have something to hide. MIS managers and their staff are far more likely to notice irregularities than are end-user managers, who may know little more about the information technology than what it costs. The MIS department is best served by bringing these situations to management's attention and by working to develop policies that will prevent abuse.

TYPES OF GENERAL CONTROLS OVER MANAGEMENT INFORMATION SYSTEMS

Fundamentally, MIS controls can be classified as *general controls* which relate to all MIS activities and *application controls* which relate to specific MIS tasks. General controls are treated first. According to the American Institute of Certified Public Accountants,

> General controls comprise (a) the plan of organization and operation of the EDP activity, (b) the procedures for documenting, reviewing, testing, and approving systems or programs and changes thereto, (c) controls built into the equipment by the manufacturer (commonly referred to as "hardware controls"), (d) controls over access to equipment and data files, and (e) other data and procedural controls affecting overall EDP operations.[3]

In addition, the author has appended a sixth part on information center controls. This six-part breakdown of general controls for management information systems is as follows:

I. MIS department controls
II. System and program development controls
III. Hardware and software controls
IV. Data center controls
V. Security controls
VI. Information center controls

This breakdown represents an updating of the general controls originally set forth by the American Institute of Certified Public Accountants. In the next chapter, a detailed questionnaire (Questionnaire 1) will be presented for general controls. In the material to follow, only a brief overview of each part will be given, followed by its major sections. This background will be sufficient to assist the reader in gaining an understanding of the questions found in Questionnaire 1.[4]

I. MIS Department Controls

The first of the general controls focuses on the plan of organization and operation of the MIS department. It looks at the normal management functions undertaken by MIS managers, that is, planning, organizing, directing, and controlling MIS activities relating to overall MIS department activities. Within this framework, the following areas are explored:

A. General considerations

B. Strategic MIS plans

C. Disaster recovery plans

D. Total quality management (TQM) program

E. Organization structure controls

F. Personnel standards

G. Performance appraisal

II. System and Program Development Controls

Procedures can be designed to control the development process of systems and programs, as well as subsequent changes. Of great importance is the degree of documentation practiced by the MIS department. Too often, this important aspect is ignored by systems and programming personnel in favor of more challenging MIS tasks. Poor internal control of MIS methods and procedures reflects on the department's management. Basic categories of system and program development controls, then, cover:

A. General considerations

B. Control over methods and procedures

C. Systems and programming development procedures

D. Control over changes

E. Control over documentation

III. Hardware and Software Controls

Although hardware and software vendors have made considerable improvements over the years to their products, there is still need to ensure that there are procedures in place to recover from hardware and software problems. Hence, there is need to review the area for adequacy so that data integrity is maintained. Typically, hardware and software controls include the following:

A. General considerations

B. Parity checks and echo checks

C. Duplication checks and dual heads

D. Overflow and sign checks

E. Operating system controls

F. Built-in software controls

G. Changes to built-in software controls

IV. Data Center Controls

The focus here is on evaluating the efficiency of the data center operations, that is, the physical environment in which the hardware platforms operate. The data center should be arranged so that there is a smooth flow of information processing. Also, an important concern is the adequacy of MIS management via its data centers to meet the processing needs of its customers internally as well as externally to the MIS department. Typical data center controls cover:

A. General considerations

B. Control over access to data center

C. Control over computer operators

D. Control over tape and disk librarian

E. Control over computer maintenance

V. Security Controls

Basically, security controls cover contingencies that are not adequately encompassed by other controls. They focus on computer platforms of various types whereby the data used as input, processed, and the resulting output is secure throughout the entire input-process-output stages. The net result is that the data are not altered in any shape or form while under the control of the computer. This area refers not only to securing information processing within the internal MIS organization, but also to those activities that are external to it. Most computer installations have security controls covering:

A. General considerations

B. Data communications and networking controls

C. Infosecurity controls

D. Program controls

E. Equipment log

F. Physical access controls

G. Fire protection

H. Media protection

VI. Information Center Controls

Information center controls relate to many of the controls set forth in the previous five sections. That is, general controls over the entire MIS department are, to a degree, set forth in this section for information centers. Only this time, the focus is on assisting end users from the organization's functional units on an as-needed basis. From this viewpoint, the information center controls are as follows[5]:

A. General considerations
B. Planning an overall strategy for information centers
C. Hardware and software integration
D. Organization of information centers
E. Staffing of information centers
F. Training of end users
G. Control and security over information centers

These controls are applicable to centralized information centers or to those found in the functional end-user departments.

TYPES OF APPLICATION CONTROLS OVER MANAGEMENT INFORMATION SYSTEMS

Complementary and supplementary to general controls are application controls. While general controls are related to organization factors, personnel, and equipment, application controls focus on the operational aspects of management information systems. For the systems development manager, no design job is complete without adequate internal controls. The systems analyst should make certain that the final design allows no one person full responsibility over an entire operation; the clearest example is in payroll, where one person with complete responsibility can defraud an organization. Built-in check points ensure that what has been processed agrees with predetermined totals. To a degree, these controls relieve the need for detailed checking and reviewing.

Referring again to the *AICPA's Statement on Auditing Standards No. 3,* "Application controls relate to specific tasks performed by EDP. Their function is to provide reasonable assurance that the recording, processing, and reporting of data are properly performed. There is considerable choice in the particular procedures and records used to effect application controls. Application controls often are categorized as 'input controls,' 'processing controls,' and 'output controls.'"[6] This breakdown can be expanded to include other application controls (i.e., database, data communications and networking, and end user controls) deemed appropriate for today. Thus, the types of application controls can be segregated as follows:

I. Input controls
II. Processing controls
III. Output controls
IV. Database controls
V. Data communications and networking controls
VI. End user controls

This breakdown builds upon the application controls originally set forth by the American Institute of Certified Public Accountants. In the next chapter, a detailed questionnaire (Questionnaire 2) will be set forth for application controls. In the material to follow, only an introduction to each part will be given, followed by its major sections. As with Questionnaire 1, this background will be sufficient to assist the reader in gaining an understanding of the questions found in Questionnaire 2.[7]

It should be noted that internal and external auditors/consultants, including EDP auditors, also have a special interest in application controls. Similarly, stockholders, creditors, and the government want assurance that processed data, whether on PC, mini, or mainframe platforms, are reliable when transmitted from one source to another. Control points for checking the accuracy of processed information and the distribution of control over one specific area are essential.

I. Input Controls

Control of input is defined as use of the procedural controls necessary to handle data prior to computer processing. Input data must be handled very carefully since they are the most probable source of errors in the entire management information system. If errors are created anywhere between the origination point and input the computer equipment, they will be carried throughout the entire system. In order to keep errors to a minimum, the following procedural controls over input data are available.

A. General considerations
B. Verification methods
C. Input control totals
D. External labels

II. Processing Controls

Extensive programmed controls are always advisable for PC, mini, and mainframe platforms since undetected errors can have serious and far-reaching consequences. Programmed control steps should be included as a part of the platform's internally stored instructions, thereby resulting in increased accuracy.

In addition, the extent of computer-programmed controls includes the requirements of the particular run and the capabilities of the equipment. Since most computer applications are slowed by the speeds of input/output units, the central processor generally has more than sufficient time to perform the necessary control checks. Therefore, the number of programmed controls is dependent upon the needs of the application. They can be classified as follows:

A. General considerations
B. Validation checks and tests
C. Computer control totals
D. Internal labels
E. Error routines

III. Output Controls

The role of a computer platform as a control center is further accentuated when output controls are present. Whereas input controls ensure that all data are processed, output controls assure that results are reliable. The latter promotes operational efficiency within the computer area over programs, processed data files, and machine operations. Output controls also ensure that no unauthorized alterations have been made to data under control. They are classified as follows:

A. General considerations
B. Output control totals
C. Control by exception
D. Control over operator intervention

IV. Database Controls

Just as computer-programmed controls are essential for an effective system, the same can be said for database controls. Without adequate database controls, important data items found in on- and off-line files can be lost or destroyed. If loss or destruction should occur, certain recovery procedures must be undertaken to recreate these essential data items. Through the use of the foregoing programmed controls, the systems analyst can help ensure, to a large degree, that file data are not destroyed during processing. Today, database controls should be an integral part of as well as facilitate a client/server architecture. From this broad perspective, database controls include the following:

A. General considerations
B. Database management systems
C. Supervisory protection program

D. File record controls

E. Physical safeguard controls

V. Data Communications and Networking Controls

Data communications and networking controls are necessary to facilitate a two-way flow of information inside and outside the MIS organization. The real purpose of data communication and networking controls is to assure MIS management that data sent have been properly received and not altered in the process. Similarly, data communications and networking are of great concern to users who rely on data transmissions for accuracy and completeness of data. During data communications, great emphasis is placed on preventing unauthorized access to sensitive organization information. Because of the emergence of local area networks, metropolitan area networks, and wide area networks, there is also need to evaluate these networks. Thus, a complete evaluation of data communications and networking requires a review of a number of areas:

A. General considerations

B. Network management

C. On-line processing controls

D. Data monitoring controls

E. Diagnostic controls

F. Local area network controls

G. Metropolitan area network controls

H. Wide area network controls

VI. End-User Controls

Although information centers are covered in Section VI of Questionnaire 1, there is need to assess controls over end users who do not interface with any type of information center and those who do. In many cases, end users have sufficient computer background to bypass the information centers. Essentially, the soft controls approach set forth earlier in the chapter comes into play. Hence, the evaluation of this approach is found in this section. From this perspective, end-user controls are set forth as follows:

A. General considerations

B. End-user systems development controls

C. End-user hardware and software controls

D. End-user database and data communications controls

E. End-user audit controls

F. End-user security controls

For the most part, compliance by end users with a soft controls approach is difficult although a positive attitude among MIS management is very helpful.

GUIDELINES TO ASSIST MIS MANAGEMENT IN CONTROLLING THE MIS ORGANIZATION AND END USERS

A *first* guideline is that MIS personnel under MIS management not only know the importance of MIS controls, but put their knowledge of MIS controls to work on a day-to-day basis, especially when working with end users. As discussed in the chapter, general controls and application controls center on specific items that need to be implemented precisely for desired results. Failure to implement MIS controls at the proper time and place generally leads to undesirable consequences.

A *second* and very important guideline for MIS management is that what is planned must be also controlled effectively. That is, there is need to control organizationwide computing activities by a soft controls approach. This approach provides incentives for both MIS personnel and end users to adhere to MIS standards and procedures. Such freedom replaces the rigid controls approach and generates an environment throughout the organizationwide computing activities that encourages experimentation. In turn, important breakthroughs can happen. In effect, a soft controls approach is an indirect and easy-to-use approach that can be used for day-to-day computing operations, as opposed to a traditional rigid controls approach.

Tied in with the previous guidelines is a *third* one centering on the need to train MIS personnel in the ins and outs of MIS controls. This is particularly true of systems analysts and programmers. The rationale is that these people need to include the proper types of controls at the appropriate level in their design and programming efforts. Failure to school systems analysts and programmers will result in conflict with the company's auditors whether internal or external. In particular, the EDP auditors will be criticizing the systems analysts and programmers for not including the proper controls in the new MIS, especially at strategic control points. Also, they will be questioning the data's integrity and security in its day-to-day operations. In essence, the auditors will be reviewing an organization's systems for the appropriate level of MIS controls. The incorporation of appropriate MIS controls is mandatory so that the auditors will give systems their final stamp of approval.

To assist in the successful implementation of information technology by end users, a *fourth* guideline focuses on centralizing the authority for purchasing hardware and software under the jurisdiction of centralized and functional end-user information centers. End users should consult these information centers to learn what works best in terms of hardware and software for specific applications in their functional units. In turn, both MIS personnel and end users should work together to justify the investment in information technology and to make sure it is consistent with MIS standards.

A *fifth* guideline relates to an effective interface between the MIS department and end users. This interface can take the direction of MIS personnel assisting end users through centralized or functional end-user information centers. Another interfacing approach is sharing of information among end users through controlled media, such as MIS newletters or company-sponsored user groups. Essentially, interfacing with end users can assist MIS personnel in acting as troubleshooters and inform end users of problems and corrective measures to prevent them in the future.

A *sixth* guideline relates to controlling the growth of end-user computing in a responsible and progressive manner that introduces end-user computing in ways that are sensitive to end-user needs and interests today and tomorrow. This includes establishing and maintaining training programs based on the identified needs of end users as well as establishing and maintaining standards for the use of computer platforms, in particular, microcomputers. In addition, this relates to monitoring the use and security of systems and data throughout end-user computing. Overall, if end-user computing is approached from a forward-looking perspective, the rewards for the entire organization can be extremely far reaching.

NOTES

1. *Statement on Auditing Standards (SAS) No. 55, Consideration of the Internal Control Structure in a Financial Statement Audit,* sections 6 through 11, New York: AICPA, 1988.

2. Richard M. Steinberg and Raymond N. Johnson, ''Implementing SAS No. 55 in a Computer Environment,'' *Journal of Accountancy,* August 1991, pp. 60–68.

3. *Statement on Auditing Standards (SAS) No. 3, The Effects of EDP on the Auditor's Study and Evaluation of Internal Controls,* New York: AICPA, 1974, p. 3, para. 7. Also refer to *Statement on Auditing Standards (SAS) No. 9, The Effect of an Internal Audit Function on the Scope of the Independent Auditor's Examination,* New York: AICPA, 1976, and *Statement on Auditing Standards (SAS) No. 48, The Effects of Computer Processing on the Examination of Financial Statements,* New York: AICPA, 1984.

4. Questionnaire 1 is an extensive reworking of the questionnaire that appeared in Robert J. Thierauf and George W. Reynolds, *Effective Information Systems Management,* Columbus, Ohio: Charles E. Merrill Publishing Company, 1982, pp. 301–312.

5. Refer to Robert J. Thierauf, *Effective Information Centers: Guidelines for MIS and IC Managers,* New York: Quorum Books, 1988.

6. *Statement on Auditing Standards (SAS) No. 3, The Effects of EDP on the Auditor's Study and Evaluation of Internal Controls,* New York: AICPA, 1974, pp. 3–4, para. 8.

7. Questionnaire 2 is an extensive reworking of the questionnaire that appeared in Robert J. Thierauf and George W. Reynolds, *Effective Information Systems Management,* Columbus, Ohio: Charles E. Merrill Publishing Company, 1982, pp. 317–324.

15

Evaluation of the MIS Organization

OUTLINE

INTRODUCTION TO EVALUATION OF THE MIS ORGANIZATION

The potential for loss associated with management information systems is growing with increasing complexity and degree of automation. Because computer programs rather than human beings perform many of the checks and verifications necessary to ensure accuracy and completeness of data and file records, the end result is that management information systems are exposed to the possibility of loss from several sources, including input errors or omissions, improper controls within the MIS, inadequate systems design, fraud or theft, and failure to comply with legislated or other standards and procedures. In addition, the potential for loss can be expanded when old systems are modernized. Although the number of errors generally does not increase as a result of moving from, say, a manual system to a computer-based MIS, the effects of any one error can be much greater. Moreover, tracing an error is considerably more difficult. From both viewpoints, the need for determining the effectiveness of MIS controls has increased. Essentially, this is the rationale for the comprehensive MIS questionnaire set forth in this final chapter.

In the previous chapter, controls were separated into two major categories, general and application, and identified important control features for both categories. This chapter will further describe these control areas in the form of a complete MIS questionnaire. Before this two-part questionnaire is presented, the potential for computer crime that is faced by the typical MIS manager is set forth along with approaches to overcome it or, at least, reduce the company's exposure to it over time. Additionally, an introduction to generalized audit software is presented as a means to detect ongoing irregularities and deficiencies of day-to-day MIS operations.

PRINCIPLES OF EVALUATING THE MIS ORGANIZATION

A starting point for evaluating the MIS organization is to think in terms of making such an evaluation on a periodic basis. Hence, there is need for the *Principle of Periodic Evaluation of the MIS Organization.* This periodic evaluation by internal and external auditors/consultants should go beyond selecting certain areas of the MIS organization. Instead, there should be a thorough, complete, and objective evaluation of all aspects of the MIS department at least once a year by someone outside the department itself. This could be undertaken by MIS consultants within or outside the organization as well as internal and external auditors. The particular circumstances will dictate which is best. Additionally, sensitive areas that are under the control of functional end-user departments should receive the same level of evaluation as that of the MIS department. In this manner, important organization data will be evaluated such that their integrity and security are not compromised.

Next, the *Principle of Correcting MIS Managerial and Operational Problems* centers on problems found in the two-part MIS questionnaire. In turn, these problems are evaluated by internal and external auditors/consultants and are presented to MIS management for corrective action. Failure to undertake the necessary corrective action by MIS management may result in additional damage to the organization in terms of MIS operations and the organization's financial results. The principal reason for highlighting present problems via the two-part MIS questionnaire is to improve the total MIS organization.

Related to the evaluation of the MIS organization is the *Principle of Assessing the Level of Risk* as related to exposure to computer crime. The best way to look at data and computer security is from a commonsense point of view. MIS management should ask: What am I protecting, and what is the cost to do it? The answers are to assess the risk and select the security approach based on the cost and/or benefit. Security can be divided into two major sectors: protection of the physical equipment and the computer room, and protection of the data from misuse and abuse. Each has subsets. A discussion of this important topic in terms of computer risk and computer crime is found later in the chapter.

Related to the preceding principle is the *Principle of Detecting and Overcoming Computer Crime*. Currently, there are a number of audit approaches (as will be discussed in this chapter) to detect computer crime. Emphasis is typically placed on computer-assisted audit software. However, there is need to go a step further and eliminate or reduce conditions that are conducive to computer crime. Because of the importance of this area, it is covered in some depth.

RELATIONSHIP OF CURRENT RESEARCH TO EVALUATE THE MIS ORGANIZATION

As stated in Chapter 14, a number of MIS control problems have been disclosed by current research. However, one is related directly to the evaluation of the MIS organization: *lack of an independent third party to review MIS operations*. This problem drew the most negative responses from the small- and large-size organizations surveyed, thereby ranking number one not only currently, but also in the previous round of research. This problem is a key one: if MIS personnel know that their operations are not evaluated thoroughly on a periodic basis, there is a natural tendency to do less than expected. But more importantly, those personnel who want to commit computer crime tend to have a license to steal. Hence, it is highly recommended that MIS management utilize the two-part MIS questionnaire as an instrument used by an objective third party. Although this MIS questionnaire can be used by an MIS manager, the end result is generally too much subjectivity. What is needed is an honest and objective viewpoint by parties outside the MIS organization, that is, internal and external auditors/consultants.

ROLES OF THE AUDITORS

Over the years, the rapid development of computerized systems led top management to demand an appropriate response from their MIS managers. Interrelated files, high-speed transmission, magnetically stored information, database management systems, data communication networks, distributed processing systems, minicomputers, and PCs changed the way financial and operating results were recorded and reported. As accounting and operational data were calculated and stored increasingly on all types of computers, management's control and auditing needs became more complex. MIS management was confronted with the question of how to perform effective reviews of computerized activities. The typical response to this question was, and is, to employ EDP auditors. Currently, the auditing profession can be divided into two major divisions: external auditing and internal auditing. The EDP auditor may function in either environment. To understand the EDP auditor's role better, the differences in the functions of external and internal auditors are discussed initially.

External Auditors

External auditing is an independent appraisal function of an organization that is external to it. Most organizations, either voluntarily or in accordance with regulations of some type, such as those for registrant corporations of the Securities and Exchange Commission (SEC), have an annual audit of their financial statements conducted by an independent certified public accounting firm. In this context, the independent certified public accountants (CPAs) are external auditors. The primary objective of an external audit is to be able to express an opinion about the quality of an organization's financial statements. Hence, the external auditors are concerned primarily with the reliability of financial information.

Internal Auditors

Internal auditing, like external auditing, is an independent appraisal function. The internal auditors' main function within an organization under top management's sanction is to examine and evaluate the entity's activities. Internal auditors' primary function is to assist top management in meeting its responsibilities. In doing so, the internal auditors are responsible for safeguarding the organization's assets, assuring the accuracy and reliability of accounting records, promoting operational efficiency, and adhering to organization policies and regulatory and legal obligations. Internal auditors are almost always concerned with the adequacy of the controls over MIS and, in most cases, with the cost-effectiveness of the procedures used. In addition, their ranks include EDP auditors who are specialists in computer processing.

Typically, EDP auditors supply technical computer skills and expertise to the audit function whether internal or external. As more advanced information technology is used by organizations to manage their resources and to record, monitor, and report activities and financial conditions, technology affects the procedures and techniques used to achieve audit objectives. Therefore, whether the audit function is internal or external, the audit function's need for computer expertise increases as the technological sophistication of the financial and operational environment increases. In many organizations, the auditor's emphasis has shifted from evaluating and testing processing results to evaluating and testing MIS controls. Many of these controls are incorporated into computer programs or exercised within the organization's MIS function.

Essentially, EDP auditors evaluate and test the more technically complex computer controls and procedures and develop and apply computer-assisted audit techniques, in particular, audit software. In most cases, it is no longer possible to verify manually the computer procedures used to summarize, calculate, and categorize data. As a result, audit software and other computer-assisted audit techniques are used.

CONTROL OVER COMPUTER CRIME BY MIS MANAGEMENT

Although the first computer crime, per the Equity Funding Corporation, that was widely publicized occurred many years ago, there are valuable lessons to be learned that are applicable to the present and the future. More specifically, the Equity Funding debacle, like all disasters caused by human actions, offered insights into computer crime for MIS management to think about for the future. A number of questions were raised by this disaster. In addition to criminal culpability and civil liability, the questions involved the sufficiency of regulatory procedures affecting publicly owned companies, such as life insurance companies, and the adequacy of prevailing assumptions about the responsibilities of various kinds of professions and occupations—accountants, lawyers, actuaries, investment bankers, and security analysts—in relation to organizations like Equity Funding. Equally important, the integrity of MIS management and its staff was open to question.

The demise of Equity Funding represents the tip of the iceberg that must be understood by MIS management and, one hopes, eliminated. With or without top management prodding, the MIS manager must make security planning and implementation a priority because the stakes are enormous. Some decisions could easily involve tens of millions of dollars. In view of this important responsibility, the MIS manager should not be making such decisions personally, but should be passing on assessments of the hazards, the costs of security measures, and recommended actions. It is up to top management to decide the level of permitted risk—trade-offs—to assure that it is acceptably low and reasonable in cost. They must be convinced that, in the event of failure, recovery will still be possible and relatively efficient.

Figure 15.1
Primary Causes of Infosecurity Problems

65 percent	Errors and omissions
13 percent	Dishonest employees
8 percent	Loss of supporting intrastructure, including power, communications, water, sewer, transportation, fire, flood, civil unrest, strikes
6 percent	Disgruntled employees
5 percent	Water, not related to fires and floods
3 percent	Outsiders, including viruses, hackers, espionage, dissidents and malcontents of various kinds and ex-employees who have been away for more than six weeks

Source: Russell Kay, "Business and Law Enforcement: Partners Against Computer Crime," *Infosecurity News*, November/December, 1992, p. 13.

Current Research on Computer Crime

Typically, computer crime is just one element of the infosecurity problems found in MIS organizations today. As shown in Figure 15.1, errors and omissions comprise the bulk of the causes of infosecurity problems, that is, approximately two-thirds (65 percent) according to current research. In contrast, problems related to computer security can be as high as 22 percent (13 percent for dishonest employees, 6 percent for disgruntled employees, and 3 percent for outsiders). No matter the percentage for computer crime, one can ask: How much do computer criminals reap from their activities? The correct answer is that no one knows for sure. One problem is that victims seldom report the crimes for fear that the publicity will be bad for business or make them a target of other criminals. Although there are many estimates of how much money is lost to computer crime, MIS management tends to place little faith in any published figures.[1]

To try to place current figures in perspective, the following research estimates are given. Hackers caused about $164 million worth of damage in 1991, according to the *1992 IPA Computer Virus and Hacker Study*. The study was conducted for the Information-Technology Promotion Agency of Japan's Ministry of International Trade and Industry and published by USA Research, Inc. (Portland, Oregon). The same study reports that viruses caused $1.077 billion worth of damage in 1991. At approximately the same time, the accounting firm of Ernst & Young conducted a survey that yielded an estimated figure of $3 billion for the annual cost of computer crime.[2]

Other estimates of costs for specific types of computer-related crime damage are currently given. The cost of telephone toll fraud has been rising dramatically over the past few years. The two-volume 1992 study *Toll Fraud & Telabuse* (published by Telecommunications Advisors, Inc, Portland, Oregon) estimates the cost of toll fraud at over $2 billion in 1991, which is expected to increase thereafter. These estimates are based on statements made by representatives of the major long-distance carriers and on user-group reports. A 1992 survey of telecommunications managers by Complementary Solutions Inc. (Atlanta, Georgia) found that over 25 percent of organizations has been victims of toll fraud. They cite estimates by unnamed industry experts that fraud damage added up to more than $1.2 billion in 1991, with the average incident costing approximately $44,000.[3]

CONDITIONS CONDUCIVE TO COMPUTER CRIME

Because of the ever-present problem of computer crime of any type, MIS management must work hard to minimize its risk. That risk is highest in those systems that affect the cash flow of the organization (payroll, accounts payable, and billing) or that guard important assets of the company (inventory and accounts receivable). If any of the following conditions is present, then that risk is heightened:

- Management has paid little attention to the risk of computer crime, saying, ''that couldn't happen here.''
- No separation of sensitive job functions, such as authorization of payment and issuance of check.
- Low employee morale and little loyalty toward the organization.
- Access to computer files or computer programs is not tightly controlled.
- No record is kept of who has access to computer files or computer programs.
- No vacations by so-called trusted employees.

A thorough analysis of these conditions indicates that MIS management is very lax in promoting effective control over personnel and operations. In such an environment, the perpetrators find it easy to obtain all the information they need for their fraudulent acts from the system. In fact, the elements of challenge and game playing are found in such situations. In some cases, MIS managers' claim that their computer systems are safe and cannot be penetrated encourages eager programmers who look at the intellectual challenge of pitting their minds against the computer. These people usually become frustrated with their success unless there is some way they can take credit publicly for their achievements. One perpetrator who claims to have gained over $1 million from his deeds said that aside from making money rapidly, his motive was to see how far he could go with his crime before he stopped and informed his victim of his acts. He was confident that the victim could not find evidence of his act even if he confessed.

Approaches to Overcome Computer Crime

Currently, there are a number of approaches to deal with computer crime or, at least, try to keep it as low as possible. Rather straightforward ones include the following:

- Assign responsibility for the finite units in a system.
- Separate duties of those using and those changing the system.
- Limit access to the physical facility and to the data.
- Assign accountability for the data.
- Require journals, including work records, at terminals.
- Track variances to make sure that they are accounted for.

In addition to these approaches, a thorough audit of the total MIS organization is an effective way to overcome computer crime. This important subject area will be covered in the next section.

From an overview standpoint, a practical approach to overcome computer crime is to identify initially what areas should be protected. The specific hazards and risks to which each area is exposed need to be addressed. To help MIS managers get a handle on this item, a cost or value needs to be assigned to each exposure to computer crime. For example, the cost of repairs or replacement value can be calculated. Next, the MIS manager determines the expected occurrence or probability of the exposure, taking into account any and all protective measures that the company already has in place. The number of people who have an opportunity to inflict a particular kind of damage is a large factor in determining the probability of occurrence. If the MIS manager has difficulty in assigning the value or probability of each occurrence, it is probably because the organization is examining too large an exposure. Instead, it should be broken down into subsets. The relative annual cost can be determined from a chart that plots the impact of a loss, say, from $1 million to $20 million, *vertically* over ten increments, and the probability of occurrence, ranging from several times a day to once in twenty years, *horizontally* over ten increments.

Once the total cost is determined, the MIS manager can take one of three protective measures against computer crime: *First,* do nothing by tolerating the exposure. *Second,* lower the dollar impact in case the loss does occur. *Third* lower the probability of the loss. Although insurance is an option, protection measures should be taken to give the greatest reduction in exposure for the cost. Typically, this turns out to be either a protective measure such as controls and procedures, or some access control that operates across a wide set of exposures and reduces total exposure by reducing a whole set of smaller exposures. In essence, successive protective measures should be applied until the level of total exposure to computer crime reaches that of an acceptable business risk.

STARTING POINT FOR EFFECTIVE AUDIT PRACTICES

As a starting point for effective audit practices, MIS management and end users must look beyond themselves to those individuals whose sole task is to evaluate the degree of systems controls, the internal and external auditors/consultants, to evaluate and verify the effectiveness of internal controls across the entire organization where computer crime can be easily undertaken. However, four things must occur before the auditors/consultants can be effective:

- Corporate senior management must ensure that the proper auditability mandate is established for the entire organization.
- MIS personnel must pay closer attention to building in adequate controls for computerized applications.
- Internal (and EDP) auditors must be involved in the systems design function and subsequent audits of computerized applications while external auditors must review the end results.
- All auditors involved in the organization's information systems must gain sufficient knowledge to meet their new responsibilities.

If any one of the four is missing, auditability and control will typically remain elusive.

Overall, MIS management must not abdicate its responsibility for systems controls, but rather must get end users as well as internal (and EDP) auditors involved in building the necessary controls at the design stage. This is opposed to the "add-on approach" that has been employed too often in the past by many organizations. The involvement of the audit control functions in all phases of management information systems is absolutely necessary and proper in today's more complex MIS environment, especially in light of increasing computer crime. The growth of data communications and networking to connect facilities at remote locations in a distributed data processing environment is one example of how new technology has complicated the control of computer crimes, not to mention normal information processing problems and irregularities.

Challenges Confronting the Auditors

Today, internal and external auditors/consultants are involved in a major way in evaluating controls relating to computerized MIS. This is the result of their relative independence in reviewing internal controls in end-user areas as well as in information processing. It is important to note, however, that although the auditors/consultants are used effectively in reviewing systems controls and in making control recommendations, the responsibility for these controls properly resides with MIS management and end-user groups responsible for the preparation and processing of transactions, record keeping, and resulting management reports. The role of the auditors/consultants is to judge the adequacy of controls and to recommend control improvements. Responsibility to implement and maintain appropriate controls resides with the MIS function and end-user organizations.

In fulfilling their tasks, a number of challenges confront the auditors/consultants of computerized operations:

- The comparative invisibility of data, files, and transactions
- The changing of input data in a variety of ways before they become output
- Centralizing or aggregating activities or transactions
- Resequencing of the steps of traditional information processing procedures
- Integration of information processing functions, which frequently has the side effect of eliminating formerly available audit trails
- Creation of new applications throughout an organization's operations
- The problem of supporting management information systems of far greater complexity than traditional manual operations

It also should be noted that today's typical organization is highly dependent on the operation of its management information systems in its conduct of business. This places a high priority on the auditing and control functions.

The recognition that today's information technology is a source of problems and challenges to the auditors/consultants should not obscure the fact that the same information technology can serve as a considerable aid to auditability and control. The computer is a powerful device for accomplishing its intended tasks of computing, data communications, process control, and so forth. It is also an ideal instrument for keeping records and producing information about its own activities and the nature of its work. Such records as statistics and analyses of its own activities can often be compiled concurrently with the main task it performs. If these capabilities can be exploited by the auditors/consultants, they can be very powerful and useful tools for their work.

Hackers and the Auditors

One important item confronting the organization and its auditors/consultants not noted previously is hacking. Rigging computers for fraud or malice is often undertaken within the organization. For example, at American Telephone & Telegraph Company (London office), three technicians used a computer to funnel company funds into their own pockets. At the General Dynamics Corporation's space division (San Diego), an employee plotted to sabotage the company by wiping out a computer program used to build missiles. And at Charles Schwab & Company headquarters (San Francisco), some employees used the stock brokerage firm's computer system to buy and sell cocaine. As these examples suggest, employees have found ways to misuse their companies' computer systems. Although publicity about computer wrongdoing has often focused on outside hackers' gaining entry to systems to wreak havoc, insiders are proving far more adept at creating computer mayhem.[4]

Organization employees are using company management information systems to line their own pockets or to seek revenge because they did not get a promotion or because of other perceived or real slights. Whatever the motive, computer misdeeds are creating significant problems for small and large organizations as well as for their internal and external auditors/consultants. Although figures for damages from computer abuse are scarce, some organizations report internal frauds involving losses of more than $1 million. Even more costly are losses from disrupted operations or from repair of the damage. Typically, employees are the ones with the skill, the knowledge, and the access to do bad things to an organization's MIS. They are the ones, for example, who can most easily plant a "logic bomb" (a program triggered by a specific time or event) which can crash an organization's computer system. Although most companies quickly fire the employees without publicity, dishonest or disgruntled employees pose a far greater problem than most in MIS management realize. These mischievous deeds may go on for a long time before being caught. In fact, sometimes these hacking problems are not discovered until after the employee's departure.

MIS management and the organization's auditors/consultants should recognize and rectify the problems related to hackers. In a typical organization, the primary problem is poor systems administration: that is, users are allowed to select easily guessed passwords. Directory permissions are poorly set and proper process accounting is neglected. Utilities to counter these problems exist for every operating system, yet they are not widely used. In addition, many systems administrators are not provided with current information from MIS management to help them secure their systems.

There is a lack of communication between vendors and MIS management and inside the corporate community as a whole. Rather than inform everyone of problems when they are discovered, vendors keep information in secret security databases or channel it to a select few through electronic-mail lists. This does little to help the situation and, in fact, only makes matters worse because many hackers have access to archives of the information sent in these mailing lists. Another major problem in system security comes from telecommunications equipment. The various Bell Operating Companies have long been the target of hackers, and many hackers know how to operate both corporate and central office systems better than the technicians who do so for a living. Increased use of computer networks has added a whole new dimension of insecurity. If a computer is allowed to communicate with another on the same network, every computer in the link must be impenetrable or the security of all sites is in jeopardy.

All of these problems are the ultimate responsibility of MIS management, who must put in place the proper tools to secure their total MIS organization against intrusion. If hackers can get their hands on critical information of the organization and manipulate this information to their advantage, this should be enough to get started on solving these problems. It is recommended that the staff of MIS management explore the potential risk from hackers as well as develop appropriate methods and procedures to keep the organization virtually free of their efforts.

GENERALIZED AUDIT SOFTWARE

To assist internal and external auditors/consultants, in particular, EDP auditors, generalized audit software exists because, in the normal course of events, many different audits require similar audit tasks (e.g., adding files, formatting reports), and this software can be adapted easily to carry out these tasks in different environments. Essentially, this software can be adapted quickly to the specific objectives of an audit. Generalized audit software is usually more cost-effective than customized software written specifically for a job.

Auditors/consultants use generalized audit software to examine the information held on computer files and to carry out audit tests, such as verification of calculations and totals or analyses produced; an example would be the evaluation and summation of old inventory balances. This software can be used to create and print additional analyses of data for audit purposes, such as the calculation of total inventory holdings in excess of current demand or total receivables that exceed credit limits. In addition, it can be used to examine the state of the data held on the file in order to provide totals of unusual items, such as customers without any credit limit or inventory issues with invalid dates; and select and print data from the file for subsequent examination, either as a sample of normal data or because it falls within the auditor's definition of unusual, such as customer credit balances over a certain amount or unusual discount terms. A listing of auditor software tools for accessing and processing application data is found in Figure 15.2.

Generalized Audit Software for Microcomputers

A generalized audit software program consists of integrated applications that can be useful in virtually any audit setting. In the past, this software was used only on computer mainframes. Currently, auditors run their software on the client's mainframe, directly accessing client files for analysis. Even though this is still an effective process, acquiring and using audit software designed for a computer mainframe are expensive and technically complex. The alternative is using microcomputer-based audit software. Clearly, this is ineffective when client files are so large that they would inundate a microcomputer. However, for small and some medium-sized applications, microcomputer-based audit software represents an inexpensive and readily usable auditing tool.

The key facets of microcomputer-based audit software are input, processing, and output. That is, the auditor is concerned with getting client data into the microcomputer, manipulating the data, and producing output that documents the audit. Typical generalized microcomputer-based audit software packages are

Figure 15.2
Audit Software Tools for Accessing and Processing Application Data

Audit Software Tool	*Description of Use*
1. Generalized audit software packages	Foots, identifies exceptions, selects, and analyzes data.
2. Customized audit software	Performs specialized audit functions not provided by generalized audit software packages.
3. Microcomputer-based audit software	Automates audit workpapers and analytical procedures. Refer to Figure 15.3 for typical software.
4. Application audit software packages	Centers on applications with common audit objectives, such as accounts receivable and accounts payable.
5. Query functions and report writers	Relates to installations that have purchased such software.
6. Embedded audit data collection	Relates to telephone, banking, insurance, and similar industries where it is not practical to use other audit software.
7. System utility software and service aids	Sets up audit software, e.g., copying or sorting files.
8. Time-sharing programs	Relates to analytical reviews, such as balance sheet analysis, operating analysis, and financial analysis.
9. Public databases and bulletin boards	Shares information with others, obtaining difficult to get public data.

given in Figure 15.3 along with their key features. Using one of these generalized audit software packages, a typical audit application is accounts receivable. In this situation, the microcomputer is used to select and print confirmations to test for the existence of specific accounts receivable, produce an aging of account receivables in order to help analyze collectibility, and extract a schedule of invoices for testing. As such, the confirmation, bad-debt review, and invoice selection processes are fully automated.

Automated Workpaper Software

In addition to generalized audit software, there are programs known as workpaper or trial balance software. Such software simplifies the preparation of financial statements by integrating the audit workpapers, schedules, and trial balances. When the auditor enters adjustments and reclassifications, related schedules and financial statements are updated automatically. These programs are valuable time-saving tools since they streamline some of the tedious work of preparing financial statements. A number of stand-alone and template packages (that are used in

Figure 15.3
Typical Generalized Microcomputer-Based Audit Software Packages

Generalized Audit Software Tool	*Description of Package*
ACL Plus (ACL Services, Ltd., Vancouver, British Columbia Canada)	This audit program offers speed and advanced features. Its functionality leads to complexity and its menus can overwhelm the user. The documentation is good.
Applaud (Premier International, Chicago, Illinois)	This audit program offers a menu-driven method of programming that tends to simplify the audit process somewhat. Features include extensive report generation capabilities, a strong on-screen record layout feature, and a print preview for easy output production. Also, database manipulation capabilities are offered in a relatively easy-to-use package.
Easytrieve Plus/PC (Pansophic Systems, Inc. Lisle, Illinois)	This audit program has an English-like language for programming that allows the product to be customized extensively. The microcomputer version of Easytrieve is designed to be used in conjunction with mainframe Easytrieve.
IDEA (American Institute of CPAs, New York, New York)	This audit program does not offer customization through programming or report generation. This may be an ideal package for the auditor who wants to use generalized software but is concerned about his or her lack of the technical skills necessary to use such software.

conjunction with a spreadsheet) are available. Typical programs are Accountant's Trial Balance, AuditCube, Express Workpapers, FAST! Financial, FAST/CPA, focus: ABC, and Pre-Audit. For these tools, prices are generally for site licenses, which vary with the number of users. In some cases, a single-user price is also available.

EFFECTIVE MIS MANAGEMENT TO EVALUATE THE MIS ORGANIZATION

The potential for loss associated with management information systems is growing with increasing complexity, exposure, and automation. Today, computer programs rather than human beings perform many of the checks and verifications necessary to ensure accuracy and completeness of data and records. This development has exposed management information systems to the possibility of loss from several sources, including input errors or omissions, improper controls within the system, inadequate systems design, fraud or theft, and failure to comply with legislated or other standards and procedures. It is from this viewpoint that the need for determining the effectiveness of MIS controls has increased. Basically, this is the rationale for the comprehensive MIS questionnaire set forth in this final chapter.

TWO-PART MIS QUESTIONNAIRE

The MIS audit function of internal and external auditors/consultants, including EDP auditors, is shifting from the evaluation and verification of processing results—that is, data files, records, and reports—to the evaluation and verification of the controls that ensure the continuing accuracy and reliability of processing results. This emphasis is resulting in new internal and external audit approaches and techniques that take into account a TQM viewpoint, an extension of traditional internal audit responsibilities, as MIS management seeks assurance that computer application systems are accurate and reliable. In light of this trend, a questionnaire can be employed to evaluate systems controls. As noted in the prior chapter, the questionnaire is divided into two parts: general controls and application controls.

Purposes of the Two-Part MIS Questionnaire

The *first* purpose of the two-part MIS questionnaire is to aid internal and external auditors/consultants, including EDP auditors, to perform a comprehensive audit of an organization's management information systems. The questionnaire focuses on appraising the accomplishment of MIS objectives in the areas of systems, programming, and operations; the ability of MIS management to perform their assigned functions of planning, organizing, directing, and controlling in their assigned areas; the adequacy of the organization's information centers; and the adequacy of managerial MIS decisions and actions in moving toward stated objectives. Hence, its questions appraise the management of MIS resources.

Going beyond the appraisal of managerial capabilities, a *second* purpose is to appraise the adequacy of controls over MIS operations and their operating procedures, along with the adequacy of control over end users. It also informs MIS management of operating problems that need to be corrected for greater efficiency and economy of operations. Within this framework, MIS personnel and end-user operating policies, computer facilities, and the operating environment are reviewed in terms of their contribution (or lack of contribution) to operating efficiency or cost savings. A secondary purpose of the two-part MIS questionnaire, then, is oriented toward evaluating the efficiency and effectiveness of operational activities on a day-to-day basis.

Inclusion of both the managerial and operational aspects provides a logical framework for a thorough and comprehensive evaluation of any management information system. Evaluating both aspects leads to improved operations in most areas. In addition, because managerial and operational activities are complementary and supplementary to one another, they should be treated as such and resolved accordingly. This combined approach allows a question to be asked from two different perspectives. For example, in the area of operational activities, What are the working conditions like in the data center? Would one enjoy working under these conditions? A look around the computer room for any capital equipment extras might just provide the answer. Quiet, comfortable air-conditioning and sophisticated, machine protecting (not sprinklers on the ceiling) fire prevention equipment make the data center more pleasant and safe. But of even greater significance from the standpoint of managerial activities, the presence of these extras indicates a concern and commitment by MIS management which probably extend to other areas more difficult to measure, such as staffing, policies, funding, and training. Thc physical layout of the equipment in the data center, then, is indicative of the amount of thought that went into the design of other aspects under MIS management's direction.

How to Use the MIS Questionnaire

The two-part MIS questionnaire does not give answers but simply asks questions. If the questions are all answered "yes," the function or area under investigation is operating as desired. On the other hand, if there are some "no" answers, it is experiencing difficulty, and the negative answers must be expanded upon in writing. If the question does not apply, the "N.A." (not applicable) column is checked. The questionnaire serves as a tool to analyze current MIS activities. But more importantly, it allows the auditors/consultants to synthesize those elements causing difficulties and deficiencies. The capability to assess all negative answers helps separate real problems from symptoms. This will be apparent in the sample case study at the end of the chapter.

Once the auditors/consultants have diagnosed the real problems and the difficulties and deficiencies surrounding them, they are ready to assess the level of performance for the function or area being investigated. Many times, performance is far below expectations. Subsequent recommendations provide a basis for an oral presentation and a written report to improve operations.

GENERAL CONTROLS—AN OVERVIEW

General controls for evaluating the MIS organization provide a framework for determining the degree of managerial and operational control. Extenuating circumstances may relate to a management information system, thereby creating the need for questions and investigations not covered in this part of the questionnaire. The individual reviewing the system must exercise judgment in this regard. Whether or not additional questions are appended, the MIS questionnaire is so designed that a minimum degree of control is maintained throughout the MIS organization.

MIS Questionnaire 1—General Controls

General controls as found in Questionnaire 1 (refer to Figure 15.4) comprise these categories:

I. MIS Department Controls
II. System and Program Development Controls
III. Hardware and Software Controls
IV. Data Center Controls
V. Security Controls
VI. Information Center Controls

These categories correspond to those found in the prior chapter. Answering these questions in Questionnaire 1 results in a comprehensive approach to evaluate general controls over the MIS organization.

APPLICATION CONTROLS—AN OVERVIEW

Questions for evaluating application controls represent the second part of the MIS questionnaire. Within each area, initially the focus is on general considerations. Because the remaining areas are somewhat technical, their focus is oriented toward the operations aspects of a management information system in some depth.

MIS Questionnaire 2—Application Controls

Application controls and detailed questions about them are set forth in Questionnaire 2 (refer to Figure 15.5). The structure for this questionnaire is as follows:

I. Input Controls
II. Processing Controls
III. Output Controls
IV. Database Controls
V. Data Communications and Networking Controls
VI. End-User Controls

This breakdown corresponds to that found in the prior chapter. Answers to these questions provide a comprehensive approach for evaluating application controls

Figure 15.4
MIS Questionnaire 1—General Controls

	Yes[1]	*No*[2]	*N.A.*[3]
I. *MIS Department Controls*			
A. *General Considerations*			
1. Is the MIS organization under the direction of a qualified manager?	___	___	___
2. Are the MIS long-range strategic plans adequate for meeting the organization's objectives?	___	___	___
3. Has MIS management made ample plans for handling the organization's future growth?	___	___	___
4. Does MIS management employ current hardware and software in its computer operations?	___	___	___
5. Does MIS management exert the necessary leadership to get adequate funding for the MIS organization?	___	___	___
6. Does MIS management utilize a cost/benefit analysis to justify their information technology?	___	___	___
7. Does MIS management review its operations with the view of outsourcing all or part of its operations?	___	___	___
8. Does MIS management recognize that picking the right outsourcer is more complex than comparing price?	___	___	___
9. Is there a proper segregation of functions between MIS personnel and end users so that there is good internal control over operations?	___	___	___
10. Does the provision for establishing MIS controls originate outside the MIS department, i.e., from internal and external auditors?	___	___	___
B. *Strategic MIS Plans*			
1. Does MIS management have MIS strategic plans from the short range to the long range?	___	___	___
2. Are the MIS strategic plans well defined and adequate for effective control?	___	___	___
3. Are the MIS strategic plans integrated with organization objectives, goals, and strategies?	___	___	___
4. Are the MIS strategic plans reviewed by senior corporate management and the MIS organizationwide committee?	___ ___	___ ___	___ ___
5. Do the MIS strategic plans include a provision for determining specific budgeted amounts for the coming year and up to five years?	___	___	___
6. Do the MIS strategic plans provide a control method for comparing budget amounts to actual	___	___	___

1—indicates a favorable condition; 2—indicates a condition that needs to be explained in writing; 3—not applicable.

	Yes [1]	No [2]	N.A. [3]
results for the coming year?			
7. Is there a control procedure for bringing important variations from budgeted amounts to the attention of management?	___	___	___
8. Is there a control method for ensuring that corrective action has been carried out?	___	___	___
C. *Disaster Recovery Plans*			
1. Is the formalized plan for disaster recovery under the control of MIS management?	___	___	___
2. Is there a disaster recovery plan in place in the event of an equipment malfunction, fire, a loss of power, sabotage, a natural disaster, and the like?	___	___	___
3. Are there emergency provisions for the recovery of extremely critical items, such as on-line data files and programs?	___	___	___
4. Is there a backup computer system available on short notice?	___	___	___
5. Does the disaster recovery plan include at least one of the following: alternative site(s) within the organization, a reciprocal agreement between MIS departments in different organizations, a vendor who offers cold- and hot-site disaster recovery facilities, or a comparable type disaster recovery arrangement?	___	___	___
6. Are disaster recovery procedures reviewed periodically for relevancy to the times?	___	___	___
D. *Total Quality Management (TQM) Program*			
1. Does MIS management have a TQM program in place for the total MIS organization which includes end users?	___	___	___
2. Does MIS management have a TQM program in place that is under the direction of a qualified TQM team?	___	___	___
3. Does MIS management have a TQM help desk in operation that can assist MIS personnel and end users in better understanding the organization's TQM program?	___	___	___
4. Does the TQM program include a consensus TQM statement, a plan for quality improvement, and a working relationship with vendors for quality improvement?	___	___	___
5. Does the TQM program for systems development include a focus on a positive working relationship with end users, a detailed listing of system specifications that are desired by end users, and walkthroughs that are useful to understand the system as designed?	___	___	___
6. Does the TQM program for software improvement include the capability to establish and revise	___	___	___

	Yes[1]	No[2]	N.A.[3]
the software quality improvement plan, to define and adjust software metrics, to monitor quality metrics and check with customers, to focus on zero defects software, to provide for adequate testing of software, and to improve the software engineering process?			
7. Does the TQM program for daily operations include a production schedule that follows a logical flow to assist end users in meeting their processing requirements, a provision for production reruns that minimizes the interruption of end-user processing requirements, and a provision on the dates and times of system maintenance to minimize the interruption of end-user processing requirements?	___	___	___
8. Does the TQM program for systems and program maintenance include a provision for dates and times of systems and program enhancements; a provision for updates to hardware.,software, and data communications; and a help desk to respond to myriad problems that end users may have?	___	___	___
9. Does MIS management have a feedback mechanism in place to report on the strengths and shortcomings of the organization's TQM program with the focus of improving the program over time?	___	___	___
E. *Organiztaion Structure Controls*			
1. Is the MIS department operating as a separate unit without direct control over the organization's assets?	___	___	___
2. Is the MIS organization chart current?	___	___	___
3. Are the major MIS personnel groups located in the MIS department organizationally and physically separate from one another?	___	___	___
4. Are systems and programming personnel forbidden to operate the computer for regular processing runs?	___	___	___
5. Are all computer operators frequently transferred to operate different programs?	___	___	___
6. Do internal and external auditors check periodically on the operations of the MIS department?	___	___	___
7. Does MIS management recognize that the total MIS organization needs to be reviewed periodically for relevance to current times?	___	___	___

		Yes[1]	No[2]	N.A.[3]
	8. Does MIS management consider downsizing, i.e., rightsizing, the total MIS organization to reflect changed operating conditions?	___	___	___
F.	*Personnel Standards*			
	1. Is there a thorough investigation of MIS personnel conducted prior to hiring?	___	___	___
	2. Is there an adequate formal orientation and training program for new employees?	___	___	___
	3. Is there an adequate training program for current MIS personnel?	___	___	___
	4. Is there provision for backup personnel in key MIS positions?	___	___	___
	5. Is there job rotation for monotonous or tedious tasks to overcome psychological fatigue?	___	___	___
	6. Is there a career path for all MIS personnel so that they can identify with the organization?	___	___	___
	7. Are employees about to be discharged removed from critical areas to prevent harm to MIS operations?	___	___	___
	8. Are critical areas controlled from access by unauthorized personnel?	___	___	___
	9. Have performance standards been established for MIS personnel?	___	___	___
G.	*Performance Appraisal*			
	1. Is a performance appraisal program employed at least annually?	___	___	___
	2. Does the performance appraisal program focus on the individual's performance in accomplishing desired goals?	___	___	___
	3. Does the performance appraisal program provide a means for observation to identify personnel for merit increases, promotions, transfers, and dismissals?	___	___	___
	4. Does the performance appraisal program assist MIS management in specifying the developmental needs of MIS personnel who have promotion potential?	___	___	___
	5. Does the performance appraisal program motivate employees by providing feedback on their performance?	___	___	___
	6. Is performance appraisal an integral part of career planning for MIS personnel?	___	___	___

II. *System and Program Development Controls*

A.	*General Considerations*			
	1. Does the MIS organization have a formal management approach to systems and program development?	___	___	___

	Yes[1]	No[2]	N.A.[3]
2. Does this approach include the best systems and program development methodologies, such as structured and object-oriented analysis, design, and programming?	___	___	___
3. Does this approach include a TQM approach that will assure the highest level of quality assurance for the final system?	___	___	___
4. Does this approach include end-user involvement whereby end users accept full responsibility for and commitment to the ultimate success of the MIS project?	___	___	___
5. Are formal requests for new or revised systems prepared by users and submitted with proper authorization signatures?	___	___	___
6. Is a cost/benefit analysis performed to ensure that the conceptual system will economically produce results?	___	___	___
B. *Control over Methods and Procedures*			
1. Does the system allow for an efficient work flow?	___	___	___
2. Have work simplification methods been employed to improve the work flow?	___	___	___
3. Have safeguards been established against possible irregularities?	___	___	___
4. Are exception items normally handled by experienced personnel?	___	___	___
5. Are there methods and procedures in effect to recognize bottlenecks and eliminate them?	___	___	___
6. Is there final approval by the applicable levels of management, appropriate end users, and the proper MIS personnel before methods and procedures are implemented?	___	___	___
C. *Systems and Programming Development Procedures*			
1. Do systems and programming managers break down their projects into 80-hour tasks so that MIS personnel can be held responsible and accountable for results?	___	___	___
2. Do systems and programming managers make sure that standard documentation procedures are followed?	___	___	___
3. Do written procedures for maintenace of systems and programs provide for formal requests for changes, approval by authorized managers, and testing of changes?	___	___	___
4. Do systems and programming managers review their projects to make sure that they meet their intended objectives?	___	___	___

		Yes[1]	*No*[2]	*N.A.*[3]
5.	Are internal auditors included in system and programming projects to ensure that appropriate audit and control features are included in the systems?	___	___	___
6.	Are systems and programming development procedures reviewed periodically by an independent third party for relevancy to the times?	___	___	___

D. *Control over Changes*

1.	Is there a control mechanism in place for making appropriate system and program changes?	___	___	___
2.	Does this control mechanism include a provision for approval?	___	___	___
3.	Are all system and program changes immediately documented, including the reason for the changes?	___	___	___
4.	Are all systems and procedures manuals kept current?	___	___	___
5.	Are written memorandums issued to appropriate personnel concerning the changes?	___	___	___
6.	Are the internal and external auditors appraised of important changes?	___	___	___

E. *Control over Documentation*

1.	Has MIS management instituted a program of effective documentation throughout the MIS department that defines the appropriate level of detail?	___	___	___
2.	Have documentation procedures been established for systems analysts, programmers, and other MIS personnel?	___	___	___
3.	Is there adequate documentation for starting, operating, restarting, and shutting down the computer system?	___	___	___
4.	Ia documentation undertaken by qualified personnel?	___	___	___
5.	Do the internal and external auditors check periodically for adequate documentation?	___	___	___

III. *Hardware and Software Controls*

A. *General Considerations*

1.	Are hardware controls that are built into the equipment considered in the acquisition of PC and computer mainframe platforms?	___	___	___
2.	Are there formal procedures to recover from hardware and software errors?	___	___	___
3.	Is there adequate control over the operating system software?	___	___	___
4.	Is there adequate control over changes to the operating system software?	___	___	___

	Yes[1]	No[2]	N.A.[3]
5. Are hardware and software controls an integral part of security controls?	___	___	___
6. Do the internal and external auditors review periodically the adequacy of hardware and software controls?	___	___	___
B. *Parity Checks and Echo Checks*			
1. Does hardware parity checking (i.e., a method for checking data as they are transferred by adding a zero or 1 bit) detect errors that are caused by losing or adding extra bits?	___	___	___
2. Is there a method for reporting parity checking errors so that they can be corrected immediately?	___	___	___
3. Is echo checking (i.e., a feedback mechanism for echoing a character of data back from the point of transmission to its original source) employed by the computer platforms?	___	___	___
4. Are parity checks and/or echo checks employed for data communications equipment to ensure accuracy of data transmission?	___	___	___
5. If there is an echo check failure, is processing stopped to determine the reason?	___	___	___
C. *Duplication Checks and Dual Heads*			
1. Does the built-in hardware require that two independent components perform the same operation and compare results?	___	___	___
2. If there are differences between the two operations, is an error condition indicated so that computer processing is halted?	___	___	___
3. Are duplicate checking errors brought to the attention of a field-service engineer for prompt corrective action?	___	___	___
4. Are dual heads (i.e., a method for reading or writing by two magnetic heads, read-write heads, or dual read heads, to check on the accuracy of one another) employed by the computer platforms?	___	___	___
5. If errors are detected by the dual heads, is processing stopped to determine the reason?	___	___	___
D. *Overflow and Sign Checks*			
1. Is overflow checking (i.e., a method of indicating that a counter or accumulator in the computer's arithmetic unit has been exceeded) employed by the computer's arithmetic unit?	___	___	___
2. Is a sign check (i.e., a method for indicating that an arithmetic value has not the required positive or negative sign) employed by the computer platform?	___	___	___

	Yes[1]	No[2]	N.A.[3]
3. If there is an overflow or a sign check problem, does it result in halting of computer processing for immediate correction?	___	___	___
4. Are overflow and sign checks an integral part of the field service engineer's tests?	___	___	___
E. *Operating System Controls*			
1. Are control features imbedded in the vendor-supplied operating system to detect and report hardware malfunctions and software errors?	___	___	___
2. Is the vendor-supplied operating system subjected to the same control procedures as those applied to application programs?	___	___	___
3. Is the vendor-supplied operating system subjected to the same control over changes as those applied to application programs?	___	___	___
4. Are there written procedures for vendor-supplied operating system maintenance?	___	___	___
F. *Built-In Software Controls*			
1. Does every system application developed include the necessary built-in software controls for efficient and effective processing?	___	___	___
2. Are end users involved in determining what built-in software controls are needed for daily operations?	___	___	___
3. Does the MIS department utilize the latest versions of purchased software to realize more of the advanced features, including improved controls?	___	___	___
4. Does the MIS management stress the need to meet the demands of internal and external auditors in terms of required built-in software controls?	___	___	___
5. Are there sufficient antivirus procedures included in the built-in software controls to ensure that the data and software are amply protected?	___	___	___
6. Is there sufficient documentation of built-in software controls to satisfy internal and external auditors?	___	___	___
G. *Changes to Built-In Software Controls*			
1. Does MIS management stress the philosophy of "ease to use" for end users when systems are changed by systems analysts and programmers to accommodate new software controls?	___	___	___
2. Does MIS management stress the need to change built-in software controls that can improve system's performance?	___	___	___
3. Does MIS management stress the need for designing flexible systems to meet changing requirements for built-in software controls?	___	___	___
4. Does MIS management require that its systems analysts and programmers work with software vendors to make sure that problem fixes, updates,	___	___	___

	Yes[1]	No[2]	N.A.[3]
new versions, etc., are in agreement with the organization's built-in software controls?			
5. Is there sufficient feedback from end users and the internal and external auditors to systems analysts and programmers for making appropriate changes to built-in software controls?	___	___	___
IV. *Data Center Controls*			
A. *General Considerations*			
1. Are there concern and commitment of MIS management for an efficient data center?	___	___	___
2. Does MIS management engage in productivity improvement of the data center? (Productivity improvement depends on the ability first to measure existing conditions and then to assess changes in these variables that result from an improvement effort.)	___	___	___
3. Is the data center adequately managed so that users' data processing needs are met?	___	___	___
4. Are the working conditions in the data center conducive to high-quality work?	___	___	___
5. Does the physical layout of equipment in the data center allow for a smooth work flow?	___	___	___
6. Are manufacturer's temperature and humidity requirements fulfilled?	___	___	___
7. Is there a periodic surprise audit of the data center by internal and external auditors?	___	___	___
B. *Control over Access to Data Center*			
1. Are only authorized persons allowed to enter the data center?	___	___	___
2. Is there a list of authorized persons who are allowed to enter the data center?	___	___	___
3. Are badges, coded cards, or the like, issued for authorized entry to the data center?	___	___	___
4. Are policies in effect to reduce possible collusion in the data center?	___	___	___
C. *Control over Computer Operators*			
1. Does the MIS operations manager exercise sufficient control over computer operators for efficient operations?	___	___	___
2. Does the MIS operations manager have sufficient control over the computer console operators to prevent unauthorized program changes and entry of data through the console?	___	___	___
3. Are computer operator instructions detailed enough that they can recover from unusual operating conditions?	___	___	___
4. Is the computer operator's manual accessible for ready reference?	___	___	___

	Yes[1]	No[2]	N.A.[3]
5. Are computer operators rotated periodically for improved internal control so that no one operator has complete control over one or more computer programs and processing runs?	___	___	___
D. *Control over Tape and Disk Librarian*			
1. Are the tape and disk library maintained under the supervision of a librarian?	___	___	___
2. Are the tape and disk library controlled during all shifts?	___	___	___
3. Are the magnetic tape and disk catalogue maintained?	___	___	___
4. Is a record of all borrowers of magnetic tapes and disks maintained?	___	___	___
5. Do internal and external auditors periodically review the operations of the tape and disk library?	___	___	___
E. *Control over Computer Maintenance*			
1. Is the data center free of dust, dirt, etc., for efficient operations?	___	___	___
2. Are field-service engineers sufficiently qualified to undertake regular as well as abnormal computer maintenance?	___	___	___
3. Is the computer equipment properly maintained, that is, is there provision for periodic maintenance (say, daily, semiweekly, etc.)?	___	___	___
4. Are parts of magnetic tape and disk drives cleaned often to reduce input/output errors?	___	___	___
V. *Security Controls*			
A. *General Considerations*			
1. Are there procedures in place that focus on authentication? (Authentication is the process of specifying that users are who they claim to be.)	___	___	___
2. Are there procedures in place that focus on authorization? (Authorization involves determining whether a user has legitimate access to a resource and allowing the owner of a resource to define who has what types of access to the resource.)	___	___	___
3. Are required security controls fully understood and implemented by systems and programming personnel?	___	___	___
4. Are required security data controls sufficient to ensure that all input and output data and corrections to data have been processed properly and accurately?	___	___	___
5. Is there a surprise audit of the MIS department for detecting fraud, theft, collusion, embezzlement, sabotage, and irregularities?	___	___	___

	Yes[1]	No[2]	N.A.[3]
6. Does the MIS department utilize antivirus software to detect computer viruses?	___	___	___
7. Are required security controls reviewed periodically by an independent third party to make sure that they serve their intended purpose?	___	___	___
B. *Data Communications and Networking Controls*			
1. Does MIS management work with users in developing and implementing security controls over data communications and networking aspects of daily operations?	___	___	___
2. Does the MIS department have the time and expertise to develop and put in place security controls for local, metropolitan, and wide area networks?	___	___	___
3. Does the MIS department develop appropriate security controls for electronic network processing, that is, image processing within the organization and electronic data interchange (EDI) outside the organization with trading partners?	___	___	___
4. Does the MIS department utilize a single sign-on as opposed to a multiple sign-on that enables a single password to control each user's access across the network?	___	___	___
5. Does the MIS department make use of at least one type of data encryption (a method of scrambling data so an eavesdropper cannot read it) on a network, a private key (two users on a network share a single key that encrypts and decrypts messages), or a public key (all recipients on a network share a common key)?	___	___	___
6. Does the MIS department make use of other transmission controls on a network as part of an effective security scheme to prevent data alteration or loss? That is, are the following controls used where deemed appropriate: hash totals, record sequence checking, transmission logging, transmission error correction, and retransmission controls?	___	___	___
7. Does the MIS department make use of virus detection software to keep data and programs secure on a network?	___	___	___
8. Does MIS management utilize a help desk to assist users in understanding and maintaining security controls on a network?	___	___	___
9. Are security controls reviewed periodically by an independent third party for their adequacy	___	___	___

Yes[1] No[2] N.A.[3]

in a data communications and networking environment?

C. *Infosecurity Controls*

1. Does MIS management have (where necessary) a password system that limits user access to specific files, directories, and databases, and automatically disables user's access after three repeated log-on failures? ___ ___ ___
2. Does MIS management have in place (where necessary) user-IDs that are associated with individual users and are the computer equivalent of a person's name? ___ ___ ___
3. Does MIS management have in place (where necessary) security codes or keys that are associated with algorithms and share certain characteristics with both passwords and user-IDs? ___ ___ ___
4. Does MIS management have in place (where necessary) password tokens that look like pocket calculators (although they may have only a few keys) and generate and display a different password each time its owner logs on? ___ ___ ___
5. Does MIS management require that its data encryption method use either the Data Encryption Standard (DES), proprietary algorithms, or both? ___ ___ ___
6. Does MIS management have in place (where necessary) the newer infosecurity control devices,that is, biometric devices, expert system-based systems, fiber optics, and satellite communications? ___ ___ ___
7. Does MIS management have in place (where necessary) security audits that maintain a log of network events, including invalid log-on attempts and program use? ___ ___ ___
8. Does MIS management require that its infosecurity controls include virus detection to protect its data and programs from unexpected viruses? ___ ___ ___
9. Does MIS management provide a help desk on infosecurity controls that can be useful to all employees who experience problems getting onto their systems or other organizational systems? ___ ___ ___
10. Are infosecurity controls reviewed periodically by an independent third party for their adequacy? ___ ___ ___

D. *Program Controls*

1. Are computer programs stored in a safe location where they are controlled by a tape and disk librarian? ___ ___ ___
2. Are computer programs duplicated on a magnetic ___ ___ ___

	Yes[1]	No[2]	N.A.[3]
tape or disk and stored in a safe storage area as back-up for emergency conditions?			
3. Does each program have a computer-run book that is available to the console operator for meeting any contingency during the processing of the program?	___	___	___
4. Does an independent third party periodically conduct a surprise audit of computer programs to make sure they serve their intended purposes?	___	___	___
E. *Equipment Log*			
1. Is a daily equipment log prepared so that computer operating time can be monitored?	___	___	___
2. Does the equipment log contain program identification, start time, stop time, production time, test time, downtime, and unusual conditions?	___	___	___
3. If there is an installed computer device for recording time, does the internal auditor periodically check the equipment log time against the usage for falsification of computer time?	___	___	___
4. Does the internal auditor periodically check the equipment log (when the run was completed) against the library record (when the program tape or disk was returned) for time discrepancies?	___	___	___
5. Is a copy of the computer console typewriter output delivered to the internal auditor at the end of each day? (It is highly recommended that the internal auditor initial the printout at the start of his or her workday.)	___	___	___
F. *Physical Access Controls*			
1. Does MIS management consider physical access controls an integral part of its total security program?	___	___	___
2. Does MIS management employ the proper level of physical access controls?	___	___	___
3. Are the cards and keys employees carry easy to use so that proper access to computing facilities is no hassle for authorized employees?	___	___	___
4. Does MIS management keep abreast of newer physical access controls and install them where appropriate to make a secure environment even more secure?	___	___	___
G. *Fire Protection*			
1. Is the computer area housed in a fire-sensitive, non-combustible structure?	___	___	___
2. Have the proper number of fire and smoke detection devices been installed in the computer room?	___	___	___
3. Are there heat and fire detection devices inside the major computer equipment?	___	___	___
4. Are required paper supplies and other combustible materials in excess of the minimum requirements, stored away from the computer area?	___	___	___

	Yes[1]	No[2]	N.A.[3]
5. Does the computer area have automatic fire extinguishing equipment to protect personnel, the building, the equipment, and supplies?	___	___	___
6. Does insurance cover losses by fire, water, power failure, fraud, sabotage, and natural catastrophe?	___	___	___
H. *Media Protection*			
1. Are magnetic tapes and disks stored at the proper temperature and humidity levels?	___	___	___
2. Are magnetic tapes and disks stored away from exposure to accidental alteration by extreme heat or cold?	___	___	___
3. Are magnetic tapes and disks stored in a safe place so there is no possibility of alteration by magnets?	___	___	___
VI. *Information Center Controls*			
A. *General Considerations*			
1. Does MIS management consider the computing needs of end users critical to the operations of the MIS department?	___	___	___
2. Is there a well-thought-out and developed plan by MIS management that centers on an overall strategy for developing and maintaining information centers?	___	___	___
3. Do the information centers, whether they are centralized or decentralized in end-user functional units, meet the needs of end users?	___	___	___
4. Is an appropriate amount being allocated to meet current needs of end users using centralized and/or decentralized information centers?	___	___	___
5. Is an increasing percentage of the computing budget being allocated to meet future needs of end users using centralized and/or decentralized information centers?	___	___	___
B. *Planning an Overall Strategy for Information Centers*			
1. Are the organization's information centers an integral part of MIS management's overall strategy to support end users more effectively over the long term?	___	___	___
2. Is there an adequate feedback mechanism from end users to MIS management regarding the capability of centralized and/or decentralized information centers to meet their needs?	___	___	___
3. Is there a tie-in of information center management with office automation management (charged with updating office equipment, methods, and procedures) so that "the right hand knows what the left hand is doing"?	___	___	___
4. Is the coming budget for all information centers	___	___	___

	Yes[1]	No[2]	N.A.[3]
adequate to cover the acquisition of hardware, software, and other expenses (operations, maintenance, and similar items) necessary to realize their overall goals?			
C. *Hardware and Software Integration*			
1. Is the acquisition of hardware and software aimed primarily at the end user rather than the other way around?	___	___	___
2. Is the acquisition of hardware and software handled in such a way that end users are in agreement with the procurement process?	___	___	___
3. Is there a periodic review of the hardware and software acquisition process by an independent third party to ensure that the organization is keeping with the times?	___	___	___
4. Do the end users have the proper background to make the selection of computer hardware and software for a specific application?	___	___	___
5. If the end users do not have the proper background for justifying and making the selection of the appropriate hardware and software, are the information centers or a comparable organization resource a way out of this dilemma?	___	___	___
6. Is there an approved company policy for integrating hardware and software purchased by end users through information centers with those of the MIS department itself?	___	___	___
7. Are the hardware and software to be purchased capable of tying in with the company's present and future systems?	___	___	___
8. Do the hardware and software to be purchased from the same equipment vendor allow for economies of scale in price, training, maintenance, etc.?	___	___	___
9. If the programming to be undertaken exceeds the capability of end users, is there provision to assist them or possibly turn the job over to the MIS department?	___	___	___
D. Organization *of Information Centers*			
1. Are the information centers, whether they are centralized or decentralized, under the direction of capable managers? Do they practice managerial functions versus accentuating only the technical aspects of their jobs?	___	___	___
2. Are the information centers taking the necessary steps to set up appropriate structures for integrating LAN-basd PCs with the organization's computer mainframe?	___	___	___
3. Is the information centers' organization structure considered appropriate by end users? That is, do	___	___	___

	Yes[1]	No[2]	N.A.[3]
end users feel there is a "good fit" among themselves, their jobs, and the services offered by the information centers?			
4. Is the information centers' organization structure designed to minimize conflict between MIS personnel and end users?	___	___	___
5. Is the information centers' organization structure reviewed periodically to ensure it is relevant to the times?	___	___	___
6. Does the MIS organizationwide committee give direction to the organization's information centers?	___	___	___
7. Does MIS management recognize the need for and importance of end-user groups as well as support them?	___	___	___
E. *Staffing of Information Centers*			
1. Does the MIS department recognize the importanceof acquiring the best-suited MIS personnel to staff the information centers whether centralized or decentralized?	___	___	___
2. Does the MIS department encourage its MIS personnel to consider the information centers a desirable career opportunity?	___	___	___
3. Does the information centers' staff understand the behavioral problems of working with and through people?	___	___	___
4. Are MIS personnel who are assigned to the information centers considered to be capable of resolving or, at least, reducing conflict that may arise on occasion?	___	___	___
5. Is there an attempt by MIS management to appropriate changes in information center staffing when there is a shift in the organization's corporate culture?	___	___	___
6. Are information centers reviewed periodically by MIS management to ensure proper staffing?	___	___	___
F. *Training of End Users*			
1. Has MIS management reviewed the various approaches to training end users in order to find the appropriate one(s)?	___	___	___
2. Are the in-house information center training programs directed toward meeting the needs of end users versus those needs that the information center is capable of fulfilling?	___	___	___
3. Does the information center training staff have the proper credentials and real world experience to give the appropriate end-user training and is it perceived by end users as such?	___	___	___
4. Is the information center training staff geared to teaching new material resulting from changing information technology?	___	___	___

	Yes[1]	No[2]	N.A.[3]
5. Does the information center training staff provide a means to improve the *productivity* of management, their staff, and operations personnel?	___	___	___
6. Does the information center training staff stress TQM requirements throughout their training programs?	___	___	___
7. Do the information center training programs allow for evaluation of the training after it has been delivered?	___	___	___
8. Are the information center training programs reviewed by the organizationwide MIS committee?	___	___	___
G. *Control and Security over Information Centers*			
1. Do the organization's information centers periodically review their control mechanisms over the acquisition of computer hardware and software so that end users feel they are an integral part of the organization's computing capabilities?	___	___	___
2. Are information centers reviewed periodically by MIS management so that they are cost-effective? That is, the benefits received exceed their costs by an acceptable margin?	___	___	___
3. Are the organization's information centers reviewed periodically by MIS management to ensure that they are meeting end-user needs?	___	___	___
4. Are there sufficient controls in place to avert theft or destruction of information center hardware and software?	___	___	___
5. Are there sufficient controls in place to safeguard end-user projects that are under way?	___	___	___
6. Are passwords and security lists used (if deemed appropriate) to give access to information center hardware?	___	___	___
7. Are the organization's information centers locked at the appropriate times (such as in the evenings) so that unauthorized personnel cannot gain access to the computing facilities?	___	___	___
8. Are the organization's information centers reviewed periodically by an independent third party to ensure that proper control and security measures are in place?	___	___	___

Figure 15.5
MIS Questionnaire 2—Application Controls

	Yes[1]	No[2]	N.A.[3]
I. *Input Controls*			
A. *General Considerations*			
1. Does MIS management require that input controls be made an integral part of its systems?	___	___	___
2. Are appropriate input controls instituted by MIS management to reflect changing conditions of input methods and procedures, such as from a computer mainframe–based processing mode to a LAN-based processing mode?	___	___	___
3. Does MIS management require that input controls start with input processing methods and procedures?	___	___	___
4. Do input controls provide assurance that data received for processing have been properly authorized, have been converted accurately into a machine-processible medium, and have not been lost, suppressed, added, duplicated, or otherwise improperly changed?	___	___	___
5. Are input controls sufficiently adequate to allow movement of data between one processing step and another plus between departments?	___	___	___
6. Are input controls sufficient to handle these input categories: entry of transactions, file maintenance transactions, inquiry transactions, and error correction transactions?	___	___	___
7. Do input controls allow for the detection of errors and correction of originating data?	___	___	___
8. Are the methods and procedures for controlling the conversion of input to a machine-processible form reviewed periodically?	___	___	___
9. Are input controls reviewed periodically by an independent third party to make sure they serve their intended purpose?	___	___	___
B. *Verification Methods*			
1. Are all original transaction data verified where necessary?	___	___	___
2. Are all important data fields verified to ensure accuracy of input data using such methods as key verification and self-checking digits?	___	___	___
3. Are all significant codes used to record data verified for accuracy?	___	___	___
4. If input is obtained from written documents or	___	___	___

1—indicates a favorable condition; 2—indicates a condition that needs to be explained in writing; 3—not applicable.

Yes[1] No[2] N.A.[3]

over the telephone, is the degree of accuracy adequate?

5. If conversion equipment and data transmission equipment are used to convert or transmit data (input), is adequate verification being performed? ___ ___ ___
6. Are adequate procedures in effect for tracing and correcting input errors? ___ ___ ___

C. *Input Control Totals*

1. Are control totals established before sending data for computer processing? ___ ___ ___
2. If no control totals are used, is there som eother means of establishing input control, such as hash totals or record count totals? ___ ___ ___
3. Are input control totals passed from run to run to ensure that all transactions are in fact processed throughout the entire system? ___ ___ ___
4. Are all input documents prenumbered and accounted for by an independent count so that all transactions received are processed? ___ ___ ___
5. Is an input control total log maintained and reconciled to processing and output control totals? ___ ___ ___
6. Is responsibility fixed for errors on input documents so that corrective action can be taken? ___ ___ ___
7. Are input error correction methods properly controlled to ensure that actual correction and reentry into the system are accomplished? ___ ___ ___

D. *External Labels*

1. Do external labels contain sufficient information for their effective use? ___ ___ ___
2. Is there an adequate procedure for documenting magnetic tape and disk labels in the computer area? ___ ___ ___
3. Are codes or serial numbers used in addition to or in place of a word description? ___ ___ ___

II. *Processing Controls*

A. *General Considerations*

1. Are processing controls required by MIS management fully understood and implemented by the programming staff? ___ ___ ___
2. Do processing controls provide assurance that programmed instructions have been performed as intended? That is, are all transactions processed as authorized, no authorized transactions omitted, and no unauthorized transactions added? ___ ___ ___
3. Are processing control totals verified against input control totals at appropriate points in the processing cycle? ___ ___ ___
4. Are processing controls verified against output ___ ___ ___

		Yes[1]	No[2]	N.A.[3]
	controls for accuracy and completeness of processed data?			
	5. Do processing controls provide assurance that the proper data files are updated?	___	___	___
	6. Do processing controls detect file manipulation errors?	___	___	___
	7. Do processing controls allow for the detection and correction of incorrect input data?	___	___	___
	8. Are processing controls reviewed periodically by an independent third party to make sure that they serve their intended purpose?	___	___	___
B.	*Validation Checks and Tests*			
	1. Is sequence checking used to verify the input data?	___	___	___
	2. Are data fields checked for correct type of data—alpha, numeric, zero, blank, mathematical sign, and special characters?	___	___	___
	3. Are limit or reasonableness tests used?	___	___	___
	4. Do programs test input data for valid codes?	___	___	___
	5. Do code numbers, such as account number and inventory number, make use of the self-checking digit technique?	___	___	___
	6. Is there a comparison of field value or code against a table of allowed values or codes?	___	___	___
	7. Are printouts or halts provided when invalid codes are detected?	___	___	___
	8. Do programs make use of check points when processing must be restarted?	___	___	___
	9. Do computer loading routines include tests to verify successful loading?	___	___	___
C.	*Computer Control Totals*			
	1. Do computer progrms provide continuance of input control? That is, are input controls reconciled with processing controls for run-to-run controls?	___	___	___
	2. Are these control techniques integrated in the various computer programs: balancing totals, cross-footing balance check, zero balancing, and proof figures?	___	___	___
	3. Are the completeness and accuracy of the various files checked during processing?	___	___	___
	4. Are changes in program rate tables and other data initiated in writing and under the control of authorized personnel?	___	___	___
	5. Are all halts, excluding end-of-job, recorded and retained for audit?	___	___	___
	6. Are program changes retained for audit?	___	___	___
D.	*Internal Labels*			
	1. Are internal header and trailer labels used on all tapes and disks?	___	___	___

	Yes[1]	No[2]	N.A.[3]
2. Do header labels have adequate information—program identification, reel or disk number, date created, and date of obsolescence?	___	___	___
3. Do internal trailer labels contain appropriate information—block count, record count, data totals, and end-of-label?	___	___	___
4. Do programs test for internal header labels each time a new tape or disk is accessed to determine whether the proper input data are being used?	___	___	___
5. Are internal trailer labels generated for all magnetic tapes or disks?	___	___	___
E. *Error Routines*			
1. Are all instructions to computer operators set forth in writing for effective processing control as well as handling error conditions?	___	___	___
2. Are console operators cautioned not to accept oral instructions or to contact programmers directly when errors are found?	___	___	___
3. Do programs test for valid codes in input data, and are halts or error messages printed out when invalid codes are detected?	___	___	___
4. Is there an adequate program procedure for identifying, correcting, and reprocessing errors?	___	___	___
5. Are all halts and error conditions printed out in exception report form and retained for audit?	___	___	___
III. *Output Controls*			
A. *General Considerations*			
1. Are output controls required by MIS management?	___	___	___
2. Are appropriate output controls instituted by MIS management to reflect changing conditions of output methods and procedures, such as from a computer mainframe–based processing mode to a LAN-based processing mode?	___	___	___
3. Are output control totals reconciled with input and processing controls?	___	___	___
4. Do output controls assure the accuracy and completeness of processed data?	___	___	___
5. Do output controls assure that computer system output be distributed to authorized persons only?	___	___	___
6. Do output controls allow for the detection and correction of processed data?	___	___	___
7. Are the methods and procedures for controlling output reviewed periodically by an independent third party?	___	___	___
8. Are outputs compared on a test basis by internal and external auditors to original transaction data for accuracy and completeness as well as sufficient security?	___	___	___

	Yes[1]	No[2]	N.A.[3]
9. Are critical output documents counted and the ending number maintained by the internal auditor?	___	___	___
10. Are system outputs distributed to authorized users only?	___	___	___
B. *Output Control Totals*			
1. Can output data be compared with predetermined control totals or by hash or record count totals?	___	___	___
2. Are there output controls over data processed against data and reports, listings, or other output media?	___	___	___
3. Are provisions made within the system to reconstruct files in the event that the current files are damaged or destroyed?	___	___	___
4. Are corresponding transactions being stored in reprocessible form for emergency conditions?	___	___	___
5. Is there an output control audit by an independent third party on a periodic basis?	___	___	___
C. *Control by Exception*			
1. Are exception conditions recognized by the computer program and are such conditions printed out and routed to authorized personnel?	___	___	___
2. Are all exception items immediately and properly investigated?	___	___	___
3. Is corrective action undertaken for all exception items?	___	___	___
4. Is there a periodic verification of master file balances, such as inventory and payroll, to correct erroneous data and check for irregularities?	___	___	___
5. Are outputs periodically tested by internal and external auditors for comparison with original source documents?	___	___	___
D. *Control over Operator Intervention*			
1. Are procedures in force that prevent access of operators and other unauthorized personnel to programs for a computer mainframe–based platform?	___	___	___
2. Is the console typewriter paper serially numbered and are numbers accounted for at the end of the shift?	___	___	___
3. If the console typewriter is a CRT rather than a typewriter device, are messages from and instructions to the computer captured in a hard-copy form via a diskette, magnetic tape, printer, or the like?	___	___	___
4. Is there a periodic review of the computer con-	___	___	___

	Yes[1]	No[2]	N.A.[3]
sole log by the internal and external auditors for error messages caused by operator interventions or for indications that processing and checking are being bypassed?			

IV. *Database Controls*

A. *Geneeral Considerations*

	Yes	No	N.A.
1. Are database controls an integral part of a client/server architecture?	___	___	___
2. Does the client/server architecture facilitate the use of database controls for daily operations?	___	___	___
3. Do database controls prevent the processing of the wrong files?	___	___	___
4. Do database controls detect errors during file manipulation?	___	___	___
5. Do database controls allow for the correction of database errors?	___	___	___
6. Is there a database administrator (DBA) responsible for the definition, organization, protection, efficiency, content, and TQM of the organization's database?	___	___	___
7. Does the database administrator work with users in finalizing the database design?	___	___	___
8. Does the database management system (DMS) have procedures to restrict unauthorized access to data?	___	___	___
9. Is the DBMS adequately controlled by a DBA or a responsible person?	___	___	___
10. Are there adequate controls to prevent access to the organization's databases when not under the control of the DBMSs?	___	___	___
11. Does the DBA or a responsible person review periodically the DBMSs to ensure that no unauthorized changes have been made?	___	___	___
12. Are all changes to the DBMS library approved and logged by the DBA or a responsible person?	___	___	___
13. Is there a database review performed by an independent third party to ensure that proper controls are in place over the contents and access to the database?	___ ___	___ ___	___ ___

B. *Database Management Systems*

	Yes	No	N.A.
1. Is there a database management system used that represents a collection of data managed by a single software system?	___	___	___
2. Is the appropriate organization model being used, that is, hierarchical, networking, relational, or object?	___	___	___

	Yes[1]	No[2]	N.A.[3]
3. Is the database management system appropriate for the organization? That is, is it centralized or decentralized for efficient and effective processing?	___	___	___
4. Does the database management system assist in integrating distributed databases?	___	___	___
5. Does the database management system facilitate data integrity and data security?	___	___	___
6. Does the database management system facilitate interoperability (involves the interrelationship of computer architectures and applications across a network) and open client/server computing (cuts across most of or the entire organization)?	___	___	___
7. Are the latest advances in database management systems, such as client/server relational DBMS and object-oriented DBMS, reviewed periodically by the DBA manager for possible implementation?	___	___	___
C. *Supervisory Protection Program*			
1. Is a supervisory protection program in place to solve the problem of concurrent updating and the resulting loss of data?	___	___	___
2. Does the DBA control the use of supervisory protection programs?	___	___	___
3. Does the supervisory protection program allow for priority in the updating process?	___	___	___
4. Are periodic tests made of the supervisory protection program to ensure that it is working properly?	___	___	___
D. *File Record Controls*			
1. Is there adherence to the "grandparent-parent-child" concept of file maintenance (i.e., the preservation of three days of successive output files with the corresponding data transactions)?	___	___	___
2. Is at least one generation of data files maintained in a location away from the regular storage area?	___	___	___
3. Is there a periodic dump of data files to ensure the capability of recoverng in case of an emergency?	___	___	___
4. Are all disk files accounted for periodically by the DBA as well as the internal or external auditors?	___	___	___
E. *Physical Safeguard Controls*			
1. Are there safeguards to ensure that data files are not dumped, lost, or misused while awaiting processing?	___	___	___
2. Are the data files adequately protected against fire, smoke, and water?	___	___	___

	Yes[1]	No[2]	N.A.[3]
3. Is off-premise storage used for duplicate computer programs and vital files?	___	___	___
4. Are physical safeguards reviewed periodically by the internal or external auditors for adequacy?	___	___	___

V. *Data Communications and Networking Controls*

A. *General Considerations*

	Yes[1]	No[2]	N.A.[3]
1. Does MIS management recognize that the mantra of network management for the next several years will be the integration of disparate, incompatible data communications and networking systems?	___	___	___
2. Does MIS management recognize that the value of computers is based more on what they are connected to than on the computers themselves?	___	___	___
3. Does MIS management utilize network analyses to understand better the strengths and weaknesses of its data communications and networking operations?	___	___	___
4. Does MIS management recognize the need for controls over the following: terminals, modems, multiplexers and concentrators, front-end communication processors, and central processing units?	___	___	___
5. Does MIS management recognize the need for interconnectivity where transported information is useful only if it can be understood at the receiving end?	___	___	___
6. Does MIS management utilize net management middleware where appropriate that provides software designed to allow system integration across heterogeneous platforms?	___	___	___
7. Does MIS management recognize the need to reduce the number of protocols in a data communications and networking environment so as to minimize the amount of protocol conversion, which can be time-consuming and costly?	___	___	___
8. Does MIS management require that data communications and networking controls are understood and implemented by MIS personnel and end users?	___	___	___
9. Do data communications and networking controls allow for the detection and correction of transmitted data?	___	___	___
10. Are data communications and networking controls reviewed by an independent third party to assure that they serve the purpose for which they were intended?	___	___	___

Yes[1] No[2] N.A.[3]

B. *Network Management*

1. Does MIS management recognize the need to put in place network management to plan, oversee, and make appropriate changes to its organizationwide networking activities? ___ ___ ___
2. Does MIS management recognize that inadequate network planning opens the organization to the risk of network overload or even failure? ___ ___ ___
3. Does network management engage in a cost/benefit analysis of present and future networking structures so that there is a cohesive vision to drive network investments in a rational and cost-effective way? ___ ___ ___
4. Does network management include in its network plans the identification of managerial and technical personnel needed to maintain and upgrade appropriate levels of network service? ___ ___ ___
5. Does network management focus on the identification of improvements that cut costs, improve services, and allow for more efficient use of tools and network staff? ___ ___ ___
6. Does network management pursue the establishment of service benchmarks and the means for tracking improvements over time? ___ ___ ___
7. Does network management support multiple platforms, such as DOS, Unix, SNA, and ISDN, and accommodate sophisticated, network-knowledgeable users of these platforms? ___ ___ ___
8. Has network management incorporated client/server computing into its day-to-day data communications and networking operations? ___ ___ ___
9. Does network management employ user feedback to determine what data communications and networking operations work and what do not work? ___ ___ ___
10. Does network management employ a one-stop help desk that goes beyond taking messages by walking users through some basic diagnostics and identifying the proper way to solve the problem? ___ ___ ___

C. *On-Line Processing Controls*

1. When input/output terminals are used for data communications, are these control techniques used: message identification (identifies each message received by the computer), message transmission control (assures that all messages transmitted are actually received), and message parity check (verifies the accuracy of the message sent)? ___ ___ ___

	Yes[1]	No[2]	N.A.[3]
2. Are message counts, character counts, and the like, performed to ensure that the data transmission is correct and no messages are lost?	___	___	___
3. Is there adequate control over terminals in case it is necessary to retrnsmit the data?	___	___	___
4. Is access to confidential information properly controlled?	___	___	___
D. *Data Monitoring Controls*			
1. Is there a monitoring routine which counts the number of unsuccessful attempts to enter the system?	___	___	___
2. Are all attempted access violations immediately reported and followed up with corrective action?	___	___	___
3. Do terminals include locking devices to prevent unauthorized use?	___	___	___
4. Does the security system include interrupt and call-back features?	___	___	___
E. *Diagnostic Controls*			
1. Are diagnostic programs, in conjunction with a supervisory program, used to detect and isolate error conditions for proper corrective action?	___	___	___
2. Are there sufficient on-line programmed controls to handle the following conditions: restart the program in question, reexecute the faulty instruction, switch control to an error routine, initiate a switchover to another on-line system, shut down part of the system, and halt the system?	___	___	___
3. Are checkpoint records developed as processing occurs, in case of a restart?	___	___	___
4. Are there manual emergency procedures to handle a halt in the computer system?	___	___	___
F. *Local Area Network Controls*			
1. Is there one or more LAN managers who report to MIS management to oversee the proper development and daily operations of LANs in the organization?	___	___	___
2. Does LAN management use a proactive approach? That is, are they able to spot LAN problems before they happen?	___	___	___
3. Does LAN management make use of software network monitors and analyzers to get a feel for day-to-day operations of its LANs?	___	___	___
4. Do these software monitors and analyzers report trends in network usage, number of errors, specific packet types, and other parameters over selected intervals?	___	___	___
5. Does LAN management use baselining	___	___	___

Yes[1] *No*[2] *N.A.*[3]

(sampling activity over time and identifying normal performance through averages, means, and other statistical calculations to establish a profile or baseline for the organization's LANs)?

6. Does LAN management use software network monitors and analyses that gather data from across the network and take action in response to what they learn? ___ ___ ___
7. Does LAN management recognize the importance of a terminate- and step resident (TSR) program loaded on PCs connected to a LAN? (TSRs are an essential component of a LAN. Loaded onto each PC, they are the types of programs that enable the PC to communicate with the network interface card [NIC] and, in turn, to the file server.) ___ ___ ___
8. Does LAN management provide for recovery planning of its LANs? That is, is there an alternative LAN someplace else or some other way of restoring lost computing and communications capability? (Many organizations use backbone networks.) ___ ___ ___
9. Does LAN management use appropriate layers of security in its local area networks? ___ ___ ___
10. Does LAN management change passwords every 30 to 45 days and distribute them only on a need-to-know basis? ___ ___ ___
11. Does LAN management have a network virus protection solution that keeps viruses from infiltrating the network operating system? ___ ___ ___
12. Does LAN management adhere to established networking standards so that an open systems architecture can be implemented in a LAN environment? ___ ___ ___

G. *Metropolitan Area Network Controls*

1. Is there one or more MAN managers who report to MIS management to oversee the proper development and daily operations of MANs in the organization? ___ ___ ___
2. Does MAN management use a proactive approach to spot MAN problems before they happen? ___ ___ ___
3. Does MAN management use software monitors and analyzers to spot trends in network usage, number of errors, specific packet type, and other parameters over selected intervals of time? ___ ___ ___
4. Does MAN management provide for recovery ___ ___ ___

Yes[1] *No*[2] *N.A.*[3]

planning of its MANs? That is, is there a MAN someplace else or some other way of restoring lost computing and communications capability?

5. Does MAN management use multiple layers of security in its metropolitan area networks?
6. Does MAN management use network control software that provides internetwork access control lists, using individual serial numbers for servers, together with the ability to define the level of interaction one server in the network can have with another server? (In this manner, there is an internet password where one server can communicate with another such that MAN management can control the levels of access between servers.) ___ ___ ___
7. Does MAN management work with its internal and external auditors in developing a flexible auditing approach to MANs? That is, can audit procedures be changed to meet changing MAN operating modes? ___ ___ ___
8. Does MAN management use network control software that allows for maintaining continuity of operations and availability of important data? That is, is disk mirroring used whereby data are written and maintained on two disks simultaneously? ___ ___ ___
9. Does MAN management use network control software that combines disk mirroring with the concept of fault-tolerant computing that uses redundant, multiple CPUs to provide nonstop MAN networking? ___ ___ ___
10. Does MAN management provide appropriate security capabilities that maintain a balance of control, flexibility, and ease of use? ___ ___ ___
11. Does MAN management have in place a virus protection solution that keeps the MAN free of viruses? ___ ___ ___
12. Does MAN management adhere to established networking standards so that an open system architecture can be implemented in a MAN environment? ___ ___ ___

H. *Wide Area Network Controls*

1. Is there a tie-in of wide area networks with local area networks and metropolitan area networks such that organizationwide computing is facilitated? ___ ___ ___

Additional questions can be found under G. Metropolitan Area Networks: that is, change the term MAN to WAN.

	Yes[1]	No[2]	N.A.[3]
VI. *End-User Controls*			
A. *General Considerations*			
1. Does MIS management recognize that the corporate culture of the organization has a great impact on end-user computing?	___	___	___
2. Is the organization's corporate culture supportive of a soft controls approach?	___	___	___
3. Does MIS management stress education and training of end users via its centralized and decentralized information centers?	___	___	___
4. Does MIS management try to accommodate end users who are performing their own computing and bypassing functional end-user information centers?	___	___	___
5. Does MIS management try to reduce end-user/MIS conflict by providing end users with more direct operational control using a soft controls approach?	___	___	___
6. Does MIS management respond to the unique needs of end users that normally are too small for traditional systems development?	___	___	___
7. Does MIS management recognize the need for data integrity and correctness of processing results by end users?	___	___	___
8. Does MIS management recognize the increasing needs of end users to analyze data and produce reports and respond to their queries?	___	___	___
B. *End-User Systems Development Controls*			
1. Does MIS management work with end users directly via the functional end-user information centers and indirectly through company publications to ensure compatibility with current MIS systems development tools?	___	___	___
2. Do functional end-user information centers assist end users in acquiring systems development tools and training them in their usage?	___	___	___
3. Do end users who develop systems on their own feel free to call upon the MIS department when they need help?	___	___	___
4. Do end users have the support of the MIS organization to meet changing requirements, including information needs and temporary throwaway systems created to respond to one-time situations?	___	___	___
5. Do end users have the support of MIS management to deal with difficulties experienced when working with vendors of systems development tools?	___	___	___

	Yes[1]	No[2]	N.A.[3]
6. Do systems development efforts by end users serve the interests of the total organization versus self-serving interests?	___	___	___
C. *End-User Hardware and Software Controls*			
1. Is there an end-user policy of MIS management regarding the purchase of either computer hardware or software?	___	___	___
2. Is this policy acceptable to end users in terms of purchasing hardware and software whether end users operate on their own or go through functional end-user information centers?	___	___	___
3. Does this policy for acquiring hardware and software recognize the fact that if the organization must continually share information among departments, standards should exist so that similar hardware and software are in use and problems in transferring data across the organization are minimized?	___	___	___
4. Does this policy recognize that if only specialized hardware or software can provide a solution, the policy should be more lenient in allowing a variety of hardware and software?	___	___	___
5. Does MIS management recognize from an overall standpoint that standardization of a hardware and software policy is preferable because it reduces problems in incompatible hardware and software, saves time in transferrring data throughout the organization, and increases the availability of hardware to other end users within and outside departmental boundaries?	___	___	___
D. *End-User Databases and Data Communications Controls*			
1. Is there a policy of MIS management that provides for database integrity by end users? That is, do all databases whether local or centralized contain the same data when under the control of end users?	___	___	___
2. Is there a policy of MIS management that provides for database security by end users? That is, are all data items secure and free of access by unauthorized personnel when under the control of end users?	___	___	___
3. Is there provision for backup of database files in terms of day-by-day processing by end users?	___	___	___
4. Is there provision by MIS management for recovery of database files under the control of end users?	___	___	___
5. Is there provision by MIS management to main-	___	___	___

	Yes[1]	No[2]	N.A.[3]
tain integrity of data communications for end users on a day-to-day basis?			
6. Are end-user data communications and networks secure and free of access by unauthorized personnel?	___	___	___
7. Do end users with the assistance of MIS management routinely change passwords and authority lists so that unauthorized access is minimized?	___	___	___
	___	___	___
8. Does MIS management have a recovery plan in place, especially for end-user LANs and their server-based backups?	___	___	___
9. Is there provision by MIS management to recreate entire networks that are used daily by end users in case of fire, floods, and the like?	___	___	___
E. *End-User Audit Controls*			
1. Is a soft controls approach of MIS management disseminated through centralized or decentralized information centers in the form of end-user methods and procedures manuals?	___	___	___
2. Do end-user controls contained in these manuals mirror those of the established controls practiced by the MIS department, including TQM requirements?	___	___	___
3. Do end users who undertake computing on their own adhere to control factors that are logical and are acceptable to internal and external auditors?	___	___	___
4. Are end-user controls adequate over sharing of department data? That is, no one end user has complete control over specific data?	___	___	___
5. Are end-user controls sufficient that internal and external auditors can follow complete information trails, i.e., from inputs through processing to outputs?	___	___	___
6. Are sufficient end-user controls in effect to highlight inconsistent data that are created in different ways or with different assumptions which are subsequently used as if they were the same?	___	___	___
F. *End-User Security Controls*			
1. Does MIS management stress a logical, commonsense approach to end-user security?	___	___	___
2. Are passwords, encryption, audit trails, usage logs, etc., employed by end users to provide needed security over access to data and program files?	___	___	___
3. Does MIS management stress the need for end users to back up data in a secure location in	___	___	___

	Yes[1]	No[2]	N.A.[3]
the form of data diskettes or disks in case of the need for recovery from hardware or software malfunctions?			
4. Does MIS management stress that one of the best methods of securing data stored on computer mainframes is to allow end users only downloading of data files needed for manipulation and stored on PCs?	___	___	___
5. If MIS management allows end users to gain write access authorization for computer mainframe resources, are the data transferred from the PCs captured on the computer mainframe as transaction files and used later to update master files, thereby facilitating reconstruction if it becomes necessary?	___	___	___
6. Does MIS management require that end users secure physically sensitive data files so that they cannot be removed from the premises and read by unauthorized individuals?	___ ___	___ ___	___ ___
7. Does MIS management require that unprotected program diskettes be secured so that they cannot be copied without authorization, which may violate licensing agreements with software vendors?	___	___	___

throughout the MIS organization, that is, not only the MIS department, but also the degree of control over end users.

SAMPLE CASE STUDY—APPLICATION OF THE MIS QUESTIONNAIRE TO COMPUTER SECURITY

The executive vice president of the Newcomb Company just finished reading an article on computer fraud. The article started with a discussion of the Equity Funding Corporation of America, which had some gaping holes in its computer security and control methods. Officials in Equity used the corporation's computer to create false insurance policies and to inflate the apparent financial status of their corporation. The fall of Equity Funding and other companies discussed in this article has made it clear to the executive vice president that there is a real threat to the company from inside its data center. Thus, he reasoned that systems personnel, with their highly specialized knowledge and skills and their easy access to operating hardware and software, can rob or defraud the company and go undetected for months, possibly indefinitely.

In view of the possibility of computer theft, fraud, and the like, in the MIS area, he called in the company's outside auditors. While meeting with them, he stressed the need for going beyond the normal audit and spending the bare minimum of two weeks during the interim review work on the MIS department alone. Although this extended the scope of the regular audit, the executive vice president felt that money spent investigating this area in great detail would be of benefit to the company. This is particularly true since the company manufactures and sells consumer products that can be easily sold on the outside.

Evaluation of Computer Security Problems

The outside auditors brought in MIS consultants from their staff. Being accustomed to reviewing computer systems in depth, they used the entire two-part MIS questionnaire as set forth in Figures 15.4 and 15.5. After a thorough review of the data center, the outside MIS consultants concluded that most controls were operating as intended, with the exception of security controls. Because of major problems in this area, two subsections on security controls are set forth in Figure 15.6. Although additional subsections from this section plus other sections of the questionnaire could have been included since some answers were negative, evaluation of the questions in Figure 15.6 does highlight important ongoing deficiencies in the operation.

In answer to question 2 (D. Program Controls), computer programs and supporting materials maintained in the tape and disk library are accessible to all company personnel, thereby allowing anyone to get hold of a program and alter it. Similarly, per question 3, the computer department is deficient in its method of handling changes to the computer run book. Referring to question 1 (E. Equipment Log), even though a daily equipment log is maintained, no one checks

Figure 15.6
Sections D and E of V. Security Controls—Questionnaire 1

	Yes	*No*	*N.A.*
D. *Program Controls*			
1. Are computer programs stored in a safe location where they are controlled by a tape and disk librarian?	X	___	___
2. Are computer programs duplicated on a magnetic tape or disk and stored in a safe storage area as back-up for emergency conditions?	___	X[1]	___
3. Does each program have a computer-run book that is available to the console operator for meeting any contingency during the processing of the program?	___	X[2]	___
4. Does an independent third party periodically conduct a surprise audit of computer programs to make sure they serve their intended purposes?	___	X[3]	___
E. *Equipment Log*			
1. Is a daily equipment log prepared so that computer operating time can be monitored?	___	X[4]	___
2. Does the equipment log contain program identification, start time, stop time, production time, test time, downtime, and unusual conditions?	X	___	___
3. If there is an installed computer device for recording time, does the internal auditor periodically check the equipment log time against the usage for falsification of computer time?	___	___	X
4. Does the internal auditor periodically check the equipment log (when the run was completed) against the library record (when the program tape or disk was returned) for time discrepancies?	___	X[5]	___
5. Is a copy of the computer console typewriter output delivered to the internal auditor at the end of each day? (It is highly recommended that the internal auditor initial the printout at the start of his or her workday.)	___	X[6]	___

1. Computer programs and supporting materials maintained in the tape and disk library are available to computer personnel without written authorization.

2. There is a computer run for each program available to the console operator. However, there is no control over changes to the computer run book, nor over who initiates them.

3. Because this is the first real audit of computer programs, there have been no surprise audits in the past.

4. Although daily logs of computer time are maintained, they are incomplete since computer operators and programmers testing programs fail to log in and out.

5. Because of the work load of the internal auditors, there is no time to check the equipment log against the library record, even periodically.

6. Again, because of the workload of the internal auditors, there is no attempt to check the computer console typewriter output.

to make sure that all computer time is accounted for. Thus, there are many cases where available computer time is unexplained. The "no" answers to questions 4 and 5 indicate that the internal auditors have too great a work load to undertake an adequate job of reviewing MIS controls.

Recommendations to Improve Computer Security

Overall, the main thrust of the negative answers in Figure 15.6 is that managerial control over computer security leaves a lot to be desired. This was the essential content of the verbal presentation that the outside MIS consultants made to the executive vice president. As one computer person said, "In the area of security controls, things are loose as a goose." To rectify this problem, their *first* recommendation revolved around improved managerial controls over computer processing time as well as the programs themselves. The current situation is such that a programmer could obtain a program, alter it by using the computer, and return it—and no one would be the wiser. This gives computer personnel the capability of stealing the company blind by altering payroll, inventory, and other programs.

A *second* recommendation is that a computer tape and disk records librarian be hired to monitor and maintain the computer records library and issue computer programs and supporting materials to authorized personnel only. In this manner, there is a complete record of what programs were used, by whom, and at what time. If there is any question regarding the altering of computer programs and related materials, the individual can be identified. Additionally, the MIS consultants suggested that the systems and programming manager establish effective controls over computer run books and changes to them. In this manner, computer operators will have up-to-date instructions for meeting any emergency condition.

A *third* recommendation centers on the proper maintenance of daily equipment logs. The outside consultants recommended that the internal auditors have the responsibility of reviewing this log time sheet for irregularities. A typical example of a computer irregularity is testing a computer program that has proved to be operational for a long time. Additional recommendations based on problems found in other sections of the two-part MIS questionnaire were presented. However, these represent the typical security problems encountered in the engagement and recommendations to overcome them.

GUIDELINES TO ASSIST MIS MANAGEMENT IN EVALUATING THE MIS ORGANIZATION

A *first* guideline relating to the evaluation of the MIS organization by MIS management centers on spending an adequate sum on internal auditing. Today, MIS and internal audit managers report that there is increasing senior corporate management concern about potential loss due to total computerization of the organization. The net result is greater emphasis on, and consequently more spending for, the development of audit and control tools and techniques. While increased expenditures for MIS controls will probably have only a limited impact, internal audit costs can be expected to increase in the future if internal auditors are to fulfill a significant role in the MIS and end-user processing environment.

A *second* guideline refers to the need for continuous training of auditors in the latest audit techniques. Senior corporate management as well as the regulatory agencies and the general public have tended to rely increasingly on both internal auditors and external auditors to protect organizations against the hazards of inadequate control in management information systems. However, investigations typically reveal a dangerous gap: auditing and control procedures for MIS have failed to keep pace with the introduction of new technology and new concepts in MIS design.

To assist auditors in their everyday tasks, a *third* guideline is needed, namely, utilization of commercially available application audit software. Purchased software packages have shown that data processing functions can be largely standardized to meet the needs of different organizations. Audit software tasks for common applications such as accounts receivable, accounts payable, general ledger, payroll, and inventory can be similarly standardized. Basically, application audit software is developed to achieve common audit objectives. Those functions are then precoded into the package and its associated documentation. Typically, the auditor saves time and effort since audit functions are predefined. Of course, it may be necessary to alter the functions somewhat, depending on the particular audit concerns, but this flexibility is built into the software.

There is need for a *fourth* guideline that recognizes that many end users are using new information technology that is over their heads and need help. As a service to the entire organization, the auditors need to steer end users in the right direction: an information center under the jurisdiction of the MIS department. Tied in with the preceding guideline is a *fifth* one that centers on end users' making use of a cost/benefit analysis to assess the feasibility of new information technology. The less rigid or nonexistent cost/benefit evaluation can present a problem to the total organization. Different criteria may be used to create estimates, and the risk of inappropriate choices and unnecessary purchases increases. It is even worse when there is no cost/benefit analysis at all. In the final analysis, large sums of information technology money may be wasted by legitimate end users.

No matter how information technology is employed, there is need for a *sixth* guideline that centers on the single most effective control mechanism: education. Experience has shown that after initial training, update sessions and end-user groups are good ways of maintaining awareness. Training programs should orient end users to risks and demonstrate that controls fulfill an obvious, agreed-upon need. End users who have experienced the effects of poor controls may help others understand the need for control.

NOTES

1. Russell Kay, ''Business and Law Enforcement: Partners Against Computer Crime,'' *Infosecurity News,* November/December 1992, p. 13.

2. Russell Kay, ''Calculating the Cost of Computer Crime,'' *Infosecurity News,* November/December 1992, pp. 1 and 12.

3. Ibid., p. 12.

4. William M. Carley, ''In-House Hackers: Rigging Computers for Fraud or Malice Is Often an Inside Job,'' *The Wall Street Journal,* August 27, 1992, pp. A1 and A4.

Bibliography

Banker, R. D., R. J. Kauffman, and M. A. Mahmood, eds. *Managing Information Resources in the 1990s*. Harrisburg, PA: Idea Publishing, 1990.

———. *Managing Information Technology in a Global Society*. Harrisburg, PA: Idea Group Publishing, 1991.

———. *Strategic Information Technology Management: Perspectives on Organizational Growth and Competitive Advantage*. Harrisburg, PA: Idea Group Publishing, 1993.

Beaumont, J. R. *Information Resource Management*. Stoneham, MA: Buttworth-Heinemann, 1992.

Bjorn-Andersen, N., K. Eason, and D. Robey. *Managing Computer Impact,* M. Ginzberg, ed. Norwood, NJ: Ablex Publishing Corporation, 1986.

Breslawski, S., J. Fowler, R. Stegman, and G. Yaverbaum. *Microcomputer Applications for Managers: A Hands-on Approach*. Harrisburg, PA: Idea Group Publishing, 1990.

Burton, P. F., and J. H. Petrie. *Information Management Technology: A Librarian's Guide,* Second Edition. New York: Chapman & Hall, 1990.

Christoff, K. *Managing the Information Center*. New York: HarperCollins College, 1990.

Cortez, E. M., and E. J. Kazlauskas. *Managing Information Systems and Technologies: A Basic Guide for Design, Selection, Evaluation and Use*. New York: Neal-Schuman Publishers, Inc., 1986.

Couger, J., and R. A. Zawacki. *Motivation and Managing Computer Personnel*. New York: John Wiley & Sons, Inc., 1980.

Davis, G. B., and T. R. Hoffmann. *Managing Information: How Information Systems Impact Organizational Strategy*. Homewood, IL: Irwin Professional Publishing, 1993.

Deans, C., and K. Karwan, eds. *Global Information Technology Applications: Focus on the Organization and Its Functional Areas*. Harrisburg, PA: Idea Group Publishing, 1993.

Dickson, G. W., and J. C. Wetherbe. *The Management of Information Systems*. New York: McGraw-Hill, Inc., 1985.

Emery, J. C. *Management Information Systems: The Critical Strategic Resource*. New York: Oxford University Press, 1987.

Gaydasch, A. *Principles of EDP Management*. Reston, VA: Reston Publishing Company, 1982.

Gibson, C. F., and B. B. Jackson, eds. *The Information Imperative: Managing the Impact of Information Technology on Business and People*. New York: Free Press, 1987.

Gray, P. *Management of Information Systems*. New York: Dryden Press, 1989.

Guimaraes, T. *Managing Information Technology with Outsourcing*. Harrisburg, PA: Idea Group Publishing, 1993.

Horton, F. W., Jr. *Information Resources Management: Harnessing Information Assets for Productivity Gains in the Office, Factory and Laboratory*. Englewood Cliffs, NJ: Prentice-Hall, Inc., 1985.

Hurtubise, R. *Managing Information Systems: Concept & Tools*. West Hartford, CT: Kumarian Press, Inc., 1984.

Hussain, D., and K. M. Hussain. *Information Management*. Englewood Cliffs, NJ: Prentice-Hall, Inc., 1989.

———. *Managing Computer Resources,* Second Edition. Homewood, IL: Richard D. Irwin, Inc., 1987.

Irving, R. H., and C. A. Higgins. *Office Information Systems Management Issues and Methods*. New York: John Wiley & Sons, Inc., 1991.

Kanter, J. *Managing with Information,* Fourth Edition. Englewood Cliffs, NJ: Prentice-Hall, Inc., 1992.

Keen, P.G.W. *Every Manager's Guide to Information Technology: A Glossary of Key Terms and Concepts for Today's Business Leader*. Boston, MA: Harvard Business School Press, 1991.

Kerr, J. M. *The IRM Imperative: Strategies for Managing Information Resources*. New York: John Wiley & Sons, Inc., 1991.

Khosrowpour, M. *Information Technology and Organizations: Challenges of New Technologies*. Harrisburg, PA: Idea Group Publishing, 1993.

———. *Micro-Based Information Systems: Development and Management*. Harrisburg, PA: Idea Group Publishing, 1993.

———. *Microcomputer Systems Applications: A Hands-on Managerial Approach*. Harrisburg, PA: Idea Group Publishing, 1993.

Khosrowpour, M., and D. Amoroso, eds. *Managing Microcomputer Technology as an Organizational Resource*. Harrisburg, PA: Idea Group Publishing, 1991.

Khosrowpour, M., and G. Yaverbaum, eds. *Information Technology Resources Utilization and Management: Issues and Trends*. Harrisburg, PA: Idea Group Publishing, 1990.

Kowlakowski, F., and L. Mcelyea. *Enterprise Analysis: Managing Knowledge Information Assets*. Englewood Cliffs, NJ: Prentice-Hall, Inc., 1993.

Kraemer, K. L., W. H. Dutton, and A. Northrup. *The Management of Information Systems*. New York: Columbia University Press, 1981.

Kraemer, K. L., J. L. King, D. E. Dunkle, and J. P. Lane. *Managing Information Systems: Change & Control in Organizational Computing*. San Francisco, CA: Jossey-Bass, Inc., Publishers, 1989.

Langer, S., ed. *Compensation in the MIS-DP Field*. Crete, IL: Abbott, Langer & Associates, 1987.

Lockwood, L. *Appraising MIS Personnel*. Carmel, IN: Sams, 1992.

Lucas, H. C., Jr. *Managing Information Services*. New York: Macmillan Publishing Company, Inc., 1989.

MacIsaac, M. *Handbook of IS Management,* Third Edition. New York: Warren, Gorham & Lamont, Inc., 1991.

Martin, E. W., and D. DeHayes. *Managing Information Technology*. New York: Macmillan Publishing Company, Inc., 1991.

McGee, J., and L. Prusak. *Managing Information Strategically: Increase Your Company's Competitiveness and Efficiency by Using Information As a Strategic Tool*. New York: John Wiley and Sons, Inc., 1993.

Osterle, H., et al. *Total Information Systems Management Guidelines and Examples on How to Get More Value Out of Your Information System*. New York: John Wiley and Sons, Inc., 1993.

Palvia, S., P. Palvia, and R. Zigli, eds. *The Global Issues of Information Technology Management*. Harrisburg, PA: Idea Group Publishing, 1992.

Ruthstrom, C. R., and C. A. Dykman. *Information Systems for Managers: Casebook*. St. Paul, MN: West Publishing Company, 1992.

Sager, M. *Managing Advanced Information Systems*. Englewood Cliffs, NJ: Prentice-Hall, Inc., 1990.

Sprague, R. H., and B. C. McNurlin. *Information Systems in Practice,* Third Edition. Englewood Cliffs, NJ: Prentice-Hall, Inc., 1992.

Szewczak, D., and C. Snodgrass, eds. *Management Impacts of Information Technology: Perspectives on Organizational Change and Growth*. Harrisburg, PA: Idea Group Publishing, 1991.

Targowski, A. *The Architecture and Planning of Enterprise-Wide Information Management Systems*. Harrisburg, PA: Idea Group Publishing, 1990.

Thierauf, R. J. *A Manager's Complete Guide to Effective Information Systems: A Questionnaire Approach*. New York: Free Press, 1983.

———. *Effective Information Centers: Guidelines for MIS and IC Managers*. Westport, CT: Quorum Books, 1988.

———. *New Directions in MIS Management: A Guide for the 1990s*. Westport, CT: Quorum Books, 1988.

———. *Executive Information Systems: A Guide for Senior Management and MIS Professionals*. Westport, CT: Quorum Books, 1991.

———. *Creative Computer Software for Strategic Thinking and Decision Making: A Guide for Senior Management and MIS Professionals*. Westport, CT: Quorum Books, 1993.

Thierauf, R. J., and G. W. Reynolds. *Effective Information Systems Management*. Columbus, Ohio: Charles E. Merrill Publishing Company, 1982.

Thomsett, R. *Third Wave Project Management: A Handbook for Managing the Complex Information Systems of the 1990s*. Englewood Cliffs, NJ: Prentice-Hall, Inc., 1992.

Umbaugh, R. E., ed. *Handbook of MIS Management,* First Edition. Boston, MA: Warren, Gorham & Lamont, Inc., 1985.

———. *Handbook of MIS Management,* Second Edition. Boston, MA: Warren, Gorham & Lamont, Inc., 1988.

———. *Handbook of IS Management,* Third Edition. Boston, MA: Warren, Gorham & Lamont, Inc., 1991.

———. *Handbook of IS Management, 1993–94 Yearbook.* Boston, MA: Warren, Gorham & Lamont, Inc., 1993.

Wittry, E. *Managing Information Systems: An Integrated Approach.* Dearborn, MI: Society of Manufacturing Engineers, 1987.

Index

About the Author

ROBERT J. THIERAUF is Professor of Information and Decision Sciences at Xavier University, Cincinnati, Ohio. Formerly a staff accountant (CPA) and consultant at Coopers & Lybrand, Thierauf has written extensively on management information systems, management science, and computers. He is the author of 28 books, nine under the Quorum Books imprint.

ISBN 0-89930-838-4

EAN

9 780899 308388 90000

HARDCOVER BAR CODE